READY FOR TAKE-OFF
AKTUELLE DEUTSCHE EXPORTARCHITEKTUR
CONTEMPORARY GERMAN EXPORT ARCHITECTURE

READY FOR TAKE-OFF
AKTUELLE DEUTSCHE EXPORTARCHITEKTUR
CONTEMPORARY GERMAN EXPORT ARCHITECTURE

Herausgeber Editors
Anna Hesse
Peter Cachola Schmal

DAM DEUTSCHES ARCHITEKTURMUSEUM

HATJE CANTZ

Inhalt Contents

Vorworte Forewords

6 Bundesminister für Verkehr, Bau und Stadtentwicklung
German Federal Minister of Transport, Building and Urban Affairs
Wolfgang Tiefensee

8 Deutsches Architekturmuseum
Anna Hesse, Peter Cachola Schmal

Aufsätze Essays

12 Welche Rolle spielen »deutsche Werte« und »Sekundärtugenden« für den Erfolg des Architekturexports?
What Role Do "German Values" and "Secondary Virtues" Play in Successfully Exporting Architecture?
Anna Hesse, Peter Cachola Schmal

Interviews mit with
16 Stefan Helming, Deutsche Gesellschaft für Technische Zusammenarbeit
24 Spencer de Grey, Foster + Partners
34 Dominique Perrault, Dominique Perrault Architecture
40 Kees Christiaanse, Kees Christiaanse Architects & Planners
Geführt von Conducted by Anna Hesse, Peter Cachola Schmal

48 Deutschlands Baukultur und das System der Stararchitekten
Germany's Building Culture and the Star Architecture System
Claus Käpplinger

54 Von »deutscher Form« zur »Weltform«?
Zur Geschichte des deutschen Architekturexports
From "German Form" to "International Form"?
On the History of German Architectural Export
Wolfgang Voigt

66 *Ready for Take-Off* – Lohnt sich der Weg ins Ausland?
Ready for Take-Off: Is Venturing Abroad Worth It?
Thomas Welter

76 Deutsche Ingenieurleistungen – im Ausland hoch geschätzt
German Engineering Services: Highly Regarded Abroad
Klaus Rollenhagen, Tatjana Steidl

Projekte Projects

86 Architekturbüro Deutschland

104 Barkow Leibinger Architekten

110 Behnisch Architekten

116 BeL

122 Carsten Roth Architekt

128 Gerber Architekten

134 GKK + Architekten

140 Ingenhoven Architekten

146 J. Mayer H.

152 Kirsten Schemel Architekten

158 KSP Engel und Zimmermann

164 KSV Krüger Schuberth Vandreike

170 Pysall Ruge Architekten

176 Sauerbruch Hutton

182 Staab Architekten

188 Wandel Hoefer Lorch + Hirsch

Anhang Appendix

196 Architekturexport:
Deutsche Planer auf der Architekturbiennale in São Paulo
Exporting Architecture:
Germany at the Architecture Biennial in São Paulo
Sally Below, Moritz Henning

202 Autoren und Interviewpartner Authors and Interview Partners

206 Bildnachweis Credits

Vorwort
Bundesminister für Verkehr, Bau und Stadtentwicklung
Wolfgang Tiefensee

Die Produkte der deutschen Industrie stellen international einen Wertbegriff dar. Einen ebenso guten Ruf genießen die Dienstleistungen der deutschen Planer. Sie stehen für technisch hochwertige Bauten mit hohen Standards bei Energieeffizienz und Nachhaltigkeit. Leistungen aus dem Bereich dessen, was gemeinhin als Baukunst verstanden wird, erwartet man international jedoch bislang eher selten aus Deutschland. Zu Unrecht: Architektur »Made in Germany« besitzt neben ihren Stärken in der technischen Ausführung, der Projektsteuerung und der besonderen Berücksichtigung des städtischen Kontextes auch ein hohes gestalterisches Niveau. Architektur in und aus Deutschland kann sich im weltweiten Kreativitätswettbewerb sehen lassen.

Der »Wettbewerb der Ideen« auf der Architekturbiennale in São Paulo Ende letzten Jahres bot Deutschland ein hervorragendes Forum, um sein baukulturelles Potenzial zu präsentieren. Unter dem Motto *Ready for Take-Off* gelang es dem Deutschen Architekturmuseum auf eindrucksvolle Weise, sechzehn Architektur- und Ingenieurbüros in der ganzen Breite ihres Leistungsspektrums zu zeigen. Die deutsche Präsenz hat sich ausgezahlt und über die brasilianische Industriemetropole hinaus Aufmerksamkeit in ganz Südamerika erregt. Die Zahl von 150 000 Besuchern im großen Biennalegebäude bestätigt dieses breite Interesse.

Brasiliens Wirtschaft hat sich in den letzten Jahren gut entwickelt, das Land steuert auf einen stabilen Wachstumskurs zu. Ein Indikator hierfür ist die beeindruckende Expansionskraft der Industriemetropole São Paulo. Für jeden Besucher ist die rasante Ausbreitung der Stadt ins Umland unmittelbar erfahrbar. Der rapide Wachstumsprozess der mittlerweile zwanzig Millionen Einwohner zählenden Stadtregion zeigt sich als kaum noch steuerbar. Wie in anderen schnell gewachsenen Städten Südamerikas beginnt nun vor diesem Hintergrund eine architektonische und städtebauliche Qualitätsdebatte, die auch international nach innovativen Lösungen fragt.

In Nachbarschaft zu den ausgestellten Leistungen Oskar Niemeyers und des Pritzker-Preisträgers Paulo Mendes da Rocha konnte nur ein baukulturell hochwertiger, das breite Spektrum der deutschen Planungsleistungen repräsentierender deutscher Biennale-Beitrag bestehen. São Paulo hat sich hierfür neben der Architekturbiennale in Venedig als ein weiterer Ort von weltweiter Bedeutung erwiesen. Deshalb haben wir gerne zum zweiten Mal eine deutsche Teilnahme unterstützt und wollen dieses Engagement fortsetzen, nicht zuletzt auch, um die Exportchancen deutscher Planungsleistungen zu erhöhen.

Die Verbesserung der Voraussetzungen und die Verbreitung des Bewusstseins für eine qualitätvolle gebaute Umwelt ist auch weiterhin eines der Hauptanliegen der »Initiative Architektur und Baukultur«. Baukultur ist kein feststehendes Postulat, sondern muss permanent neu mit Inhalten ausgefüllt und gelebt werden. Uns geht es um die Voraussetzungen für eine Baukulturpolitik, die sowohl national als auch international die Chancen guten Planens und Bauens herausstellt und damit sowohl in der Alltagsarchitektur als auch bei herausragenden Bauaufgaben Hervorragendes möglich macht.

Ich danke dem Deutschen Architekturmuseum für seinen gelungenen Biennale-Beitrag, der nun auch in seinem eigenen Haus in Frankfurt am Main zu sehen ist. Er hat dazu beigetragen, die Leistungen der deutschen Architekten und Ingenieure auch als baukulturellen Wertbegriff international hervorzuheben.

Foreword
German Federal Minister of Transport, Building and Urban Affairs
Wolfgang Tiefensee

The products of German industry set international benchmarks of quality. German planners are held in similarly high regard. They stand for technically sophisticated buildings with high standards of energy efficiency and sustainability. Yet the international community rarely holds such high expectations of Germany in the field of what is widely regarded as the art of architectural design. Unjustifiably so, for the strengths of architecture "Made in Germany" lie not only in its technical execution, project management, and sensitivity to the urban context, but also in its high standards of creative design. Architecture in and from Germany can compete with the worldwide competition in terms of creativity.

The "competition of ideas" at the Architecture Biennial in São Paulo late last year provided Germany with an excellent platform on which to showcase its architectural potential. Under the motto *Ready for Take-Off*, the Deutsches Architekturmuseum gave an impressive insight into the wide range of abilities and achievements of sixteen architectural and engineering firms. Germany's participation in this event has paid off, drawing attention not only in São Paulo itself, but throughout South America. Visitor numbers in the region of 150,000 bear witness to the enormous interest that was generated.

In recent years, the Brazilian economy has developed, and the country is moving toward stable growth. One indicator of this is the rate of expansion in the industrial metropolis of São Paulo. The speed at which the city is spreading into the surrounding areas is clearly evident to anyone who visits. With a population already at the 20 million mark, the scale of expansion has become barely manageable. As in other South American cities that have undergone rapid growth, the situation has triggered a debate on the quality of architectural and urban development and an international quest for innovative solutions.

Alongside works by Oscar Niemeyer and Pritzker laureate Paulo Mendes da Rocha, the German contribution to the Biennial had to be of the highest architectural quality, representing the broad spectrum of Germany's planning and design abilities. In this respect, São Paulo has proved to be yet another internationally important venue, to rank with the Venice Architecture Biennial. So we were delighted to lend our support a second time to Germany's participation in the event and we wish to continue to do so, not least in order to enhance the export opportunities for German architectural, engineering, and planning services.

Raising awareness of the importance of quality in the built environment and improving the conditions under which this can be achieved remain two of the primary concerns of the Architecture and Building Culture Initiative. Building culture is not a fixed given; it has to be constantly replenished and invigorated. We are concerned with laying the foundations for a policy of building culture that highlights the opportunities for good planning and architecture both nationally and internationally, so that excellence can be achieved not only in major building projects, but also in everyday architecture.

I wish to thank the Deutsches Architekturmuseum for their outstanding contribution to the Biennial, which can now be seen in the museum itself in Frankfurt am Main. This exhibition has helped to draw international attention to the capacity of German architects and engineers to establish a concept of value in building culture.

Vorwort
Deutsches Architekturmuseum
Anna Hesse, Peter Cachola Schmal

Seit einigen Jahren lässt sich weltweit das Aufkommen eines internationalen Starsystems in der Architektur beobachten: In der Hoffnung auf eine Wiederholung des »Bilbao-Effekts« mitsamt seinen vielfältigen positiven Auswirkungen, wird häufig auf Markenarchitektur und -architekten gesetzt. Besonders in Deutschland kamen und kommen vielfach internationale Stararchitekten zum Zuge, um prestigeträchtige Gebäude zu errichten. Manche dieser Stars hatten ihren endgültigen Durchbruch mit Bauten in Deutschland. Jedoch kann zurzeit, in der Nachfolge von Altmeistern wie Walter Gropius und Mies van der Rohe, kein deutscher Architekt zu dieser Gruppe der internationalen »Starchitects« gezählt werden. Nichtsdestotrotz kommen in den letzten Jahren zunehmend deutsche Architekten und Ingenieure im Ausland zum Zuge, allerdings auf wesentlich breiterer Basis. Es gibt also durchaus eine rege Nachfrage architektonischer Leistungen aus Deutschland.

Erstmalig wurde 2007 ein deutscher Beitrag für die Internationale Architekturbiennale São Paulo (BIA) speziell für den Biennale-Pavillon konzipiert und dort vom 10. November bis 16. Dezember 2007 präsentiert. Im Jahr 2005 war eine bereits existierende Ausstellung für diesen internationalen Transfer umgewandelt worden. Dies unterstreicht die gestiegene Bedeutung der BIA São Paulo für den Auftraggeber, die Bundesrepublik Deutschland, vertreten durch das Bundesministerium für Verkehr, Bau und Stadtentwicklung (BMVBS). Ähnlich wie beim bereits mehrfach durchgeführten Auswahlverfahren für den deutschen Beitrag zur Architekturbiennale in Venedig wurde erstmals ein Wettbewerb für Ausstellungsideen vom BMVBS ausgeschrieben. Als Gewinner ging das Konzept des Deutschen Architekturmuseums (DAM) aus dem Rennen hervor und dessen Direktor Peter Cachola Schmal wurde als Generalkommissar verpflichtet.

In der Ausstellungsinstallation *Ready for Take-Off* werden die als »charakteristisch deutsch« gehandelten Architekturqualitäten wie technische Innovation, Detailqualität, Einbindung in den städtebaulichen Kontext oder die Berücksichtigung von Ökologie und Nachhaltigkeit hervorgehoben und den ebenfalls »klassisch deutschen« Sekundärtugenden wie Ordnung, Gründlichkeit, Ehrlichkeit, Disziplin, Pünktlichkeit oder Zuverlässigkeit gegenübergestellt: In einen schwarz-rot-goldenen Teppich, der einer überdimensionalen deutschen Fahne ähnelt, sind diese Begriffe auf Deutsch und Portugiesisch eingewoben – in der brasilianischen Nationalfarbe Grün. Insgesamt sechzehn Architekturbüros und ihre jeweiligen Ingenieurpartner werden mit einem aktuellen Exportprojekt vorgestellt. Die typische Arbeitsweise dieser Planer wird zudem anhand der Darstellung eines bereits fertiggestellten Bauwerks in Deutschland demonstriert. Modelle, Pläne und Fotos der Projekte werden in großen aufgeklappten Aluminiumkoffern präsentiert, welche das weltweite Reisen und Arbeiten der deutschen Architekten symbolisieren. Die Rimowa-Koffer und der in einem Spezialverfahren bedruckte Dura-Teppich stellen selbst als Produkte typische qualitätvolle und unverwüstliche »Made in Germany«-Exportartikel dar.

Die Auswahl der deutschen Planer konzentriert sich auf Architekturbüros, die in Folge eines Wettbewerbgewinns oder eines Direktauftrags aktuell ihr erstes bedeutendes Projekt im Ausland realisieren. Dabei reicht die Bandbreite von jungen Talenten wie BeL, Kirsten Schemel Architekten, KSV Krüger Schuberth Vandreike und Pysall Ruge Architekten über etablierte Büros wie Carsten Roth Architekt, Gerber Architekten, GKK + Architekten, Staab Architekten sowie Wandel Hoefer Lorch + Hirsch

Foreword
Deutsches Architekturmuseum
Anna Hesse, Peter Cachola Schmal

For some years now, we have seen an international celebrity system emerging in the world of architecture: branded architecture and famous names are sought out in the hope of reviving the so-called Bilbao Effect, with all its positive impact. Germany has been, and still is, particularly proactive in inviting internationally renowned star architects to create prestigious buildings. Indeed, some of these celebrities made their breakthrough by designing buildings for Germany. But at the moment, not one of those stars is actually a German citizen stepping into the shoes of such past masters as Walter Gropius or Mies van der Rohe. Nevertheless, in recent years, increasing numbers of German architects and engineers have been making their mark in other countries, albeit on a much broader basis. In short, quality German architecture is in demand.

Having adapted an existing exhibition for the International Architecture Biennial São Paulo (BIA) in 2005, Germany's 2007 contribution, commissioned by the Federal Ministry of Transport, Building and Urban Affairs (BMVBS) on behalf of the German government, and presented at the Biennial Pavilion from November 10 to December 16, 2007, was the first to be specially devised for the event. This in itself testifies to the increasing importance of the São Paulo BIA for Germany. In preparation for the BIA, the BMVBS held a competition for exhibition concepts along the lines of the long-familiar selection process for the German contribution to the Venice Architecture Biennial. The winning concept was submitted by the Deutsches Architekturmuseum (DAM), and its director, Peter Cachola Schmal, was duly appointed general commissioner.

The exhibition installation *Ready for Take-Off* highlights architectural qualities generally held to be "typically German," such as technical innovation, attention to detail, sensitivity to the urban context, and awareness of ecological issues and sustainability, in addition to the "classic" secondary virtues associated with Germany, such as order, thoroughness, diligence, honesty, discipline, punctuality, and reliability. These slogans, in German and Portuguese, were woven in green, the Brazilian national color, into a black, red, and gold carpet reminiscent of an oversize German flag that was part of the show. A total of sixteen architectural firms and their respective engineering partners were represented, each showing a current export project. The typical working approach of each of these firms was demonstrated by way of a building project they had already completed in Germany. Models, plans, and photos of the projects were displayed in large, open aluminum suitcases symbolizing the worldwide travels and international work of German architects. The Rimowa cases and the specially printed Dura carpet featured in the exhibition are themselves products that typify the high-quality, built-to-last ethos behind the export commodities labeled "Made in Germany."

For the most part, the German representatives selected for the exhibition were drawn from architectural firms currently undertaking their first major project abroad, either as the result of a competition or through a direct contract. They ranged from talented newcomers such as BeL, Kirsten Schemel Architekten, KSV Krüger Schuberth Vandreike, and Pysall Ruge Architekten, to established names such as Carsten Roth Architekt, Gerber Architekten, GKK + Architekten, Staab Architekten, and Wandel Hoefer Lorch + Hirsch, including such internationally renowned players as Barkow Leibinger Architekten, Behnisch Architekten, Ingenhoven Architekten, J. Mayer H.,

und international renommierte Akteure wie Barkow Leibinger Architekten, Behnisch Architekten, Ingenhoven Architekten, J. Mayer H. oder Sauerbruch Hutton bis hin zu einer sehr großen Firma wie KSP Engel und Zimmermann mit mehreren Filialen in drei verschiedenen Ländern. Das Architekturbüro Deutschland ist ein Netzwerk von acht etablierten Architektur- und Ingenieurbüros, die einzeln und gemeinsam im Ausland tätig sind. Sie alle sind *Ready for Take-Off* für die Ausführung ihres ganz persönlichen Architekturexports.

Die vorliegende Publikation erscheint aus Anlass der Übernahme des deutschen Biennalebeitrags aus Brasilien, der in einer Ausstellung im DAM in Frankfurt am Main präsentiert wird. Neben der Darstellung der ausgewählten Projekte im In- und Ausland und einer Dokumentation der 7. BIA São Paulo beleuchtet dieser Katalog mithilfe von Beiträgen renommierter Architekturkritiker sowie erfahrener Geschäftsführer und Referenten von Architekten- und Ingenieurverbänden weitere Bereiche des Architekturexports.

Für den ursprünglichen Auftrag, den deutschen Beitrag in Brasilien zu kuratieren, geht ein großer Dank an das BMVBS und an das Auswärtige Amt, das dieses Projekt gefördert hat. Hervorragende Arbeit leistete in diesem Zusammenhang das Bundesamt für Bauwesen und Raumordnung (BBR), insbesondere Olaf Asendorf und Kerstin Schwabe. Wir danken natürlich auch allen beteiligten Architekturbüros und Fotografen für die Unterstützung der Ausstellung mit ihren Modellen, Plänen und Bildern. Hervorzuheben ist hier das Architekturbüro Deutschland, vertreten durch Matthias Burkart, Amandus Sattler und Till Schneider, für ihre Beratung bei der Konzeptfindung und für die Ausstellungsarchitektur. Den Grafikern von Surface, Markus Weisbeck, Oliver Kuntsche und Max Weber, sei gedankt für die Corporate Identity der Ausstellung und die ausgefallene Gestaltung der Kofferinhalte und dieses Katalogs. Sally Below und Annette Schotters von Sally Below Cultural Affairs machten eine hervorragende Projektkommunikation. Manuel Cuadra vermittelte wertvolle Kontakte.

In São Paulo wurden wir von vielen Menschen unterstützt, die wir hier nicht alle nennen können, die jedoch zum Gelingen der Ausstellung und des Rahmenprogramms entscheidend beigetragen haben. Unser Dank geht besonders an das Generalkonsulat der Bundesrepublik Deutschland in São Paulo, das Goethe-Institut São Paulo, die Fundação Bienal de São Paulo, die Architekturfakultät der Universidade de São Paulo sowie an Tobias May, Wolfgang Glöckner und Anne Dieterich. Dem gesamten Team des DAM möchten wir für die Unterstützung in der Vorbereitungszeit danken, besonders Anke Gabriel und Christian Walter für die Modellausleihen und den Auf- und Abbau in Frankfurt und São Paulo.

Nicht zuletzt sei unseren Sponsoren gedankt, ohne die wir *Ready for Take-Off* nicht hätten realisieren können: der Stadt Frankfurt am Main als Förderer des DAM, der Deutschen Bank Bauspar AG als Hauptsponsor der Ausstellung, der AUDI AG als Sponsor des DAM 2008, der Dorma GmbH & Co. KG für den Transport, der Dura Tufting GmbH für die Teppiche in São Paulo und Frankfurt sowie der Siteco Beleuchtungstechnik GmbH für die Leuchten in den Koffern. Weiterhin wurden wir freundlicherweise unterstützt von der Rimowa GmbH, der Röhm GmbH und der Oschatz Visuelle Medien GmbH & Co. KG und der Schenker Deutschland AG.

and Sauerbruch Hutton, and even the major firm of KSP Engel und Zimmermann, which has offices in three different countries. Architekturbüro Deutschland is a network of eight established architectural and engineering firms working both independently and jointly in other countries. They are all *Ready for Take-off* to show their own personal architectural exports.

This catalogue is published to coincide with the exhibition at the DAM in Frankfurt am Main presenting Germany's contribution to the 2007 BIA. Apart from showcasing the selected projects at home and abroad, along with a report on the 7th BIA São Paulo, the catalogue contains essays by renowned architecture critics and by experienced members of architectural and engineering bodies that shed light on further aspects of architectural export.

We wish to express our enormous gratitude to the Federal Ministry of Transport, Building and Urban Affairs (BMVBS) and to the German Foreign Office, who funded this project, for inviting us to curate the German contribution in Brazil. The work of the Federal Office for Building and Regional Planning (BBR), especially Olaf Asendorf and Kerstin Schwabe, was outstanding. We are also immensely grateful to all of the architects and photographers involved in supporting the exhibition by providing models, plans, and pictures. In particular, we wish to thank Architekturbüro Deutschland, represented by Matthias Burkart, Amandus Sattler, and Till Schneider, for their input in developing the concept and for the exhibition architecture. We are also indebted to Markus Weisbeck, Oliver Kuntsche, and Max Weber of the Surface graphic design team, who created the corporate identity for the exhibition, imaginatively orchestrated the suitcase contents, and designed this catalogue. Sally Below and Annette Schotters of Sally Below Cultural Affairs did an excellent job of ensuring smooth communications throughout the project. Manuel Cuadra introduced valuable contacts.

In São Paulo we were fortunate in having the support and assistance of many individuals, too numerous to mention here, all of whom contributed to the success of the exhibition and fringe program in important ways. Our special thanks go to the General Consulate of the Federal Republic of Germany in São Paulo, to the Goethe-Institut São Paulo, to the Fundação Bienal de São Paulo, to the Faculty of Architecture at the Universidade de São Paulo, and to Tobias May, Wolfgang Glöckner, and Anne Dieterich. We also wish to thank the entire team at the DAM for their generous support in the course of all of the preparations, most notably Anke Gabriel and Christian Walter, who arranged the loans of architectural models and the setup and dismantling of the exhibition in Frankfurt and São Paulo.

Finally, we wish to thank our sponsors, without whom we could not have realized *Ready for Take-Off:* the City of Frankfurt am Main as patron of the DAM, Deutsche Bank Bauspar AG as main sponsor of the exhibition, AUDI AG as sponsor of the DAM 2008, Dorma GmbH & Co. KG for the transport, Dura Tufting GmbH for the carpets in São Paulo and Frankfurt, and Siteco Beleuchtungstechnik GmbH for the lighting in the suitcases. We also benefited from the kind support of Rimowa GmbH, Röhm GmbH, Oschatz Visuelle Medien GmbH & Co. KG, and Schenker Deutschland AG.

Welche Rolle spielen »deutsche Werte« und »Sekundärtugenden« für den Erfolg des Architekturexports?
Anna Hesse, Peter Cachola Schmal

Ready for Take-Off
auf der 7. BIA São Paulo 2007
Ready for Take-Off
at the 7th BIA São Paulo 2007

Ready for Take-Off
auf der 7. BIA São Paulo 2007
Ready for Take-Off
at the 7th BIA São Paulo 2007

Pink Project, New Orleans, Graft
Pink Project, New Orleans, Graft

Das Konzept der Ausstellung *Ready for Take-Off* basiert auf der These, dass deutsche Planer international beliebt und gefragt sind, weil sie die »typisch deutschen« Werte und »Sekundärtugenden« verinnerlicht haben: Sie sind nicht nur im Berufsleben »fleißig«, »zuverlässig«, »ordentlich«, »pünktlich« und »pflichtbewusst«. Besonders deutlich wird dies, wenn sie sich auf internationalem Parkett bewegen. Im Vergleich mit anderen Nationen besitzt offenbar ein Großteil der Deutschen diese Charaktereigenschaften. Seit der erfolgreichen und vorbildlich organisierten Fußballweltmeisterschaft 2006 haben die Deutschen einen Teil ihrer häufig präsenten Zurückhaltung und Bescheidenheit verloren und zeigen ihre nationale Zugehörigkeit mit wahrer Freude. Eine Haltung, die in den meisten Ländern als selbstverständlich angesehen wird, die Deutschen betreffend aber immer noch für erhebliche Missverständnisse und Irritationen sorgt – nicht nur in Deutschland selbst, sondern auch in den Nachbarländern.

Diese Tugenden machen natürlich aus einem gewöhnlichen noch keinen erfolgreichen Architekten, besonders dann nicht, wenn er von Kollegen mit ähnlichen Eigenschaften umgeben ist. Langjährige Erfahrungen im Exportgeschäft zeigen jedoch, dass das gute Ansehen der Deutschen und der deutschen Bauwirtschaft beim Einstieg und der Auftragsvergabe im Ausland sehr hilfreich sein kann. Danach müssen selbstverständlich auch die planerischen Qualitäten überzeugen. Im Gespräch mit uns hat Stefan Helming, Projektleiter der Deutschen Gesellschaft für Technische Zusammenarbeit (GTZ), dieses Phänomen anhand eines Beispiels in Äthiopien anschaulich beschrieben.

Der deutsche Architekturexport erfolgt mittlerweile über verschiedene Wege direkt im Ausland oder aber von Deutschland aus. Ein Teil der am Auslandsgeschäft interessierten Architekten macht sich ganz real auf den Weg ins Ausland. Das Phänomen dieser »ausgewanderten« deutschen Planer ist so weit verbreitet, dass es eine eigene Ausstellung verdiente; daher werden wir hier nicht weiter darauf eingehen. Als besonders erfolgreich sei nur das von Deutschen geführte Büro Graft (mit Hauptsitz in Los Angeles und Berlin sowie einem Büro in Peking) genannt, das zur Zeit in Zusammenarbeit mit Brad Pitt bezahlbare Wohnungen für die Opfer des Hurrikans Katrina in New Orleans plant. Auch die jungen Sachsen m2r in London, bei uns bekannt für ihre Schwarzbergschanze Vogtland Arena in Klingenthal, stehen für diese Version des »Eigenexports«.

Ready for Take-Off dagegen präsentiert anhand ausgewählter Projekte einen aktuellen Querschnitt der tatsächlich von Deutschland aus »exportierenden« Gruppe. In der Nachfolge von großen Büros wie Albert Speer und Partner (AS&P) oder von Gerkan, Marg und Partner (gmp), die bereits seit Jahrzehnten große Bauvorhaben in Asien, Afrika und der arabischen Welt ausführen, verteilen sich die Planungen der nächsten Generationen beinahe weltweit. Ein Schwerpunkt liegt dabei auf der Europäischen Union, die als bevorzugte Region durch geringere Sprach- und Kulturbarrieren sowie durch eine einfachere Rechtslage für viele – nicht nur geografisch – am nächsten liegt. Es fällt jedoch auf, dass keine Projekte in Lateinamerika oder Afrika für die Ausstellung zu finden waren. Das Berliner Büro Staab Architekten hat zwar im vergangenen Jahr die Deutsche Botschaft in Mexiko-Stadt fertiggestellt, die jedoch nach deutschem Planungsrecht für deutsche Bauherren gebaut und nach der deutschen Honorarordnung für Architekten und Ingenieure abgerechnet wurde.

What Role Do "German Values" and "Secondary Virtues"
Play in Successfully Exporting Architecture?
Anna Hesse, Peter Cachola Schmal

The concept of the exhibition *Ready for Take-Off* is based on the hypothesis that German architects and engineers are in great demand internationally because they embody "typically German" values and secondary virtues. They are "industrious," "dependable," "orderly," "punctual," and "dutiful"—and not just in their working lives. This becomes particularly evident when they make their appearance on the international scene. Apparently, in comparison with architects from other nations, a greater number of the Germans possess these characteristics. Since their exemplary organization of the highly successful soccer World Cup in 2006, Germans have dropped something of their customary self-effacing reserve and are happy to proclaim their nationality. In most other nations, such an attitude is entirely normal, but where Germans are involved it can still cause serious misunderstandings and annoyance—not just in Germany itself, but also in neighboring countries.

Naturally, the virtues listed above do not make a successful architect out of an ordinary one, especially if he or she is surrounded by colleagues with much the same qualities. But long years of experience in the export business show that the good reputation of the Germans and the German construction industry can be extremely helpful in securing a foothold in foreign markets and obtaining commissions there. Of course, accessing these markets is only a first step; designers must then be able to convince clients of their skills. Stefan Helming, project manager of Deutsche Gesellschaft für Technische Zusammenarbeit (GTZ), discussed this phenomenon with us, using an example in Ethiopia to illustrate his case.

These days the export of German architecture takes place in various ways. In some cases it is produced directly abroad; in others it is sent from Germany. A number of architects interested in doing business abroad have moved to foreign countries. Today this phenomenon of "émigré" German planners is so widespread that it would merit an exhibition of its own; for this reason we shall not examine it in depth. Nevertheless, a few particularly successful examples can be named here: the German-run firm Graft (with its main offices in Los Angeles and Berlin and an office in Beijing) is at present designing affordable housing in New Orleans for the victims of the hurricane Katrina in collaboration with Brad Pitt; and the young architects from Saxony who head the London-based practice m2r, known here for their Schwarzberg Ski Jump, Vogtland Arena in Klingenthal, are also representative of this kind of "self-export."

Ready for Take-Off features projects that provide an up-to-date cross section of the group that actually "exports" from Germany. Works by the architects of the next generation, the successors to large offices such as Albert Speer und Partner (AS&P) or von Gerkan, Marg und Partner (gmp)—who have been erecting large projects in Asia, Africa, and Arab countries for decades—are distributed throughout much of the world. There is, however, a strong focus on the European Union; the language and cultural barriers other European countries present are less formidable, and the legal situation is simpler, making it for many the closest region—and not in a purely geographical sense. It is remarkable, however, that no projects in either Latin America or Africa could be found for this exhibition. The Berlin practice Staab Architekten did complete the German embassy in Mexico City last year, but this building was erected for a German client, was built in compliance with German planning regulations, and used the German scale of fees for architects and engineers; thus it would

Schwarzbergschanze Vogtland Arena,
Klingenthal, m2r-architecture
Schwarzberg Ski Jump, Vogtland Arena,
Klingenthal, m2r-architecture

Diplomatenviertel, Riad, AS&P
Diplomatic Quarter, Riyadh, AS&P

OAU Konferenzzentrum, Abuja, AS&P
OAU International Conference Center, Abuja, AS&P

International Conference & Exhibition Center,
Nanning, gmp
International Conference & Exhibition Center,
Nanning, gmp

Daher kann dieses Projekt nicht als typisches Exportprojekt für einen beispielhaften Bau in Lateinamerika in der Ausstellung herangezogen werden. Viele lateinamerikanische Länder scheinen ihre Märkte durch restriktive Regelungen Ausländern zu verschließen – ähnlich wie Brasilien, das Gastland der Biennale. Ob dies der alleinige Grund für das Fehlen erfolgreicher Projekte ist, müsste indes weitergehend untersucht werden.

Um besser zu verstehen, weshalb es zur Zeit keine deutschen Stararchitekten gibt, internationale Stars aber im Gegenzug gerne in Deutschland bauen und warum deutsche Architekten als Mitarbeiter in ausländischen Büros so beliebt sind, wurden mehrere renommierte europäische Architekten zum Interview gebeten. Der Engländer Spencer de Grey (Senior Executive und Head of Design im Büro Foster + Partners, London) und der Franzose Dominique Perrault (Inhaber des Büros Dominique Perrault Architecture, Paris) berichteten uns von ihren langjährigen und einschlägigen Erfahrungen mit deutschen Planern und Bauherren. Im darauffolgenden Gespräch stellte sich der Niederländer Kees Christiaanse (Inhaber des Büros Kees Christiaanse Architects & Planners, Rotterdam und Zürich, sowie Professor an der ETH Zürich) schließlich als Kenner und Liebhaber der deutschen und schweizerischen Baukultur heraus. Seiner Meinung nach steht der deutschen Baukultur in den nächsten Jahren eine rosige Zukunft bevor.

Deutsche Architekten und Ingenieure sollten daher den internationalen Vergleich nicht scheuen und mit einer gesunden Portion Selbstbewusstsein auf dem internationalen Parkett auftreten. Sie können direkt auf den guten Ruf, der ihnen vorauseilt, aufbauen.

be impossible to present it in the exhibition as a typical export project for a model building in Latin America. It seems that many Latin American countries—including Brazil, the host country of the Biennial—use restrictive regulations to close their markets to foreigners. To be able to say whether this is the sole reason for the lack of successful German projects there would require investigation in greater depth.

To gain a better understanding of why there are no German star architects at present—even though international star architects like to build in Germany—and to discover why foreign offices are so eager to recruit German architects, we interviewed a number of well-known European architects. Englishman Spencer de Grey (senior executive and head of design at Foster + Partners, London) and French architect Dominique Perrault (head of Dominique Perrault Architecture, Paris) told us about their many years of experience with German architects, engineers, and clients. Dutch architect Kees Christiaanse (head of Kees Christiaanse Architects & Planners, Rotterdam and Zurich, and professor at the ETH Zurich) revealed himself to be a well-informed admirer of the German and Swiss culture of building. In his opinion, German building culture can look forward to a rosy future.

It is clear that German architects and engineers can more than hold their own in the international arena and can venture onto the international stage with a healthy degree of self-assurance. The good reputation that precedes them offers a sound foundation upon which to build.

Flughafen Algier, gmp
Algiers airport, gmp

Stefan Helming, Deutsche Gesellschaft für Technische Zusammenarbeit
Interview, 27. Dezember 2007

DAM Herr Helming, worin genau besteht Ihre Aufgabe für die GTZ in Äthiopien?

Stefan Helming Ich bin hier Abteilungsleiter für all die Projekte, die die GTZ im Auftrag der äthiopischen Regierung realisiert. Wir haben einerseits Projekte, die von der Bundesregierung mitfinanziert werden – das sind eher Beraterprojekte. Und dann haben wir Projekte, die ausschließlich von den Äthiopiern finanziert werden, die im engeren Sinn keine Entwicklungsprojekte mehr sind. Diesen Teil leite ich. Das beinhaltet ein großes Projekt für mehrere Universitäten, ein paar Wohnungsbauprojekte sowie Bauprojekte für Gesundheitsstationen auf dem Land.

DAM Was für Ausmaße hat dieses große Universitätsprojekt? In was für einem Zeitraum soll dort gebaut werden?

SH Es sind dreizehn Universitäten an fünfzehn Standorten. Der Ursprungsvertrag geht über 1,5 Millionen Quadratmeter. Das sind über 1 000 Häuser: Studentenwohnheime, Vorlesungsgebäude, Bibliotheken und so weiter. Alles was man so braucht für einen Unibetrieb. Es sind nagelneue Universitäten auf der grünen Wiese. Wir sind ein bisschen stolz darauf, dass alles sehr schnell geht. Der Vertrag wurde Ende August 2005 abgeschlossen. Da war noch nichts geplant, geschweige denn gebaut. Baubeginn auf den ersten Baustellen war dann im April / Mai 2006, und die ersten Universitäten haben im Februar 2007 eröffnet – natürlich noch nicht mit der vollen Ausbaustufe, sondern nur für die ersten 800 Studenten. Aber die wohnen nun auf dem Campus und werden dort auch unterrichtet. Jetzt gerade hat jede Universität wieder weitere Leute aufgenommen, so dass wir an den einzelnen Universitäten nach gut zwei Jahren Projektlaufzeit schon zwischen 2 000 und 3 000 Studenten haben. Aber die Ausbaustufen gehen bis 8 000, 10 000, 12 000 Studenten, je nach Standort. Das heißt, da fehlt noch einiges.
Der Witz ist, dass das Ganze baubegleitende Planung ist, oder planungsbegleitendes Bauen. Es geht alles gleichzeitig. Wir können alles aus einer Hand machen – das ist ein Vorteil. Normalerweise gibt es immer ein Ausschreibungsverfahren, dann eine Studie, danach einen Entwurf und dann wieder eine Ausschreibung und so weiter. Das dauert so alles ewig. Wir managen das aus einer Hand.

DAM Ging der Auftrag direkt an die GTZ?

SH Der Auftrag ging direkt an die GTZ als »Programme Management Agent«, was eigentlich zwei Aufgaben beinhaltet. Die eine ist so etwas wie Bauherrenvertretung, die zweite ist »Capacity Building«, Kompetenzentwicklung für die äthiopische Bauwirtschaft. Sowohl Planung als auch die ganze Durchführung machen Äthiopier unter unserer Anleitung. Hunderte Baufirmen und Architekturbüros wagen sich an dieses riesige Uniprojekt. Ein Projekt, für das sie streng genommen eigentlich gar nicht qualifiziert sind. Aber weil sie von der GTZ »ans Händchen genommen« werden, geht es eben doch.
Schon vor etlichen Jahren gab es im Wohnungsbaubereich eine Zusammenarbeit bei der Entwicklung von Geschosswohnungsbau – damals wurde alles noch von der Bundesregierung finanziert. Eine standardisierte Bauweise mit Hohlblocksteinen wurde an die hiesigen Verhältnisse angepasst und eingeführt. Das lief erfolgreich und hat den Äthiopiern gefallen, sowohl die Art der GTZ als auch die technische Vorgehensweise. Dann hatte die Regierung noch beschlossen, auf einer anderen

Stefan Helming, Deutsche Gesellschaft für Technische Zusammenarbeit
Interview, December 27, 2007

DAM Mr. Helming, what exactly does your work for the GTZ in Ethiopia entail?

Stefan Helming I'm here as department head for all the projects undertaken by the GTZ at the request of the Ethiopian government. On the one hand, we have projects that are cofinanced by the German government—those tend to be consulting projects. And then we also have projects that are fully financed by the Ethiopians, and which are not development projects in the narrow sense. That's the part I'm in charge of. It includes a major project for several universities, a few housing construction projects, and construction projects for health-care facilities in rural areas.

DAM Just how big is this major university project? And what kind of time frame is involved?

SH It's for thirteen universities in fifteen different locations. The original contract is for 1.5 million square meters. That's more than 1,000 buildings: student residence halls, lecture buildings, libraries, and so on. All of the things that are needed for a university to operate. These are brand-new universities, greenfield developments. We are quite proud of the speed at which everything is progressing. The contract was signed at the end of August 2005. At that stage, there were still no plans, let alone any buildings. Construction work began on the first sites in April/May 2006, and the first universities opened in February 2007—of course, not to full capacity, but just for the first eight hundred students. But they are now living on the campus and being taught there. Each of the universities has just had a new intake of students, so that now, a good two years into the project, the individual universities already have between two and three thousand students. But they are aiming at capacities of eight, ten, and twelve thousand students, depending on location. So there's still a lot to be done.
The thing is that the whole project involves planning during construction, or construction during planning. It's all happening at the same time. We can do everything under one roof—that's an advantage. Usually, there's always a process of tendering, then a study, then a design, and then another round of tendering and so on. That can take forever. We manage the whole thing ourselves.

DAM Was the contract awarded directly to the GTZ?

SH The contract was awarded directly to the GTZ as so-called program management agent, which actually involves two tasks. One is more or less acting on behalf of the client, and the other is capacity development—developing skills in the Ethiopian construction industry. Both the planning and the entire implementation of the project are being carried out by Ethiopians under our supervision. Hundreds of construction companies and firms of architects are tackling this huge university project—a project for which, strictly speaking, they are not really qualified. But because they have the GTZ holding their hand, as it were, it does work.
Quite a few years ago there was a joint project in the housing construction sector to develop multistory apartment buildings. At that time, everything was still being financed by the German government. A standardized cavity block construction system was adapted to the local conditions and introduced. That went well and the Ethiopians were pleased both with the approach taken by the GTZ and with the technical modus operandi. Then the government decided to implement a modernization of

Universität Dese
Dese University

»Skill Upgrading« auf einer Baustelle
"Skill upgrading" on a construction site

Ebene die Modernisierung der äthiopischen Wirtschaft mit Deutschland als Referenz durchzuführen – als »Benchmark«, wie sie immer sagen. Das ganze nennt sich »Engineering Capacity Building«. Es bezieht sich nicht nur auf Architektur und Bauwesen, sondern auf alle technischen Zweige der Wirtschaft, Berufsschulbildung, Ingenieurfakultäten der Unis, Messwesen, Normung, Qualitätssicherung und so weiter. Folgende Geschichte wird erzählt, die wohl nicht ganz falsch ist: Die Äthiopier sind nach China und Malaysia gefahren und haben gefragt: »Wie habt ihr das denn so schnell hingekriegt hier bei euch, mit der Entwicklung im technischen Bereich?« Die Antwort war: »Das haben wir uns alles bei den Deutschen abgeguckt!« Deswegen finde ich es interessant, dass bei dieser Biennale die sogenannten Sekundärtugenden der Deutschen in den Vordergrund gestellt werden. Genau darum geht es hier: die Zuverlässigkeit, die technische Brillanz, die Innovationskraft der deutschen Ingenieure im weitesten Sinne. Da gehören auch Architekten mit dazu.

DAM Aber es ist schon sehr auf die technische Innovation ausgerichtet? Es geht nicht um das Künstlerische, oder?

SH Ja, es geht um das Bautechnische, aber nicht nur im technologischen Sinne, sondern auch im organisatorischen. Es geht auch um diese »Sekundärwerte« wie Disziplin und Fleiß, Detailgenauigkeit und Detailtreue. Dass man sich von der Qualitätsethik her nicht mit Pfusch zufrieden gibt. Es gibt in diesem Sinn eine kulturelle Dimension, aber keine künstlerische.

DAM Und wie vermitteln Sie das? Sie sind für das Projektmanagement verantwortlich, aber wie vermitteln Sie solche Werte?

SH Indem wir die Oberaufsicht über das ganze Programm führen, indem wir den Architekten, die die einzelnen Gebäude entwerfen und den Masterplan entwickeln, mit Rat und Tat zur Seite stehen, Verbesserungsvorschläge machen und den Rahmen setzen. Und indem wir später in der Bauausführung auf den Baustellen ganz konkret Leute einsetzen. Wir haben auf jeder Baustelle einen sogenannten »Site Manager«, einen Projektleiter: Das ist ein deutscher Bauingenieur oder ein Architekt. Dann haben wir sogenannte »Skill Upgrader«: Das sind deutsche Handwerksmeister, zum Beispiel Maurer, Elektriker oder Dachdecker, die ganz direkt »on the job« den Arbeitern und dem Personal der Baufirmen etwas beibringen und die »deutschen« Werte und Standards vermitteln. Das meiste wird einfach auf der Baustelle vorgeführt. Wir machen auch ein bisschen Theorieunterricht, aber das ist vielleicht eine halbe Stunde am Abend. Als dritte Kategorie gibt es noch die »Construction Consultants«, so eine Art Unternehmensberater, die mit dem Büro der Baufirma zusammenarbeiten. Sie beraten in allen Bereichen, wie man die Prozesse verbessern kann, im Beschaffungs- und Rechnungswesen, bei der Planung und auf der Baustelle. Das führt zu einer unabhängigen Zertifizierung nach ISO 9001. Demnächst wird die erste Gruppe dahingehend untersucht, ob sie von den Prozessen und vom Management her fit und auf Weltniveau ist.

DAM Wie kam denn der ursprüngliche Kontakt zustande? Hat sich die äthiopische Regierung direkt an die GTZ gewandt oder an die deutsche Regierung?

the Ethiopian economy on a different level with Germany as their point of reference, or benchmark, so to speak. This program is known as engineering capacity development. It relates not only to architecture and construction, but also to all the technical branches of the sector, vocational training, university engineering faculties, quantity surveying, standardization, quality assurance, and so on. There's an anecdote going around that probably has a grain of truth to it. It goes like this: some Ethiopians traveled to China and Malaysia, and when they were there, they asked, "How did you manage to achieve so much technical progress so quickly?" The answer was, "By copying what the Germans do!" That's why I find it interesting that at this Biennial the so-called secondary virtues of the Germans have been highlighted. That's exactly what it's all about here: reliability, technical brilliance, the innovative prowess of German engineers in the broadest sense. And that includes the architects.

DAM But it's all very much about technical innovation, rather than art, isn't it?

SH Yes, it is about construction techniques, not only in the purely technological sense, but also in terms of organization. It's also about such secondary values as discipline and diligence, precision and attention to detail, about an ethos of quality that simply refuses to accept shoddy workmanship. In that respect, yes, there is a cultural dimension, but not necessarily an artistic one.

DAM And how do you get that across? You're in charge of project management, but how do you convey values like those?

SH By supervising the entire program, by providing advice and hands-on assistance to the architects designing the individual buildings and drawing up the master plan, by suggesting improvements and staking out the framework. And by deploying certain people on the building site during construction. On every building site we have a "site manager," a project manager who is a German structural engineer or architect. And then we have what we call "skill upgraders": qualified German tradesmen such as bricklayers, electricians, or roofers who pass on their skills directly, on the job, to the laborers and employees of the construction companies and who convey their "German" values and standards in that way. Most of that is simply demonstrated on the building site. We also do some theoretical instruction, but that's only for about half an hour in the evening. As a third category, there are so-called construction consultants who work closely with the office of the construction company. They provide consulting in all areas regarding ways of improving processes, not only in procurement and accounting, but also in planning and on-site. That results in an independent certification according to ISO 9001. The first group is about to be assessed to see whether their processes and management are up to international standards.

DAM How was the contact initially set up? Did the Ethiopian government approach the GTZ directly or did they contact the German government?

SH Both. The GTZ has been involved in all kinds of projects in Ethiopia since the 1960s that have nothing to do with construction work. But the GTZ has been repeatedly and increasingly involved in training engineers—so that is a leitmotif. For instance, in the engineering faculty at the country's first and oldest university in Addis Ababa, there's a bronze plaque commemorating the inauguration of the

Einführung einer neuen standardisierten Bauweise
Introduction of a new, standardized construction method

Auf dem Weg zur Zertifizierung
On the way to certification

Auf der Baustelle in Axum: Bau eines Wohnheims in Beton-Skelettbauweise
On a construction site in Axum: construction of a residence hall using a concrete skeleton construction method

SH Beides. Die GTZ ist bereits seit den 1960er-Jahren in Äthiopien mit allen möglichen Projekten vertreten, die mit dem Bauwesen nichts zu tun haben. Aber immer wieder tritt die GTZ verstärkt im Bereich der Ingenieurausbildung auf – das ist schon ein Leitmotiv. Zum Beispiel gibt es in der Ingenieurfakultät an der alten, ersten großen Universität in Addis Abeba eine bronzene Plakette, die daran erinnert, dass die Fakultät von Bundespräsident Heinrich Lübke eingeweiht wurde. Daran sieht man die Kontinuität. Das ganze ist wie ein Kompliment an die deutsche Entwicklungshilfe. Die Äthiopier sagen: »Wir kennen euch, wir schätzen euch und wir vertrauen euch. Und jetzt geben wir euch einen Auftrag für Programme, die gar nicht von eurer Regierung gezahlt werden, sondern die wir selbst bezahlen, mit unserem eigenen Geld.« Man kennt sich, da gibt es keine großen Brücken zu schlagen.

DAM Wie viel Geld bekommen Sie für das Management des Universitätsprojekts?

SH Das ganze Projekt hat einen Wert von 250 Millionen Euro. Die Leute sagen immer, wenn das Projekt in Deutschland wäre, dann könnte man das mindestens um den Faktor zehn erhöhen. Einfach deswegen, weil hier die Baukosten natürlich viel geringer sind. Wir können die Leute bezahlen, die wir nach Äthiopien schicken. Das sind ungefähr einhundert deutsche Experten. Die werden alle nach unserem deutschen Tarifvertrag bezahlt. Zusätzlich bekommen wir noch so viel, dass es eben auskömmlich ist. Wir sind keine profitorientierte Firma, wir müssen auf unsere Kosten kommen. Die normalen »Overheads« werden noch bezahlt. Da bleiben keine großen Gewinne übrig, aber es wird alles rundum komfortabel bezahlt. Von höchster Ministerebene wird auch immer nachgeprüft, und es gibt regelmäßige Treffen. Wir können sagen, dass dieses Bauprogramm schneller und preiswerter ist als jedes andere, das bisher in diesem Land realisiert wurde. Man kann es schwer mit Deutschland vergleichen, aber der Quadratmeterpreis liegt zwischen 110 und 120 Euro. Das ist natürlich keine Spitzenarchitektur und das ist auch keine Luxusausführung. Es sind Hohlblocksteine und Stahlbetongerippe, aber es sind solide Bauten. Diese Technologie wurde vor ein paar Jahren von der GTZ in Äthiopien eingeführt. Mit Hohlblocksteinen und Trägerelementen, die gegossen werden. Sehr wenige Elemente, aus denen man aber sehr viel bauen kann. Es sind immer wieder dieselben normierten Einzelteile. Daraus ergeben sich große Rationalisierungseffekte, es ist einfach kostensparend. Äthiopien ist ein armes Land, das ärmste Land der Erde: Dort muss man billig bauen.

DAM Haben Sie die äthiopischen Architekten und Ingenieure, die an diesem Projekt arbeiten, ausgewählt?

SH Die äthiopische Regierung hat gesagt, dass im Lauf des Projekts alle Baufirmen und alle Architekturbüros, die irgendein Interesse zeigen, daran teilnehmen sollen. Das heißt, es ist fast wie mit Schulklassen. Zuerst haben wir eine Gruppe von Firmen, die für ein Baulos teilnehmen. Wenn die fertig sind, dann kommen die nächsten Firmen für das nächste Baulos. Wir haben im Augenblick über zwanzig Baufirmen und acht bis zehn Architekturbüros. Zusätzlich gibt es noch eine andere Vorgabe, die auch entwicklungspolitisch sehr wichtig ist: Die Generalunternehmer – wir haben an jedem Standort einen Generalunternehmer, zum Teil sogar mehrere – müssen Subunternehmen zum Beispiel für Ausbaugewerke beauftragen, damit das Ganze eine regionale Komponente erhält. Teilweise handelt es sich um sehr abgelegene

faculty by German president Heinrich Lübke. That in itself speaks for continuity. The whole thing is something of a compliment to German development aid. The Ethiopians take the view that, "We know you, appreciate you, and trust you. And now we're going to give you a contract for programs that aren't even being paid by your government, but by us, with our own money." Both sides know each other; there are no major gulfs to be bridged.

DAM How much money do you get for managing the university project?

SH The project as a whole has a value in the region of 250 million euros. People always say that if the project was in Germany, it would be at least ten times that amount. That's simply because construction costs here are, of course, much lower. We can pay the people we send to Ethiopia. That's about a hundred German experts, all paid according to our German tariff. And in addition to that we get enough to break even. We're a not-for-profit organization. The usual overheads are covered. That means there's not much in the way of profit, but there's enough to cover everything comfortably. The highest levels of government make constant checks and there are regular meetings. We can say that this construction program is faster and more economical than anything ever undertaken in this country. It can't really be compared with Germany, but prices run to about 110 to 120 euros per square meter. Of course, we're not talking about deluxe architecture here; these are cavity block systems and reinforced concrete shells, but they're solid buildings. The GTZ introduced this technology to Ethiopia a few years ago. Cavity block systems and cast load-bearing elements—very few elements, with which it is possible to build a great deal. The same standardized components are used. The result is enormously cost-effective rationalization. Ethiopia is a poor country, the poorest country on Earth. You have to build cheaply there.

DAM Did you choose the Ethiopian architects and engineers involved in this project?

SH The Ethiopian government said that in the course of the project, all the construction companies and architectural firms with an interest in doing so should take part. In other words, it's a little like a classroom situation. First, we have a group of companies involved in one construction phase. Once they've finished, the next company comes in for the next construction phase. At the moment, we have more than twenty construction companies and between eight and ten architectural firms. Besides that, there is another stipulation that is of considerable importance in terms of development policy: the general contractors. We have a general contractor, and sometimes even more than one, at each location. They have to commission subcontractors, for instance for fittings, so that the whole thing takes on a regional component. Some of the sites are very remote. So at the same time, it is a regional development project that creates employment locally. In some cases we have had to build up companies that didn't exist before and ensure that they run operations that are needed, such as making windows or building stairwells.

DAM Were the German experts who came to Ethiopia specially trained for this task?

SH We recruited them on the open market. A lot of them had already worked for German construction companies abroad, such as Bilfinger Berger and the like—

Universität Dire Dawa: der neue Vorlesungssaal
Dire Dawa University: the new lecture hall

Auf der Baustelle in Dire Dawa:
Produktion der Hohlblocksteine
On a construction site in Dire Dawa:
production of hollow blocks

Standorte. Es ist somit gleichzeitig ein Regionalentwicklungsprojekt, damit auch Beschäftigungseffekte vor Ort eintreten. Firmen, die es dort zum Teil gar nicht gibt, müssen wir vor Ort erst aufbauen und dafür sorgen, dass sich die Betriebe bilden, die benötigt werden, zum Beispiel um Fenster oder Treppenhäuser zu bauen.

DAM Wurden die deutschen Experten, die nach Äthiopien gekommen sind, für diese Aufgabe in Deutschland speziell geschult?

SH Die haben wir am Markt rekrutiert. Viele von ihnen sind schon mit deutschen Baufirmen im Ausland tätig gewesen. Mit Bilfinger Berger und so weiter, die üblichen Firmen, die in den Golfstaaten, Saudi-Arabien oder Nigeria bauen. Einige hatten noch nicht in Entwicklungsländern gearbeitet, sondern nur in Deutschland in der Bauwirtschaft. Wir haben sie dann vor Ort selbst ein bisschen geschult, aber nicht sehr intensiv.

DAM Das heißt, Sie sind davon ausgegangen, dass diese Experten direkt in die Arbeit einsteigen können?

SH Ja, und das haben sie auch getan. Was das Bauen angeht, sind sie fit. Das sind gute Leute aus der Branche. Und jetzt müssen sie natürlich diese zusätzliche Aufgabe des »Capacity Building« übernehmen – das fällt einigen leichter als anderen. Da herrscht zum Teil natürlich eine andere Mentalität. Wenn ich aus Deutschland komme, dann würde ich sagen: »Diese Wand, die sie gebaut haben, die ist schief, die muss wieder abgerissen werden.« Als Entwicklungshelfer würde ich stattdessen sagen: »Na komm, letzte Woche war die noch viel schiefer und krummer. Die haben sie doch schon besser gemacht und sie wird schon nicht umfallen.« Da muss man sich dann, was Qualitätsansprüche angeht, schon ein wenig auf die örtlichen Standards einstellen.

DAM Kommen die Deutschen denn generell gut an in Äthiopien? Ist ein gutes Bild der Deutschen vorhanden? Sind Sie persönlich sofort positiv aufgenommen worden?

SH Ja, wir sind sehr positiv aufgenommen worden. Die Äthiopier sind ja aus freien Stücken auf die Deutschen zugekommen. Wir haben hier ein hohes Ansehen. Das hängt natürlich mit verschiedenen Faktoren zusammen. Vielleicht zunächst einmal damit, dass Deutschland hier nie Kolonialmacht war, gewissermaßen politisch unverfänglich ist. Man kann uns keine finstern Motive unterstellen, wie es mit Franzosen, Engländern oder Italienern passiert. Wir sind auch keine Weltmacht wie die Amerikaner, denen man aus diesem Grund misstraut. Zudem haben wir eine für die Leute vertrauenerweckende Art. Nach dem Motto: »Es ist zwar nicht so einfach, mit den Deutschen zu arbeiten, die sind vielleicht nicht so diplomatisch oder geschickt im zwischenmenschlichen Umgang wie manche andere, aber wenn man sich dann mit ihnen verträgt und sich an sie gewöhnt hat, dann sind sie sehr zuverlässig und bleiben am Ball. Sie lassen sich nicht von jeder Kleinigkeit verschrecken.« Das sind, glaube ich, die Merkmale, die man hier schätzt.

the usual companies who do construction work in the Gulf states, Saudi Arabia, or Nigeria. Some of them had never worked in developing countries before, but only in the German construction industry. We did give them some training locally, but nothing intensive.

DAM Which means that you assumed these experts could fit into the job right away?

SH Yes, and they did. As far as construction work goes, they're on the ball. These are good workers from within the industry. And now, of course, they have to take on the additional task of capacity building—which some of them take to more readily than others. Needless to say, there can sometimes be a difference in mentality. If I come from Germany, I'm going to say, "That wall you've built isn't straight. It has to be torn down again." As a development aid worker I'm more likely to say, "Well, OK, that wall is a lot better than it was last week. You've improved it and it isn't going to fall down." So you do have to adapt a little to local standards.

DAM Are the Germans generally well regarded in Ethiopia? Do they have a good image? Were you yourself made to feel welcome right away?

SH Yes, we have been made very welcome. After all, the Ethiopians did approach the Germans themselves. We are very highly regarded here. Of course, that has to do with a number of different factors. First of all, perhaps, because of the fact that Germany was never a colonial power here, so that makes us politically uncontroversial. We cannot be accused of ulterior motives, which might well be the case with the French, the British, or the Italians. And we're not a superpower like the Americans, who are distrusted for that reason. What's more, we do inspire trust in a way, along the lines of: "It may not be easy working with the Germans, they may not be as diplomatic or as socially skilled as some others, but once you get used to them and if you get along with them, they are very reliable and they stay on the ball. And they don't balk at the slightest little problem." Those, I think, are the characteristics that are appreciated here.

Auf der Baustelle in Debre Markos:
die zukünftige Mensa und Veranstaltungshalle
On a construction site in Debre Markos:
the future cafeteria and event hall

Spencer de Grey, Foster + Partners
Interview, 2. Oktober 2007

Commerzbank, Frankfurt am Main,
Foster + Partners

DAM Herr de Grey, ich würde gerne über Deutschland und Deutsche in Ihrem Unternehmen sprechen. Stefan Behling ist der einzige deutsche Senior-Partner, während neun von siebzig Partnern deutsch sind. Gilt das gleiche Verhältnis für Ihre 1 200 Mitarbeiter?

Spencer de Grey Ja, Deutschland ist mit über 200 Architekten, die für uns arbeiten, nach Großbritannien das zweitgrößte in diesem Unternehmen vertretene Land. Unsere Beziehung zu deutschen Architekten, Studenten und Deutschland im Allgemeinen ist so alt wie unser Architekturbüro. Ich kann mich noch erinnern, als ich vor fünfunddreißig Jahren dazustieß und wir für Willis Faber Dumas – unser erstes wichtiges Projekt – tätig wurden; damals interessierten wir uns für die Art und Weise, wie Architekten in Deutschland ausgebildet wurden, ihren gestalterischen Ansatz und vor allem ihr besonderes Augenmerk für technische Aspekte. Ihr Interesse für Struktur und Bauweisen stand in Einklang mit den Überzeugungen und der Philosophie unseres Büros. Auch schon ganz zu Beginn, als wir nur dreißig oder vierzig Mitarbeiter hatten, arbeiteten bereits ein oder zwei deutsche Architekten für uns. Wir haben die Beiträge, die die deutschen Architekten in dieses Büro einbrachten, immer außerordentlich zu schätzen gewusst. Ich glaube, es gibt eine sehr enge Verbindung zwischen unserem Gestaltungsansatz, unseren Interessen und – obwohl man dies nie verallgemeinern kann – der strategischen Sichtweise von Architekten und Studenten in Deutschland. Im Laufe der Zeit ist die Beziehung zwischen dem Büro und Deutschland immer enger geworden. Natürlich gab es kritische Momente, vor allem was die Commerzbank und den Reichstag betrifft. Das waren zwei außerordentlich bedeutende Projekte, für die wir zunächst hier in London arbeiteten. Leute wie Stefan Behling sowie eine Reihe von weiteren deutschen Architekten arbeiteten an diesen Projekten – viele von ihnen kamen aufgrund dieser Aufträge zu uns. Als der Gestaltungsbereich dann nach Deutschland verlagert wurde – sowohl nach Frankfurt, als auch nach Berlin – gründeten wir Büros vor Ort mit deutschen und internationalen Architekten aus London sowie Architekten, die wir vor Ort angeworben hatten. Das führte natürlich in der Folge zur Gründung des Berliner Büros. Es war zunächst als Projektbüro für die Bauphase des Reichstagsgebäudes gedacht. Mittlerweile arbeiten siebzig oder achtzig Leute in Berlin. Es ist unser größtes Büro im Ausland, was zeigt, wie sehr wir den Beitrag, den die deutschen Architekten für unser Büro geleistet haben und weiterhin leisten, bewundern und respektieren.

DAM Obwohl es natürlich nicht gerade politisch korrekt ist, verallgemeinernde Aussagen über Personen oder bestimmte Personengruppen zu treffen, möchte ich Sie dennoch fragen, ob es so etwas wie »typisch deutsche« Eigenschaften oder Stärken bei den entsprechenden Mitarbeitern gibt?

SdG Ja, mit derlei Verallgemeinerungen muss man vorsichtig sein. Ich möchte trotzdem sagen, dass es da ein Engagement und eine Begeisterung gibt, die bemerkenswert sind. Das hat vielleicht mit den Hochschulen und der Ausbildung in Deutschland zu tun. Man ist fasziniert von der Art und Weise, wie die Dinge zusammenkommen, wie sie funktionieren und von der Form des grundlegenden Aufbaus und der Struktur eines Gebäudes. Zudem ist eine Gründlichkeit zu beobachten, die der Philosophie unseres Architekturbüros immer sehr entsprach: Die Art und Weise wie wir uns einem Gestaltungsproblem annähern, versuchen, das Projekt und Briefing von

Spencer de Grey, Foster + Partners
Interview, October 2, 2007

DAM Mr. de Grey, I would like to talk about Germany and Germans in your firm. Stefan Behling is the only executive partner who is German, while 9 out of 70 partners are German. Does that same ratio apply to all of your staff of 1,200?

Spencer de Grey Yes, Germany is the second-largest country represented in this office, after the UK, with over 200 Germans working for us. Our relationship with German architects, German students, and Germany goes right back to the beginning of the practice. I can recall when I joined the practice thirty-five years ago, when we were dealing with Willis Faber Dumas—our first major project—we were very interested in the way that architects in Germany were trained, their approach to design and particularly their emphasis on technical matters. Their interest in structure and how buildings were built struck a chord with the beliefs and philosophy of the practice. Even in those days, right at the beginning, when we were only thirty or forty strong, there were one or two German architects working. We have always hugely enjoyed the contribution that the German architectural profession has made to this practice. I think there is a very close rapport between our design approach, our interests, and—although you can never generalize—the sort of strategic outlook of architects and students in Germany. Over the course of time, the relationship between the practice and Germany has gone from strength to strength. Obviously, there were some critical moments, notably the Commerzbank and the Reichstag. These were two highly significant projects where initially we did the work here in London. People like Stefan Behling worked on them, as did a number of other German architects—many of whom joined the office as a result of those projects. When the design effort moved to Germany—one to Frankfurt and one to Berlin—we set up local offices, comprising both German and international architects from London, as well as those recruited locally. Of course that subsequently led to the setting up of the Berlin office. It was started as a project office for the construction phase on the Reichstag. We now have between seventy and eighty people working in Berlin. It is by far our largest overseas office, which reflects how much we respect and admire the contribution that German designers have made and continue to make to the practice.

DAM Although today it is not deemed politically correct to generalize about a certain people, a certain group . . . but still, is there something where you would say, I find these to be very German traits in my collaborators, or typical strengths?

SdG Yes, one has to be careful of generalizations. I would say, however, that there is a commitment and an enthusiasm, which are very commendable traits. This probably relates to the way the schools work in Germany and the training that is offered. There is a fascination in how things come together, how things work and the sort of fundamental organization and structure of a building. There is also a thoroughness, which has always appealed to the philosophy of the practice. The way we approach a design problem to try and understand the essence of the design and the brief, and all the research that is associated with that. It is very much in keeping with the "German ethos," if that is the right expression. This complements the skills that students acquire from British architecture schools. We have always encouraged people to come to the office right after school and then work their way up through the organization—it has been a very successful approach.

Reichstag, Berlin, Foster + Partners
Reichstag, Berlin, Foster + Partners

Umbau Dresdner Hauptbahnhof,
Foster + Partners
Conversion Dresden Main Station,
Foster + Partners

Bibliothek der Philologischen Fakultät der Freien
Universität Berlin, Foster + Partners
Philology Faculty Library, Berlin Free University,
Foster + Partners

Grund auf zu verstehen sowie die Recherchearbeit, die damit verbunden ist. Das alles steht sehr im Einklang mit dem »deutschen Ethos« wenn das der richtige Ausdruck ist. Das ist eine Ergänzung der Fähigkeiten, die Studenten an britischen Architekturschulen erwerben.

DAM Hat der Auftrag für den Hauptbahnhof in Dresden auch im Berliner Büro seinen Anfang genommen?

SdG Der strategische Entwurf wird zunächst immer erst im Londoner Büro entwickelt – insbesondere in den ersten Phasen eines Projekts. Im Falle des Dresdner Bahnhofs kam das kleine Team aus Berlin nach London, während ich nach Berlin ging. Es fand also an beiden Orten satt. Später, in der Umsetzungsphase des Projekts, wurde die Arbeit natürlich vom Berliner Büro aus getätigt. Ich habe – zusammen mit anderen Kollegen – regelmäßig das Berliner Büro und die Baustelle besucht. Auf diese Art und Weise arbeiten wir gerne im Ausland, das heißt, wenn die Bereiche sich verwischen und das Büro vor Ort – das gewöhnlich viel kleiner ist als das Berliner Büro – eine Menge zu bieten hat. So war das auch mit der Freien Universität Berlin. Bei beiden Projekten gab es eine erfolgreiche wechselseitige Befruchtung durch die Kompetenzen, die sowohl in London als auch in Berlin zur Verfügung standen.

DAM Norman Foster wird in den meisten anderen Ländern als internationaler Star betrachtet, der in den heimischen Markt eindringt. So erleben Leute aus dem Ausland Ihr Architekturbüro. Das ist nicht immer von Vorteil und im Falle von Deutschland gibt es eine Menge ausländischer Architekten, insbesondere die sogenannten Stararchitekten. Ist das eine Besonderheit des deutschen Markts?

SdG Das ist eine gute Frage. Unserer Erfahrung nach – und unsere Erfahrung in Deutschland reicht mit dem Leichtathletikstadion in Frankfurt, das leider nie gebaut wurde, bis 1987 zurück – war Deutschland immer ein offener Markt. Wir wurden immer herzlich aufgenommen. Für uns ist es ein sehr wichtiges Land – nicht nur wegen der Leute, die für uns arbeiten, sondern auch weil wir gerne in Deutschland arbeiten und weil wir eine ganze Reihe von äußerst bedeutenden Projekten für unser Büro in Deutschland realisieren konnten. Ich weiß, dass es immer eine gewisse Spannung erzeugt, wenn Leute von außen kommen, um in einer Stadt oder einem Land zu arbeiten. Ich denke, diese Spannung wird es immer geben, aber das ist einfach eine Gegebenheit. Heutzutage leben viele ein sehr internationales Leben und viele Architekturbüros erhalten Aufträge im Ausland. Das ist ein allgegenwärtiges Phänomen, das auch seine Vorteile hat. In London gibt es sowohl viele US-amerikanische, als auch eine Reihe europäischer Firmen, die für Projekte hierher gekommen sind. Ich glaube, dass das für den Berufsstand der Architekten sehr gut ist. Das heißt, dass alle versuchen am Ball zu bleiben. Es ist eine Herausforderung. Wenn Architekten aus dem Ausland in Ihrer Heimatstadt arbeiten, kann dies neue Begeisterung wecken, spannend sein und andere Möglichkeiten eröffnen und ich finde nicht, dass man sich deswegen in die Ecke gedrängt fühlen sollte.

DAM Dass man ausländische Architekten nach England holt, ist ziemlich neu.

DAM Did the Dresden Main Station project originate in the Berlin office, too?

SdG Strategic design always emanates from the London office—in particular at the initial stages of a project. In the case of Dresden Station, it was a question of the small team in Berlin coming to work in London while I went to Berlin. So it was done in both locations. Later on, the realization of the project was obviously undertaken by the Berlin office. I—together with other colleagues from London—regularly visited both the Berlin office and the site. That is the way that we like to work overseas, where the divisions are blurred, and the local office—usually much smaller than the Berlin office—has a lot to offer. It was the same at the Berlin Free University. On both of those projects there was a successful cross-fertilization of skills between London and Berlin.

DAM Norman Foster is considered in most other countries to be an international star architect that comes into their local market. This is the way people overseas experience your practice. It is not always a benefit, and in the case of Germany there are a lot of foreign architects, especially the so-called star architects, working in Germany. Is that a speciality of the German market?

SdG That's a good question. I think in our experience—and our experience in Germany goes back to 1987 and the athletics stadium in Frankfurt, which sadly did not get built—Germany has always been an open market. We have always gotten a warm reception. For us it is a very important country—not only because of people coming to work here, but because we like working in Germany, and we have done a number of very significant projects for our practice in Germany. I know that there is always a tension when people come from outside to work in a city or country. I think that tension will always exist, but it is a fact of life. Today, everybody leads a very international life, and many practices are invited to work overseas. It is a pervasive phenomenon, which has its benefits. In London we have seen many American firms coming to work here, as well as a number of European firms. I think it is a good thing for the architectural profession. It keeps everybody on their toes. It is a challenge. Having overseas architects working in your hometown can lead to new enthusiasm, new excitement, new possibilities, and I don't think one should be overly defensive about it.

DAM Importing foreign architects to England is rather new.

SdG Yes, I think we are far less open as a country than Germany. It was interesting that the three finalists for the Reichstag did not include a German architect, which, at the time, I found quite extraordinary. It is very far-sighted and broad-minded for a country to commission a foreign architect for their national parliament building.

DAM Our Reichstag is now the symbol of the German Republic. And there are many architects who resent the fact that this building is by a British architect. They say, well it's fine to have an airport, a cultural building, but why do we have the Reichstag built by a foreigner? Can you understand that feeling?

SdG I do understand that, but that is an issue at the time of setting up the competition, which obviously we were not party to. The competition was open to all German architects and twelve invited overseas architects. So, by including the twelve overseas

Wettbewerbsmodell für ein Leichtathletikstadion, Frankfurt am Main, Foster + Partners
Competition model for an athletics stadium, Frankfurt am Main, Foster + Partners

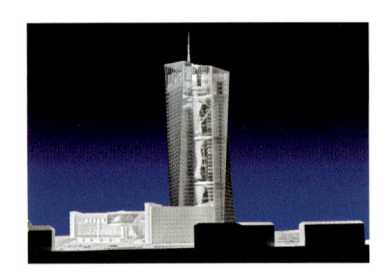

Europäische Zentralbank, Frankfurt am Main,
Coop Himmelb(l)au
European Central Bank, Frankfurt am Main,
Coop Himmelb(l)au

SdG Ja, ich glaube wir sind viel weniger offen als Deutschland. Es war interessant, dass unter den drei Finalisten für den Reichstag kein deutscher Architekt war, was ich zu jener Zeit ziemlich außergewöhnlich fand. Ein Land muss schon sehr weitsichtig und aufgeschlossen sein, um einen ausländischen Architekten für sein nationales Parlamentsgebäude zu beauftragen.

DAM Der Reichstag ist nun das Symbol Deutschlands und es gibt viele Architekten, die sich darüber ärgern, dass dieser Bau von einem britischen Architekten entworfen wurde. Sie argumentieren, dass dies für einen Flughafen oder ein kulturelles Gebäude in Ordnung sei, wenn der Reichstag jedoch von einem Ausländer gebaut werde, sei dies fragwürdig. Können Sie diese Einwände verstehen?

SdG Ja, ich verstehe das, aber es hat mit der Ausrichtung des Wettbewerbs zu jener Zeit zu tun, an der wir offenkundig nicht beteiligt waren. Der Wettbewerb stand allen deutschen und zwölf eingeladenen ausländischen Architekten offen. Indem man also diese zwölf ausländischen Architekten miteinbezog, musste man auch mit der Möglichkeit rechnen, dass einer von ihnen ausgewählt wird. Ich persönlich finde, dass dies nur die Offenheit der Deutschen zeigt, man sollte sich eigentlich darüber freuen. Und insgesamt gesehen halte ich es gar nicht für schlecht, Wettbewerbe mit einer gesunden Mischung aus Architekten vor Ort und aus dem Ausland auszurichten. Es war sehr mutig von der damaligen Regierung, so zu denken. Zudem war es ein sorgfältig organisierter und durchgeführter Wettbewerb. Ich bin natürlich nicht neutral – denn wir haben ja schließlich gewonnen – aber ich hoffe, dass das Ergebnis für sich spricht. Es war eine würdige Lösung für eine ziemlich anspruchsvolle Problematik.

DAM Die Europäische Zentralbank in Frankfurt wird nun vom österreichischen Architekturbüro Coop Himmelb(l)au gebaut. Trotzdem hat auch dieses Gebäude eine hohe symbolische Bedeutung und ist zudem ein Hochhaus.

SdG Wenn man an die Europäische Gemeinschaft glaubt und daran, dass in Europa eine Reihe von unabhängigen Ländern zusammenkommt, dann ist die Idee, dass die Architektur in Europa von europäischen Architekten gestaltet wird, doch eigentlich nur sehr positiv zu sehen. Ich meine, es ist eine gute Sache, wenn ein deutscher Architekt in Madrid oder ein englischer Architekt in Berlin arbeiten und es ist schade, dass England diesbezüglich nicht etwas offener ist. Frankreich sowie die Niederlande, Spanien und viele andere europäische Länder sind da wesentlich aufgeschlossener. Ich sähe auch uns gerne in dieser Position. Es ist in unserem Land schon besser geworden. Das Laban Center und die Tate Modern von Herzog & de Meuron waren in diesem Zusammenhang wichtig. Die steigende Anzahl ausländischer Architekten ist hier auf die Förderung von mehr öffentlichen Gebäuden durch die »Lottery« zurückzuführen. Amerikanische Firmen wie SOM, HOK und KPF sind hier in London natürlich im Rahmen vieler Projekte tätig.

DAM Ihr Berliner Büroleiter sagte mir, er möchte, dass Foster + Partners Berlin als deutsche Firma wahrgenommen wird und er das Gefühl habe, dass das Büro in allen Wettbewerben behandelt würde, als wäre es im Ausland ansässig.

architects there was always a possibility that one of them might have been selected. Personally, I think it illustrates the broadmindedness of the German people—it is something which should be celebrated. More generally, I don't think it is a bad thing to have healthy competitions with people from overseas as well as with local architects. It was very courageous of the government of the day to think like that. Equally, it was a very thoroughly run, carefully organized competition. Obviously I am biased, because we were the winners . . . but I hope that the result speaks for itself. It was an honorable solution to what was actually quite a challenging problem.

DAM The European Central Bank in Frankfurt is now being built by the Austrian architects Coop Himmelb(l)au. But still it is another symbolic building, and a highrise as well.

SdG If one believes in the European community and in Europe as a coming together of a number of independent countries, then the idea that the architecture of Europe can be built by European architects is something to be very positive about. I think that a German architect working in Madrid or an English architect in Berlin is very positive, and my only regret is that England is not more open-minded. France has been quite open-minded in its approach, as well as the Netherlands and Spain and many other European countries. I would like us to be in that same league. I do think there has been improvement in this country. Obviously the Laban Center and Tate Modern by Herzog & de Meuron were important. The increase here in overseas architects mainly resulted from the lottery and its funding of more public buildings. Of course, American firms like SOM, HOK, and KPF also do a lot of work here in London.

DAM Your Berlin office manager told me that he would like Foster + Partners Berlin to be recognized as a German firm. He says that in all the competitions he has the feeling they are being treated like foreigners. And he would like the public to view them as a local firm.

SdG We have a substantial body of work in Germany, and I think that although we might not be recognized as a local firm, I hope that we might be recognized as an important global firm with particular relevance to the architecture of Germany. I think that would be a more appropriate position to be in, because inevitably we bring with us a design philosophy and an approach to problem-solving that emanates from London. The relationship to our local offices is a very important point. The fact that there is a constant dialogue and cross-fertilization of ideas, as well as visits between the offices, is different from the way that some other larger firms work, where the local offices become autonomous branch offices in their own right.

DAM Another aspect is the issue of the so-called star architects. It is a new phenomenon insofar as this topic has been a public matter for some time now. There seems to be something good about this discussion as the general public is getting more interested in architecture. How do you feel about this?

SdG It is interesting to consider which way round it is. Has the general public become interested in architecture because a number of architects have been given this so-called star status, or is it the fact that, for other reasons, the general public have become more interested in architecture? Is it because they rather enjoy visiting new

SdG Es gibt in Deutschland ein großes Auftragsvolumen und ich hoffe, obwohl wir nicht als einheimisches Büro betrachtet werden, dass man uns dennoch als wichtiges globales Unternehmen anerkennt, welches eine besondere Relevanz für die Architektur in Deutschland hat. Das wäre wohl eine etwas angemessenere Rolle, denn wir bringen schließlich eine Designphilosophie und einen Problemlösungsansatz mit, der unverkennbar aus London kommt. Die Beziehung zu unseren lokalen Büros ist ein sehr wichtiger Punkt. Die Tatsache, dass es einen konstanten Dialog und wechselseitigen Austausch von Ideen sowie Besuche zwischen den Büros gibt, unterscheidet uns von jenen Firmen, bei denen die lokalen Büros zu eigenständigen autonomen Niederlassungen werden.

DAM Ein anderer Aspekt sind die sogenannten Stararchitekten. Es ist insofern ein neues Phänomen, da es erst seit einiger Zeit zu einem öffentlichen Thema geworden ist. Diese Debatte scheint den positiven Aspekt mit sich zu bringen, dass sich die Allgemeinheit nun mehr für Architektur interessiert. Wie sehen Sie das?

SdG Es fragt sich, was zuerst kam. Interessieren sich die Leute plötzlich für Architektur, weil einigen Architekten der sogenannte Starstatus verliehen wurde, oder ist es so, dass sich das breite Publikum aus anderen Gründen nun mehr für Architektur interessiert? Macht der Besuch von neuen Gebäuden vielleicht einfach Spaß? In Großbritannien ist das sicherlich so. Folglich musste man auch eine Reihe von Hauptakteuren auf der architektonischen Bühne bestimmen. Es könnte also auf einen dieser Gründe zurückzuführen sein oder vielleicht auch auf beide zugleich. In der Architektur geht es am Ende darum, einen guten Job zu machen und das bestmögliche Gebäude zu entwerfen und dies ist die Motivation für jeden hier.

DAM Aber war es bei Frank Lloyd Wright nicht genauso? Eine einzelne Figur mit einer großen Menge von Leuten hinter sich?

SdG Ja, das ist richtig und das trifft auch auf jemanden wie Christopher Wren zu, als er St. Pauls baute. Er hatte ein Team mit sehr talentierten Architekten, die später in ihrer Zeit eine Spitzenposition einnahmen. Ich glaube nicht, dass das Konzept neu ist, dass ein großes oder erfolgreiches Architekturbüro eine berühmte Persönlichkeit an seiner Spitze hat. Ich denke, das gibt es schon seit vielen Jahren. Es ist allerdings neu, dass diese Persönlichkeiten nun einem breiteren Publikum bekannt sind. Das ist gut für die Architektur. Je mehr Leute in der Lage sind, sich durch ein Gebäude wie den Reichstag mit Normans Namen zu identifizieren, desto größer, so könnte man sagen, ist vielleicht auch das allgemeine Interesse an Architektur, das dadurch kultiviert wird. Dieser Prozess ist maßgeblich, um Barrieren zwischen dem Publikum, Gebäuden und den Architekten aufzulösen, sodass es ein besseres Verständnis für unsere Bemühungen geben kann. Ich sehe das sehr positiv.

DAM Eine Debatte, die wir in Deutschland haben, dreht sich um die Frage, warum wir nicht einen einzigen Namen eines deutschen Architekten nennen können, der einen solchen Starnimbus hätte. Welche Personen kommen Ihnen in den Sinn, wenn ich Sie frage, wer heutzutage diese Symbolfiguren in Deutschland sind?

SdG Oh, da denke ich an Behnisch, von Gerkan und Marg, Ingenhoven und mir würden noch einige andere einfallen. Es gibt eine ganze Reihe von Namen in Deutschland,

buildings? Which has certainly happened in this country. As a result of that there has been the need to identify a number of key players on the architectural stage. It could therefore be either of those reasons or it might be a bit of both. In the end, architecture is about doing the best possible job you can, designing the best possible building you can, and that is the thing that motivates everybody here.

DAM But wasn't it the same with Frank Lloyd Wright? A single figure with a whole lot of people behind him.

SdG Yes, that is true and it is also true of somebody like Christopher Wren when he built St. Paul's. He had a very talented team including architects who later became leading architects of their time. I don't think the phenomenon of having a large or successful practice, with one key celebrated individual, is new. I think it has existed for many years. What is new is that those individuals have become more widely known. This is a good thing for architecture. The more people who are able to identify with Norman's name through a building like the Reichstag, you could argue that the more interest is cultivated in architecture more generally. This process is essential to breaking down barriers between the general public, buildings, and architecture, so that there is a better understanding of what we are trying to do. I think this is very positive.

DAM A debate we have in Germany revolves around why it is hard to identify a single German architect's name with that movement of personal cultism. Let me ask you, which figures would come to your mind if asked who are these single, symbolic figures in Germany nowadays?

SdG Oh, I think of Behnisch, von Gerkan and Marg, Ingenhoven, I could go on. There are a number of people in Germany that one could identify. It is very cyclical. There are moments when a country has a great reputation for the architecture it produces and a number of people associated with it. If you look at the United States, for instance, in the fifties and sixties there were a whole string of extremely well-known American architects, while more recently there have been fewer. In England it was probably the reverse. In the fifties and sixties there weren't very many names, but when James Stirling started to practice and was successful through competitions like Stuttgart Staatsgalerie, English architecture or architects became better known. It's a roller coaster. France, too, has a number of architects that have a world reputation.

DAM German engineers are exporting a lot, especially their expertise, and working with a lot of high-profile architects, but I don't remember any exact circumstances where I have seen the name Foster and one of those engineers. Is it because you work a lot with Arup?

SdG We work both with Arup and with Buro Happold but we have worked with many German engineers such as the late Professor Pichler, Werner Sobek, Leonhardt Andrä + Partner and Schmidt Reuter on German projects. Of course, we work an enormous amount with German construction firms, and cladding firms in particular, so in a way that's another sort of entrée into Germany. Many projects have emerged in this way. We have always enjoyed having a close relationship with people who

Staatsgalerie Stuttgart,
Stirling Wilford & Associates
Stuttgart Staatsgalerie,
Stirling Wilford & Associates

die man nennen könnte. Das ändert sich immer wieder. Es gibt Zeiten, da genießt ein Land großes Ansehen für seine Architektur, die es produziert und für eine Reihe von Personen, die damit in Verbindung stehen. Wenn man zum Beispiel in die USA schaut, gab es dort in den Fünfziger- und Sechzigerjahren eine ganze Reihe von sehr bekannten amerikanischen Architekten, während es in den letzten Jahren weniger sind. In England war es vielleicht umgekehrt. In den Fünfziger- und Sechzigerjahren gab es nicht viele berühmte Namen, aber als James Stirling die Bühne betrat und mit Wettbewerben wie für die Stuttgarter Staatsgalerie erfolgreich war, bescherte dies der englischen Architektur einen größeren Bekanntheitsgrad. Es ist wie eine Achterbahn. Frankreich hat auch einige Architekten, die weltweiten Ruhm genießen.

DAM Deutsche Ingenieure exportieren viel, vor allem ihre Fachkenntnisse. Sie arbeiten mit vielen hochrangigen Architekten zusammen, aber ich kann mich an keine konkreten Umstände erinnern, bei denen der Name Foster in Verbindung mit einem dieser Ingenieure aufgetaucht wäre. Liegt das daran, dass Sie sehr viel mit Arup arbeiten?

SdG Wir arbeiten mit Arup und auch Buro Happold, aber wir haben auch mit vielen deutschen Ingenieuren an deutschen Projekten zusammengearbeitet wie dem kürzlich verstorbenen Gerhard Pichler oder Werner Sobek, Leonhardt, Andrä + Partner sowie Schmidt Reuter. Und wir kooperieren natürlich in großem Umfang mit deutschen Bauunternehmen und insbesondere Fassadenverkleidungsfirmen, dies ist eine andere Form des Zugangs nach Deutschland. Viele Projekte sind auf diese Weise zustandegekommen. Wir haben schon immer eine enge Beziehung mit den Leuten gepflegt, die die Dinge umsetzen und deutsche Firmen haben etwas Besonderes: Die Tatsache, dass die meisten von ihnen noch Familienbetriebe oder relativ kleine Firmen sind. Die Art und Weise wie man kommunizieren und eine enge Beziehung mit einer bestimmten Person in einem Unternehmen aufbauen kann, hat immer stark zum Erfolg beigetragen. Das ist in England tendenziell nicht so einfach, wo die Firmen oft eher Großunternehmen sind und sich der Dialog entsprechend schwieriger gestaltet. Dieser Aspekt ist sicherlich für unsere enge Bindung an Deutschland maßgeblich.

DAM Matthias Schuler von Transsolar und seine Konzepte über passive Solartechnologie scheinen sehr gut zu Ihren Vorstellungen zu passen.

SdG Ja, wir arbeiten mit ihm im Rahmen einer ganzen Reihe von Projekten zusammen und auch da gibt es eine große Übereinstimmung zwischen unserem von Nachhaltigkeit geprägten Ansatz und Aspekten des Energieverbrauchs. Deutschland steht an der Spitze ökologischen Denkens und wir begrüßen diese Verbindung. Die Commerzbank bot uns eine besondere Gelegenheit, in großem Rahmen Erfahrungen mit einem höchst nachhaltig konzipierten Gebäude zu machen, und es gab diese glückliche Verbindung zwischen uns, der Commerzbank und mit den Grünen in der Stadt Frankfurt. Die Idee, dass jedes einzelne Büro im höchsten Gebäude Europas auf natürliche Weise belüftet werden soll, wurde in den Wettbewerbsvoraussetzungen klar definiert und später weiterentwickelt. Jedes Bauprojekt ist eine Art Abenteuer, denn anders als bei Autos gibt es keine Prototypen oder die Möglichkeit, ein Gebäude vorab einem Test zu unterziehen. Man baut es und es ist eine einmalige Sache; dafür benötigt man die geballte Erfahrung des Gestaltungsteams, das sich diese durch zuvor geleistete Arbeit erworben hat.

make things and there is something very special about German companies. The fact that a lot of them are still family run or quite small organizations, the way you can communicate with and build a strong relationship with an individual in a company has always been a great success. That tends to be more difficult in England, where organizations are often more corporate and the dialogue more difficult to establish. This factor is certainly a manifestation of a bond between us and Germany.

DAM Matthias Schuler of Transsolar and his concepts of passive solar technology seem to fit very well with your concepts, as well.

SdG Yes, we are working with him on a number of projects, so again I think there is a very strong rapport there between our approach to sustainability and energy use. Germany leads the world in that thinking and we enjoy that relationship. The Commerzbank was an extraordinary opportunity for us to explore on a large scale a highly sustainable building, and it was a happy conjunction between ourselves, the Commerzbank, and the City of Frankfurt, which in those days was run by the Green Party. The idea, though, that you can naturally ventilate every single office in the highest building in Europe was clearly defined at the competition stage and was developed thereafter. Every building project is always a bit of an adventure because, unlike motorcars, there is not the ability to prototype and test your building. You build it, it's a one-off, and yes, it requires all the experience of the designer team based on all the work that they have done previously.

Dominique Perrault, Dominique Perrault Architecture
Interview, 20. Dezember 2007

Velodrom, Berlin,
Dominique Perrault Architecture
Velodrome, Berlin,
Dominique Perrault Architecture

DAM Herr Perrault, wie viele deutsche Architekten arbeiten derzeit in Ihrem Büro?

Dominique Perrault Es sind zurzeit acht deutsche Architekten. Das heißt 10 Prozent.

DAM Und an welchen Projekten arbeiten diese Architekten?

DP Im Moment sind sie mit einem österreichischen Projekt in Wien beschäftigt und entwickeln Projekte für Bauherren in Deutschland oder in der Schweiz. Zudem arbeiten sie an Projekten in anderen europäischen Ländern, zum Beispiel in Großbritannien. Dort liegt der Schwerpunkt ihrer Arbeit. Sie sind zwischen dreißig und fünfzig Jahre alt und sind für bautechnische Details oder die Überwachung der eigentlichen Baustelle zuständig. Sie sind keine jungen Architekten. Nicht sehr alt, aber auch nicht zu jung.

DAM Wurden sie speziell von Ihnen ausgewählt, da es für ein deutsches oder österreichisches Projekt wichtig ist, dass jemand die Sprache beherrscht?

DP Absolut. Die Sprache und ihre Auffassungsgabe, denn es gibt, insbesondere in den Bauphasen, Unterschiede zwischen den Abläufen in Frankreich und in Deutschland. In Deutschland und Österreich ist jede Phase klar definiert, aber in Frankreich sind die Unterscheidungen subtiler.

DAM Hatten Sie bisher viele Aufträge für Projekte in Deutschland? Ich weiß, dass eines Ihrer großen Projekte das Velodrom in Berlin war.

DP Nein, noch nicht. Ich erwarte, dass ich einige neue Projekte in Deutschland erhalten werde, aber nach dem Velodrom und dem Schwimmbad (1992–1999) habe ich mein Büro in Berlin geschlossen, weil es keine Arbeit mehr gab. Das war eine mehr als verrückte Zeit, aber die Dinge haben sich geändert und Deutschland befindet sich jetzt in einer anderen Phase. Es ist möglich, dass wir einen Auftrag für ein neues Projekt bekommen, wir werden sehen.

DAM Wie waren Ihre Erfahrungen in Berlin oder mit deutschen Architekten, die in ihrem Büro in Paris arbeiten? Was können deutsche Architekten Ihrer Ansicht nach sehr gut und worin sind sie schlecht?

DP Ich finde, dass die Herangehensweise von deutschen Architekten die von französischen sehr gut ergänzt, denn sie gehen bei der Entwicklung von Projekten methodisch vor. Zudem meine ich, dass die Beziehung zwischen Ingenieuren und Architekten in Deutschland sehr gut ist. Auf jeden Fall besser als in Frankreich. Deutsche Ingenieure sind sehr erfindungsreich, sie entwickeln Ideen und Konzepte. Der Austausch von Ideen zwischen deutschen Architekten und Ingenieuren funktioniert sehr gut. Wir arbeiten zum Beispiel mit Bollinger + Grohmann aus Frankfurt zusammen. Es gibt einen echten Austausch über das architektonische Konzept und das gleiche gilt für das Statikkonzept. Das ist kein so undurchdringliches Feld: Deutsche Architekten sind in der Lage, eine Verbindung zwischen architektonischen und technischen Abläufen herzustellen. Sie ziehen das Projekt während der Entwicklungsphase durch und treiben es voran, aber sie können auch Vorzeichnungen machen, insbesondere mit einer funktionalen und sehr pragmatischen Bewertung. Und ich

Dominique Perrault, Dominique Perrault Architecture
Interview, December 20, 2007

DAM Mr. Perrault, how many German architects are working in your firm at the moment?

Dominique Perrault There are eight German architects in the office right now. That's 10 percent.

DAM What kind of projects do they work on in your office?

DP At the moment they are working on an Austrian project in Vienna, and they are developing projects for clients in Germany or Switzerland. Also they are working on projects in other European countries, for example in the UK. That's where their main work is focused. They are between thirty and fifty years of age. And they work on construction details, or supervise the actual site. They are not young architects. Not very old, but not too young.

DAM Did you choose them especially because you have a German or an Austrian project where it is important that they speak the language?

DP Absolutely. The language and also their perceptiveness, because there are differences between the processes in France and in Germany, especially in the construction phases. In Germany and Austria each phase is very clearly defined, but in France the distinctions are a little more flexible.

DAM And have you had many projects in Germany? I know that one of your big projects was the Velodrome in Berlin.

DP No, not yet. I expect to get some new projects in Germany but after the Velodrome and the swimming pool (1992–1999) I closed my office in Berlin because there was no work. It was the craziest time, but now things have changed, it's a different period in Germany. It's possible that we might get a new project. We will see.

DAM What kind of experiences have you had with German architects working in your firm in Paris or when you were working in Berlin? What do you think German architects can do very well, and what would you say they do very badly?

DP In my opinion, the approach used by German architects complements the approach of French architects very well, because they have a method of developing projects. Also, as I see it in Germany, the relationship between engineers and architects is very good. Better than it is in France, definitely. In Germany engineers are highly imaginative, they develop technical ideas and concepts. The exchange of ideas between German engineers and architects works very well. For example, we are working with Bollinger + Grohmann from Frankfurt. You can get a real exchange of ideas about the architectural concept and the same applies for the static concept. You know, it is not an impervious field. German architects are able to develop a link between architecture and technical development. For them it is possible to push and promote the project during the development phases, but they can also work on preliminary sketches, especially with a functional, very rational and pragmatic evaluation. And I think this is very good, because French architects are more conceptual and a little more abstract perhaps, or . . .

Schwimmbad, Berlin,
Dominique Perrault Architecture
Swimming pool, Berlin,
Dominique Perrault Architecture

Europäischer Gerichtshof, Luxemburg,
Dominique Perrault Architecture
European Court of Justice, Luxembourg,
Dominique Perrault Architecture

Tenniszentrum, Madrid,
Dominique Perrault Architecture
Tennis center, Madrid,
Dominique Perrault Architecture

glaube, das ist sehr gut, denn die französischen Architekten sind vielleicht etwas konzeptueller und abstrakter in ihrem Ansatz, oder …

DAM … philosophischer vielleicht?

DP Ja, genau. Und diese Art von Austausch zwischen zwar verschiedenen, dennoch nicht gänzlich unterschiedlichen Denkweisen ist sehr gut. In meinem Büro organisieren wir Workshops mit Architekten, die aus verschiedenen Ländern kommen und das hat außerordentlich positive Auswirkungen. Auch wenn es vielleicht nicht ganz einfach ist, ist es sehr interessant, derartige Prozesse in Gang zu setzen.

DAM Sie haben gerade gesagt, dass die Franzosen in gewisser Weise konzeptueller sind. Würden Sie sagen, die Deutschen sind innovativer?

DP Nun ja, deutsche Architekten sind von der Industriemacht ihres Landes sehr überzeugt; wenn sie zum Beispiel in reicheren Ländern bauen, dann ist das manchmal sehr gut. Aber in ärmeren Ländern ist das vielleicht schwieriger, denn es ist nicht einfach, den deutschen Standard als Norm anzuwenden. Manchmal sind die Entwürfe von deutschen Architekten zu teuer, denn sie verwenden viele hochwertige Materialien.

DAM Ist Ihr Büro in unterschiedlichen, das heißt armen und reichen Ländern tätig? Oder liegt Ihr Schwerpunkt eher in der industrialisierten Welt?

DP Wir haben Projekte in Asien, das ist anders, und auch in Italien. Im Moment entwickeln wir ein Projekt in Neapel, aber es ist nicht einfach, das Geld für ein solches Vorhaben zu bekommen. Auch in Spanien ist es anders, dort hat man ein anderes Verhältnis zu Qualität und Geld.

DAM Empfinden Sie sich als Star? Gibt es Länder, die speziell bei Ihnen anfragen, weil sie ein architektonisches Projekt von Ihnen umgesetzt haben möchten?

DP Ja, aber das kommt auf den Auftrag an. Wir sind in den Bau des europäischen Gerichtshofes in Luxemburg eingebunden, ein sehr großes Projekt, sowie des Tenniszentrums in Madrid und der Universität in Seoul, Korea.

DAM Haben Sie diese Aufträge erhalten, weil Sie einen Wettbewerb gewonnen haben?

DP Ja, alle. Aber wir verlieren auch – manchmal gewinnen wir, aber meistens verlieren wir!

DAM Sind Sie der Meinung, dass es deutsche Architekten gibt, die internationale Berühmtheit erlangt haben?

DP Ja, es gibt einige sehr gute deutsche Architekturbüros, die berühmt sind. Zum Beispiel von Gerkan. Das ist meistens der erste Name der genannt wird, aber es gibt auch andere. Um ehrlich zu sein, ich bevorzuge Architekten wie Behnisch oder Ingenhoven. Ich finde, diese Architekten sind sehr interessante Personen.

DAM . . . philosophical, maybe?

DP Yes, exactly. And this kind of exchange between two different mind-sets which are not miles apart is very good. In my office we organize workshops between different architects coming from different countries, and it is very, very positive. Though it might not be very easy, it is very interesting to develop this kind of process.

DAM You just said that the French are more conceptual. Would you say the Germans are innovative?

DP Well, German architects are very confident about their nation's industrial power, and sometimes it's very good if they are building something in rich countries. But it could be more difficult when you are in poor countries, because it is not so easy to apply the German standard, the norm. Sometimes the conceptions German architects produce are too expensive, because they use a lot of high-quality materials.

DAM Does your firm work in different countries—poor and rich countries? Or do you focus more on the industrialized world?

DP We work in Asia, which is different, and also in Italy. At the moment we are developing a project in Naples but it is not easy to get the money to build this kind of project. In Spain it is also different. It is a different relationship to quality and money.

DAM Do you feel like a star? Are there countries that ask you especially because they want a piece of your architecture?

DP Yes, but it depends on the job. We are involved in constructing the European Court of Justice in Luxembourg, a big project, and the tennis center in Madrid, another big project, and the university in Seoul, Korea.

DAM Did you get these commissions because you won a competition?

DP Yes, all of them, absolutely. But we also lose—sometimes we win, but normally we lose!

DAM Would you say there are German architects who are internationally famous?

DP Yes, you have some very good, important German architectural offices that are famous. For example von Gerkan. It's the first name people mention usually, but there are also others. To be honest I prefer architects like Behnisch, like Ingenhoven. I think these architects are very exciting people.

DAM At the moment we are talking about the lack of German star architects. Have you heard about young, up-and-coming architects from Germany in the last couple of years?

DP No, I don't know any. It's a little bit curious if you compare Germany and Austria. In Austria you have some famous architects, Hans Hollein or Wilhelm Holzbauer, now he is an old man, but he is famous. Coop Himmelb(l)au with Wolfgang Prix for example,

Universität, Seoul,
Dominique Perrault Architecture
University, Seoul,
Dominique Perrault Architecture

Hans Hollein in Wien
Hans Hollein in Vienna

DAM Im Moment spricht man vom Mangel an deutschen Stararchitekten. Haben Sie in den letzten zwei Jahren von jungen und aufstrebenden deutschen Architekten gehört?

DP Nein, ich kenne keinen. Es ist seltsam, wenn man Deutschland und Österreich vergleicht. In Österreich gibt es einige berühmte Architekten, Hans Hollein oder Wilhelm Holzbauer, er ist mittlerweile ein alter Mann, aber er ist berühmt. Und zum Beispiel Coop Himmelb(l)au mit Wolfgang Prix oder Gustav Peichl. Ich weiß nicht, warum es solche Leute nicht in Deutschland gibt. Das Niveau ist sehr gut und es gibt viele sehr moderne und außerordentlich interessante Gebäude. Wirklich sehr viele. Nicht nur im Hinblick auf bauliche Qualität, sondern auch was den Entwurf betrifft. Ich bin kein Deutscher, daher weiß ich nicht, warum das so ist. Ich kann mir nicht erklären, warum es diese bestimmte Starqualität bei euch im Moment nicht gibt. Vielleicht lastet aus psychologischer Sicht die Geschichte noch zu schwer, aber es gibt ja jetzt eine neue Generation: Diese wird sich freier fühlen und ich sehe das nicht als Problem.

or Gustav Peichl. I don't know why you don't get this in Germany. The level is very good, and you have a lot of very modern and very, very interesting buildings. A lot. Not just the quality of construction, but the design, too. I don't know exactly why, because I am not German. I don't know why you don't get this specific star quality. Maybe they are not free from a psychological point of view, because of the weight of history, but I think there is a new generation. A new generation will feel freer and I don't see it as a problem.

Wilhelm Holzbauer in Amsterdam
Wilhelm Holzbauer in Amsterdam

Kees Christiaanse, Kees Christiaanse Architects & Planners
Interview, 11. Januar 2008

Bürogebäude Holzhafen, Hamburg,
Kees Christiaanse und Astoc
Holzhafen office building, Hamburg,
Kees Christiaanse and Astoc

DAM Herr Christiaanse, was war Ihr erster Kontakt mit dem Bauen in Deutschland?

Kees Christiaanse Ich war Partner im Büro von Rem Koolhaas, beim OMA. Koolhaas selbst war mehr im angelsächsischen, im asiatischen und im amerikanischen Raum tätig. So blieb dann Mitteleuropa als mein Territorium übrig. Dadurch war ich sehr häufig für Vorträge in Deutschland. Wir haben damals auch angefangen an eingeladenen Wettbewerben in Deutschland und an Preisgerichten teilzunehmen. Und so bin ich schon vor 1990 im deutschen Umfeld gelandet. Daraus hat sich dann alles weitere entwickelt.

DAM Wie kam es dann dazu, dass Sie 1991 eine Dependance Ihres Rotterdamer Büros in Köln eröffneten?

KC Das war anlässlich des Hamburger Bauforums. Ich war zu dieser einwöchigen Veranstaltung, von Baudirektor Egbert Kossak ins Leben gerufen, eingeladen worden; sie bestand aus einem Workshop mit Meisterklasse und Vorträgen. Dazu wurden etwa zehn international bekannte Architekten eingeladen und diese mussten innerhalb einer Woche für einen spezifischen Teil von Hamburg einen Entwurf vorlegen. Die Mitarbeiter wurden unter talentierten Studenten aus Deutschland ausgewählt. Mir wurden die späteren Partner von Astoc zugeteilt, die damals in Aachen im letzten Jahr studierten und gerade den Schinkel-Preis gewonnen hatten. Seitdem arbeiten wir zusammen. Sie haben zunächst als Praktikanten für uns gearbeitet oder wir haben gemeinsam an Wettbewerben teilgenommen. Dann haben sie Diplom gemacht und wir haben uns überlegt, dass wir eine Dependance gründen, mit ihnen als Geschäftsführern: So ist das Büro in Köln entstanden.

DAM Weshalb wollten Sie speziell mit Deutschen zusammenarbeiten? Hatten Sie während des Bauforums etwas Besonderes an Ihren zukünftigen Partnern entdeckt? Oder war es einfach eine Erweiterung zum niederländischen Büro?

KC Nein, ich fand die deutsche Kultur besonders angenehm, sehr interessant und auch sehr nuanciert und habe mich dort von Anfang an sehr zu Hause gefühlt – besonders in Städten wie Hamburg und Berlin. Es gibt ja auch eine lange urbane Tradition in Deutschland, die es in anderen Ländern, oder jedenfalls in den Niederlanden, nicht gibt. Die Niederlande sind nach dem Krieg zu einem suburbanen Land geworden. Die deutschen Städte haben dagegen eine wahnsinnig eindrucksvolle Tradition, sowohl von der Bausubstanz als auch von der Kultur her. Das hat mich von Anfang an sehr interessiert und da habe ich mich auch sehr wohlgefühlt. Deswegen habe ich aus eigener Initiative einen zweiten Schwerpunkt auf Deutschland gelegt. Später habe ich auch noch eine Frau aus Wien geheiratet und danach war ich natürlich noch viel mehr dort, im Osten. So hat sich das verfestigt und zusammen mit dem in Köln gegründeten Büro weiter verdichtet. Das hatte zur Folge, dass ich eine Doppelkarriere verfolgt habe: Ich war gleichzeitig niederländischer und deutscher Architekt. So kam ich an die TU Berlin als Professor für Städtebau. Diese Position hatte ich sieben Jahre lang (1996–2003). Dort hat es mir so gut gefallen, dass ich Anfang 2000 mit meiner Familie nach Berlin gezogen bin. Da wären wir auch geblieben, wenn ich kein Angebot von der ETH Zürich bekommen hätte, was drei Jahre später wieder zum Umzug geführt hat. Aber Zürich liegt ja auch im deutschsprachigen Raum und es gibt dort sehr viele Deutsche. Seitdem haben wir

Kees Christiaanse, Kees Christiaanse Architects & Planners
Interview, January 11, 2008

DAM Mr. Christiaanse, what was your first experience of building in Germany?

Kees Christiaanse I was a partner in the firm of Rem Koolhaas, at the OMA. Koolhaas himself was more involved in Asia and America, so Central Europe became my territory. That meant that I was often in Germany in connection with commitments there. Around that time, we were starting to participate in competitions in Germany and to serve on jury panels. And so I ended up working in a German context even before 1990. Everything else just developed from there.

DAM How did it come about that you opened a branch of your Rotterdam firm in Cologne in 1991?

KC That was connected with the Bauforum in Hamburg. It was a one-week event, arranged by the city's director of planning, Egbert Kossak, consisting of a workshop with a master class and lectures. Ten internationally renowned architects were invited to attend and each had to present a design for a specific part of Hamburg within one week. The staff was selected from a pool of talented German students. I was allocated some final-year students from Aachen who had just won the Schinkel Prize and went on to become partners in Astoc. We've been working together ever since. Initially, they worked for us as interns, and then, after they graduated, we decided to found a branch with them as directors. That's how the office in Cologne started up.

DAM Why did you want to work with Germans, in particular? Did you notice something special about your future partners during the Bauforum? Or was it simply an extension of the Dutch office?

KC No, I found German culture particularly appealing, very interesting and subtly nuanced; I felt right at home there from day one—especially in cities like Hamburg and Berlin. There's a long urban tradition in Germany that simply doesn't exist in other countries—at least not in the Netherlands. The Netherlands became a suburban country after the war. But the German cities have an incredibly impressive tradition, both architecturally and culturally. That caught my interest right from the start, and I felt very much at ease there. That's why I chose to make Germany my second focal point. Later, I married a Viennese woman, and, of course, I started spending a lot more time there, in the east. So that all came together with the Cologne office. The upshot of it all was that I pursued a dual career as a Dutch and as a German architect. That's how I became professor of urban planning at the TU Berlin—a position I held for seven years (1996–2003). I liked it there so much that I settled in Berlin with my family. And we would have stayed there, had it not been for an invitation from the ETH Zurich, which prompted us to move again three years later. But Zurich is also part of the German-speaking world and there are a lot of Germans there. Since then, we've had a branch in Zurich instead of Cologne, and use it as our base for German projects, especially in southern Germany.

DAM Did you see Germany as an especially suitable place to pursue your main interest, urban planning?

KC In actual practice, there are not many urban planners in Germany. There is a relatively large number of architects, but only a handful of firms working in urban

HafenCity, Hamburg, nach einem Masterplan von Kees Christiaanse und Astoc
HafenCity, Hamburg, in line with a master plan by Kees Christiaanse and Astoc

Masterplan Shenyang, KCAP
Master plan for Shenyang, KCAP

statt in Köln eine Niederlassung in Zürich und arbeiten von dort aus an unseren deutschen Projekten, insbesondere im süddeutschen Raum.

DAM Haben Sie denn speziell in Deutschland eine Möglichkeit für Ihr Schwerpunktthema Städtebau gesehen?

KC In der Praxis gab es wenige Städtebauer in Deutschland. Es gibt verhältnismäßig viele Architekten, aber nur wenige Büros, die im Städtebau arbeiten. Das heißt, es war eine Nische für uns und wir waren auf diesem Gebiet auch innovativ. Man könnte außerdem sagen, dass in dieser Zeit besonders interessante Projekte entstanden sind, zum Beispiel die IBA Emscher Park und die Auseinandersetzung mit Stadtbrachen sowie die Erschließung der ostdeutschen Städte. Das heißt, in dem Moment, als wir anfingen, Städtebau zu betreiben, war die Lage in Deutschland extrem günstig.

DAM Ist es denn auch weiterhin so, dass Sie parallel Städtebau- und Hochbauthemen bearbeiten?

KC Ja, das ist so geblieben. Bei mir ist es mittlerweile sogar fast so, dass ich weltweit vor allem komplexe Städtebauprojekte mache; mein Schwerpunkt liegt beim Städtebau.

DAM Wenn Sie von weltweiten Projekten sprechen, in welchen Ländern sind Sie zurzeit unterwegs?

KC Ziemlich viel in England und Irland, auch in Dänemark. Wir arbeiten in der Schweiz, in Frankreich und in China, und hier und da an ganz »exotischen« Stellen.

DAM Wie problematisch ist es dort, dass Sie, im Unterschied zum deutschsprachigen Raum, die Sprache nicht kennen und keine Lebenserfahrung im Land selbst haben, zum Beispiel in China?

KC Das geht natürlich nur mit Partnerbüros und lokalen Angestellten, die die Sprache beherrschen. Man braucht eine Antenne und eine Nase für die wichtigen Leute, die mitarbeiten und einem helfen können. Man benötigt nicht unbedingt eine große Erfahrung in solch einem Land.

DAM Wie viele deutsche Mitarbeiter haben Sie denn in Ihren Büros und an der Hochschule?

KC In unserem Büro in Rotterdam arbeiten ungefähr achtzig Leute. Ich denke, dass so 25 Prozent davon Deutsche sind. In unserem Büro in Zürich arbeiten ungefähr zehn Leute, davon sind sieben oder acht deutsch. An der Architekturfakultät der ETH Zürich sind über 50 Prozent der wissenschaftlichen Mitarbeiter Deutsche, und bei mir am Lehrstuhl sind es sogar ungefähr 70 Prozent. Das ist ein weitverbreitetes Phänomen: Wenn man zum Beispiel die bekannten Büros in London besucht, dann sind erhebliche Teile der Mitarbeiter deutsch.

planning. That meant that there was a niche for us in that field, in which we were also quite innovative. What's more, it can also be said that some particularly interesting projects came up during this time, such as the Emscher Park IBA, the issue of how to develop urban gap sites, and the regeneration of eastern German cities. In other words, at the very time when we embarked on urban planning, the situation in Germany was very favorable.

DAM And do you still work on urban planning and construction projects at the same time?

KC Yes, that hasn't changed. In fact, it's gotten to the point where I tend to work mainly on complex urban planning projects all over the world; my main focus is on urban planning.

DAM Speaking of worldwide projects, which countries are you working in at the moment?

KC Quite a lot in England and Ireland, and also in Denmark. We're working in Switzerland, in France and in China, and there are one or two quite "exotic" sites.

DAM What problems do you come up against in places where, unlike the German-speaking world, you don't know the language and have no experience of actually living there—in China, for instance?

KC Of course, that can only work in partnership with local firms and local employees who do speak the language. You need to have an intuitive feel for the key people who can work with you and help you. You don't necessarily have to have a great deal of experience in the country itself.

DAM How many German co-workers do you have in your offices and at the university?

KC Our office in Rotterdam currently employs about eighty people. I think that about 25 percent of them are Germans. There are about ten people in our Zurich office, seven or eight of whom are German. At the architecture faculty of the ETH Zurich more than half the assistants are Germans and that ratio is probably about 70 percent among the academic staff. It's a widespread phenomenon. If you look at the well-known architectural firms in London, for instance, you'll find that a considerable proportion of the staff is German.

DAM Do you think that German architects build and work abroad because contracts and work in Germany were thin on the ground for a while?

KC That is certainly the case. Germany went through a period of crisis for about ten or fifteen years that brought the entire construction sector to its knees—with repercussions right up to the present day, leading to a brain drain right across the board, especially in architecture. You could even go so far as to say that the most talented designers have left the country and are now working in the leading international firms. But there are signs of change on the horizon. Some of these architects

China Central Television Station (CCTV),
Peking, OMA (Rem Koolhaas, Ole Scheeren)
China Central Television Station (CCTV),
Beijing, OMA (Rem Koolhaas, Ole Scheeren)

DAM Glauben Sie denn, dass deutsche Architekten im Ausland bauen und arbeiten, weil es eine Zeit lang in Deutschland nicht genügend Aufträge und Jobs gab?

KC Das ist bestimmt so. In Deutschland gab es eine zehn- bis fünfzehnjährige Krise, in der die ganze Baukultur zusammengebrochen ist. Sie hat bis jetzt gedauert und hat zu einem »Braindrain« auf mehreren Ebenen geführt, insbesondere in der Architektur. Man könnte fast sagen, dass die besten Entwerfer ins Ausland verschwunden sind und jetzt bei den besten internationalen Büros arbeiten. Aber derzeit gibt es erste Anzeichen dafür, dass sich dies ändert. Manche dieser Architekten haben zehn Jahre lang im Ausland gearbeitet, sind jetzt fünfunddreißig bis vierzig Jahre alt und denken sich: »Vielleicht gehe ich nun zurück nach Deutschland und eröffne mein eigenes Büro. Jetzt zieht die Wirtschaft gerade wieder an. Es gibt viele Architekten, die aufgehört haben zu arbeiten, sodass es in bestimmten Städten einen gewissen Mangel an Architekten gibt. Jetzt kehre ich wieder zurück.« Ich spüre auch bei unseren Mitarbeitern in Rotterdam und Zürich sehr stark ein ähnliches Bedürfnis. Sie fragen uns: »Warum müssen die deutschen Projekte alle von Köln aus gemacht werden? Wir sind auch deutsch, wir wollen auch gerne für das Büro Projekte in Deutschland realisieren.«

DAM Wofür schätzen Sie Ihre deutschen Mitarbeiter am meisten? Werden sie ganz breit gefächert eingesetzt oder gibt es einen Bereich, in dem sie besonders gut sind?

KC Ich habe natürlich eine ganz präzise Auswahl von guten Leuten. Ich finde, die deutsche Grundausbildung ist sehr gut und daher besitzen sie grundlegende Fähigkeiten. Wir picken uns die guten Entwerfer raus, aber das ist nicht sehr repräsentativ. Das ist einfach speziell in unserem Büro und an meinem Lehrstuhl so.

DAM Dass Sie viel Wert auf entwerferische Fähigkeiten legen?

KC Ja, genau. Aber viel wichtiger sind eigentlich eine breite architektonische Ausbildung, Eloquenz und eine gewisse »Zivilisiertheit«, die sehr wichtig für den Umgang mit Bauherren und Politikern ist. Und eine gewisse soziale Kompetenz: Bescheidenheit oder Zurückhaltung hinsichtlich des persönlichen Auftretens erzeugen eine positive Entspanntheit und Lockerheit. Gleichzeitig sind meine deutschen Mitarbeiter im Allgemeinen sehr strukturiert und daher sind einige besonders geeignet als Projektverantwortliche, sie arbeiten sehr gut als Teamleiter.

DAM Kann man denn daraus auch auf die deutschen Mitarbeiter an der ETH Zürich schließen? Wenn es so eine breite und gute Ausbildung in Deutschland gibt, wieso bleiben die Wissenschaftler dann nicht in Deutschland?

KC Erstens werden sie an der ETH sehr gut bezahlt, zweitens ist die Schule hervorragend organisiert und auf Qualität ausgerichtet. Es gibt dort keine Professoren, die nur ihr Gehalt kassieren und sich nie zeigen. Die Anforderung, sich zu profilieren und Qualität zu zeigen, muss erfüllt werden, ansonsten kann man sich dort nicht lange halten. An der ETH zu arbeiten, stellt somit eine ständige Herausforderung dar. Die Schweiz bildet wahrscheinlich zu wenige Akademiker aus, sodass sie diese »importieren« muss. Da sind die Deutschen naheliegend, weil sie die Sprache beherrschen. Die Schweizer tun sich manchmal wegen ihres Schweizerdeutsch etwas schwer mit dem Hochdeutsch.

have been working abroad for ten years, are now in their thirties and forties, and are thinking, "Maybe I'll go back to Germany and set up my own practice. The economy is recovering. There are lots of architects who have stopped working, so there's a shortage of architects in some cities. It's time to go back." I've felt a strong sense of that among our staff in Rotterdam and Zurich. They're asking us, "How come the German projects all have to be run from Cologne? We're German, too; we'd like to work on the firm's German projects as well."

DAM What do you appreciate most about your German staff? Are they represented across the board, or is there one area in which they have a particular aptitude?

KC Needless to say, I select able workers very carefully. I think the German training is fundamentally very good and so they have excellent basic skills. We do pick out the good designers, but that doesn't really give an accurate picture. That just happens to be the case in our office and in my university department as well.

DAM The fact that you value design skills?

KC Yes, exactly. But what is much more important is for them to have broad-based architectural training, and to be articulate and cultivated, all of which are very important when dealing with clients and politicians. They also have to have social skills: modesty and reticence in their personal approach generates a positive atmosphere that is relaxed and laid-back. At the same time, my German staff tends to be very organized, which makes some of them particularly suited to project management, because they are good team leaders.

DAM Does this also apply to the Germans on the staff at ETH Zurich? If Germany has such good, broad-based training, why don't these academics stay in Germany?

KC First of all, they are very well paid at the ETH, and second, the school is extremely well organized and geared toward quality. You won't find any professors there who simply pocket their salaries and don't bother to show their faces. If you don't make your mark and achieve certain standards of quality, you won't last long there. So, working at the ETH is a constant challenge. Switzerland probably trains too few academics, which is why they have to "import" them. And Germans are the obvious choice, because they speak the language. The Swiss sometimes have problems with High German because of their Swiss German.

DAM Germany doesn't seem to have any star architects at the moment. Because of that, Germans are not as high profile abroad as they are at home. On the other hand, a lot of foreign stars have won contracts in Germany. For instance, Norman Foster did the Reichstag conversion in Berlin. Can you explain why—apart from the "modesty" you mentioned earlier—German architects are not so well known internationally?

KC I think that still has something to do with the Second World War. First of all, there was an incredible brain drain because of the National Socialists and the war. The country's finest architects disappeared off to America as early as the 1930s. Those who were already stars became stars again in the USA. So it can't be said that Germany doesn't produce star architects. After the Second World War, two factors played a major role: one was that Germans felt they shouldn't draw attention to

Science City ETH Zürich, KCAP
Science City, ETH Zurich, KCAP

DAM Zurzeit scheint es in Deutschland keine Stararchitekten zu geben. Dadurch entgeht den Deutschen, dass sie im Ausland genauso wahrgenommen werden wie im eigenen Land. Im Gegenzug haben jedoch viele ausländische Stars Aufträge in Deutschland bekommen, zum Beispiel hat Norman Foster den Reichstag in Berlin umgebaut. Haben Sie außer der bereits erwähnten »Bescheidenheit« eine Begründung dafür, weshalb deutsche Architekten international nicht sehr bekannt sind?

KC Ich glaube, das hat immer noch mit dem Zweiten Weltkrieg zu tun. Erstens hat es wegen der Nationalsozialisten und wegen des Kriegs einen unglaublichen »Braindrain« gegeben. Schon in den 1930er-Jahren sind die besten Architekten nach Amerika verschwunden. Die damaligen Stars sind in den USA auch wieder zu Stars geworden. Deswegen kann man nicht sagen, dass Deutschland keine Stars produzieren kann. Nach dem Zweiten Weltkrieg spielen zwei Faktoren eine wichtige Rolle: Der eine Faktor war, dass man sich nach außen nicht zeigen oder laut werden durfte: »Wir müssen still sein und gut arbeiten.« Und der zweite war, dass es erstmal eine große Wiederaufbau-Nachfrage im eigenen Land gab. Das hat zu einer langen Periode geführt, in der man sich »in splendid isolation« ausschließlich den eigenen Bauaufgaben zugewandt hat. Dies ist erst in letzter Zeit ein wenig aufgebrochen worden. Es gibt jetzt wieder deutsche Stars.

DAM Wen würden Sie denn einen deutschen Star nennen?

KC Sauerbruch und Hutton zum Beispiel, die sind auch weltweit im Kommen, Barkow Leibinger …

DAM Wobei dies ja jeweils zwei Partner sind, die nur zur Hälfte deutsch sind.

KC Ich weiß nicht, ob es damit etwas zu tun hat. Von Gerkan ist ein Star in China, absolut. Steidle wäre es geworden, wenn er weiter gegangen wäre. Man kann nicht sagen, dass es keine deutschen Stars gibt. Es wird auch in Zukunft wieder mehr geben. Zurzeit gibt es durch diese Auslandserfahrungen eine extrem interessante Gruppe junger deutscher Architekten, die in zehn bis fünfzehn Jahren zu den Stars gehören werden.

DAM Die zurzeit noch in großen ausländischen Büros arbeiten und dann ihre eigenen Büros in Deutschland aufmachen könnten?

KC Genau. Und es gibt noch etwas, was zu dieser Baukrise in den letzen Jahren hinzukam: Bauaufgaben in Deutschland gehörten zu den besten der Welt, sowohl vom Honorar als auch vom Ausbaustandard her. Die Honorare sind in den letzten zehn Jahren leider den Bach hinuntergegangen. Dadurch ist es für deutsche Architekten auch von Interesse, in der Schweiz oder den Niederlanden zu bauen, was vorher wegen der niedrigen Honorare, die dort geboten wurden, nicht interessant war. Das heißt, es gibt ganz einfache Faktoren, die zu dieser Situation führen. Grundsätzlich glaube ich nicht, dass Deutschland ein Land ist, das keine Stars hervorbringt.

themselves or make too much noise. "We have to keep quiet and work well." And the second factor was the enormous reconstruction task in their own country. That led to a lengthy period of splendid isolation when they concentrated solely on their own construction needs. That has relaxed somewhat in recent years. Now there are German stars again.

DAM Who would you describe as a German star?

KC Sauerbruch and Hutton for instance—they're gaining international recognition—or Barkow Leibinger . . .

DAM Both of those are partnerships, in which only one half is German.

KC I don't know whether that has anything to do with it. Von Gerkan is a star in China, certainly. Steidle would have become one if he had continued. So you can't say there aren't any German stars. And there will be more of them in the future. At the moment, because of their experience abroad, there's an extremely interesting group of young German architects who will be among the stars of tomorrow, in about ten or fifteen years.

DAM You mean the ones who are currently working in major firms abroad and who could go on to set up their own practices in Germany?

KC Exactly. And in recent years there's been another thing besides the construction crisis itself. Building projects in Germany used to be the best in the world, both in terms of the fees paid and in terms of the quality of fittings. But in the last ten years, the fees have unfortunately plummeted. That has made it more attractive for German architects to build in Switzerland or the Netherlands, which used to be less appealing because of the low fees. In other words, there are some very simple factors that have led to this situation. Basically, I don't think Germany is a country that doesn't produce stars.

Deutschlands Baukultur und das System der Stararchitekten
Claus Käpplinger

Zollverein School, Essen, SANAA

BMW Welt, München, Coop Himmelb(l)au

Mercedes-Benz Museum, Stuttgart, UN Studio

Phaeno, Wolfsburg, Zaha Hadid

Herzog & de Meuron, Zaha Hadid, Wolf D. Prix (Coop Himmelb(l)au), Kazuyo Sejima + Ryue Nishizawa (SANAA), Norman Foster, Frank O. Gehry, David Chipperfield, Richard Meier, Daniel Libeskind, Jean Nouvel, Ben van Berkel (UN Studio), Peter Zumthor oder Dominique Perrault sind nur einige wenige Namen, die im letzten Jahrzehnt das Bild von Architektur in Deutschland entscheidend geprägt haben. Omnipräsent scheint der Anteil ausländischer Architekten am deutschen Baugeschehen zu sein, wenn man den internationalen, aber auch den inländischen Publikationen folgt. Denn viele der prominentesten Projekte wie etwa das Jüdische Museum (Daniel Libeskind) oder das Velodrom (Dominique Perrault) in Berlin, die Allianz Arena (Herzog & de Meuron) oder die neue BMW Welt (Coop Himmelb(l)au) in München, das Mercedes-Benz Museum (Ben van Berkel) in Stuttgart, das Diözesanmuseum in Köln (Peter Zumthor), die Universitätsbibliothek in Cottbus (Herzog & de Meuron) oder das Phaeno-Zentrum in Wolfsburg (Zaha Hadid) wurden von ausländischen Architekten konzipiert und gebaut. Sogar das bedeutendste Gebäude des deutschen Staates, der Bundestag im ehemaligen Reichstagsgebäude, wurde nicht von einem deutschen Architekten, sondern vom Briten Norman Foster realisiert.

Was ist nur mit der Architektur deutscher Architekten? Wieso haben ausländische Architekten einen so hohen Einfluss auf das Bauen in Deutschland? Diese Fragen drängen sich nicht nur vielen ausländischen Besuchern auf, deren Kenntnis deutscher zeitgenössischer Architektur oft gering ist. Sie pilgern zumeist wegen der Werke internationaler Architekturgrößen nach Deutschland. Denn kein anderes westliches Land zeigte sich in den letzten Jahrzehnten wohl so offen und besitzt heute eine so hohe Dichte an bedeutenden Werken ausländischer Architekten wie Deutschland. Daniel Libeskind, David Chipperfield oder Wolf D. Prix erhielten hier sogar ihre ersten Großaufträge, noch bevor sie in ihren Heimatländern einer breiteren Öffentlichkeit bekannt wurden. Dagegen waren bis vor wenigen Jahren nur sehr wenige deutsche Architekten international bekannt. Mit Gottfried Böhm, Otto Steidle, Frei Otto, Ludwig Leo, Oswald Matthias Ungers, Günter Behnisch und Hans Kollhoff erschöpfte sich lange Zeit die Kenntnis renommierter deutscher Architekten im Ausland, was sich nun dank einer internationaler agierenden jüngeren Architektengeneration allmählich verändert.

Ausländische Architekten scheinen im Gegensatz zu ihren deutschen Kollegen über eine besondere Aura und Kreativität zu verfügen, sofern man der medialen Verbreitung ihrer Persönlichkeit und Werke vertrauen will. Sie erscheinen oft redegewandter und selbstsicherer und können die wesentlichen Ideen ihrer Konzeptionen einer breiteren Öffentlichkeit leichter und schneller vermitteln. Wo nicht wenige deutsche Architekten langatmig erst den städtebaulichen Kontext sowie die konstruktiven und funktionalen Details zu erläutern versuchen, scheinen viele ausländische Architekten, weit erhoben über alle Widrigkeiten des Alltags, zu sehr bildhaften und einprägsamen Präsentationen fähig, die auch der Baulaie rasch verstehen kann.

Zudem verfügen sie aufgrund ihrer oftmals anders gearteten Baukulturen über einen Marketingvorteil. Geübter in diskursiven Wettbewerbsverfahren, die schon lange die Baukulturen Frankreichs, Großbritanniens oder der Niederlande dominieren, demonstrieren sie den Vorteil einer gekonnten Vermittlung. Persönlichkeit und öffentliches Auftreten besitzen in solchen Verfahren mehr Gewicht als in den lange Zeit in Deutschland üblichen anonymen Wettbewerbsverfahren. In letzteren werden

Germany's Building Culture and the Star Architecture System
Claus Käpplinger

Herzog & de Meuron, Zaha Hadid, Wolf D. Prix (Coop Himmelb(l)au), Kazuyo Sejima + Ryue Nishizawa (SANAA), Norman Foster, Frank O. Gehry, David Chipperfield, Richard Meier, Daniel Libeskind, Jean Nouvel, Ben van Berkel (UN Studio), Peter Zumthor, Dominique Perrault—these are just some of the names that have shaped the face of architecture in Germany over the course of the past decade. International and national publications give the impression that foreign architects are omnipresent on the German building scene. After all, many of the most high-profile projects of recent years, such as the Jewish Museum (Daniel Libeskind) and the Velodrome (Dominique Perrault) in Berlin, the Allianz Arena (Herzog & de Meuron) and the new BMW Welt (Coop Himmelb(l)au) in Munich, the Mercedes-Benz Museum (Ben van Berkel) in Stuttgart, the Diocesan Museum in Cologne (Peter Zumthor), the University Library in Cottbus (Herzog & de Meuron) and the Phaeno center in Wolfsburg (Zaha Hadid) were designed and built by foreign architects. Even the most important government building in Germany—the Bundestag in the former Reichstag building— was built by British architect Norman Foster, rather than by a German architect.

So what about the buildings by German architects? Why do foreign architects have such an enormous influence on building in Germany? It is not just our many visitors from abroad, some of whom may have little knowledge of contemporary architecture, who are asking these questions. For the most part, these visitors come to Germany to see the works of renowned international architects. For no other country in the Western world has been so open to amassing such a high proportion of works by outstanding foreign architects. Daniel Libeskind, David Chipperfield, and Wolf D. Prix are among those who received their first major commissions in Germany, at a time when they were little known to the broader public in their home countries. By contrast, until quite recently, only a handful of German architects—Gottfried Böhm, Otto Steidle, Frei Otto, Ludwig Leo, Oswald Mathias Ungers, Günter Behnisch, and Hans Kollhoff—had widespread recognition, though this situation is gradually changing thanks to the younger generation of architects now active on the international scene.

Unlike their German colleagues, foreign architects seem to be associated with a certain aura of creativity, if the portrayal of their image and works in the media is anything to go by. They often seem more eloquent and self-assured than their German colleagues, with a capacity to convey the essence of their ideas more easily and succinctly to a wider audience. Whereas German architects do have a tendency to launch into long-winded explanations of the urban context and the structural or functional details of their buildings, many of their foreign colleagues seem able to rise above such everyday matters and give memorable presentations full of powerful imagery that even the layperson can readily grasp.

What is more, they often come from a very different architectural culture, which actually gives them an advantage on the market. They have honed their communicative skills in the more discursive style of competition that has long prevailed in France, the UK, and the Netherlands, where personal charisma and public speaking often carry more weight than in the anonymous competition process that has been the norm in Germany for many years. In the latter case, the client and the architect generally have nothing to do with each other until the decision has been reached, followed by an often laborious process of building up mutual understanding and trust.

Reichstag, Berlin, Foster + Partners
Reichstag, Berlin, Foster + Partners

Gottfried Böhm
Gottfried Böhm

Frei Otto
Frei Otto

Kulturzentrum, Wolfsburg, Alvar Aalto
Cultural center, Wolfsburg, Alvar Aalto

Bauherr und Architekt nicht schon während des Wettbewerbs miteinander konfrontiert, sondern erst nach der Entscheidung, der dann nicht selten ein recht mühsamer Verständnis- und Vertrauensbildungsprozess folgt.

Die Konzeptionen deutscher Architekten sind konstruktiv, kontextuell und funktional oftmals durchdachter. Sie sind jedoch häufig weniger bildhaft und verlieren sich nicht selten in Details, da sie primär an Fachleute adressiert sind. Deutsche Architekten sind zudem oft pragmatischer und überschreiten ihre Budgets seltener so extrem wie manche internationalen Architekturstars, die dank ihres öffentlichen Auftretens und ihrer Wirkung die Bauherren zu zusätzlichen Investitionen zu bewegen verstehen. Geprägt von einer Alltagsbaukultur, die vom Realismus des Bauens und nicht von der Attraktivität der Ideen dominiert wird, können sich viele deutsche Architekten den Baulaien oft nur schwer verständlich machen. Dieser »Nachteil« fällt umso mehr ins Gewicht, wenn es sich um prominente Bauprojekte mit großer öffentlicher Wirkung wie etwa Museen oder Theater handelt.

So scheiterte beispielsweise vor wenigen Jahren selbst einer der prominentesten deutschen Architekten kommunikativ vor einer Gruppe US-amerikanischer Alumni, denen er seinen Entwurf vorstellen wollte. Allzu rasch verlor er sich in Erläuterungen seiner vielen konstruktiven Details, wofür ihm zusätzlich auch die englischen Fachbegriffe fehlten. Wo die Anwesenden vor allem die zugrundeliegende Idee begreifen wollten, wurden ihnen ausführlich erst der städtebauliche Kontext und dann die Konstruktion erläutert.

Doch die große Präsenz ausländischer Architekten in Deutschland scheint nicht nur eine Folge ihrer kommunikativen und konzeptionellen Fähigkeiten zu sein. Schon lange vor dem Starkult der Architekturszene bemühte man sich in Deutschland um ausländische Architekturgrößen, die man gezielt einlud. In der Zeit nach dem Zweiten Weltkrieg waren die Wünsche nach Anerkennung, kulturellem Austausch und Integration in die »westliche Wertegemeinschaft« die Hauptmotive für eine besondere Offenheit des Landes gegenüber ausländischen Architekten, wie sie sonst nur noch in manchen Schwellenländern der »Dritten Welt« zu finden war. Die Internationale Bauausstellung (IBA) 1957 in Berlin oder die Erweiterung von Wolfsburg waren prominente Schauplätze dieser Bemühungen und standen am Beginn der Präsenz ausländischer Architekten in Deutschland.

Dem Kulturzentrum von Alvar Aalto in Wolfsburg (1962) folgten in den Jahren eines wirtschaftlich immer erfolgreicheren Landes unter anderem das HEW-Gebäude von Arne Jacobsen in Hamburg (1965), das Rathaus in Marl von Van den Broek en Bakema (1966), das FU-Hauptgebäude von Candilis-Josic-Woods und Schiedhelm mit Jean Prouvé in Berlin (1973) oder die zahlreichen Bauten von Dissing und Weitling in Mainz, Castrop-Rauxel oder Düsseldorf. Dennoch blieb die Präsenz ausländischer Architekten noch relativ punktuell auf wenige Orte begrenzt. Erst ab den späten 1960er-Jahren weitete sich ihr Engagement aus, nicht zuletzt aufgrund höherer Architektenhonorare und umfangreicherer Architektenleistungen, die das Bauen für ausländische Architekten in Deutschland attraktiv machten, aber deutsche Architekten Projekte im Ausland scheuen ließen – unter anderem ein Grund, weshalb deutsche Architekten lange Zeit international kaum bei Wettbewerben präsent waren, bot doch das eigene Land genügend Möglichkeiten zu bauen.

Though the designs by German architects are often better conceived in terms of structure, context, and function, they may well come across as rather dry, for they are frequently laden with details aimed primarily at a specialist audience. Added to this, German architects often take a more pragmatic approach and so are less likely to overstep their budget as outrageously as an international star architect with the kind of clout and public persona that can persuade clients to invest that little bit more. Shaped by a culture of everyday architecture that is dominated more by the reality of building than the appeal of a vision, many German architects find it hard to communicate their ideas to the layperson. This puts them at a disadvantage when it comes to tabling designs for prestigious projects with a major public impact, such as museums or theaters.

To give an example: a few years ago, one of Germany's leading architects found himself in a situation where he was unable to communicate the essence of his design to a group of U.S. alumni. He soon became bogged down in detailed structural explanations, for which, to make matters worse, he simply did not have the specialist English vocabulary. While his audience was interested mainly in grasping the underlying idea, what it got was a detailed exposé of the urban context and the structure.

It would seem, however, that the presence of so many foreign architects in Germany is not just a result of their communicative and conceptual abilities. Germany was already wooing star architects from abroad long before the architectural scene had embraced the cult of celebrity. In the postwar years, Germany's wish for recognition, cultural exchange, and integration into the international community were the main factors that motivated the nation to open its doors to foreign architects on a scale otherwise seen only in developing countries of the so-called Third World. The 1957 IBA in Berlin and the expansion of Wolfsburg were major arenas in this development and, as such, marked the beginning of Germany's love affair with foreign architects.

As the economy went from strength to strength, Alvar Aalto's cultural center in Wolfsburg (1962) was soon followed by Arne Jacobsen's HEW building in Hamburg (1965), the Marl town hall by Van den Broek en Bakema (1966), the main university building of the FU Berlin by Candilis, Josic, Woods, and Schiedhelm together with Jean Prouvé (1973) as well as numerous buildings by Dissing und Weitling in Mainz, Castrop-Rauxel, and Düsseldorf. But even then, the work of foreign architects still remained limited to a relatively small number of specific locations. It was not until the late 1960s that things really took off, partly due to the generous architectural fees and other benefits that made Germany a particularly attractive workplace for architects from other countries, while at the same time making German architects more reluctant to embark on projects abroad—another reason why, at a time when their own country offered plenty of opportunities, German architects rarely participated in international competitions.

It was the rise of postmodernism in the 1970s, with the Abteiberg Museum in Mönchengladbach (Hans Hollein), the Berlin IBA 1978–1987 (Rob Krier and others), the Museumsufer and Römerberg developments in Frankfurt am Main (Charles Moore and others), that made the presence of foreign architects in Germany a nationwide phenomenon. At the time, postmodernism was very much geared toward the cult of celebrity, internationality, and media publicity, putting architecture in the spotlight as never before and making it a keystone of new urban and commercial marketing

James Stirling vor der Jury für das Wissenschaftszentrum Berlin
James Stirling addressing the jury for Wissenschaftszentrum, Berlin

Städtisches Museum Abteiberg,
Mönchengladbach, Hans Hollein
Abteiberg City Museum,
Mönchengladbach, Hans Hollein

Wohnbebauung Ritterstraße, Berlin,
Rob Krier
Residential project, Ritterstrasse, Berlin,
Rob Krier

Mit dem Aufkommen der Postmoderne in den Siebzigerjahren, mit dem Museum auf dem Abteiberg in Mönchengladbach (Hans Hollein), der Internationalen Bauausstellung Berlin 1978–1987 (Rob Krier und andere), dem Museumsufer und der Römerberg-Neubauten in Frankfurt am Main (Charles Moore und andere) wurde die Präsenz ausländischer Architekten zu einem Breitenphänomen. Sehr bewusst setzte damals die Postmoderne auf den Starkult, auf Internationalität und Medialität, was der Architektur eine wahrscheinlich nie zuvor erreichte populäre Wirkung einbrachte und sie zu einem zentralen Baustein neuartigen Stadt- und Unternehmensmarketings werden ließ. Auf breiter Front bemühten sich dann seit den Achtzigerjahren nicht nur kleine und mittelgroße Städte, sondern zunehmend auch private Bauherren um internationales Flair und Beachtung durch die Verpflichtung ausländischer Architekten. James Stirlings Braun Melsungen AG, Zaha Hadids Vitra-Feuerwehrhaus in Weil am Rhein, Frank O. Gehrys Energie-Forum in Bad Oeynhausen, Jean Nouvels Technologiezentrum in Wismar, David Chipperfields Literaturmuseum in Marbach, Richard Meiers Hans-Arp-Museum in Rolandseck oder Peter Zumthors Bruder-Klaus-Kapelle in Wachendorf sind nur wenige Beispiele wie präsent heute die Werke internationaler Größen selbst noch in den kleineren Orten Deutschlands sind.

Wirtschaftlich exportorientert, verfolgt man in Deutschland vielleicht auch stärker als andernorts die Entwicklungen im Ausland und ist zugleich häufig mehr auf die internationale Außenwirkung bedacht – in einem Land, das sich kulturell seiner Selbst immer noch nicht völlig gewiss und auf der Suche nach dem Eigenen ist. In der geografischen Mitte Europas gelegen, hat Deutschland immer wieder viele sehr unterschiedliche Kultureinflüsse aufgenommen und verarbeitet. Zumal dieses Land über kein dominantes kulturelles Zentrum verfügt und keine seiner vielen Architekturschulen heute ein klar fassbares internationales Profil besitzt, welches Orientierung im In- und Ausland bieten könnte. So gibt es in Deutschland nur wenige eigene Stars, dafür aber eine relativ entwickelte Baukultur im Alltag.

Die deutsche Architektur besitzt somit einen schwer fassbaren Vielklang und keine dominante Stimme – als Potenzial und Last zugleich. International geschult und redegewandter tritt heute eine neue deutsche Architektengeneration auf die Bühne, die im In- und Ausland gerade mit ihren oft unterschätzten Stärken wie Konstruktivität, Nachhaltigkeit und Funktionalität auf sich aufmerksam zu machen versteht. Interessanterweise arbeiteten viele Architekten dieser neuen Generation zuvor für ausländische Büros, die in Deutschland bauten.

strategies. By the 1980s, not only were small towns and provincial cities vying for media attention and international kudos by engaging foreign architects, but private clients, too, were jumping on the bandwagon. James Stirling's Braun Melsungen AG, Zaha Hadid's Vitra Fire Station at Weil am Rhein, Frank O. Gehry's Energy Forum in Bad Oeynhausen, Jean Nouvel's Technology Center in Wismar, David Chipperfield's Literature Museum in Marbach, Richard Meier's Hans Arp Museum in Rolandseck and Peter Zumthor's Bruder-Klaus Field Chapel in Wachendorf are but a few examples of the extent to which internationally renowned architects are represented in even the smaller towns in Germany.

In an exporting nation like Germany, there may be a tendency to follow trends abroad more keenly than elsewhere. At the same time, as a country that still has to find its feet and regain a certain confidence in its own cultural heritage, Germany is perhaps more sensitive to how it is perceived abroad. Located as it is at the geographic center of Europe, Germany has always absorbed many very different cultural influences. Germany is a country with no predominant cultural center and, for all its many architectural colleges, no single school of architecture that projects a clearly recognizable national or international profile. As a result, though Germany has only a handful of homegrown star architects, it does have a relatively highly developed general building culture.

And so, German architecture might be described as a polyphonic orchestration without a dominant voice. While this may be a disadvantage, it is also a source of great potential. A new, more eloquent, and internationally versed generation of German architects is now entering the arena, fully capable of marketing their hitherto underestimated strengths in the fields of construction, sustainability, and functionality. Interestingly, many of them previously worked for foreign architectural firms building in Germany.

Werk Pfieffewiesen der B. Braun Melsungen AG, Stirling Wilford & Associates mit Walter Nägeli
B. Braun Melsungen AG's Pfieffewiesen factory, Stirling Wilford & Associates with Walter Nägeli

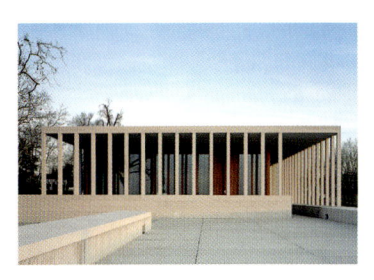

Literaturmuseum der Moderne, Marbach, David Chipperfield
Museum of Modernist Literature, Marbach, David Chipperfield

**Von »deutscher Form« zur »Weltform«?
Zur Geschichte des deutschen Architekturexports**
Wolfgang Voigt

Gericht, Tokio, Ende & Böckmann, 1887
Court of law, Tokyo, Ende & Böckmann, 1887

Deutschland ist Exportweltmeister in vielen Branchen, bisher jedoch nicht in der Architektur. Davon, dass auf diesem Sektor zurzeit aber auffällige Erfolge zu verzeichnen sind, handelt diese Ausstellung. Warum sich die deutschen Architekten mit dem Ausland lange schwer taten, erklärt sich durch einen Blick auf die Geschichte.[1]

Die Ausgangslage im 19. Jahrhundert war nicht günstig. Nicht das in zahlreiche Fürstentümer zersplitterte Deutschland, sondern Großbritannien und mehr noch das von der Revolution von 1789 dynamisierte Frankreich waren die kulturell dominierenden Mächte. Die zuerst 1851 veranstalteten Weltausstellungen zogen das interessierte Publikum eher nach London und Paris als in die deutschen Residenzstädte. Wer die perfekte Metropole der Belle Époque sehen wollte, fand diese nicht in Berlin, sondern an der Wiener Ringstraße und im von Baron Haussmann umgestalteten Paris. Die dort angesiedelte École des Beaux-Arts war lange Zeit die weltweit einflussreichste Architekturschule, die ihren akademischen Stil über alle Kontinente verbreitete. Selbst wenn es wie heute einen internationalen Markt für Architekturentwürfe gegeben hätte, das Ausland hätte diese kaum in Deutschland nachgefragt.

Gewiss gab es Ausnahmen: Leo von Klenze durfte die Neue Eremitage in Sankt Petersburg bauen und sein Rivale Friedrich von Gärtner das Königsschloss in Athen, jedoch waren dies nicht auf einem freien Markt erhaltene, sondern durch dynastische Verbindungen der regierenden Fürstenhäuser entstandene Aufträge. Auch gab es aufstrebende souveräne Staaten, die sich vom gezielten Architekturimport einen Modernisierungsschub versprachen. So geschah es in Japan, wo 1887–1891 die Berliner Architekten Ende & Böckmann eingeladen wurden, das Parlament und andere Staatsbauten in Tokio zu errichten,[2] oder im osmanischen Reich, wo deutsche Architekten und Ingenieure nach 1900 die Bagdad-Bahn mit ihren Bahnhöfen bauen durften. Das üblichere Muster der Ausfuhr von Ideen und Talenten aus Deutschland war jedoch die Auswanderung und das politische Exil, wie beispielsweise die Flucht Gottfried Sempers nach der gescheiterten Revolution von 1848 nach Paris und London.

Gegen Ende des 19. Jahrhunderts begann sich das Blatt zu wenden. Das seit 1871 vereinigte Deutschland Bismarcks entwickelte eine wirtschaftliche Dynamik, die es vor Großbritannien zur stärksten Industrienation werden ließ. Wissenschaft und Kunst blühten, das Kaiserreich blickte euphorisch in die Zukunft. Mit Nachdruck nahmen sich Architekten und Gestalter der Aufgabe an, die schnell gewachsenen und als chaotisch empfundenen Städte zu ordnen und für alles einen neuen, angemessenen Stil zu suchen. Die Konzepte waren oft ausländischen Ursprungs, wie die aus England übernommene Arts-and-Crafts-Bewegung und die Idee der Gartenstadt, allerdings gelang es in Deutschland besonders gut, die neuen Impulse wirkungsvoll zu bündeln.

Eine wichtige Rolle spielte dabei die Kunstschulreform, welche die Ausbildung in angewandter Kunst und Architektur von akademischen Zöpfen befreite und mit lebensnahem Werkstättenunterricht verband. Später sollte sich daraus das 1919 gegründete Bauhaus entwickeln. An deutschen Technischen Hochschulen wurde der Städtebau erstmals als wissenschaftliche Disziplin behandelt. Nun waren es deutsche Leistungsschauen, die das fremde Publikum anzogen: die Internationalen Städtebauausstellungen von Berlin (1910) und Düsseldorf (1912) sowie die Kölner Werkbundausstellung von 1914.

From "German Form" to "International Form"?
On the History of German Architectural Export
Wolfgang Voigt

While German exports lead the world market in many fields, architecture, to date, has not been one of them. However, remarkable successes are currently being achieved in this sector, as this exhibition aims to show. A glance at history can explain why German architects have had such a low profile abroad for so long.[1]

In the nineteenth century, the situation was hardly favorable. Europe's cultural power was concentrated mainly in Great Britain and in dynamic, post-revolutionary France, rather than in Germany, which was then a loosely bound league of many sovereign states. With the inception of the universal expositions known as the World's Fair in 1851, visitors flocked to London and Paris. The ideal cities of the Belle Époque were not Berlin but Vienna, with its Ringstraße, and Paris, with its boulevards by Baron Haussmann. For many years, the École des Beaux-Arts was the most influential school of architecture in the world, disseminating its academic style across every continent. Even if there had been an international market for architectural design in those days, as there is now, few foreign clients would have considered looking to Germany.

Of course, there were exceptions: Leo von Klenze was commissioned to build the New Hermitage in Saint Petersburg, and his rival, Friedrich von Gärtner, designed the Royal Palace in Athens. But these were not free-market commissions; they were contracts awarded through the dynastic loyalties of the ruling aristocracy. On the other hand, there were emerging nation-states that specifically aspired to enhance their modernization by importing foreign architecture. One of these was Japan, where Berlin architects Ende & Böckmann were invited to build the parliament building and other state buildings in Tokyo between 1887 and 1891.[2] Another was the Ottoman Empire, where German architects and engineers constructed the Baghdad railway and its stations from 1900 onward. For the most part, however, German ideas and talents were exported by means of emigration and political exile, as in the case of Gottfried Semper, who fled to Paris and London in the wake of the ill-fated revolution of 1848.

By the late nineteenth century, the tide was beginning to turn. Germany, united since 1871, with Bismarck as chancellor, developed a dynamic economic upswing that saw it overtake Britain as the leading industrial nation. The arts and sciences blossomed and the German empire looked euphorically to the future. Architects and designers eagerly embraced the task of structuring the rapidly growing cities that were perceived as chaotic and of finding a new and fitting style for everything. Though many of their concepts originated in other countries, such as the Arts and Crafts movement and the idea of the Garden City, both from Britain, the Germans proved singularly adept at adopting these new movements to great effect.

One major factor in this was the so-called *Kunstschulreform,* which meant that training in the applied arts and architecture was freed from the constraints of the academic system and combined with hands-on workshop teaching, paving the way for the foundation of the Bauhaus in 1919, and introducing urban planning as a recognized discipline at technical universities for the first time. From here on, it was the German expositions that drew the foreign crowds: the international architecture expositions in Berlin (1910) and Düsseldorf (1912) and the 1914 Werkbund exhibition in Cologne.

Bahnhof der Bagdadbahn, Istanbul,
Otto Ritter und Helmut Conu, 1908
Baghdad Railway Station, Istanbul,
Otto Ritter and Helmut Conu, 1908

Die Zukunft der deutschen Form,
Hermann Muthesius, 1915
The Future of German Form,
Hermann Muthesius, 1915

Dem 1907 gegründeten Deutschen Werkbund gelang das Kunststück, die reforminteressierten Kreise aus Industrie und Politik mit den Gestaltern in einen einflussreichen Verband unter dem Motto der Qualitätsarbeit zusammenzubringen.[3] Werkbundarchitekten wie Theodor Fischer, Peter Behrens, Walter Gropius, Max Berg und Heinrich Tessenow – um nur die wichtigsten Namen zu nennen – durften Bauten errichten, die heute zum Kanon der Architekturmoderne gehören. Nicht zufällig zog damals der junge Charles-Édouard Jeanneret, der sich später Le Corbusier nannte, ganz bewusst nach Deutschland, um in den Büros von Peter Behrens und Theodor Fischer zu lernen. Das Werkbundmodell war so erfolgreich, dass sich in der Schweiz, Österreich, Tschechien und Ungarn bald eigene Werkbünde etablierten.

Die führenden Mitglieder des Werkbundes waren nicht frei von den imperialen Phantasien des späten Kaiserreiches. Im Hochgefühl des Erfolgs planten sie bereits für den Export. In seiner zu Beginn des Ersten Weltkriegs verfassten Schrift *Mitteleuropa* forderte der liberale Politiker und Werkbundmitglied Friedrich Naumann für Deutschland die Vormachtstellung auf dem europäischen Festland und eine führende Rolle in der Weltwirtschaft, was vor allem eine Schwächung Frankreichs und Englands bedeutet hätte.[4] Die Kolonien dieser Länder boten ihren Industrien exklusive Absatzgebiete. Im britischen Empire reichten die Territorien, in denen sich auch die Architekten des Mutterlandes entfalten durften, von Indien bis Kanada und von Ägypten bis Südafrika. Der Kolonialbesitz der »verspäteten Nation« der Deutschen war vergleichsweise bescheiden, und entsprechend unbedeutend waren Städtchen wie Windhoek im heutigen Namibia oder Tsingtau in China, denen deutsche Architekten ihren Stempel aufdrückten. Sie waren winzig im Vergleich zu den britisch ausgerichteten Metropolen wie Kairo, Bombay, Neu-Delhi und Hong Kong oder zum strahlenden Casablanca der Franzosen.

In Deutschland erwartete man nach einem siegreich beendeten Weltkrieg eine Umkehrung der Verhältnisse. Hermann Muthesius sah die »deutsche Form« zur »Weltform« werden. Es genüge nicht, »die Welt zu beherrschen, […] sie zu finanzieren, sie zu unterrichten, sie mit Waren und Gütern zu überschwemmen«. In Zukunft gehe es darum, der Welt »das Gesicht zu geben. Erst das Volk, das diese Tat vollbringt, steht wahrhaft an der Spitze der Welt; und Deutschland muss dieses Volk werden.«[5]

Die deutsche Niederlage von 1918 und der Verlust der Kolonien machten solche Hoffnungen zunichte. Der Traum, im Kielwasser der Weltmacht »deutsche Form« unter Einschluss der Architektur im Ausland zu verbreiten, hatte sich erledigt. Die Deutschen waren isoliert, an der *Exposition internationale des arts décoratifs* in Paris 1925 durften sie nicht teilnehmen. Walter Gropius fand einen Ausweg im Konzept der *Internationalen Architektur,* die er im gleichen Jahr als erstes Bauhausbuch präsentierte: Ein Querschnitt geplanter und gebauter Beispiele aus vielen Ländern, der die Avantgarde der Moderne als einheitliche Bewegung darstellte, die über Grenzen hinweg dieselben Ziele verfolgte. Zur Weißenhofsiedlung des Werkbundes in Stuttgart 1927 wurden demonstrativ ausländische Architekten eingeladen, darunter Victor Bourgeois und Le Corbusier als Vertreter Belgiens und Frankreichs, mit denen man zuvor Krieg geführt hatte. Der Weißenhof markierte den Durchbruch der modernen Bewegung in Deutschland, die im Ausland zunehmend Eindruck machte. Deutsche Architekten wurden Mitglieder der Congrès internationaux d'architecture

The Deutscher Werkbund, founded in 1907, succeeded in getting reform-minded industrial and political circles to join forces with designers in an influential organization that pinned the idea of "quality workmanship" to its mast.[3] Werkbund architects such as Theodor Fischer, Peter Behrens, Walter Gropius, Max Berg, and Heinrich Tessenow—to name but a few of the most important—were able to create buildings that have become icons of modernist architecture. It was no coincidence that the young Charles-Édouard Jeanneret, who later called himself Le Corbusier, chose to come to Germany to hone his skills in the offices of Peter Behrens and Theodor Fischer. So successful was the Werkbund model that Switzerland, Austria, Czechoslovakia, and Hungary soon established their own Werkbunds.

The leading members of the Werkbund were not immune to the imperial fantasies of the late *Kaiserreich*. In the euphoria of success, they were already planning for the export market. The liberal politician and Werkbund member Friedrich Naumann published his treatise *Mitteleuropa,* written at the beginning of the First World War, calling for German hegemony in continental Europe and a leading role in the world economy, which first and foremost would have involved a weakening of France and Britain.[4] Both of these countries had colonies providing exclusive markets for their goods. The British Empire, where, needless to say, British architects were able to exercise their talents, stretched from India to Canada and from Egypt to South Africa. The colonial territories of "latecomer" Germany were relatively modest by comparison, and the towns where German architects could make their mark were smaller, less important ones such as Windhoek in what is now Namibia or Tsingtau in China. They paled into insignificance by comparison with the British-ruled cities of Cairo, Bombay, New Delhi, and Hong Kong, or the scintillating French-ruled city of Casablanca.

Germany fully expected the tables to turn once they had won the war. Hermann Muthesius could already envisage "German form" becoming "international form." This, he went on, "involves more than simply ruling the world . . . financing it, teaching it, or flooding it with wares and goods. It has to do with giving the world a new face. The people that accomplishes this feat will truly stand at the top of the world. And Germany must be this people."[5]

Those high hopes were dashed in 1918 with the defeat of Germany and the loss of its colonies. The dream of disseminating "German design," including architecture, across the globe as a world power was well and truly over. Germany was isolated and was not allowed to participate in the 1925 Exposition internationale des arts décoratifs in Paris. Walter Gropius found a solution in the form of *International Architecture*—a concept he presented that same year in the very first Bauhaus book: a cross section of planned and built examples from many different countries, portraying avant-garde modernism as a single movement *sans frontières,* united in its pursuit of the same goals. A point was made of inviting foreign architects, including Victor Bourgeois and Le Corbusier, as representatives of Belgium and France, with whom Germany had so recently been at war, to participate in the Werkbund's Weissenhofsiedlung project. The Weissenhofsiedlung marked the breakthrough in Germany of the modern movement that was already making such an impact elsewhere. German architects became members of the Congrès internationaux d'architecture moderne (CIAM), which held its second congress in Frankfurt am Main in 1929. The

Internationale Architektur (Bauhaus-Bücher 1),
Walter Gropius, 1925
International Architecture (Bauhaus Books 1),
Walter Gropius, 1925

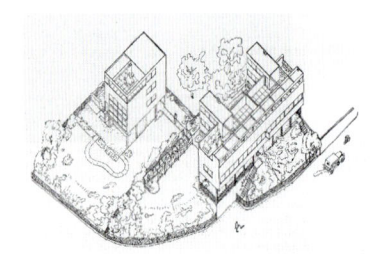

Isometrie von zwei Häusern in der Weißenhofsiedlung, Stuttgart, Le Corbusier, 1927
Isometry of two buildings on the Weissenhof estate, Stuttgart, Le Corbusier, 1927

Haus Salomon, Haifa, Robert Friedmann, 1937
Salomon building, Haifa, Robert Friedmann, 1937

Jewish National Fund, Haifa, Josef Klarwein, 1937
Jewish National Fund, Haifa, Josef Klarwein, 1937

moderne (CIAM), deren zweiter Kongress 1929 in Frankfurt am Main stattfand: der Bann war damit gebrochen. Ernst May und der Schweizer Hannes Meyer zogen 1930 für einige Jahre an der Spitze vielköpfiger Architektenteams in die Sowjetunion, um bei der Gründung neuer Industriestädte zu helfen.

Nachdem die Isolation überwunden war, machte die nationalsozialistische Herrschaft ab 1933 alles zunichte. Was folgte, war Architekturexport in seiner schädlichsten Form – Aderlass durch die erzwungene Emigration der jüdischen Kollegen und der exponiertesten Architekten der Avantgarde. Die einst für deutsche Städte entwickelte Architekturmoderne brachten diese nun in ihre Gastländer mit. In absurder Umkehrung von Hermann Muthesius' Vision von 1915 halfen sie tatsächlich, an den Orten des Exils zwischen Kalifornien und Palästina eine »Weltform« der Architektur zu verbreiten, jedoch nicht mehr im Namen ihres einstigen Vaterlandes.[6] Das 1933 geschlossene Bauhaus, dessen Lehre im Exil wieder erblühte und heute als Ikone der Geschichte der Moderne verehrt wird, war zu diesem Zeitpunkt schon keine deutsche Sache mehr.

Eine weitere, nicht weniger verzerrte Variante des Exports folgte im Zweiten Weltkrieg, als Hunderte von Ingenieuren und Architekten in die von deutschen Truppen besetzten Länder ausschwärmten, um ihre Tüchtigkeit durch den Bau von Landepisten, Straßen, Brücken, Bunkern, Geschützstellungen, Flugzeughangars und Konzentrationslagern unter Beweis zu stellen. Statt der Kolonien hatte man nun die besetzten Gebiete im Osten. Für die dort gelegenen Städte und Dörfer wurden auf deutschen Reißbrettern Planungen entwickelt, welche die Herrschaft über die unterworfenen »Untermenschen« für alle Zeiten manifestieren sollten.[7]

Nach 1945 hatten die europäischen Nachbarn von ungebetenen deutschen Architekturexporten für lange Zeit genug. Die deutschen Städte lagen in Trümmern, die Zerstörung hatte nie zuvor gekannte Ausmaße erreicht. Die große Mehrheit der im Lande gebliebenen Architekten hatte indessen keinen Anlass zur Klage, da Jahrzehnte sicherer Beschäftigung vor ihnen lagen. Die Aussicht auf ein geeintes Europa und nicht zuletzt die Erfindung der Urlaubsreise als Massenphänomen ließen die nationalen Vorurteile schwächer werden. Der Austausch von Ideen war nun weniger behindert, was den Reimport der nach 1933 verpönten Architekturmoderne, die sich während des Nationalsozialismus nur in einigen Industriebauten entfalten durfte, erleichterte.

In Westdeutschland boten die Jahrzehnte des Wiederaufbaus den Architekten ein goldenes Zeitalter. Man hatte so viel zu tun, dass der Gedanke an Export gar nicht aufkam. In den aufstrebenden Ländern der »Dritten Welt«, die ihre Kolonialherrschaft abschütteln konnten, entwickelten sich inzwischen erstmals Ansätze eines internationalen Marktes für Ingenieur- und Architekturleistungen. Mehr als fürs Ausland interessierten sich die Kollegen jedoch dafür, die Konditionen des »Wirtschaftswunders« im eigenen Land möglichst lange zu erhalten. Das Ergebnis war die Schaffung nach innen gerichteter defensiver Strukturen, etwa in Gestalt der Honorarordnung für Architekten und Ingenieure (HOAI) und der ab Ende der Sechzigerjahre eingerichteten Architektenkammern. Dafür gab es gute Gründe, aber zweifellos ging es auch darum, als Berufstand für weniger gemütliche Zeiten nach dem Aufbauboom gerüstet zu sein.

spell was broken. In 1930, Ernst May and the Swiss architect Hannes Meyer set off for the Soviet Union, where they spent several years heading a large team of architects involved in building new industrial cities.

But Germany's newfound escape from isolation was soon to be thwarted. With the rise to power of the National Socialists in 1933, the country began exporting architecture in the most damaging way of all—through the massive brain drain triggered by the forced emigration of Jewish colleagues and, with them, some of the country's finest avant-garde architects. They brought with them into exile the modernist architecture they had once developed for German cities. And so, in an absurd reversal of Hermann Muthesius's 1915 vision, they did indeed help to spread their "international design" all the way from California to Palestine—but not in the name of their former "fatherland."[6] The teachings of the Bauhaus, which was forced to close its doors in 1933, blossomed in exile to become a beacon of modernism. But by then it was no longer a German institution.

Another, no less distorted, variation of Germany's design exports occurred in the Second World War, when hundreds of engineers and architects set forth into occupied territories to demonstrate their skills as builders of runways, roads, bridges, bunkers, aircraft hangars, and concentration camps. Instead of its colonies, Germany now had its *Lebensraum* in Eastern Europe. On German drawing boards, plans were drawn up for the towns and villages there, designed to manifest German supremacy over the "inferior races" for all eternity.[7]

Post-1945, Germany's European neighbors had had quite enough of such unsolicited architectural exports to last them a long time. The cities of Germany lay in ruins. The scale of the devastation was unprecedented. Most of the architects who had stayed had little to complain about, for they clearly had enough work to keep them busy for years. As visions of a united Europe took shape and the wider public began to discover the joys of foreign holidays, nationalistic prejudices and resistance to outside ideas were tempered. This made it easier to re-import the modernist architecture that had been so disparaged under the National Socialist regime since 1933 that it had been tolerated only in the occasional industrial building.

In West Germany, the postwar decades of reconstruction were a golden age for architects. There was so much to be done at home that export was simply not a priority. In the developing countries of the so-called Third World, which had shaken off the fetters of colonial rule, an international market began to emerge for engineering and architectural services. But German architects and engineers were more interested in maintaining the status quo of their own "economic miracle." The result was the creation of such inward-looking structures as a fixed tariff scale (known as the *Honorarordnung für Architekten und Ingenieure,* or HOAI) for architects and engineers and the establishment of Chambers of Architects in the late 1960s. Laudable as some of their aims may have been, these moves were also undoubtedly aimed at feathering the profession's nest in preparation for less-profitable times ahead.

While major construction companies that had already been active abroad even before the First World War successfully set about once more building up business abroad, architects were happy to leave foreign projects entirely to the devices of

Artilleriebunker, Longues-sur-Mer, Organisation Todt, 1942
Artillery bunker, Longues-sur-Mer, Organisation Todt, 1942

Deutscher U-Boot-Bunker, Bordeaux, um 1941
German U-boat bunker, Bordeaux, around 1941

Während die großen Baufirmen, die schon vor dem Ersten Weltkrieg im Ausland tätig waren, dieses Feld nun mit Erfolg erneut beackerten, überließen die Architekten das Auslandsgeschäft fast ganz der Konkurrenz. Vor allem die großen US-amerikanischen Architekturbüros waren hier seit den Fünfziger- und Sechzigerjahren in die Offensive gegangen und profitierten dabei von der allgemeinen Bewunderung für die damals noch kaum in Frage gestellte Konsumkultur des »American Way of Life«. Als mit der westdeutschen Baukrise von 1974/75 die Dauerkonjunktur des Aufbaus zu Ende ging, waren die deutschen Kollegen somit nicht darauf vorbereitet, ihre brachliegenden Potenziale in den Export zu lenken. Zwar waren einige Architekten in den Ländern des Nahen und Mittleren Ostens erfolgreich. Aber auch hier waren Architekten aus anderen Ländern früher eingestiegen und erhielten die besseren Aufträge. Konstantinos Doxiadis' Masterplan für Bagdad und Louis Kahns Parlament in Dhaka seien hier als Beispiele für die spektakulärsten Projekte genannt.

In den Achtzigerjahren öffnete sich Westdeutschland demonstrativ wie zuvor kein anderer Staat den ausländischen Architekten. Dies geschah zuerst in Westberlin, wo es galt, auf internationalem Niveau die Modernisierung der in prekärer Insellage gelegenen Metropole zu betreiben. Das ausländische Engagement bei der Internationalen Bauausstellung in Berlin (IBA) 1978–1987 wurde zum Vorbild für das ganze Land und nach der Wiedervereinigung auch für den Umbau der Hauptstadt und den Aufbau in den neuen Bundesländern. Umgekehrt hatte der Drang der ausländischen Kollegen nach Deutschland auch eine materielle Seite, denn hier konnte man dank der für alle geltenden komfortablen Honorarordnung für die gleiche Leistung mitunter mehr verdienen als zu Hause. Was als defensive Marktregulierung im Interesse der einheimischen Berufsgenossen begonnen hatte, sorgte nun für noch mehr Konkurrenz im eigenen Land.

Das Überspringen der Ländergrenzen fand somit lange nur in einer Richtung statt. Inzwischen hat sich die Welt jedoch dramatisch verändert. Die Globalisierung und das Internet haben nicht nur die Kommunikation revolutioniert und die Vorstellungen von Nähe und Ferne auf den Kopf gestellt. Die Einbindung Chinas und vieler anderer Länder in die westliche Ökonomie begünstigte die Entstehung eines Weltmarkts für Architektenleistungen – wovon lange Zeit nur geträumt wurde. Davon profitiert heute eine wachsende Zahl deutscher Architekten, die sich angesichts der andauernd flauen Baukonjunktur nach Ende des »Aufbau Ost« auf das Wagnis im Ausland einlassen. Selbst eine stetig zunehmende Zahl kleinerer und junger Büros hat es geschafft, Kontakte aufzubauen, Wettbewerbe für sich zu entscheiden und in Asien, im europäischen Ausland und sogar in den USA zu bauen. Der Abstand zu den auf internationalem Parkett über mehr Erfahrung verfügenden Konkurrenten aus den USA, Großbritannien, Frankreich und den Niederlanden besteht noch immer, aber die Deutschen haben sichtbar aufgeholt.

Zwei große deutsche Büros, von Gerkan Marg und Partner (gmp) und Albert Speer und Partner (AS&P), fallen durch Intensität und Volumen ihres Engagements im Ausland aus dem Rahmen. Die Internationalisierung ihrer Arbeit ist so weit fortgeschritten, dass in manchen Jahren mehr als die Hälfte ihrer Bauten und Projekte für ferne Standorte entwickelt worden sind. Mit Entwürfen für China begann der weltweit als Stadtplaner tätige Albert Speer 1994, Meinhard von Gerkan und Volkwin Marg folgten vier Jahre später. Als um die Jahrtausendwende die deutsche Baukonjunktur

their foreign colleagues. Leading U.S. architectural practices had been proactively making inroads in this field since the 1950s and 1960s, buoyed by a widespread admiration for the consumerist mind-set embodied by the "American way of life." The West German construction industry crisis of 1974–75 that marked the end of a long and uninterrupted period of growth caught German architects and engineers unprepared and unable to shift their focus to potential export markets. Though a handful of German architects did win some important contracts in the Middle East, their colleagues from abroad, having prepared the ground long before, picked the cream of the crop. Constantinos Doxiadis's master plan for Baghdad and Louis Kahn's parliament building in Dhaka are just two examples of some of the more spectacular of these projects.

In the 1980s, West Germany, more than any other country, demonstratively opened its doors to foreign architects. It all began in West Berlin, where there was a keen interest in modernizing the city, an island of Western democracy set in socialist Eastern Europe, to bring it up to international standards. The involvement of foreign architects in the 1978–1987 IBA architectural exhibition inspired the whole country and set the benchmark for the post-reunification restructuring of Berlin as the German capital and the redevelopment of the former East German states. On the other hand, there was also a financial incentive involved in this influx of foreign architects to Germany, for the tariff structures designed to ensure a comfortable income often meant that they could command considerably higher fees than they might have expected in their own countries for the same work. In other words, what had originally been put in place as a self-preserving instrument of market regulation had now become a source of increased competition on the domestic market.

For many years, international architectural activity was a one-way street. But the world has changed dramatically. Globalization and the Internet have revolutionized communication and radically altered our perception of distance. With China and many other countries entering the arena of the Western economy, an international market for architecture has emerged on a scale that was once the stuff of dreams alone. This development has benefited a growing number of German architects who, faced with a construction industry still in the doldrums since the flurry of post-reunification redevelopment slowed down, have taken the step of looking for work abroad. Even small and recently founded architectural firms have been succeeding, in increasing numbers, to establish contacts, win competitions, and build their designs in Asia, in neighboring European countries, and even in the United States. Though they still have some way to go to catch up with their American, British, French, and Dutch rivals, the Germans have clearly narrowed the gap.

Two leading German firms, von Gerkan Marg und Partner (gmp) and Albert Speer und Partner (AS&P), are exceptions to the rule in terms of the intensity and sheer volume of their international contracts. Indeed, so strongly is their work directed toward the international market that in some years more than half their buildings and projects are in distant locations. Albert Speer, internationally active as an urban planner, began designing for China back in 1994, with Meinhard von Gerkan and Volkwin Marg following in his footsteps just four years later. When the German construction industry collapsed at the turn of the millennium, von Gerkan Marg und Partner were able to compensate by focusing more strongly on projects abroad. As a result,

Bauentwurfslehre (38. Auflage),
Ernst Neufert, 2005
Architects' Data (38th edition),
Ernst Neufert, 2005

einbrach, gelang von Gerkan, Marg und Partner die Kompensation durch verstärkte Anstrengungen im Ausland. So waren im Jahr 2005 von insgesamt 72 Projekten nur noch 22 in Deutschland angesiedelt und bereits 28 in Asien.

Zwei weitere Exportphänomene sind in diesem Zusammenhang von Interesse. Das eine erinnert an frühere Wellen der Emigration. Viele der an deutschen Hochschulen ausgebildeten jungen Architekten gehen direkt nach Rotterdam, London, Madrid, Basel oder Wien und anderswohin. Die Niederlassungsfreiheit in der EU macht es möglich. Leichter als im Inland gelang dort in den letzten Jahren der Einstieg in geregelte Arbeitsverhältnisse. Die jungen Deutschen in den Niederlanden oder in Frankreich sind die Enkel der Kriegsgeneration, die man einst als Besatzer im Land hatte. Mit diesen haben sie außer der Sprache allerdings nicht mehr viel gemein, ihre Jugend prägte nicht mehr die Hitlerjugend, sondern der Spanienurlaub und die *Sesamstraße*.

Das zweite Phänomen betrifft die in alle Welt verschifften deutschen Bauhandbücher und vor allem eine Zeitschrift: Der Welterfolg des seit 1936 verlegten »Neufert« – ein Standardwerk zur Bauentwurfslehre, der inzwischen in achtzehn Sprachen erscheint und eine Gesamtauflage zwischen 1,5 und 2 Millionen Exemplaren erreicht haben dürfte –, verbreitet deutsche Standards und die »deutsche Mentalität«, soweit sie sich auf das praktische Bauen beziehen, in alle technologisch entwickelten Länder der Erde. Einen auffälligen Export schafft auch die expandierende Zeitschrift *Detail* aus München, die in sieben Sprachen erscheint und nach Angaben des Verlags in 80 Ländern ihre Leser findet. Die sorgfältige Durcharbeitung selbst der kleinen Dinge kann man von den Deutschen lernen, das ist die nicht zu unterschätzende Botschaft zwischen den Zeilen.

Aber zurück zum eigentlichen Export, unter dem wir nicht die Abwanderung von Menschen oder das Verschicken von Büchern, sondern die Ausfuhr von Entwürfen verstehen. Interessanterweise gelingt das »Aufholen« im Ausland ohne Aufbietung der sogenannten Stararchitekten. Inzwischen gelingt es offenbar, den Starrummel des Auslands mit einem Angebot zu unterlaufen, in dem weniger auffällige Kriterien in den Vordergrund rücken; so zum Beispiel die hohen einheimischen Standards bei energiesparender Bautechnologie, die in den neuerdings an Umweltschutz interessierten USA auf großes Interesse stoßen. Nachhaltigkeit spielt weltweit in der Architektur eine immer wichtigere Rolle, und auf diesem Feld haben die einheimischen Kollegen etwas vorzuzeigen. Unter dem Titel »Why are they greener than we are?« berichtete die New York Times kürzlich über den großen Vorsprung der Mitteleuropäer in Sachen der »green architecture«.[8]

Die durchaus doppelgesichtige Honorarordnung und der Drang zur absichernden »Verregelung« haben die Planermentalität hierzulande jahrzehntelang spezifisch geprägt. »Deutsche Gründlichkeit« und ein neues Umweltbewusstsein haben andererseits eine reflexive Haltung[9] hervorgebracht, die alles in Betracht zieht, die Probleme tiefer ergründet und der ersten wie der letzten Phase des Projekts dieselbe Aufmerksamkeit widmet – weil sie alle von Bedeutung sind. Während im Inland heute oft nur der verzögernde und verteuernde Aspekt solchen Planens wahrgenommen wird, können die deutschen Architekten im Ausland gerade damit punkten. Nach dem Zweiten Weltkrieg war die Bundesrepublik um ein Selbstbild aus Demut

in 2005, only twenty-two of their seventy-two projects were in Germany, whereas no fewer than twenty-eight were in Asia.

There are two other export phenomena worth mentioning. One of these is reminiscent of earlier waves of emigration. Many young architecture graduates from German universities go straight to Rotterdam, London, Madrid, Basel, Vienna, and elsewhere. The freedom of work and residence under the EU has made this possible. And in recent years, it has been easier to find a steady job there than at home. The young Germans working in the Netherlands and France are the grandchildren of the wartime generation who occupied those countries. But apart from the language, they have little in common with their grandparents. Their formative years were shaped not by the Hitler Youth, but by holidays in Spain and by *Sesame Street*.

The second of these phenomena involves the worldwide distribution of German construction manuals, and above all of one particular periodical: the internationally acclaimed *Neufert*—an essential reference work for designing and planning buildings, launched in 1936 and now issued in eighteen languages with a circulation of between 1.5 and 2 million. These publications disseminate German standards and the German approach to practical construction work throughout all the technologically developed countries on Earth. Another remarkable export in this field is the ever-expanding Munich-based periodical *Detail,* published in seven languages and with a readership, according to the publishers, in eighty countries. What we can read between the lines here is the message, not to be underestimated, that German architects and engineers do indeed have something worthwhile to say about painstaking attention to even the smallest detail.

But let us return to the question at hand—neither the emigration of talent nor the distribution of reading matter, but the export of actual designs. It is interesting to note that Germany has been closing the gap abroad even without a stable of celebrity architects. Clearly, German architects are able to compete in an otherwise starstruck market by offering something that puts less ostentatious criteria to the fore—such as the high standards of German energy-saving construction technology that are now garnering considerable interest in a more environmentally aware United States. Sustainability is playing an increasing role and, again, the Germans have something to offer here. A recent *New York Times* article titled "Why Are They Greener Than We Are?" reported on the enormous lead that Central Europeans have when it comes to "green" architecture.[8]

For decades, architects' attitudes have been shaped by the double-edged sword of Germany's tariff regulations and security-driven red tape. Yet, on the other hand, German thoroughness and a new ecological awareness have also spawned a "reflexive" approach[9] that involves taking every aspect into consideration, carefully weighing problems, and devoting the same attention to detail at every stage of the project, from beginning to end—because they are all important. Though often viewed in Germany itself as time-consuming and expensive, it is precisely this approach that gives German architects the edge on the foreign market. After the Second World War, the Federal Republic of Germany was eager to adopt an image of humility and modesty that would help to obliterate the Nazi era and its bombastic architecture. At the Berlin Interbau exhibition of 1957, a canon of new values was launched

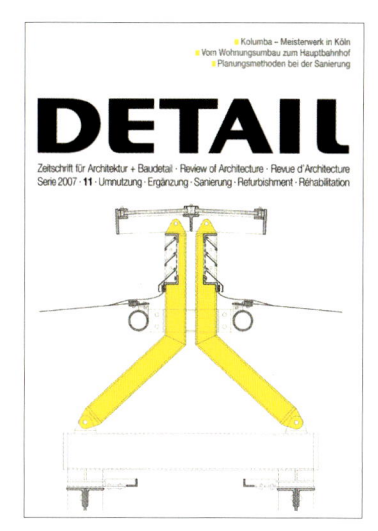

Die Zeitschrift *Detail*, Nr. 11, 2007
The magazine *Detail*, No. 11, 2007

Tripoli Gate, Tripolis, Jo Franzke Architekten,
Fertigstellung 2009
Tripoli Gate, Tripoli, Jo Franzke Architekten,
completion: 2009

und Bescheidenheit bemüht, das die NS-Herrschaft und ihre steinern-dröhnende Bauvergangenheit vergessen machen sollte. Auf der Berliner Interbau von 1957 wurde mit dem Slogan »Leicht, heiter, wohnlich, festlich, farbig, strahlend, geborgen« ein Kanon neuer Werte in Umlauf gebracht. In diesem Geiste entstand auch 1958 der betont leicht und gläsern gebaute Pavillon von Egon Eiermann und Sep Ruf auf der Brüsseler Weltausstellung, und vierzehn Jahre später das schwebende Olympiadach in München von Günter Behnisch und Frei Otto. Natürlich waren beide Bilder Klischees, das zu verdrängende alte ebenso wie das heitere neue. Noch ging es nicht darum, dem Ausland Entwürfe zu verkaufen, die Architektur stand explizit im Dienst nationaler Sympathiewerbung.

Eine Generation später ist die Demokratie gefestigt, und das Land ist derart mit der EU verwachsen, dass die Gesten von einst nicht mehr zwingend sind. So kann der deutsche Beitrag zur Architekturbiennale von São Paulo, *Ready for Take-Off,* mit einem neuen oder doch eher alten Wertekanon operieren, der nicht das Image des Landes im Blick hat, sondern direkt auf ein Produkt und die Kompetenz seiner Anbieter gerichtet ist. Darin spielt übrigens der Gedanke einer spezifisch »deutschen« Architektur, die sich in Gestalt und Stil von anderen Ländern auf markante Weise abheben würde, keine Rolle mehr. Je weiter man von Deutschland entfernt ist, desto weniger wird der Tugendkatalog mit Argwohn betrachtet. Brasilianische Besucher der Biennale sahen sich an die Fähigkeiten erinnert, die dort noch immer den deutschen Einwanderern zugeschrieben werden, und an die bei deutschen Autos und Maschinen stets nachprüfbaren Vorzüge des »Made in Germany«. Gern hätte das Land, hieß es, selbst mehr davon ...

Lily Hollein, die in São Paulo den benachbarten Beitrag Österreichs kuratierte, hat mit ihrer Einschätzung, bei *Ready for Take-Off* handele es sich wohl um eine »knallharte Marktstrategie«, keineswegs unrecht.[10] Der Akzent liegt in der Tat auf »Markt«, und damit befinden wir uns in sicherer Entfernung von den deutschen Auftritten vor 1945, die allzu häufig von Machtansprüchen und Sendungsbewusstsein getragen waren. Und im Gegensatz zum Ernst der architektonischen Demutsgesten der Nachkriegszeit darf heute ein Stück Selbstironie dabei sein.

1 Siehe hierzu auch Wolfgang Voigt, »Zur Vorgeschichte deutschen Architekturexports im 19. und 20. Jahrhundert«, in: Ingeborg Flagge u. a. (Hrsg.), *Architektur in Deutschland (DAM-Jahrbuch* 2002), München 2002, S. 13–19.
2 Vgl. Michiko Meid, *Der Einführungsprozeß der europäischen und der nordamerikanischen Architektur in Japan seit 1542 (Veröffentlichung der Abteilung Architektur des Kunsthistorischen Instituts der Universität Köln,* 11), Köln 1977.
3 *100 Jahre Deutscher Werkbund,* hrsg. von Winfried Nerdinger, Ausst.-Kat. Pinakothek der Moderne, München; Akademie der Künste, Berlin, München u. a. 2007.
4 Bernd Nicolai, »Der Deutsche Werkbund im Ersten Weltkrieg – eine Gratwanderung«, in: *100 Jahre Deutscher Werkbund* 2007 (wie Anm. 3), S. 70–74.
5 Hermann Muthesius, *Die Zukunft der deutschen Form (Der Deutsche Krieg,* 50), Stuttgart und Berlin 1915, S. 35.
6 Vgl. Bernd Nicolai, Stichwort »Architektur«, in: Claus-Dieter Krohn (Hrsg.), *Handbuch der deutschsprachigen Emigration 1933–1945,* Darmstadt 1998, S. 691–703.
7 Vgl. hierzu Niels Gutschow und Barbara Klain, *Vernichtung und Utopie. Stadtplanung Warschau 1939–1945,* Hamburg 1994.
8 Nicolai Ouroussoff, »Why Are They Greener Than We Are?«, in: *The New York Times Magazine,* 20. Mai 2007.
9 Ullrich Schwarz prägte den Begriff der »reflexiven Moderne« für die deutsche Architektur der Gegenwart, vgl. Ullrich Schwarz (Hrsg.), *Neue Deutsche Architektur. Eine Reflexive Moderne,* Ostfildern 2002.
10 Vgl. »Die Stadt im Abverkauf«, in: *Der Standard* (Wien), 24. November 2007.

with the slogan "Light, serene, livable, festive, colorful, radiant, sheltering." It was in this spirit that Egon Eiermann and Sep Ruf designed the distinctly filigree, glass-built German pavilion for the 1958 World's Fair in Brussels, followed fourteen years later by the lightweight tentlike roof of the Olympic stadium in Munich created by Günter Behnisch and Frei Otto. Of course, both these images—the old-style architecture they sought to banish and the brave new architecture they embraced—were merely clichés. Both were specifically aimed at gaining homegrown popularity rather than appealing to a foreign market.

Now, a generation later, German democracy is so stable and the country so fully integrated into the EU that such gestures are no longer needed. This means that the German contribution to the São Paulo Architecture Biennial, *Ready for Take-Off*, can deploy a new or, perhaps more correctly, an old canon of values that is not primarily concerned with the country's image but focuses instead on the product itself and the competence of the suppliers. In that respect, the notion of a specifically "German" architecture with a style and formal vocabulary that is markedly different from that of other countries no longer plays a role. The farther you are from Germany, the less negatively the list of virtues is viewed. Brazilian visitors to the Biennial found themselves reminded of the very skills that are still attributed to their own German immigrant population, and of the proven merits of cars and machinery "Made in Germany." Rumor has it that the country would like more of the same . . .

Lily Hollein, who curated the neighboring Austrian contribution to the São Paulo Biennial, described *Ready for Take-Off* as "hard-nosed marketing strategy."[10] Her observation is not entirely wide of the mark, for the accent is indeed on "marketing." This puts it light years away from Germany's pre-1945 presentations, which were all too often steeped in a sense of mission and a will to power. What's more, in contrast to the earnest gestures of humility in the postwar era, Germans are now able to laugh at themselves a little.

Ready for Take-Off
auf der 7. BIA São Paulo 2007
Ready for Take-Off
at the 7th BIA São Paulo 2007

---

1   See among others Wolfgang Voigt, "Zur Vorgeschichte deutschen Architekturexports im 19. und 20. Jahrhundert," in Ingeborg Flagge et al., eds., *Architektur in Deutschland* [DAM-Jahrbuch 2002] (Munich, 2002), pp. 13–19.
2   See Michiko Meid, *Der Einführungsprozeß der europäischen und der nordamerikanischen Architektur in Japan seit 1542* [Veröffentlichung der Abteilung Architektur des Kunsthistorischen Instituts der Universität Köln, 11] (Cologne, 1977).
3   Winfried Nerdinger, ed., *100 Jahre Deutscher Werkbund*, exh. cat. Pinakothek der Moderne, Munich; Akademie der Künste, Berlin (Munich, 2007).
4   Bernd Nicolai, "Der Deutsche Werkbund im Ersten Weltkrieg—eine Gratwanderung," in *100 Jahre Deutscher Werkbund* 2007 (see note 3), pp. 70–74.
5   Hermann Muthesius, "The Future of German Form," in Tim and Charlotte Benton, eds., *Form and Function: A Sourcebook for the History of Architecture and Design 1890–1939* (London, 1975).
6   See Bernd Nicolai, headword "Architektur," in Claus-Dieter Krohn, ed., *Handbuch der deutschsprachigen Emigration 1933–1945* (Darmstadt, 1998), pp. 691–703.
7   See Niels Gutschow and Barbara Klain, *Vernichtung und Utopie. Stadtplanung Warschau 1939–1945* (Hamburg, 1994).
8   Nicolai Ouroussoff, "Why Are They Greener Than We Are?" in *The New York Times Magazine*, May 20, 2007.
9   Ullrich Schwarz coined the term "reflexive modernism" for contemporary German architecture; See Ullrich Schwarz, ed., *New German Architecture: A Reflexive Modernism* (Ostfildern, 2002).
10 See "Die Stadt im Abverkauf," in *Der Standard* (Vienna), November 24, 2007.

Ready for Take-Off – Lohnt sich der Weg ins Ausland?
Thomas Welter

Die Chancen und Möglichkeiten des Planens und Bauens im Ausland, oder kurz der Architekturexport, sind in aller Munde. In Architekturzeitschriften und in den Feuilletons der großen Tageszeitungen liest man regelmäßig Artikel über die Realisierung von Prestigebauten ausländischer Staaten oder Großinvestoren durch deutsche Architekten sowie über die Konzeption ganzer Städte durch deutsche Stadtplaner. Besonders im Ausland, so scheint es, werden große Projekte verwirklicht und können Architekten viel Geld verdienen.

Doch ist der Architekturexport angesichts der Tatsache, dass 40 Prozent der rund 40 000 Architekturbüros in Deutschland Einmannbüros sind und weitere 40 Prozent maximal vier Beschäftigte inklusive Inhaber haben, überhaupt ein Thema für die Mehrheit der Architekten und Stadtplaner in Deutschland? Die Zahlen scheinen dagegenzusprechen: Gerade einmal 5 Prozent der Architekten in Deutschland haben Projekte im Ausland durchgeführt.

Ist die hohe Aufmerksamkeit, die dem Thema von Politik, Medien, Kammern und Verbänden entgegengebracht wird, nicht übertrieben? Ergibt es angesichts des kleinen Adressatenkreises überhaupt Sinn, dass die Bundesregierung Förderprogramme für Architekten und Stadtplaner unterhält, dass Kammern und Verbände Exportinitiativen, wie beispielsweise das Netzwerk Architekturexport der Bundesarchitektenkammer (NAX), betreiben und dass angesehene Kulturinstitutionen sich dem Thema intensiv widmen?

Ansehen und Chancen versus Risiken und Probleme

Die Akteure, die sich mit dem Planen und Bauen im Ausland beschäftigen, verweisen regelmäßig auf das Ansehen deutscher Architekten und Stadtplaner im Ausland. Dieses positive Bild basiert auf dem Ruf guter Ingenieurleistungen, eines hohen Qualitätsanspruchs, der Umsetzung technischer Innovationen und der Fähigkeit zur erfolgreichen Durchführung ganzer Projekte durch deutsche Architekten, Stadtplaner und Ingenieure.

Doch ein zweiter Blick lohnt sich, denn die Chancen und Möglichkeiten werden von vielen Akteuren relativiert. Nicht nur Inhaber mittlerer und kleinerer Architekturbüros haben Schwierigkeiten im Ausland. Auch von großen Büros ist zu hören, sie betrieben ihre Auslandsprojekte mehr aufgrund des Prestiges als aufgrund einer guten Verdienstmöglichkeit. Nicht wenige Architekten in Deutschland haben mit ihren Auslandsprojekten Geld verloren oder mussten ihretwegen sogar Insolvenz anmelden.

Die erheblichen Risiken und Probleme, die mit der Realisierung von Auslandsprojekten verbunden sind, werden häufig unterschätzt. Auslandsakquisitionen sind nicht nur für Neueinsteiger häufig teurer und zeitraubender als solche im Inland. Nicht wenige Akquisitionsversuche im Ausland sind erfolglos, denn der Umstand einer besseren Baukonjunktur in manchen Ländern führt nicht automatisch zum Erfolg. Selbst wenn Architekten einen Auftrag erhalten haben, führt die Risikoscheu deutscher Banken bei der in der Regel geringen Kapitalausstattung deutscher Büros schnell zu Finanzierungsproblemen.

Ready for Take-Off: Is Venturing Abroad Worth It?
Thomas Welter

There is a lot of talk about the potential opportunities of planning and building abroad; in short, about architectural exports. Architectural periodicals and the arts sections of leading newspapers regularly carry articles about prestigious building projects by German architects for other countries and major investors or about designs being drawn up for entire cities by German urban planners. It is easy to get the impression that in other countries, especially, there are huge projects in the pipeline and rich pickings to be had for architects.

Yet given the fact that 40 percent of Germany's 40,000 or so architectural practices are one-man operations and that a further 40 percent employ no more than four people, including the proprietor, is architectural export really an option for the majority of architects and urban planners in Germany? The figures would seem to suggest otherwise: just 5 percent of architects in Germany have actually undertaken projects abroad.

So is the high profile that is being given to this issue by politicians, the media, and the profession's own chambers and associations perhaps somewhat disproportionate? With such a small target audience, is there any point in government-funded programs for architects and urban planners or in initiatives launched by professional bodies, such as the Network for Architectural Export (NAX), or indeed in respected cultural institutions expending so much time and energy on the subject?

Reputation and potential versus risks and problems

Those involved in promoting planning and building abroad frequently point out the high esteem in which German architects and urban planners are held in other countries. This positive image is based on Germany's reputation for good engineering practice, high standards of quality, technical innovation, and the project-management skills of German architects, urban planners, and engineers.

On closer inspection, however, it appears that, for many of those involved, the opportunities available are relative. It is not just the small and medium-sized architectural firms that face difficulties abroad. Even some of the bigger players say that their foreign projects are more about prestige than profits. Indeed, quite a few architects in Germany have lost money on foreign projects or have even faced bankruptcy because of them.

The enormous risks and problems involved in undertaking a project abroad are often underestimated. Foreign acquisitions are frequently more expensive and time-consuming than projects on the domestic market—and not just for newcomers. Pitching for contracts abroad can be a fruitless undertaking, for the mere fact that the construction industry in another country is more buoyant is by no means a guarantee of success. And even when an architect does secure a contract, the modest capital of most German architectural offices is unlikely to prompt any German bank to depart from its usual conservative attitude to risk assessment, and so funding shortfalls can easily arise.

ESO Hotel am Cerro Paranal, Auer + Weber + Assoziierte
ESO Hotel on the Cerro Paranal, Auer + Weber + Assoziierte

Eine Befragung deutscher Architekten und Stadtplaner durch das NAX in Kooperation mit dem Deutschen Architektenblatt im Dezember 2007 hat ergeben, dass grenzüberschreitend tätige Architekten, Stadtplaner und Ingenieure darüber hinaus mit weiteren Schwierigkeiten konfrontiert werden.

An oberster Stelle stehen Probleme mit den Behörden vor Ort. Als ausländischer Architekt sieht man sich nicht selten mit einem protektionistischen Verhalten konfrontiert. Die Schwierigkeiten im Umgang mit Ämtern und Behörden verstärken sich aufgrund der in der Regel geringeren Kenntnisse der Gesetze, Bau- und Planungsabläufe im Zielland sowie wegen Unsicherheiten und Fehlern im kulturellen Umgang. Abhilfe würden hier einheimische Kooperationspartner schaffen; doch häufig fehlen diese bei ersten Projekten im Ausland, da der Aufbau zuverlässiger Kontakte selten kurzfristig erfolgt.

Außerhalb der Europäischen Union steht die Frage der Berufszulassung und Niederlassungsfreiheit an oberster Stelle. Nur wenige Länder außerhalb der EU erlauben einen einfachen Marktzutritt deutscher Architekten und Ingenieure. Die Anerkennung deutscher Hochschulabschlüsse und des deutschen Architektentitels ist meist mit großen bürokratischen Hürden verbunden und nicht selten werden Prüfungen und Nachweise einer langen Berufstätigkeit verlangt. Auch in größeren Büros setzt der latente Mangel an geeigneten Mitarbeitern mit Auslandserfahrung und die fehlende Bereitschaft vieler Mitarbeiter, dauerhaft im Ausland zu leben, einer grenzüberschreitenden Tätigkeit enge Grenzen.

Darüber hinaus wird häufig die Zeit unterschätzt, die für den Aufbau stabiler wirtschaftlicher Kontakte im Ausland benötigt wird. Architekten, Stadtplaner und Ingenieure erbringen sogenannte Vertrauensgüter: Sie sind im Ausland auf zuverlässige Kooperationspartner angewiesen. Hierfür sind enge persönliche Kontakte eine unabdingbare Voraussetzung. Die Investitionen an Zeit und Geld für den Aufbau dauerhafter professioneller und persönlicher Kontakte dürfen nicht unterschätzt werden. Büroinhaber müssen regelmäßig in das Zielland reisen und in bestimmten Akquisitions- und Projektphasen müssen deutsche Mitarbeiter vor Ort sein. Nicht immer spielen Gesundheit und Familie dabei mit.

Viele international arbeitende Architekten und Stadtplaner berichten über Schwierigkeiten, feste Kontakte aufgrund kultureller Unterschiede aufzubauen. Häufig besteht die Notwendigkeit, den Umgang mit ausländischen Geschäftspartnern systematisch durch interkulturelles Training zu erlernen. Es muss eine richtige, ortstypische Balance gefunden werden zwischen einem freundschaftlichen, privaten Umgang und einem klaren, am geltenden Recht orientierten Geschäftsumgang. Häufig verlassen sich deutsche Architekten und Stadtplaner auf ihre Erfahrungen im Inland. Dies ist grundsätzlich falsch und verkennt die enorme Bedeutung ortstypischen Verhaltens auch in Zeiten von Globalisierung und Internet.

Für wen lohnt sich der Weg ins Ausland?

Trotz dieser deutlichen Relativierung der Chancen realisieren einige deutsche Architekturbüros außergewöhnliche Projekte und verdienen auch Geld im Ausland. Die Unterschiede in Planungs- und Bautraditionen, die neuen Anforderungen vor Ort und

In December 2007, a poll conducted by NAX in conjunction with the *Deutsches Architektenblatt*, organ of the Federal Chamber of German Architects, indicated that this is not the only problem faced by architects, urban planners, and engineers working internationally.

At the top of the list was the difficulty of negotiating with local authorities in countries where foreign architects are often faced with protectionist attitudes. These difficulties are further compounded by the architects' own lack of knowledge of the legal system and the planning and architectural processes in the host country, as well as their unfamiliarity with cultural and social mores. Though cooperation with local companies could alleviate these problems, many embarking on their first projects abroad have had neither the time nor the opportunity to build up the necessary reliable contacts.

Outside the European Union, the issues of recognized professional qualifications and rights of domicile are the biggest hurdle. Only a few countries outside the EU allow German architects and engineers to enter the market with ease. Not only is there a lot of red tape involved in getting German university degrees and architectural qualifications officially recognized, but there is often a requirement to take exams and provide proof of long-standing professional experience, as well. Even in larger firms, a shortage of suitably qualified candidates with experience of working abroad, coupled with the reluctance of many employees to consider long-term relocation to another country, place considerable constraints on international operations.

Moreover, the time it takes to build up dependable business contacts abroad is often underestimated. Architects, urban planners, and engineers provide services based on trust. For this, they need to have reliable cooperation partners. And that means that good personal contacts are absolutely imperative. The time and expense that must be invested in establishing long-term professional and personal contacts should not be underestimated. The head of any firm has to visit the country in question on a regular basis, and, for some phases of the project, including acquisition, there have to be German co-workers on the ground. This is not always compatible with health and family issues.

Many internationally active architects and urban planners report difficulties in building up good contacts because of cultural differences. Often, systematic intercultural training is needed in order to learn how to negotiate with foreign business partners. The right and locally acceptable balance has to be found between friendly, sociable interaction and clear-cut business negotiation in accordance with the country's legal system. Many German architects and urban planners tend to rely on the experience they have gained in their home country. This is a fundamental error that fails to recognize the enormous importance of socially and culturally determined behavioral differences—even in this age of globalization and the Internet.

Who can benefit from working abroad?

In spite of these considerably relativized opportunities, some German architectural firms do undertake extraordinary projects abroad and profit from them, as well. Getting to grips with the differences in planning and building traditions, as well as

Siedlung Jiande,
Brandenfels Landscape + Architecture
Jiande Settlement,
Brandenfels Landscape + Architecture

Hauptsitz Metro AG, Moskau,
Eller + Eller Architekten
Metro AG Headquarters, Moscow,
Eller + Eller Architekten

das Kennenlernen anderer Kulturen werden als Bereicherung für das Büro empfunden und führen zu Prozess- und Projektinnovationen, die auch für Projekte in Deutschland relevant sind.

Somit stellt sich die Frage, für welche Architekten beziehungsweise welche Bürostrukturen sich der Weg ins Ausland lohnt. Die Befragung zeigt, dass die Erfolgsaussichten und organisatorischen Fähigkeiten der Büroinhaber in Bezug auf Akquisition und Durchführung ausländischer Projekte im Allgemeinen eher zurückhaltend bewertet werden. Die Chancen, Auslandsprojekte zu akquirieren und durchzuführen, werden von den Inhabern großer Büros deutlich positiver eingeschätzt als von denjenigen kleiner Büros. Auslandserfahrene Architekten sind hier deutlich optimistischer als Architekten ohne Auslandserfahrung.

Allerdings sollte man dem Vorurteil, dass der Architekturexport nur von großen Büros erfolgreich betrieben werden könne, nicht erliegen. Ausstellungen, Publikationen sowie online verfügbare Datenbanken belegen eindeutig, dass auch mittlere und kleine Betriebe erfolgreich im Ausland tätig sein können. Zur Kompensation der Einschränkungen kleiner Büros nutzen deren Inhaber häufig private Kontakte zu Kollegen vor Ort. Quelle dieser privaten Kontakte ist nicht selten ein familiärer Hintergrund oder ein längerer Auslandsaufenthalt während der Schulzeit, des Studiums oder zu Beginn des Berufslebens.

Unabhängig vom Vorhandensein tragfähiger wirtschaftlicher oder privater Kontakte sollten Architekten, Stadtplaner und Ingenieure, die im Ausland tätig sein wollen, mehrere Voraussetzungen erfüllen: Zum einem sind gute Fremdsprachenkenntnisse – möglichst auch bei einem oder mehreren Mitarbeitern – unerlässlich. Ebenso sollten interkulturelle Kompetenzen und eine große Affinität zur Kultur und den Menschen im Zielland vorhanden sein. Da die möglicherweise häufigen Auslandsreisen eine hohe körperliche und psychische Belastung bedeuten, sollten Auslandsaktivitäten durch die Familie befürwortet werden und man selbst körperlich gesund sein. In jedem Fall benötigen grenzüberschreitend tätige Büros eine stabile wirtschaftliche Basis im Inland, um etwaige Planungsverzögerungen oder ausstehende Honorare durch andere Einnahmen auffangen zu können.

Ein Auslandsengagement bedarf einer sorgfältigen Vorbereitung. Mehrere Schritte sollten im Vorfeld erledigt werden: Um eine effektive Markterschließung und einen kontinuierlichen Aufbau stabiler Kontakte ins Ausland zu gewährleisten, sollte die Festlegung eines Ziellandes beziehungsweise einer Zielregion frühzeitig erfolgen. Geeignete Länder sind solche, die über entwickelte Märkte beziehungsweise Märkte mit hohen Wachstumsraten verfügen. Insofern liegt es nahe, dass viele deutsche Architekten und Stadtplaner vor allem innerhalb der Europäischen Union und in den Wachstumsregionen Asiens und Arabiens tätig sind. Die Befragung des NAX hat eindeutig ergeben, dass die Staaten der Europäischen Union die größten Chancen für ein erfolgreiches Auslandsengagement bieten – insbesondere für kleine und mittlere Büros.

Es ist wenig ratsam, die Wahl eines Landes an einer aktuellen Nachfrage oder einem Bauboom zu orientieren. Die Bauwirtschaft und damit auch die Planungsbranche sind stark von der konjunkturellen Lage abhängig, attraktive Ziele können sich schnell

with new challenges on-site, not to mention the experience of learning about another culture, are all seen as an enrichment for the firm, leading to innovations in processes and projects that can also be applied to projects within Germany.

This brings us to the question: which architects, and which types of architectural practice, are most likely to benefit from working abroad? The poll indicated that the likelihood of success and the organizational capacities of the proprietor in terms of acquisition and implementation of international projects tended to be viewed with caution. The chances of acquiring and implementing international projects were viewed much more optimistically by the proprietors of larger firms than by their colleagues from smaller practices. Architects with international experience are themselves much more positive about this than those without.

This does not mean, however, that only the bigger offices are capable of successfully undertaking architectural exports. Exhibitions, publications, and online data banks clearly show that even small and medium-sized firms can operate successfully abroad. The proprietors of smaller firms often make use of personal contacts with colleagues abroad to compensate for other drawbacks. These personal contacts are frequently through family connections, through a previous student exchange, or through a lengthy period of study abroad or work experience at the start of their careers.

Irrespective of whether feasible business or personal contacts already exist, architects, urban planners, and engineers with a mind to work abroad do have to meet certain criteria. On the one hand, they—and preferably some of their employees—need to be able to speak a foreign language fluently. They should also have certain intercultural abilities and should have an affinity for the culture and people of the country they plan to work in. Since frequent foreign travel can also be physically and mentally demanding, they should have the support of their families and be in good health. In any case, firms operating internationally need a well-established business base at home to ensure they have a financial safety net in case of delays and in order to cover any outstanding fees.

Any project abroad requires careful preparation. Several steps have to be taken before work commences. In order to enter the market effectively and continue to build up reliable contacts abroad, it is important to decide early on which country or region to aim for. Suitable countries are those with developed markets or high growth rates. In this respect, it is understandable that many German architects and urban planners tend to work primarily within the European Union and in the growth regions of Asia and the Middle East. The NAX poll clearly indicated that the EU states offer the best opportunities for successful architectural export, especially for small and medium-sized firms.

There is little to be said for choosing a country simply on the basis of current market demand or a boom in the construction industry. The construction sector and, with that, the planning sector, are strongly affected by economic trends, and a seemingly attractive target market can quickly dry up. Language skills and cultural affinities are more important, as are existing contacts, business or personal, and the organizational capacity of the firm.

Bugatti Atelier, Molsheim, Henn Architekten
Bugatti studio, Molsheim, Henn Architekten

Fabrik PULS, Chomutov,
K+P Architekten und Stadtplaner
PULS factory, Chomutov,
K+P Architekten und Stadtplaner

ablösen. Von größerer Bedeutung sind sprachliche und kulturelle Affinitäten sowie bereits vorhandene – auch private – Kontakte und die organisatorischen Möglichkeiten des Büros.

Die Büroorganisation muss zwingend auf die Ansprüche ausländischer Kontakte eingerichtet sein. Das Vorhandensein eines Internetauftritts und Präsentationsmaterialien in den entsprechenden Sprachen, die Gewährleistung einer professionellen Bearbeitung fremdsprachiger Anrufe und E-Mails sowie ein gewisses Maß an PR und Marketing im Zielland sind hierfür Beispiele.

Grenzüberschreitende Kooperationen sollten auch branchenübergreifend eingegangen werden. Auftraggeber im Ausland fragen, stärker als in Deutschland, nach schlüsselfertigen Projekten mit einem klaren Nachweis ihrer Wirtschaftlichkeit. Der Grund für die Beauftragung deutscher Architekten liegt häufig insbesondere in der Umsetzung technischer Innovationen. Um diese Fähigkeit potenziellen Auftraggebern im Ausland zu vermitteln, ist laut der Umfrage des NAX die Mehrheit der am Auslandsgeschäft interessierten Architekten bereit, Kooperationen mit Herstellern von Bauprodukten einzugehen.

Architektenexport statt Architekturexport?

Der deutsche Planungsmarkt ist aufgrund verschiedener Sonderentwicklungen, wie beispielsweise des Baubooms infolge der deutschen Wiedervereinigung, verhältnismäßig wenig internationalisiert. Allerdings zeichnet sich hier in den letzten Jahren eine neue Entwicklung ab. Haupttriebfeder hierfür ist die stärkere Auslandsorientierung von Architekturstudenten seit Anfang der 1990er-Jahre. Nicht zuletzt angetrieben durch die schwierige berufliche Situation im Inland gehen immer mehr Studenten beziehungsweise Absolventen für einen längeren Zeitraum ins Ausland.

Die Erweiterung der Europäischen Union, die Freiheiten des EU-Binnenmarktes, die allgemeine Liberalisierung auch im Bereich der Dienstleistungen und die internationalen Kooperationen der Universitäten und Fachhochschulen fördern nicht nur den grenzüberschreitenden Austausch von Planungsleistungen, sondern auch die Wahrnehmung beruflicher Chancen im Ausland.

Es existieren keine genauen Zahlen zu den Wanderungsbewegungen deutscher Architekturstudenten sowie ausgebildeter Architekten und Stadtplaner. Generell hat die berufliche Mobilität, insbesondere des Planernachwuchses, jedoch stark zugenommen. Die meisten Architekten und Stadtplaner kehren nach einiger Zeit wieder nach Deutschland zurück, aber die im Ausland erworbenen Erfahrungen und Kontakte sind für grenzüberschreitende Projekte wichtig. Zusätzlich arbeiten vermehrt ausländische Architekten und Stadtplaner auch in Deutschland. Diese stellen nach Ihrer Rückkehr ebenfalls entscheidende Kontakte für den Architekturexport dar.

Zwar gibt es Architekten und Stadtplaner, die nach ihrem Auslandsengagement enttäuscht nach Deutschland zurückkehren, da die erfahrene Realität ihren Hoffnungen und Wünschen nicht entsprochen hat. Aber die wenigsten Heimkehrer profitieren nicht von ihren Auslandserfahrungen. Wer als Architekt oder Stadtplaner im Ausland gearbeitet hat, musste sich intensiv mit Land und Leuten auseinandersetzen.

It is absolutely imperative for the firm to be in a position to communicate with foreign clients and cater to their expectations. This includes, for instance, having a website and printed material in the relevant languages, being able to respond professionally to foreign-language phone calls and e-mails, and conducting a certain amount of PR and marketing in the target country.

International ventures should also involve intersectoral cooperation. Foreign clients are much more likely than German clients to demand turnkey projects with clear evidence of their return on investment. One of the main reasons why German architects are commissioned often lies in the implementation of technical innovations. In order to convey this skill to potential clients abroad, according to the NAX poll, most architects are willing to cooperate with manufacturers of building materials.

Exporting architects instead of architecture?

The German planning market has a relatively low level of international involvement. This is due to a number of specifically German developments, such as the construction boom following reunification. But a new trend has begun to emerge here in recent years, driven primarily by the increasingly outward-looking approach of architecture students since the early 1990s. More and more, students and graduates are committing to lengthy placements abroad, partly because there are fewer opportunities for them at home.

The expansion of the European Union, the freedoms of the EU internal market, and the liberalization of the service sector, as well as international cooperation between universities and polytechnics, have not only increased the cross-border exchange of planning and architectural services, but have also prompted more individuals to take up opportunities of working in other countries.

Although there are no precise statistics available on the movements of German architecture students or qualified architects and urban planners, it is clear that their work-related mobility has increased, especially among the younger generation of planners. Most architects and urban planners return to Germany eventually, bringing with them experience and contacts that are crucial to future international projects. There are also more foreign architects and urban planners working in Germany. They, in turn, also provide important contacts for architectural exports.

While there may be architects and urban planners who return to Germany disappointed that the everyday reality has not lived up to their hopes and wishes, very few of them have failed to profit from the experience. Working abroad as an architect or urban planner invariably means getting to know the country and people very well, finding out about the legal system and prevailing business practice, while at the same time perhaps seeing the roles of architect and client in a new light. All of which requires a considerable grasp of communicative skills and teamwork abilities—abilities that can prove useful all over the world, as well as in Germany. There is one very simple conclusion to be drawn from this: anyone seriously thinking of developing a foreign market should work abroad for a while or give an employee the opportunity of doing so, and should also invite foreign students and qualified architects from other countries to work in their office.

Deutsche Botschaft, Mexiko-Stadt, Volker Staab Architekten und Levin Monsigny
German embassy, Mexico City, Volker Staab Architekten and Levin Monsigny

Deutsches Generalkonsulat, Kaliningrad, Meuser Architekten
German consulate general, Kaliningrad, Meuser Architekten

Das Gleiche gilt für gesetzliche Vorgaben, wirtschaftliche Gepflogenheiten und ein mitunter anderes Verständnis der Rollen des Architekten und des Bauherren. Dies alles erfordert ein hohes Maß an Kommunikationskultur und Teamfähigkeit. Diese Fähigkeiten sind weltweit von Nutzen, auch in Deutschland. Aus dieser Beobachtung leitet sich eine einfache Schlussfolgerung ab: Wer ernsthaft einen Auslandsmarkt entwickeln möchte, sollte für einige Zeit im Ausland arbeiten oder seinen Mitarbeitern diese Möglichkeit einräumen sowie ausländische Studenten und fertig ausgebildete Architekten in das eigene Büro aufnehmen.

Unterstützung grenzüberschreitend tätiger Architekten, Ingenieure und Stadtplaner

International tätige Architekten, Ingenieure und Stadtplaner sind ein Exportmultiplikator für die deutsche Wirtschaft. Die als Treuhänder der Bauherren agierenden Planer beeinflussen in erheblichem Maße die Auswahl der Materialien und der Gebäudetechnik. Schätzungen zufolge generiert der Planungsumsatz der Architekten und Ingenieure einen 10- bis 20-fachen Umsatz in den Bereichen der Baustofflieferung, der Bauausführung und der Gebäudetechnik. Die Entscheidung über Materialien und Gebäudetechniken treffen grenzüberschreitend tätige Architekten und Ingenieure im Lichte ihrer im Inland erworbenen Kenntnisse und Erfahrungen. Produkte aus Deutschland stehen dabei in der ersten Reihe.

In Deutschland hat sich zur Unterstützung grenzüberschreitend tätiger Architekten, Ingenieure und Stadtplaner ein breites Netz außenwirtschaftlicher Unterstützungen und Informationen entwickelt. Neben den Auslandshandelskammern und den Botschaften der Bundesrepublik Deutschland bieten die Anlaufstelle zur politischen Flankierung von Auslandsprojekten und die SOLVIT-Streitschlichtungsstelle innerhalb der EU Unterstützung bei politischen Schwierigkeiten im Ausland. Beide Stellen sind im Bundesministerium für Wirtschaft und Technologie angesiedelt.

Meistens sind ausufernde Bürokratie in den Gastländern, wenig transparente Entscheidungsverfahren oder politische Einflussnahmen ausländischer Mitbewerber der Anlass einer solchen Unterstützung. Die Anlaufstelle zur politischen Flankierung von Auslandsprojekten hilft in allen Projektphasen: Im Rahmen internationaler Ausschreibungsverfahren oder während der Ausführung von Aufträgen.

Bei grenzüberschreitenden Problemen, die durch fehlerhafte Anwendung des EU-Rechts entstanden sind, zum Beispiel verursacht von nationalen, regionalen oder lokalen Behörden, hilft die SOLVIT-Streitschlichtungsstelle. Sie ist ein benutzerfreundlicher und kostenloser Service, der von der EU-Kommission ins Leben gerufen wurde, um EU-Bürgern und Unternehmen zu helfen, pragmatische Lösungen für ihre Binnenmarktprobleme zu finden.

Für Architekten, Ingenieure und Stadtplaner relevante Außenwirtschaftsinformationen bieten zudem das zentrale Außenwirtschaftsportal iXPOS, die Bundesagentur für Außenwirtschaft bfai und die Kammern und Verbände der freien technischen Berufe. Seit Mitte 2002 unterstützt auch die Bundesarchitektenkammer mit dem Netzwerk Architekturexport grenzüberschreitend tätige deutsche Architekten auf ihrem Weg zu neuen Märkten. Das NAX ist bestrebt, das Ansehen deutscher Architektur und die Chancen deutscher Architekten und Ingenieure im Ausland zu verbessern sowie ausländische Investoren von der hohen Planungsqualität in Deutschland zu überzeugen.

Supporting architects, engineers, and urban planners in foreign markets

Architects, engineers, and urban planners working internationally are export multiplicators for the German economy. The planners working on behalf of the clients have an enormous influence on the choice of materials and technology. The planning turnover of architects and engineers generates an estimated ten- to twentyfold turnover in the building materials, construction, and building technology sectors. Internationally active architects and engineers make decisions about materials and technical services on the basis of the knowledge and experience they have of the home market. That makes products from Germany their first choice.

Germany has developed a wide-ranging network of information and support mechanisms for architects, engineers, and urban planners working in foreign markets. In addition to the German Chambers of Industry and Commerce and the German embassies worldwide, the contact point for the political support of foreign trade projects and the SOLVIT center—both under the umbrella of the Federal Ministry of Economics and Technology—can provide assistance if political problems arise in relation to foreign trade within the EU.

Most problems requiring assistance of this kind are related to bureaucratic issues in the host country, lack of transparency in decision-making processes, or the exertion of political influence on foreign competitors. The contact point for the political support of foreign trade projects offers support at every project stage, from international tendering processes to implementation of contracts.

SOLVIT assists with cross-border problems arising as a result of an incorrect application of EU law by national, regional, or local authorities. Launched by the European Commission, SOLVIT is a free and user-friendly service aimed at helping EU citizens and companies to find pragmatic solutions to internal market problems.

Foreign trade information of relevance to architects, engineers, and urban planners can be found on the iXPOS Internet portal coordinated by the German Office for Foreign Trade in association with the chambers and guilds of the technical freelance professions. Since mid-2002, the Federal Chamber of German Architects has also been helping German architects to open up new foreign markets with its NAX. The NAX aims to enhance the image of German architecture and promote opportunities for German architects and engineers abroad, as well as convey the high quality of planning and design in Germany to foreign investors.

Deutsche Ingenieurleistungen – im Ausland hoch geschätzt
Klaus Rollenhagen, Tatjana Steidl

Deutsche Ingenieure genießen weltweit einen exzellenten Ruf. Diese Wertschätzung hat eine lange Tradition und hat bis heute viele ausländische Studenten an deutsche Hochschulen gelockt. Mit dem Ansehen deutscher Ingenieurkunst verbinden sich Begriffe wie Qualität, Organisationstalent und technische Innovation. Eine große Zahl deutscher Ingenieure ist in der Lage, diese »Vorschusslorbeeren« zu nutzen und mit herausragenden Leistungen weltweit zu bestätigen. Die in diesem Katalog vorgestellten beeindruckenden Projekte »Planned in Germany« bieten ein Beispiel für das erfolgreiche Zusammenspiel deutscher Architekten und Ingenieure bei ausländischen Bauvorhaben. Gemeinsam sorgen sie dafür, dass die Gebäude über ihre ästhetische Attraktivität hinaus auch funktional allen Wünschen von Bauherren und Nutzern genügen. In die Planerteams der meisten Projekte dieser Ausstellung sind Mitglieder des Verband Beratender Ingenieure (VBI) eingebunden, darunter so auslandserfahrene Büros wie Schlaich Bergermann und Partner, Werner Sobek, Ebert-Ingenieure, Bollinger + Grohmann, Professor Pfeifer und Partner, HL-Technik oder WPW Ingenieure. Sie alle warten nicht *Ready for Take-Off* auf den Start ins Auslandsgeschäft, sondern haben bereits aufsehenerregende internationale Großprojekte realisiert.

Vermutlich besteht in dieser Zusammenarbeit schon ein entscheidender Schritt zum Erfolg: Im Planerteam von Architekten und Fachingenieuren bieten die Partner mit Auslandserfahrung den Neueinsteigern ihr Wissen an – zu beiderseitigem Nutzen. Denn bei aller Begeisterung für deutsche Qualität im Bau und die in São Paulo hervorgehobenen »deutschen Sekundärtugenden« ist der Export von Planungsleistungen nicht ganz ohne Tücken. Ein Planer muss den Auftraggeber schon überzeugen, bevor dieser die fertige Leistung prüfen kann. Besonders für Neueinsteiger, die noch nicht mit prominenten Referenzobjekten glänzen können, liegt hierin eine ernstzunehmende Hürde.

Ingenieurleistungen – nicht nur für Gebäude

Eine Architekturausstellung kann nur einen kleinen Ausschnitt der Leistungen zeigen, die Ingenieurunternehmen ins Ausland exportieren. Ingenieure leisten einen großen Beitrag zur Gestaltung der gebauten Umwelt, nur einige dieser Projekte werden zusammen mit Architekten geplant. Ein wesentlicher Anteil der Infrastruktur, die das Funktionieren von Wirtschaft und gesellschaftlichem Leben sicherstellt, wird von beratenden Ingenieuren geplant und gestaltet: Verkehrswege mit ihren Brücken, Tunneln und Kanälen zählen ebenso dazu wie Kraftwerke und Industrieanlagen oder Strukturen für die Wasserversorgung. Bei aller Dominanz der Technik und Funktionalität wird oft übersehen, dass auch Ingenieurbauwerke durch ihre Gestalt die Umwelt maßgeblich prägen. Von Zeit zu Zeit scheinen dies selbst die Ingenieure zu vergessen, weshalb sie von ihrem berühmten Kollegen Jörg Schlaich unermüdlich daran erinnert werden, dass Ingenieurbauten auch ästhetischen Ansprüchen genügen müssen. Nicht nur mit seinen spektakulären Brücken hat Jörg Schlaich im In- und Ausland gestalterische Maßstäbe für den gesamten Berufsstand gesetzt.

Bei der Selbstverständlichkeit, mit der die Leistungen von Ingenieuren tagtäglich genutzt werden, bleibt ihr immenser Beitrag zur Baukultur oft im Hintergrund. Doch die Zeiten ändern sich, und heute verstehen sich immer mehr Ingenieure auch als Gestalter. Sie setzen ihr Wissen ein, um Form und Funktion in idealer Weise miteinander

German Engineering Services: Highly Regarded Abroad
Klaus Rollenhagen, Tatjana Steidl

The excellent reputation enjoyed by German engineers throughout the world has a lengthy tradition and continues to attract numerous foreign students to German universities. In describing the esteem in which German engineering is held, terms such as "quality," "organizational talent," and "technical innovation" are regularly used. Throughout the world, large numbers of German engineers have been able to exploit the benefits of a reputation that has preceded them and to confirm it with their exceptional achievements. The impressive projects "Planned in Germany" introduced in this catalogue are examples of successful collaboration between German architects and engineers on construction projects in foreign countries. Engineers and architects working together ensure that, as well as being aesthetically appealing, these buildings also meet all of the clients' and users' functional requirements. The design teams for most of the projects in this show are made up of members of the VBI (Verband Beratender Ingenieure / Association of Consulting Engineers), including firms with a wealth of experience abroad such as Schlaich Bergermann und Partner, Werner Sobek, Ebert Ingenieure, Bollinger + Grohmann, Professor Pfeifer und Partner, HL-Technik and WPW Ingenieure. These firms are not waiting to do business abroad, but have already completed large international projects that have received considerable acclaim.

It seems very likely that this kind of collaboration represents a decisive step on the path to success: in design teams made up of architects and specialist engineers, the partners with experience working abroad can offer the newcomers their knowledge, to the benefit of both parties. For, despite all the enthusiasm about the quality of German construction and the "German secondary virtues" that were singled out for attention in São Paulo, the export of planning services is not without its problems. The architect or engineer must be able to convince the client before the latter has a chance to inspect a completed project. Particularly for those just starting their careers, who cannot present glossy catalogues filled with reference buildings, this represents a serious obstacle.

Engineering services—not just for buildings

An architecture exhibition can show only a small selection of the services and achievements exported by engineering firms. Engineers make a major contribution to the design of our built environment, but only a number of their projects are designed in collaboration with architects. A significant part of the infrastructure that ensures the efficient functioning of business and social life is designed and planned by consulting engineers: this includes transportation and transport systems, with their bridges, tunnels, and canals, as well as power stations and industrial complexes or water supply systems. Given the dominance of technology and functionality in such projects, the fact that engineering buildings also play a major role in shaping the environment is often overlooked. Indeed, it seems as if engineers themselves forget this fact from time to time, possibly the reason their famous colleague, Jörg Schlaich, finds it necessary to remind them that engineering buildings must also meet aesthetic needs. Schlaich has established new design standards for his entire profession—and not only with his spectacular bridges.

As the achievements of engineers are taken for granted in daily life, their enormous contribution to the culture of building is not often spotlighted. But times are changing,

Dreiländerbrücke, Weil am Rhein / Huningue,
Feichtinger Architectes mit Leonhardt,
Andrä und Partner
Three-Country Bridge, Weil am Rhein / Huningue,
Feichtinger Architectes with Leonhardt,
Andrä und Partner

zu verbinden. Entsprechend hat sich die Zusammenarbeit von Architekten und Ingenieuren bei der Planung von Gebäuden gewandelt: Das Konzept der integralen Planung beschreibt die Zeit- und Kostenvorteile eines Bauherrn, der von Beginn an – bereits in der Entwurfsphase – ein Planungsteam beschäftigt, das seine Anforderungen an das zukünftige Gebäude verwirklichen kann. Im integralen Planungsprozess arbeiten die Fachingenieure als Partner der Architekten, im Team verwirklichen sie die gestalterische Idee und setzen sich dafür ein, einen gewagten Entwurf mit all seinen technischen und ästhetischen Herausforderungen zu realisieren. Die Qualität des Entwurfs wird durch die partnerschaftliche Zusammenarbeit zwischen Architekten und beratenden Ingenieuren erheblich gesteigert und garantiert das Gelingen auch komplexer Projekte. Nur wenige Ingenieure überwinden dabei allerdings die beinahe sprichwörtliche Zurückhaltung ihrer Zunft. Gerade bei der Eroberung neuer Märkte im Ausland ist zu viel Bescheidenheit jedoch fehl am Platz. Die Erkenntnis, dass auch »Klappern« zum Handwerk gehört, lässt sich für manchen beratenden Ingenieur nur schwer mit dem traditionellen Berufsethos vereinbaren.

Die Zurückhaltung hat viel mit dem Selbstverständnis beratender Ingenieure als Treuhänder ihrer Auftraggeber zu tun. Neben Planung und Gestaltung steht selbstverständlich auch die Beratung im Mittelpunkt ihrer Tätigkeit. Auf diesem Gebiet haben beratende Ingenieure den ausführenden Firmen und Generalübernehmern einiges voraus, denn sie stehen ihren Auftraggebern unabhängig von Herstellerinteressen lösungsorientiert zur Seite.

Diese Qualität wird auch im Ausland hoch geschätzt, allerdings muss ihr Vorteil oft erst vermittelt werden. So geht es beispielsweise bei der Gewährleistung von Mobilität nicht allein um den Bau von Verkehrswegen, sondern ebenfalls darum, ein funktionierendes Gesamtkonzept zu entwerfen, das an die spezifische regionale Situation anpasst ist: angefangen von der Topografie, den zur Verfügung stehenden Mitteln, regionalen Bedürfnissen und Gewohnheiten bis hin zur Frage des langfristigen Unterhalts, der Wartung und Instandsetzung. Denn wem nützt zum Beispiel ein hochmodernes Schienennetz, wenn es durch Sandstürme regelmäßig außer Kraft gesetzt wird oder beim ersten Ausfall des computergesteuerten Stellwerks zusammenbricht, weil das Personal für dessen Wartung nicht ausreichend geschult wurde?

Ob bei Lärm- und Emissionsminderung, Umwelt- und Hochwasserschutz, Abfallbehandlung oder Energieversorgung in unzugänglichen Gebieten – in vielen Regionen der Welt vertrauen die Auftraggeber auf die problembewusste und lösungsorientierte Herangehensweise deutscher Ingenieure. Sie vertrauen darauf, mit deutscher Planung, Koordination und Bauüberwachung nicht nur die technisch beste Lösung zu erhalten, sondern auch Zeit und Kosten zu sparen.

Globales Umweltbewusstsein

Das weltweit gewachsene Bewusstsein, dass Umweltschutz mehr ist als ein dekadenter Luxus der Industrienationen, hat sich zu einem Pluspunkt für deutsche Ingenieurunternehmen im internationalen Wettbewerb entwickelt: Deutschland gilt in Umweltfragen als besonders sensibel. Aus dieser hohen Aufmerksamkeit, die sich nicht zuletzt in finanzieller Förderung ausdrückt, konnte sich in Deutschland ein innovativer, leistungsstarker Umweltsektor entwickeln. Die Initiativen »Erneuerbare

and today more and more engineers see themselves as designers, too; they use their knowledge to combine form and function in an ideal way. This means that the manner in which architects and engineers collaborate in designing buildings is changing, also. The concept of integral planning defines the advantages in terms of time and costs to a client who from the very start—that is to say, at the design phase—engages a planning team that can provide him with a building that will meet his future needs. In the integral planning process, the specialist engineers work as the architects' partners. As members of the team they give built form to the design concept and apply their skills to carrying out an ambitious design, with all its technical and aesthetic challenges. The partnership between architects and consulting engineers substantially improves the quality of the design and guarantees the success of even complex projects. However, only few engineers are able to overcome the almost proverbial reserve of their profession; in conquering new foreign markets, excessive modesty is entirely out of place. But many consulting engineers still find it difficult to reconcile the realization that beating their own drum is now a part of their trade, along with their traditional professional ethics.

This reserve has much to do with the fact that consulting engineers understand their role as that of their client's trustee. In addition to planning and design, consulting advice is a central aspect of the service offered by engineers. In this area, consulting engineers have something of an advantage over general contractors and construction firms, as they provide their clients with disinterested advice and solutions that are not colored by a manufacturer's interest in selling his own products.

This independent quality is also highly regarded abroad, but in some cases the advantages it offers must first be explained. For example, in providing mobility, the concern is not just to construct transport systems but also to work out a properly functioning overall concept that is suited to the specific regional situation, starting from the topography, the means available, and the regional needs and customs, and including the question of long-term maintenance and repair work. As an example: what use to anyone is a state-of-the-art railway network that is regularly shut down by sandstorms or that breaks down the first time the computer-operated signal box fails because the maintenance staff have not been given adequate training?

Whether it be in the areas of reduction of noise or emissions, environmental or flood protection, garbage disposal or energy supply to inaccessible areas, in many regions of the world clients are willing to place their trust in the approach taken by German engineers, which shows an awareness of the problems and focuses on finding solutions to them. These clients are convinced that German coordination of planning and supervision of construction will not only deliver the technically best possible solution but, additionally, will result in savings of both time and money.

Global environmental consciousness

The growing global awareness that protecting the environment is more than just a decadent luxury only the industrialized countries can afford has developed into a bonus for German engineering firms competing in international markets. Germany is generally believed to have a heightened consciousness of environmental issues. On the basis of this awareness, which is also expressed in the form of financial

Humboldthafenbrücke, Berlin,
Schlaich Bergermann und Partner
Humboldthafen Bridge, Berlin,
Schlaich Bergermann und Partner

Flughafen Bangkok,
Murphy / Jahn mit Werner Sobek
Bangkok airport,
Murphy / Jahn with Werner Sobek

Energien« und »Energieeffizienz« des Bundeswirtschaftsministeriums zeugen davon, dass die Bundesregierung auch den Export von Dienstleistungen in diesem Bereich unterstützt.

Deutsche Ingenieurunternehmen haben sich schon frühzeitig mit allen Fragen des nachhaltigen Umwelt- und Ressourcenschutzes auseinandergesetzt – kein Wunder also, dass Länder, die erst jetzt auf diese globale Entwicklung reagieren, gerne auf deutsche Experten setzen – das Beispiel China ist unübersehbar. Auch wenn es sich zunächst nur um wenige Vorzeigeprojekte handelt, die energetisch optimiert sind und beispielsweise Wasser sparende Versorgungskreisläufe vorweisen können: Deutsche Planungsunternehmen sind erste Wahl, wenn es um ganzheitliche Konzepte geht. Gerade für die Ingenieurunternehmen gilt, was auch die Architekten erkannt haben: Umweltkompetenz ist ein herausragendes Markenzeichen für deutsche Planer im Ausland.

Trotz hoher Qualität nur eingeschränkt wettbewerbsfähig?

Bei diesen hervorragenden Voraussetzungen ist es kaum vorstellbar, dass die Ingenieurbranche beim Export ihrer Leistungen längst nicht ihr volles Potenzial ausschöpft. Die mittelständisch geprägte und aus dem freien Beruf heraus gebildete Struktur der Planerlandschaft in Deutschland erweist sich auf dem internationalen Markt als strategischer Nachteil. Es fehlen die großen Planungsunternehmen, die als »Riesen« im internationalen Wettbewerb ganz vorne stehen und bei wichtigen Ausschreibungen ihr Gewicht in die Waagschale werfen könnten. Diese Großunternehmen fungieren als »Türöffner«, indem sie weitere Aufträge an Ingenieurbüros aus dem eigenen Land vergeben. Die Sogwirkung, die bei solchen Riesenprojekten entfaltet wird, lässt sich an den Wettbewerben ablesen, die von ausländischen Mitbewerbern dieser Größenordnung gewonnen und durchgeführt werden.

Auch bei den von der Weltbank finanzierten Projekten erbringen deutsche Unternehmen zwar einen hohen Anteil an Waren- und Güterlieferungen, der Anteil der Beratungsleistungen am deutschen Gesamtvolumen dagegen fällt mit circa 21 Prozent im Vergleich zu Großbritannien (46 Prozent) oder den USA (51 Prozent) unterdurchschnittlich aus. Generell lässt sich feststellen, dass der deutsche Mittelstand, obwohl er im direkten Exportgeschäft durchaus erfolgreich ist, bei den Finanzierungs- und Förderprogrammen multinationaler Institute unterrepräsentiert ist.

Ebenso beim direkten Export ist die Frage der Kapitaldecke entscheidend, die bei den kleinen deutschen Büros oft genug zu dünn ist, um für den Sprung ins Auslandsgeschäft das nötige Durchhaltevermögen mitzubringen. Planungsbüros gehen häufig für ihre Auftraggeber weit in Vorleistung – manchmal weiter als es den Unternehmen bekommt. Im Ausland sind die Investitionen, bis die ersten Honorare fließen und schließlich die Gewinnschwelle erreicht werden kann, nochmals höher. Hinzu kommen Haftungen und Bürgschaften, welche die Firmen zusätzlich belasten. Dabei wird es den deutschen Planern auch von der Politik nicht eben leicht gemacht: Viele Maßnahmen zur Exportförderung und Risikoabsicherung von Bund und Ländern eignen sich zwar gut für Hersteller und Bauausführende, sind aber für den Export geistiger Leistungen, wie sie Ingenieure und Architekten anbieten, kaum anwendbar. Der Verband Beratender Ingenieure steht deshalb in stetigem

subsidies, an innovative, high-performance environment sector has grown up in Germany. Renewable Energy and Energy Efficiency are initiatives from the Federal Ministry of Economy and Technology that show that the federal government also supports the export of services in this sector.

As German engineering firms began early on to examine questions of sustainable protection of resources and the environment, it is not surprising that countries that are only now beginning to respond to this global development turn to German experts. Here the example of China looms large. Even though initially only a few model projects optimized in terms of energy and use were involved—for example, water-saving supply systems—the fact remains: German design firms are the first choice when it comes to comprehensive concepts. A truth already grasped by architects is equally valid for engineering firms: competence in environmental matters is a prominent trademark of German architects and engineers working abroad.

Restricted competitiveness, despite high-quality services?

Under excellent auspices such as these, one could be led to believe that the engineering sector long ago achieved its full potential in exporting its services. But the predominantly medium-scale structure of the German planning sector that developed from the concept of the self-employed individual has turned out to be a strategic disadvantage on the international market. There is a distinct shortage in Germany of the kind of large planning firms that generally take the top places in international competition and, as "giants," can throw their entire resources behind entries for such competitions. These large firms also function as "door openers" in the sense that they in turn commission other engineering firms from their own country. The "pull" that develops in such huge projects is clearly evident in the competitions that have been won and carried out by foreign competitors of this size.

In the case of projects financed by the World Bank, too, German firms provide a high proportion of the goods and materials supplied, but consultancy services amount to only a meager 21 percent of the total contribution made by German businesses to such projects, as compared with a figure of 46 percent in the UK or 51 percent in the United States. Generally speaking, medium-sized German companies, although extremely successful in direct export, are underrepresented in the financing and subsidy programs of multinational institutions.

As in the case of direct export, here too the question of the capital base is decisive. With smaller German firms, this base is often too small to provide the staying power required for expansion into foreign markets. Planning firms frequently offer their clients a variety of services in advance of payment—at times going further than is good for the firm. In working abroad, the investments made before the first fees are paid and the profit threshold is reached are even higher. Liabilities and sureties are an additional burden for the firms. In this area, politics are not particularly helpful to German planners. While eminently suitable for producers and building contractors, many measures undertaken by the federal government and the individual German states are of almost no use in exporting intellectual services of the kind offered by engineers and architects. The VBI is therefore engaged in continual discussions with the relevant ministries and the credit services industry to secure

Eidgenössische Hochschule Learning Center, Lausanne, SANAA mit Bollinger + Grohmann
Eidgenössische Hochschule Learning Center, Lausanne, SANAA with Bollinger + Grohmann

Iranische Botschaft, Bangkok, Naqsh-e-Jahan Pars
mit Professor Pfeifer und Partner
Iranian embassy, Bangkok, Naqsh-e-Jahan Pars
with Professor Pfeifer und Partner

Austausch mit den Ministerien und der Kreditwirtschaft, um diesbezüglich Verbesserungen für die Branche zu erreichen. Inzwischen hat auch die Politik erkannt, dass man diese hoch innovative Branche, die als »Türöffner« für die gesamte Bauwirtschaft dient, mit spezifischen Maßnahmen im Export fördern muss. Bis zur konsequenten Umsetzung wird allerdings noch einige Überzeugungsarbeit zu leisten sein.

Erfolgreich im Ausland – einen Königsweg gibt es nicht

Trotz der geschilderten Nachteile, die die mittelständische Struktur der deutschen Planerlandschaft im internationalen Wettbewerb mit sich bringt, ist auf der anderen Seite nicht zu übersehen, dass ebendiese differenzierte Struktur die fachliche Vielfalt, hohe Innovationsfreude und technische Qualität hervorbringt, für die die deutsche Ingenieurkunst weltweit geschätzt wird. In der Vielzahl der inhabergeführten und oft hoch spezialisierten Büros konnten sich die besonderen Kenntnisse entwickeln, mit denen erfolgreich Nischen auf internationalen Märkten besetzt werden. In vielen Ratgebern zum Export von Planungsleistungen wird daher den kleineren Unternehmen empfohlen, sich sowohl hinsichtlich ihrer Leistungen als auch regional zu konzentrieren. Einen Königsweg, der für alle Unternehmen passend wäre, gibt es dennoch nicht. Ob allein, im Verbund einer Arbeitsgemeinschaft oder im »Huckepackverfahren« mit dem deutschen Auftraggeber – im Ausland wie auf dem heimischen Markt liegt in der Fähigkeit zur Kooperation eine entscheidende Qualifikation.

Die Zusammenarbeit in interdisziplinären Planungsteams ist Voraussetzung bei komplexen Bauvorhaben. Wer die nötige Teamfähigkeit nicht mitbringt, wird im internationalen Geschäft kaum Fuß fassen. Das haben Architekten und beratende Ingenieure gleichermaßen erkannt und treten daher bei ihren Auftraggebern für einen integralen Planungsprozess ein. Durch interdisziplinäre Wettbewerbe, die Gestaltung und Technik gleichermaßen in den Blick nehmen und diese Kriterien durch eine qualifiziert besetzte Jury auch beurteilen können, wird die Kooperation von Ingenieuren und Architekten gefördert und die Qualität der Objekte maßgeblich erhöht. Auch in der Ausbildung ist es nach Ansicht des VBI dringend geboten, die Fähigkeit zu kooperativer Zusammenarbeit besser zu entwickeln.

Plattform für Planernetzwerke

In den Arbeitskreisen und Fachgruppen des VBI spielt die interdisziplinäre Zusammenarbeit eine zentrale Rolle. Auch deshalb zählt der Verband immer mehr zukunftsorientierte Architekturbüros zu seinen Mitgliedern, die in der engen Zusammenarbeit mit qualifizierten Ingenieuren eine besondere Chance sehen. Die Bildung von Netzwerken, die ihre Leistungen im In- und Ausland gemeinsam anbieten, ist eine wichtige Aufgabe, zu der auch die Verbände ihren Beitrag leisten. Auf diese Weise entstehen größere Einheiten, die den Anforderungen von Großprojekten vollständig gewachsen und zugleich flexibel sind. Auftraggeber suchen zunehmend nach einem verlässlichen Partner, der das gesamte Projekt aus einer Hand organisiert. Netzwerke eingespielter Partner können dieser Marktanforderung gerecht werden, auch wenn die einzelnen Unternehmen selbst nicht besonders groß sind. Sie steuern und verwirklichen umfangreiche Projekte, bei denen auch die Finanzierung in die Bauherrenberatung mit einfließt, bis hin zu Lösungen für den Betrieb von Industrieanlagen und -einrichtungen. Die Rechtsform solcher Zusammenschlüsse kann

improvements for the design sector. By now, politicians, too, have recognized the need for special measures to support the exports of this highly innovative sector, which can open doors for the entire construction industry. However, until this awareness begins to make an impact, a certain amount of persuasive argument is still required.

Success abroad—there is no single ideal approach

Despite the difficulties in international competition caused by the medium-sized structure of the German engineering design sector, it is impossible to overlook the fact that it is precisely this differentiated structure that provides the wide range of specialization, the delight in innovation, and the high technical quality for which German engineering is so highly regarded throughout the world. In the many—often highly specialized—firms run by the person who set them up, areas of expertise have often developed that have made it possible to fill niches in international markets. In many advisory booklets on exporting planning services, smaller firms are therefore recommended to concentrate on their particular services and to focus on a specific region. But ultimately there is no "one size fits all" approach. Whether it be alone, as part of a consortium, or in a kind of "piggyback system" with the German client, both on the home market and abroad the ability to cooperate is a decisive factor.

Complex building projects require collaboration in interdisciplinary planning teams. Those lacking the ability to work as part of a team will hardly ever be able to gain a foothold in international business. Architects and consultant engineers have realized this to equal extents and therefore try to convince their clients of the advantages offered by the integral planning process. Interdisciplinary competitions that look at both design and technology, and that, thanks to a suitably qualified jury, are also able to judge these criteria, encourage cooperation between engineers and architects and lead to a substantial improvement in the quality of buildings. The VBI believes that it is vitally necessary for these skills to be developed as an integral part of engineers' training.

Platform for networks of planners

Interdisciplinary collaboration plays a central role in the working teams and specialist groups in the VBI. This is one reason why the VBI increasingly numbers among its members forward-looking architecture firms who are convinced that close collaboration with qualified engineers can offer them special opportunities. The formation of networks that jointly offer their services at home and abroad is an important objective to which the associations also contribute. This creates larger units that are able to meet the demands of large projects but that are, at the same time, highly flexible. Increasingly, clients look for a reliable partner able to take over the entire responsibility for organizing a project. Networks of experienced partners can meet the demands of this market, even where the individual firms are not particularly large. They manage and carry out wide-ranging projects, in which the consultancy services provided for the client range from financing to solutions for running industrial complexes and facilities. Such partnerships can take very different legal forms oriented to the requirements of the target market.

Oberösterreichische Landesbibliothek, Linz,
Bez + Kock Architekten
mit Weischede, Herrmann und Partner
Upper Austria State Library, Linz,
Bez + Kock Architekten
with Weischede, Herrmann und Partner

BMW-Wintertestgelände, Arjeplog,
WPW Ingenieure
BMW winter test-driving complex, Arjeplog,
WPW Ingenieure

sehr unterschiedlich aussehen und orientiert sich am Bedarf des Zielmarktes und der Beteiligten.

Um den internationalen Marktanforderungen entsprechen zu können, ist es erforderlich umzudenken: Statt einzelner Planungsphasen muss das Endprodukt in den Fokus aller Beteiligten rücken. Ein Beispiel bietet der Markt für Bauten im Gesundheitswesen und Wellnessbereich. Hier sind Architekten, Fachingenieure und Betreiber gefordert, gemeinsam über die internationale Vermarktung ihrer Leistungen nachzudenken und dabei das fertige Produkt einer Klinik oder Kuranlage bis hin zu deren langfristigen Betrieb in den Blick zu nehmen. Der Gesundheitsbau fordert in besonderem Maße die Verbindung von technischer Präzision und höchsten Ansprüchen an Bequemlichkeit und Komfort. Es gilt, sich auf den Bedarf der Auftraggeber einzustellen, das bereits vorhandene Vertrauen in deutsche Technologie und Lösungskompetenz aufzugreifen und durch gelungene Projekte zu bestätigen.

Mit der Kombination aus Information, Schulungsangeboten und individueller Unterstützung konnte der VBI sein selbstgestecktes Ziel erreichen, den Anteil der im Ausland aktiven Unternehmen unter seinen Mitgliedern kontinuierlich zu erhöhen. Heute sind gut 20 Prozent mehr VBI-Mitglieder auf ausländischen Märkten tätig als noch 2003; darunter sind auch Konsortien, die der Verband zusammenführen konnte.

In der konstruktiven Zusammenarbeit zwischen Architekten und Ingenieuren schließt sich der Kreis: Das Erfolgsmodell deutscher Baukunst weltweit, so wie es sich in dieser Ausstellung mit Neulingen und bereits Etablierten darstellt, basiert auf Kooperation und interdisziplinärer Zusammenarbeit aller Beteiligten. Diese »Tugend« im Inland zu pflegen, heißt die Marke »Planned in Germany« weltweit zu stärken.

To successfully meet the demands of the international markets, a rethinking is necessary: instead of thinking in terms of individual planning phases, all those involved must focus on the end product. One example is the market for buildings for health facilities and wellness. Here architects, specialist engineers, and those who operate such services must consider the international marketing of their facilities in the process, focusing on the end product of a particular clinic or spa facility and on its long-term operation. Buildings for health facilities in particular demand a combination of technical precision and the highest standards of comfort and service. It is essential to respond to the client's needs, to utilize the existing confidence in German technology and its ability to deliver solutions, and to confirm this trust by delivering successful projects.

A combination of information, training courses, and individual support has enabled the VBI to achieve a goal that it set for itself, which was to continuously increase the number of member firms who are active abroad. Today a good 20 percent more VBI members work in foreign construction markets than in 2003, and this figure includes consortiums put together by the VBI.

The constructive collaboration between architects and engineers closes the circle: the success story of the worldwide German art of building, as presented in this exhibition using examples of both established firms and newcomers, is based on the cooperation and interdisciplinary collaboration of all those involved. Encouraging this "virtue" at home means strengthening the brand "Made in Germany" throughout the world.

Gründung Established
2002 in Berlin

Büros Offices
8

4a Architekten
www.architektenbuero4a.de

Allmann Sattler Wappner Architekten
www.allmannsattlerwappner.de

Chestnutt Niess Architekten
www.chestnutt-niess.de

Jan Störmer Partner
www.stoermer-partner.de

Léon Wohlhage Wernik Architekten
www.leonwohlhagewernik.de

Schneider + Schumacher
www.schneider-schumacher.de

Werner Sobek
www.wsi-stuttgart.com

Yes Architecture
www.yes-architecture.com

Kontakt Contact
Leibnizstrasse 65
10629 Berlin
Deutschland Germany

Tel +49 (0)30 31 01 21 86
Fax +49 (0)30 32 76 00 60

info@architekturbuerodeutschland.com
www.architekturbuerodeutschland.com

Architekturbüro Deutschland
Berlin

4a Architekten

Allmann Sattler Wappner Architekten

Chestnutt Niess Architekten

Jan Störmer Partner

Léon Wohlhage Wernik Architekten

Schneider + Schumacher

Werner Sobek

Yes Architecture

Wellnesspark ELSE Club
ELSE Club Wellness Park
Auslandsprojekt Foreign project

Architekten Architects
Architekturbüro Deutschland,
vertreten durch represented by
4a Architekten, Stuttgart
Matthias Burkart, Alexander von Salmuth,
Ernst Ulrich Tillmanns
Birgit Wäldin, André Georg

Ingenieure Engineers
IB Kannewischer, Baden-Baden

Bauherr Client
Krost Industrial & Building Company,
Moskau Moscow

Typologie Type
Freizeitbau Recreational building

Standort Location
Moskau, Russland Moscow, Russia

Beginn Start
Januar January 2003

Fertigstellung Completion
September 2007

Brutto-Grundfläche Gross floor area
4 250 m²

Das Baugrundstück des Wellnessparks liegt etwas außerhalb des Stadtkerns von Moskau, in einem leicht bewaldeten Gebiet mit einzelnen Wohnhochhäusern. Der ELSE Club selbst belegt die beiden unteren Etagen eines 25-geschossigen Wohnhochhauses. Als Ausdruck der veränderten Nutzung löst sich der Wellnessbereich formal völlig vom darüberliegenden Wohngebäude. Es wird ein Sockel, im Grundriss größer als die darüberliegenden Wohngeschosse, unter das Gebäude »geschoben«. Die Fassaden werden da, wo es möglich ist, großzügig verglast, um den Bezug nach außen herzustellen und den Außenbereich mit schönem Baumbestand für den Gast erlebbar zu machen. Um dem Wellnessbereich die angemessene Großzügigkeit zu geben, laufen die Räume fließend ineinander. Es entsteht eine begehbare Raumskulptur, bei der die einzelnen Funktionsbereiche »landschaftlich« miteinander verwoben sind.

The wellness park is situated just off Moscow's city center in a wooded area dotted with some residential high-rises. The ELSE Club occupies the ground and lower floors of a twenty-five-story housing block. To make the altered function of these two floors visible from outside and distinguishable from the residential floors, it was converted and enlarged as a "plinth" pushed under the high-rise. Wherever possible, its façades were largely glazed in order to offer spa customers the view of the surroundings with beautiful mature trees. To make the spa areas appear more spacious, they were designed as a series of "flowing" spaces. The result is a walk-in spatial sculpture of individual functional areas interwoven in a "scenic" fashion.

1 Grundriss Erdgeschoss
  Ground floor plan
2–4 Innenansichten
  Interior spaces
5 Eingang ELSE Club
  ELSE Club entrance

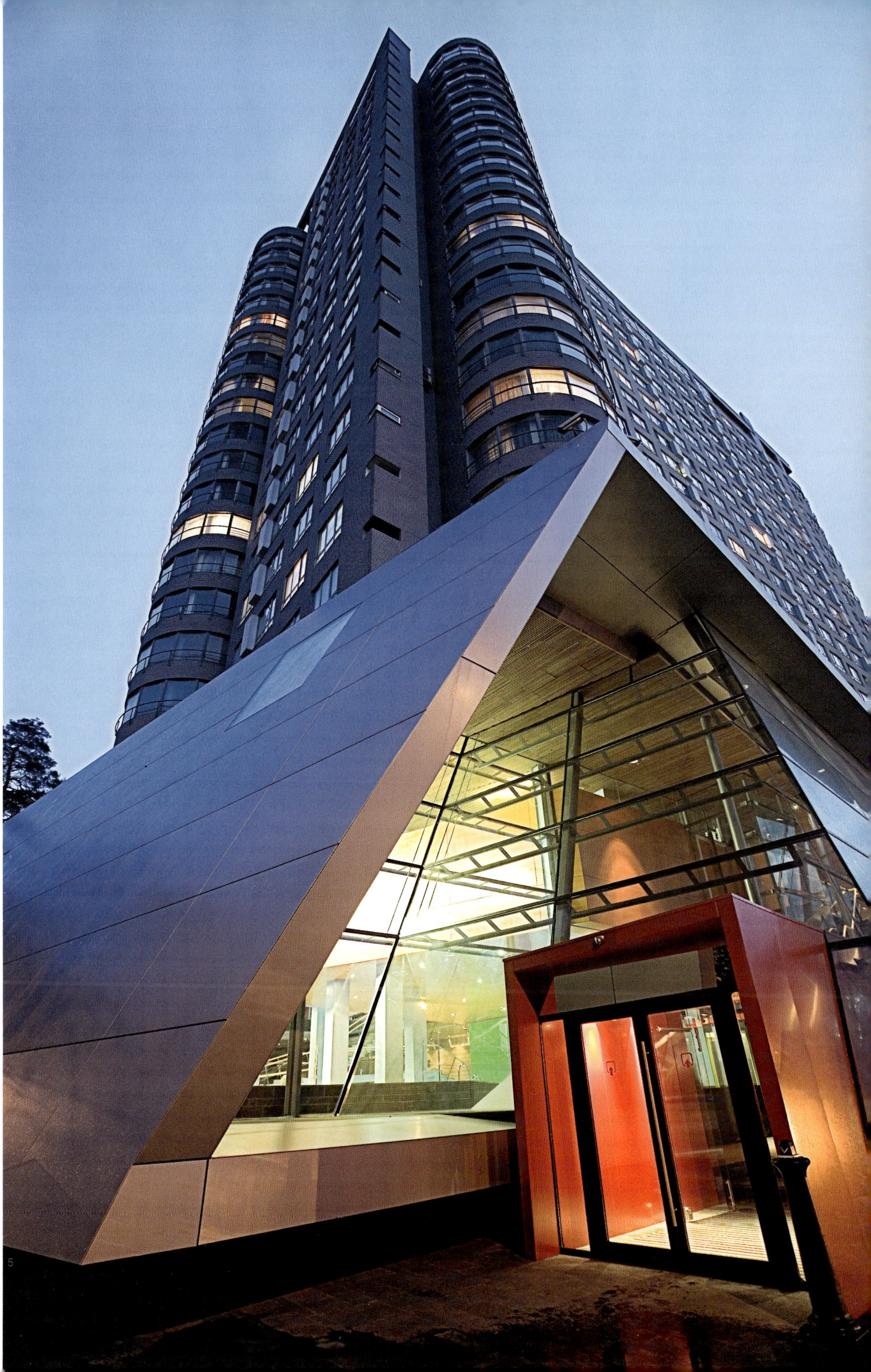
5

AUDI Terminal Paris
Paris AUDI Terminal
Auslandsprojekt Foreign project

Architekten Architects
Architekturbüro Deutschland,
vertreten durch represented by
Allmann Sattler Wappner Architekten, München
Markus Allmann, Amandus Sattler, Ludwig Wappner
Carola Dietrich, Matthias Both, Alex Wagner,
Christian Boland

Partner Partners
B/R/S Architectes Ingénieurs, Paris

Ingenieure Engineers
Werner Sobek Ingenieure, Stuttgart
Transsolar KlimaEngineering, Stuttgart
Laux, Kaiser + Partner, Stuttgart
Raible + Partner, Reutlingen
MSLicht, München Munich
BETOM Ingénierie, Frankreich France

Bauherr Client
AUDI AG / AUDI France

Typologie Type
Geschäfts- und Verwaltungsbau
Commercial and administration building

Standort Location
Paris, Frankreich France

Wettbewerb Competition
2005

Fertigstellung Completion
2009

Brutto-Grundfläche Gross floor area
10 210 m²

Dynamik, Asymmetrie und Transparenz sind die wesentlichen Gestaltungsmerkmale der AUDI-Architektur. So wird die asymmetrische Kurve als dreidimensionale, raumbildende Form zum bestimmenden Element des AUDI Terminals. Einzelne Kurvensegmente, zur Präsentation der Fahrzeuge, sind über Rolltreppen verbunden und bilden so ein Raumkontinuum. Alle anderen Funktionen, die Kundenzone, die Verwaltung oder der Servicebereich, sind orthogonal organisiert. Die Fassade ist ein wesentliches, identitätsprägendes Merkmal der Architektur. In die Haut aus Aluminiumblech werden expressive Fenster geschnitten, die im Kontrast zur geschlossenen Fassade eine besondere Bedeutung erhalten und Blicke in die Schauräume freigeben. Die exponierte Lage des Terminals Paris auf einem Gewerbestreifen zwischen zwei Verkehrswegen führte zu einem solitären Baukörper, der sich in die Gebäudetypologie der Umgebung einfügt. Die Schauräume orientieren sich übereck zur Autobahn im Süden und zur Zufahrt im Norden.

Dynamism, asymmetry, and transparency were the main design criteria for the new AUDI building. The idea of an asymmetrically curved, three-dimensional, space-defining mass became the determining design element of the AUDI Terminal. Individual segments of this "curve" contain the car showrooms, which are interconnected by escalators and thus form a spatial continuum. All the other functions of the building, i.e., the customer, administration, and service areas, are structured based on an orthogonal grid. The façade is essential to the architectural identity of the structure. Its skin of aluminium sheeting is perforated by expressively shaped windows that open up the otherwise closed-looking façade and afford views into the showrooms. The exposed position of the Paris AUDI Terminal on a narrow industrial estate between two roads prompted the designers to create a freestanding structure that matches the typology of the neighboring buildings. The showrooms are oriented across two corners: south to the highway and north to the front drive.

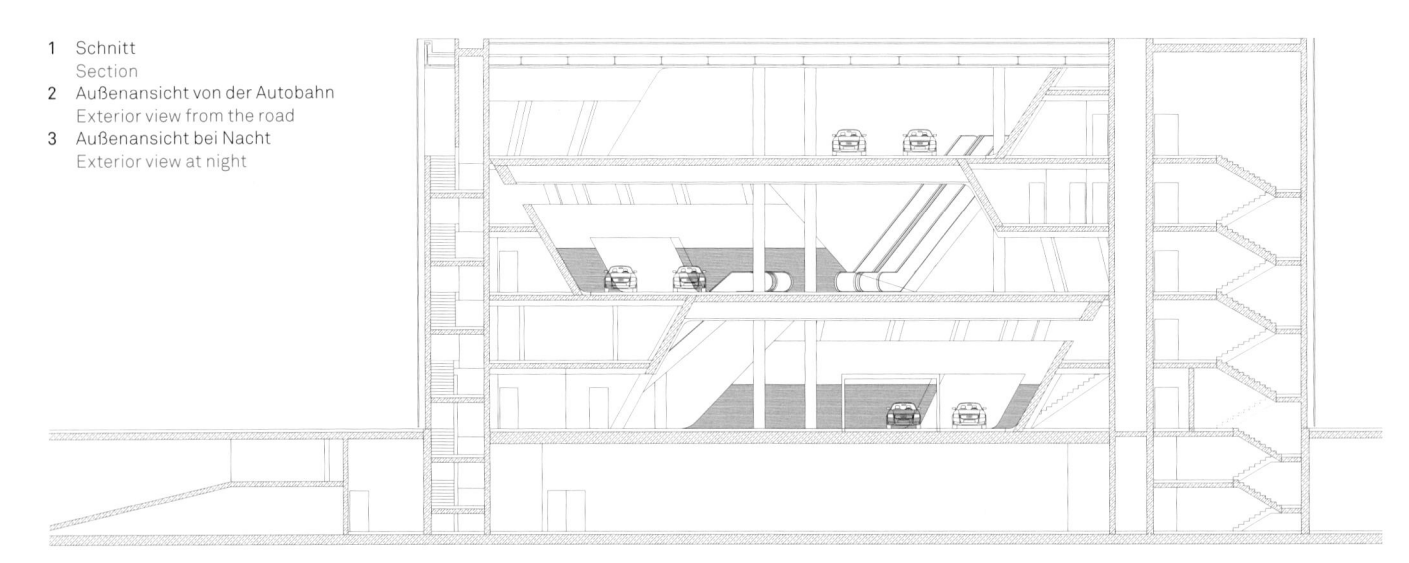

1 Schnitt
  Section
2 Außenansicht von der Autobahn
  Exterior view from the road
3 Außenansicht bei Nacht
  Exterior view at night

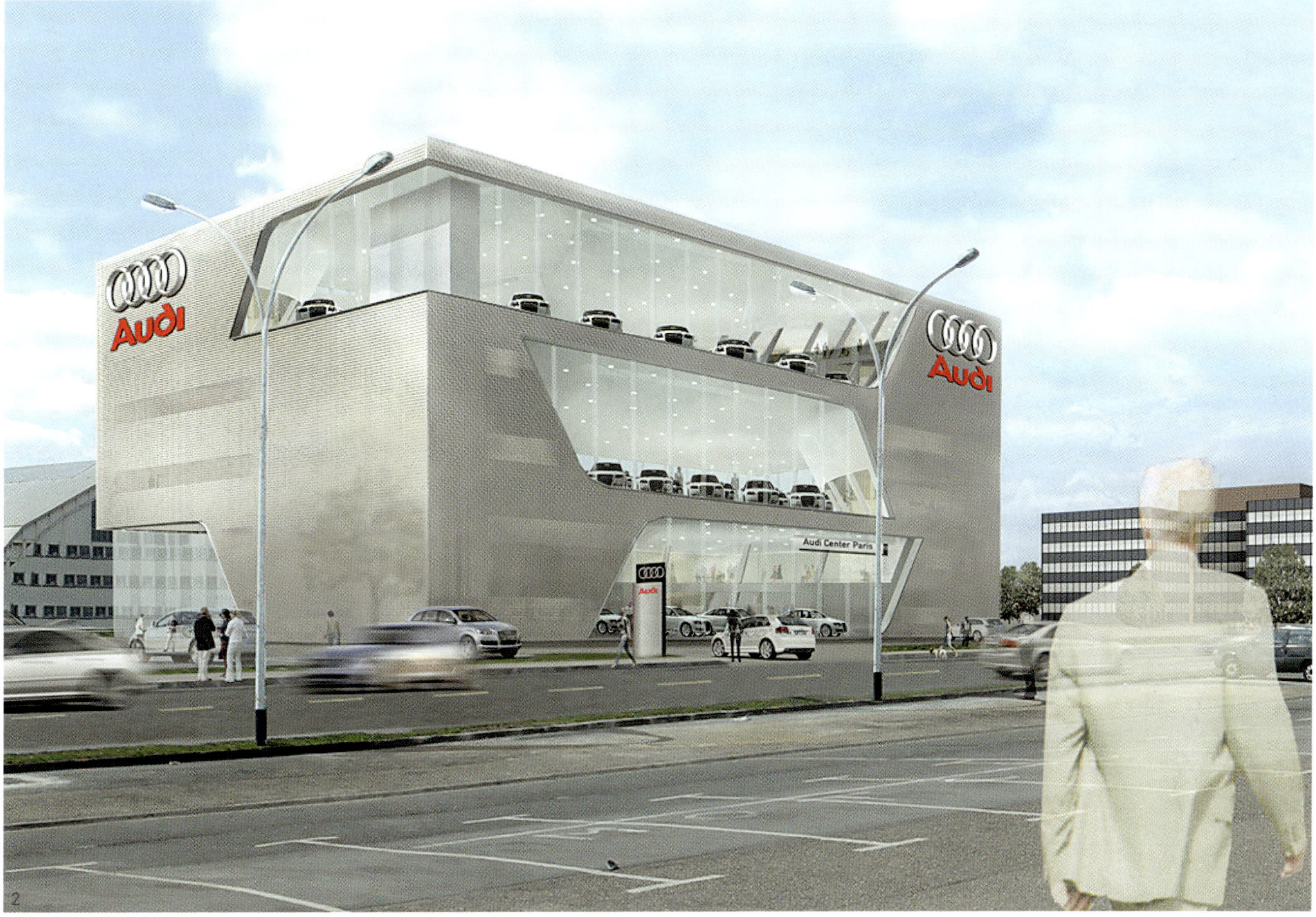

2

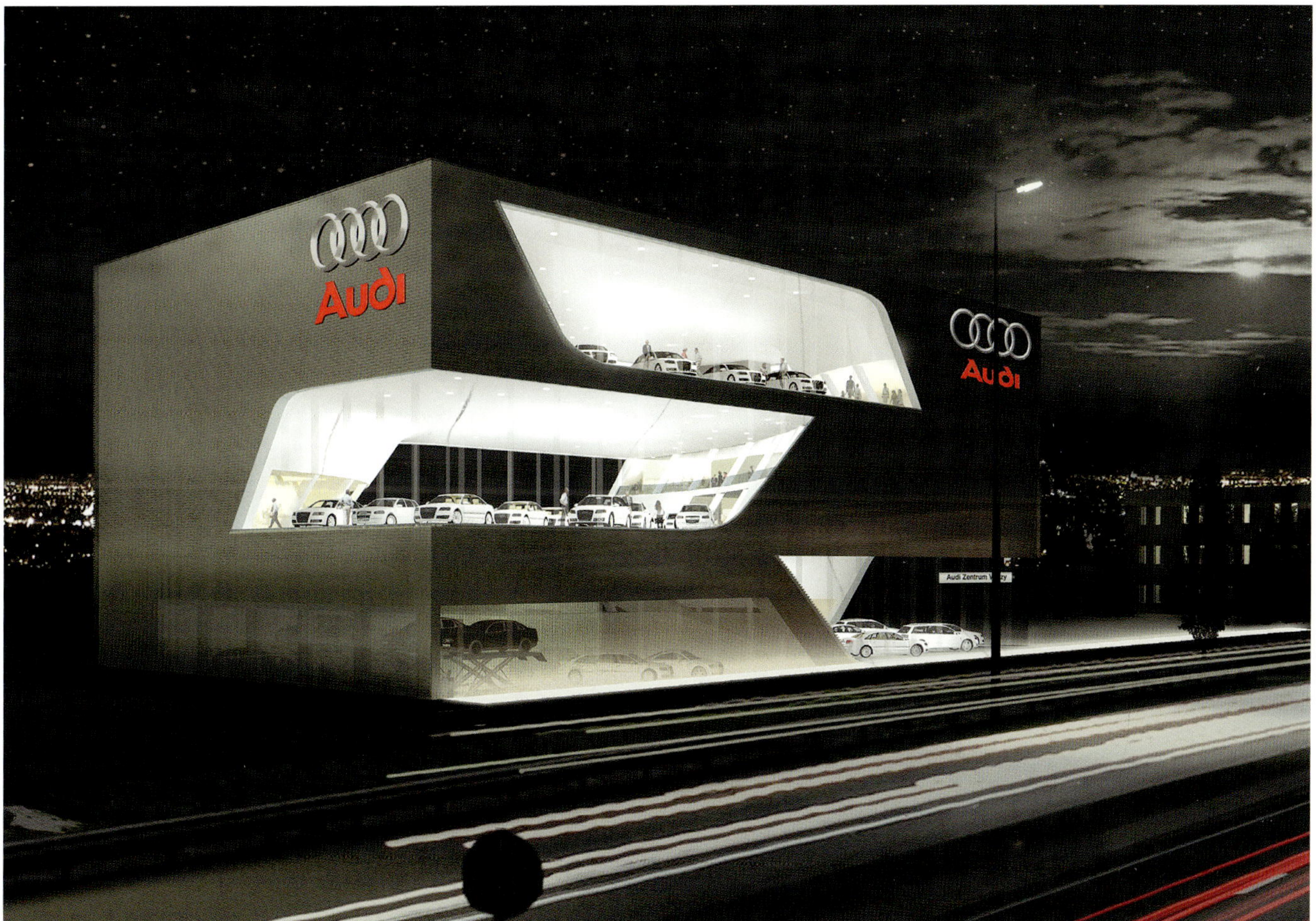

3

Sporthalle Hausburgviertel
Hausburgviertel Gymnasium
Inlandsprojekt Domestic project

Architekten Architects
Architekturbüro Deutschland,
vertreten durch represented by
Chestnutt Niess Architekten, Berlin
Rebecca Chestnutt, Robert Niess
Ulrike Vogel Marco Lösekrug, Heike Clasen Warns

Ingenieure Engineers
Eisenloffel, Sattler + Partner, Berlin
Ingenieurbüro big, Berlin
B & S Baupartner, Berlin
Ingenieurbüro Draheim, Berlin

Bauherr Client
Land Berlin, vertreten durch die SIES
State of Berlin, represented by the SIES

Typologie Type
Freizeitbau Recreational building

Standort Location
Berlin

Wettbewerb Competition
2001

Fertigstellung Completion
2007

Brutto-Grundfläche Gross floor area
1 480 m²

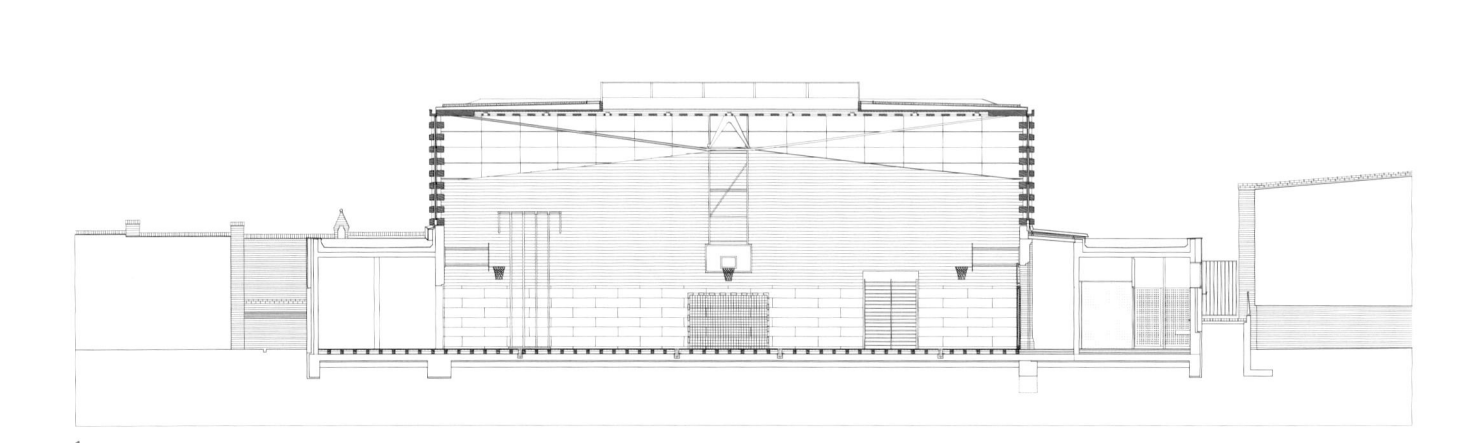

1

Die neue Doppelsporthalle wurde innerhalb des bestehenden alten Rinderstalls auf dem ehemaligen Schlachthofgelände in Berlin-Prenzlauer Berg realisiert und nimmt dessen Grundfläche und Achsen auf. Beiderseits der Hallenfläche sind Funktionalschienen als zurückhaltende eingeschossige Neubauten angegliedert. Im Westen sind darin Umkleiden und Duschen untergebracht, im Osten Geräteräume für die Innen- und Außenraumnutzung. Der Hauptzugang erfolgt durch den vorhandenen historischen Eingang in der Giebelfassade. Das bestehende Gebäude bleibt in Teilen erhalten und erlebbar. Ein Wechselspiel zwischen neuen und historischen Flächen und Räumen entsteht; Durchblicke und Einblicke bewahren und befördern die jeweilige Eigenständigkeit. Die gewählten Materialien Holz, Stahl und Glas entwickeln eine sinnliche Ästhetik, die das moderne Gebäude deutlich in der Umgebung artikuliert. Holz zeigt als Hauptmaterial der Halle die neue Nutzung der alten Industriearchitektur.

The new gymnasium actually contains two halls. It was built into the old cattle shed of the former abattoir in Berlin's Prenzlauer Berg area and uses the shed's footprint area and axes. The halls are flanked by "functional bars," i.e., modest new single-story structures for various purposes. The one on the west contains the dressing rooms and showers and the one on the east stores indoor and outdoor sports equipment. The main entrance is the historical portal in the gable wall. Parts of the historical building were preserved and will remain visible. This creates an interplay of old and new floors and rooms, which maintain their separate identities while being open to through-views as well as views from outside. The materials used—wood, steel, and glass—unfold a sensual aesthetic appeal and make the building stand out from its surroundings. Wood as the main material expresses the new use of the old industrial architecture.

1 Querschnitt
  Cross section
2 Eingang
  Entrance
3 Blick in die Sporthalle
  View into the gymnasium
4 Außenansicht
  Exterior view
5 Im Gang zwischen den Umkleiden und der Sporthalle
  In the hallway between the dressing rooms and the gymnasium

Hotel am Puschkinplatz
Hotel on Pushkin Square
Auslandsprojekt Foreign project

Architekten Architects
Architekturbüro Deutschland,
vertreten durch represented by
Jan Störmer Partner, Hamburg
Holger Jaedicke, Martin Murphy, Jan Störmer
Kasimir Altzweig, Johannes Buchholz, Daniel
Kmoch, Natalja Kopycko

Ingenieure Engineers
Werner Sobek, Stuttgart

Bauherr Client
Bell Development, Moskau Moscow

Typologie Type
Hotel- und Geschäftsbau
Hotel and commercial building

Standort Location
Moskau, Russland Moscow, Russia

Wettbewerb Competition
2006

Fertigstellung Completion
2009

Brutto-Grundfläche Gross floor area
14 725 m²

In einer erstklassigen Lage im Zentrum von Moskau wird ein neues Boutique-Hotel gebaut. Das Hotel am Puschkinplatz liegt inmitten des Moskauer Nachtlebens, in direkter Nachbarschaft zu zahlreichen Restaurants, Clubs, Theatern, Bars und Geschäften. Das Konzept eines erstklassigen Hotelumfeldes, das eine anregende Szenerie und zugleich eine Mischung aus Boutiquen, Restaurants und Abendunterhaltung bietet, zielt auf eine junge, dynamische Kundengruppe ab. Das Designkonzept verbindet diese Funktionen, sodass eine Identität für den Ort geschaffen wird; dabei werden Formen, Farben sowie unterschiedliche Materialien eingesetzt, um jeden einzelnen Bereich innerhalb des Gebäudes genau zu definieren. Ein internes Umfeld wird geschaffen, das in der Lage ist, sich anzupassen und im Laufe der Zeit zu erneuern. Es ist ein flexibles Konzept, welches Veränderungen zulässt und nicht im Augenblick verharrt.

This new boutique hotel is being built on Pushkin Square, a prime location in Moscow's city center, right in the hub of the city's nightlife, with many restaurants, clubs, theaters, bars, and shops. The concept of a first-class hotel offering an exciting, stimulating mixed scenery of boutiques, restaurants, and evening entertainment targets young and dynamic patrons. The design combines the different functions and services that define the hotel's identity. Various shapes, surface colors, and materials will be used to give every interior area its own character. This creates an adaptable environment suited for renewal as time goes on—the flexible design allows for changing conditions.

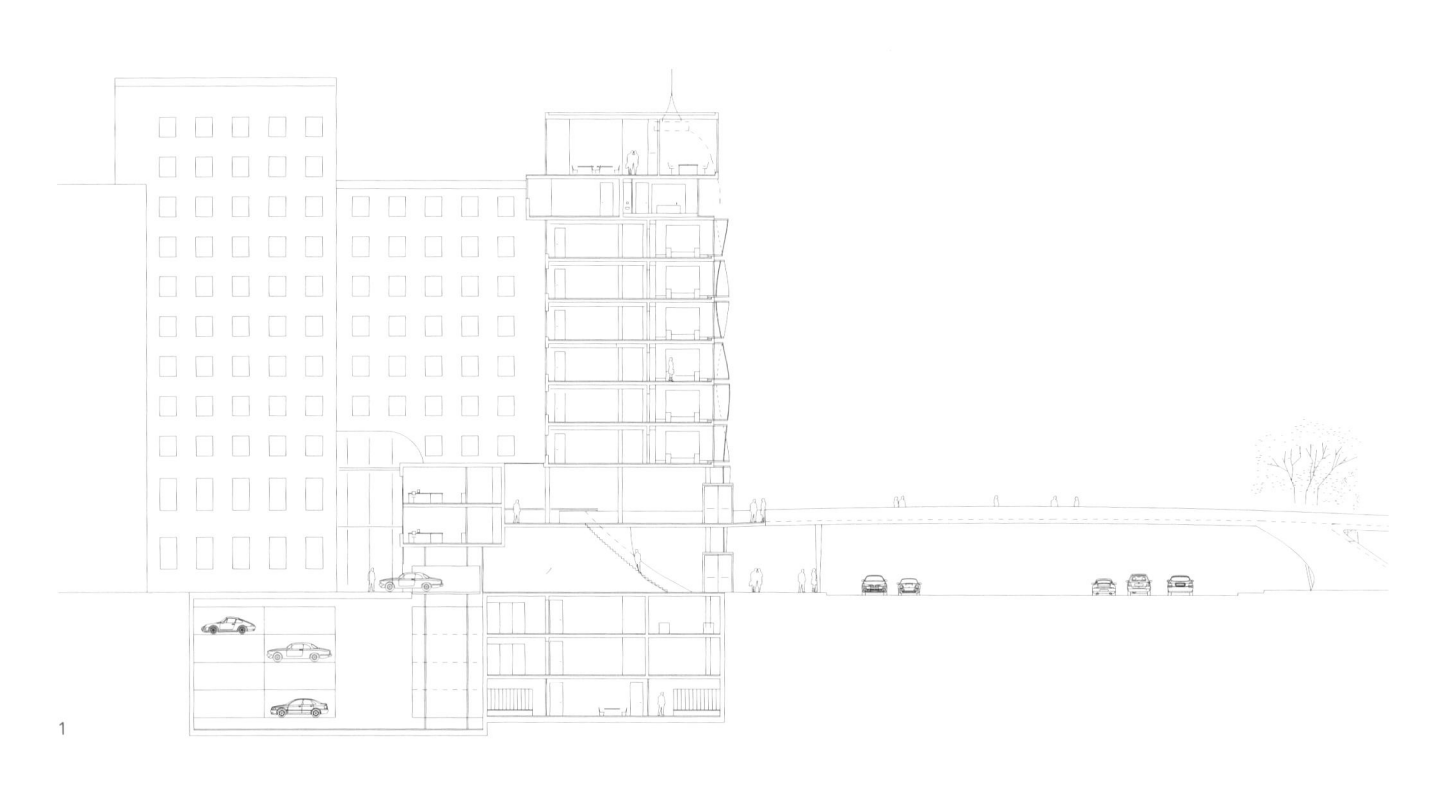

1

1 Schnitt
  Section
2–3 Restaurant im 9. Obergeschoss
  Restaurant on the 10th floor
4 Hotelzimmer
  Hotel room
5 Außenansicht
  Exterior view

SchwabenGalerie
SchwabenGalerie
Inlandsprojekt Domestic project

Architekten Architects
Architekturbüro Deutschland,
vertreten durch represented by
Léon Wohlhage Wernik Architekten, Berlin
Hilde Léon, Konrad Wohlhage (†), Siegfried Wernik
Ulrich Möller, Ulrich Vetter, Sabine Arntz, Nina
Behjati, Tilman Bock, Jörn Börner, Julia Hausmann,
Hans Josef Lankes, Jochen Menzer, Walter Miller,
Abdullah Motaleb, Lydia Rößiger, Francesca Saetti,
Tim Schmitt, Henning Schulz, Andrew Strickland,
Michael Tümmers, Iris Wagenplast

Ingenieure Engineers
Deufel Ingenieurgesellschaft mbH, Deizisau
Ingenieurbüro Scheer, Stuttgart
K+S Haustechnik, Rheinbach
Lichtvision, Berlin

Bauherr Client
Senator h. c. Rudi Häussler, Stuttgart

Typologie Type
Geschäftsbau Commercial building

Standort Location
Stuttgart-Vaihingen

Wettbewerb Competition
2000

Fertigstellung Completion
2004

Brutto-Grundfläche Gross floor area
103 000 m²

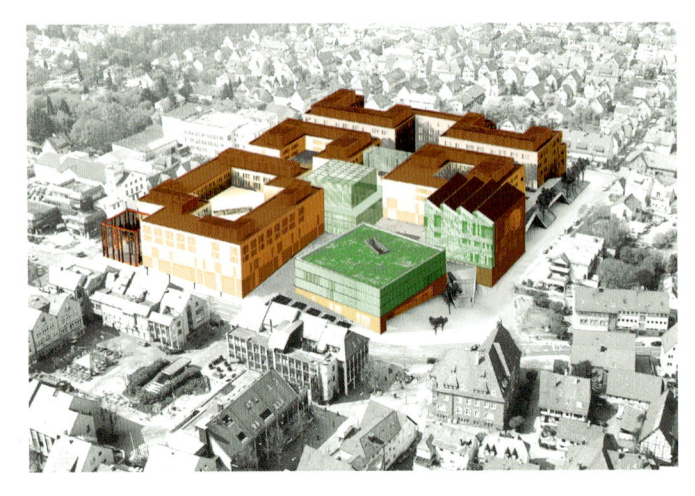

Das historische Zentrum von Stuttgart-Vaihingen bestand lange Zeit nicht aus Kirche, Rathaus und Schule, sondern aus einer Brauerei. Mit dem Wegzug dieser Industrie bestand die Möglichkeit, ein neues Stadtzentrum mit öffentlichen Räumen zu planen, die SchwabenGalerie. Statt einer amerikanischen Shopping-Mall wurde eine europäische Stadt mit öffentlichen Plätzen und Gassen entworfen, die das neue Quartier mit der Nachbarschaft verwebt. So rückt das bisher am Rand gelegene Alte Rathaus mit einem neuen Rathausplatz in die Mitte und ein weiterer höher gelegener Platz wird zum Fokus von drei Straßen. Zwischen beiden Plätzen stehen das neue Bürgerforum und die Markthalle. Weitere Baumassen gliedern sich wie Stadtbausteine in drei Blöcke mit Geschäften, Büros und einem Hotel. Das Kernstück ist ein sogenanntes Atrium, eine Glashalle, die zwei Funktionen erfüllen soll: Sie ist das winterliche Gegenstück zum offenen Platz, belichtet zugleich die Tiefgarage und zieht die Menschen hinauf.

For a long time, the main buildings in the historic center of the town of Vaihingen (now part of Stuttgart) were not, as might be expected, a church, the town hall, and a school, but a brewery complex. When the brewery company moved to another location, this opened the way for the site to be redeveloped as a new urban center, called the SchwabenGalerie (Swabia Gallery), with a number of public spaces. Instead of an American-type shopping mall, the design envisaged a European city center with public squares and alleyways that connect the new quarter to the adjoining areas. Thus the old town hall, previously on the edge of the site, and the new town hall square now form the center, while a square a bit farther up the hill has become a focal point where three streets meet. The new Civic Forum and the market hall are located between the two squares. Further buildings are subdivided urban blocks containing shops, offices, and a hotel. The centerpiece is the Atrium, a glass hall with a dual function. In the winter it acts as the indoor counterpart to the open public square; it also lights up the underground parking lot, thus leading people from there up to the ground floor.

1   Luftbild
    Aerial view
2   Außenansicht
    Exterior view
3–4 Blicke in das Atrium
    Views into the atrium

Fronius Forschungs- und Entwicklungszentrum
Fronius Research and Design Center
Auslandsprojekt Foreign project

Architekten Architects
Architekturbüro Deutschland,
vertreten durch represented by
Schneider + Schumacher, Frankfurt am Main
Kai Otto, Till Schneider, Michael Schumacher,
Christian Simons
Tim Ahlswede, Alexander Hirsch, Mathias Hoof, Hidir Ilter, Lisa Kistner, Christoph Martinek, Margarethe Mika, Natalija Miodragovic, Andreas Schneider, Ralf Seeburger, Stefano Turri, Bartek Wieczorek

Ingenieure Engineers
Bollinger + Grohmann, Frankfurt am Main
Arup GmbH, Berlin
EBP Ingenieurbüro Preisack, Perg

Bauherr Client
Fronius International GmbH, Pettenbach

Typologie Type
Verwaltungs- und Industriebau
Administration and industrial building

Standort Location
Thalheim, Österreich Austria

Wettbewerb Competition
2007

Fertigstellung Completion
2009

Brutto-Grundfläche Gross floor area
31 000 m²

Der Entwurf des Neubaus für die Firma Fronius setzt sich stark mit der Arbeitsstruktur sowie der Corporate Identity – Kontinuität und Innovation – des weltweit agierenden österreichischen Unternehmens auseinander. Dass die Zukunft auch eine Herkunft hat, drückt sich im Verhältnis der Neubauten zum bestehenden Gebäude der Gründergeneration aus. Die Fassade, welche in der Firmenfarbe ausgeführt wird, unterstreicht die Bedeutung des neuen Zentrums im Gesamtkomplex. In der Wahrnehmung und in der Kommunikation der Corporate Architecture nach außen erzählt der Komplex von der Vergangenheit, dem erfolgten Wandel und den Visionen für die Zukunft. Die Architektur vermittelt die Botschaft und die Haltung der Firma Fronius: Klarheit und Einfachheit in der Anordnung der Baukörper, offene und flexible Strukturen mit sehr guter Orientierung, eine Fassade, die einen thermischen Beitrag zur Energiebilanz liefert sowie Verwendung von erneuerbaren Energien.

The design of the new Fronius research and design center followed extensive studies of the work structure and processes as well as the corporate identity—continuity and innovation—of this internationally active Austrian company. The fact that the future also has a past is expressed in the relationship between the new structure and the existing ones built by the company's founding generation. The façades in the corporate colors underline the significance of the new center in the context of the entire complex. The exterior of this piece of corporate architecture speaks of the company's past, the changes it has experienced, and its visions for the future. With the clarity and simplicity of the building masses, the open and flexible interior structure designed for easy orientation, a thermal façade (which contributes to the building's good energy balance) and the use of renewable energy resources, the architecture expresses Fronius's corporate message and attitudes.

1–2 Außenansichten
   Exterior views
3 Innenraum
   Interior space

Haus R 128
House R 128
Inlandsprojekt Domestic project

Architekten Architects
Werner Sobek, Stuttgart

Ingenieure Engineers
Werner Sobek, Stuttgart
Transsolar KlimaEngineering, Stuttgart
SE Stahltechnik, Stammham
Hardwork, Stuttgart
Ing.-Büro F. Müller, Weissach im Tal
Baumgartner GmbH, Kippenheim
Jochen Köhnlein Gebäudeautomation, Albstadt

Bauherr Client
Ursula und and Werner Sobek, Stuttgart

Typologie Type
Wohnungsbau Residential building

Standort Location
Stuttgart

Beginn Start
1997

Fertigstellung Completion
2000

Nutzfläche Effective area
250 m²

1 Stahlkonstruktion
  Steel structure
2 Außenansicht
  Exterior view
3 Innenraum
  Interior space

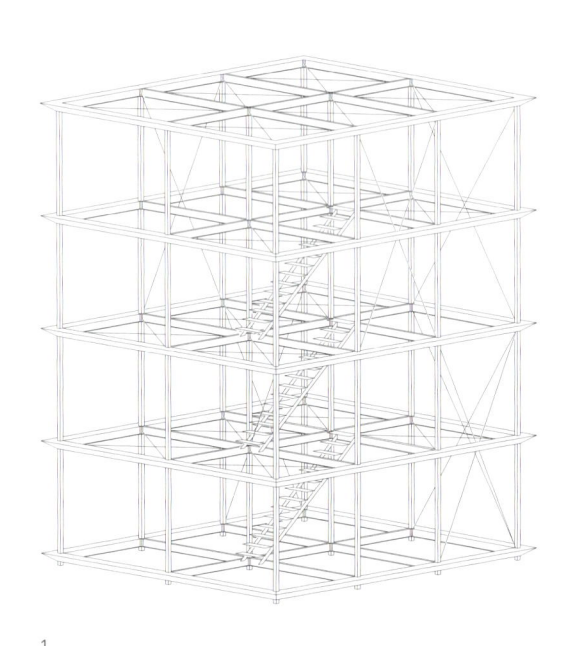

Das viergeschossige Wohnhaus befindet sich auf einem steilen Grundstück am Rand des Stuttgarter Talkessels. Es wurde als wiederverwertbares, im Betrieb emissionsfreies Nullheizenergiegebäude entworfen. Das Haus besitzt eine hochwertige Dreifachverglasung, ist modular aufgebaut und durch Steck- und Schraubverbindungen leicht auf- und abbaubar. Die Innentemperatur wird durch ein neu entwickeltes, computergesteuertes Klimakonzept geregelt. Der für Heizung und Regelungstechnik benötigte elektrische Strom wird fotovoltaisch erzeugt. Das offen liegende Tragwerk aus Stahl ist wesentliches Gestaltungs- und Gliederungselement und trägt darüber hinaus zur kurzen Bauzeit bei. Der Zugang erfolgt über eine Brücke, die an die oberste Ebene führt, in der die Küche und der Essbereich liegen. Nach unten schließen sich dann die Wohnebene, der Schlafbereich und das Kinderzimmer mit Technikbereich an. Durch eine sparsame Möblierung wurde die maximale Transparenz auch im Inneren konsequent fortgeführt.

This four-story house is situated on a steep hillside plot overlooking Stuttgart's valley basin. The house was designed as a recyclable, zero-emission, zero-energy building. It is insulated by high-quality triple glazing and consists of room modules that can easily be erected using inserted and screw joints— and can be as easily dismantled. The interior temperature is computer-controlled by a newly developed air-conditioning system. The electric power necessary for controlling the heating system is generated via photovoltaic panels. The open steel structure is an essential element of both the design and the spatial organization and also contributed to a short construction period. The house is accessed via a bridge at the top-floor level, which accommodates the kitchen and dining area. The living room, the bedroom, and the children's room, together with the service spaces, occupy the three lower floors. Maximum transparency was maintained throughout the house by sparse furnishings.

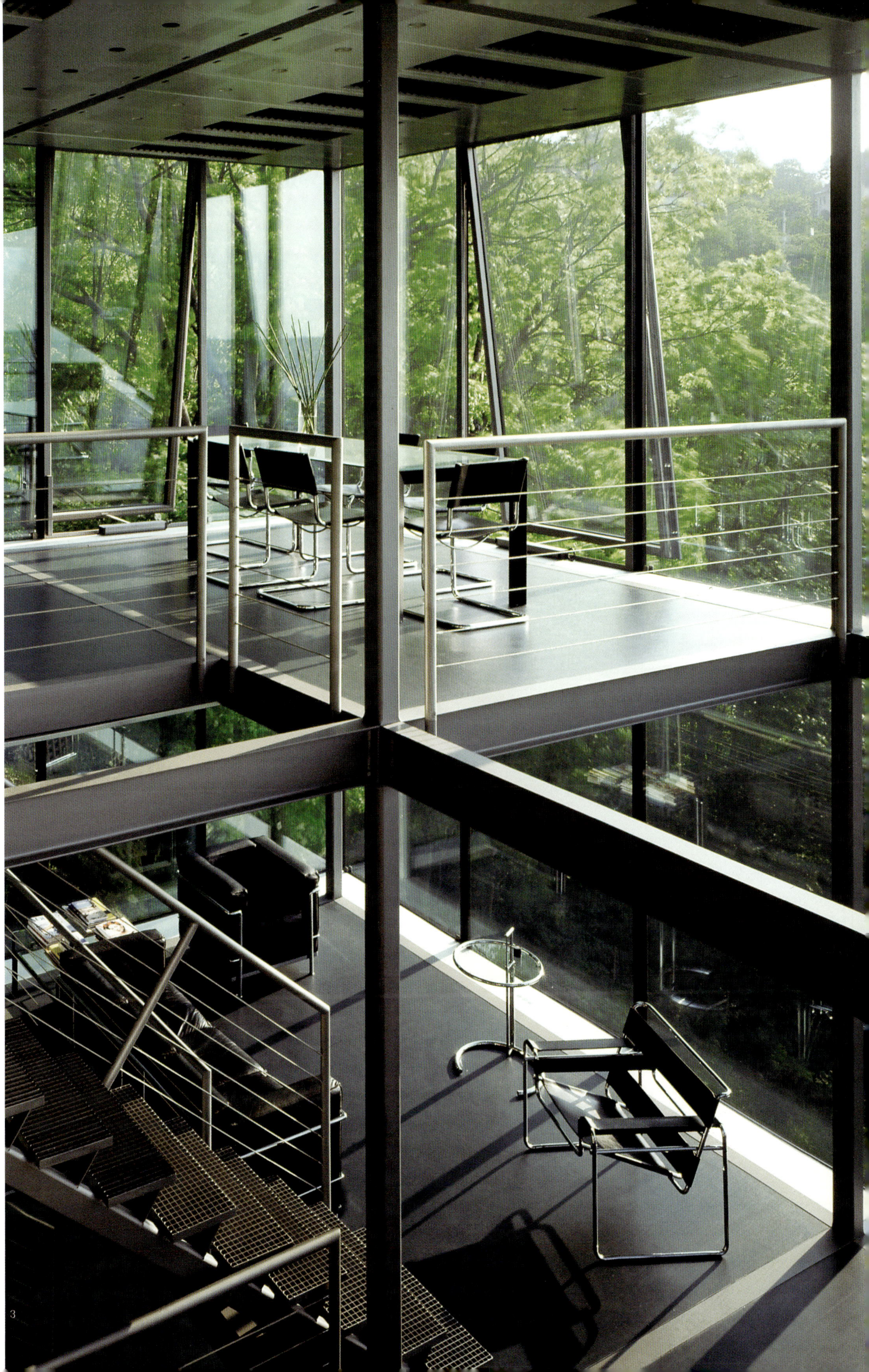

3

WCCB World Conference Center Bonn
WCCB World Conference Center Bonn
Inlandsprojekt Domestic project

Architekten Architects
Architekturbüro Deutschland,
vertreten durch represented by
yes architecture, München
Ruth Berktold, Marion Wicher
Herbert Schwarzmann, Jens Niemann, Jesko Brandi,
Ivo Hermann, Alix Pacher, Heiner Pflugfelder, Steffen
Thauer, Arnold Tisch, Winny Tran

Ingenieure Engineers
Krebs und Kiefer, Karlsruhe
Knippers Helbig, Stuttgart
Inros Lackner AG, Rostock
Schlotfeldt Licht, Berlin

Bauherren Clients
Bundesstadt Bonn
UNCC United Nations Conference Center, Bonn
SMI Hyundai Europe GmbH, Berlin

Typologie Type
Konferenz- und Verwaltungsbau mit Hotel
Conference and administration building with hotel

Standort Location
Bonn

Wettbewerb Competition
2004

Fertigstellung Completion
2009

Brutto-Grundfläche Gross floor area
75 200 m²

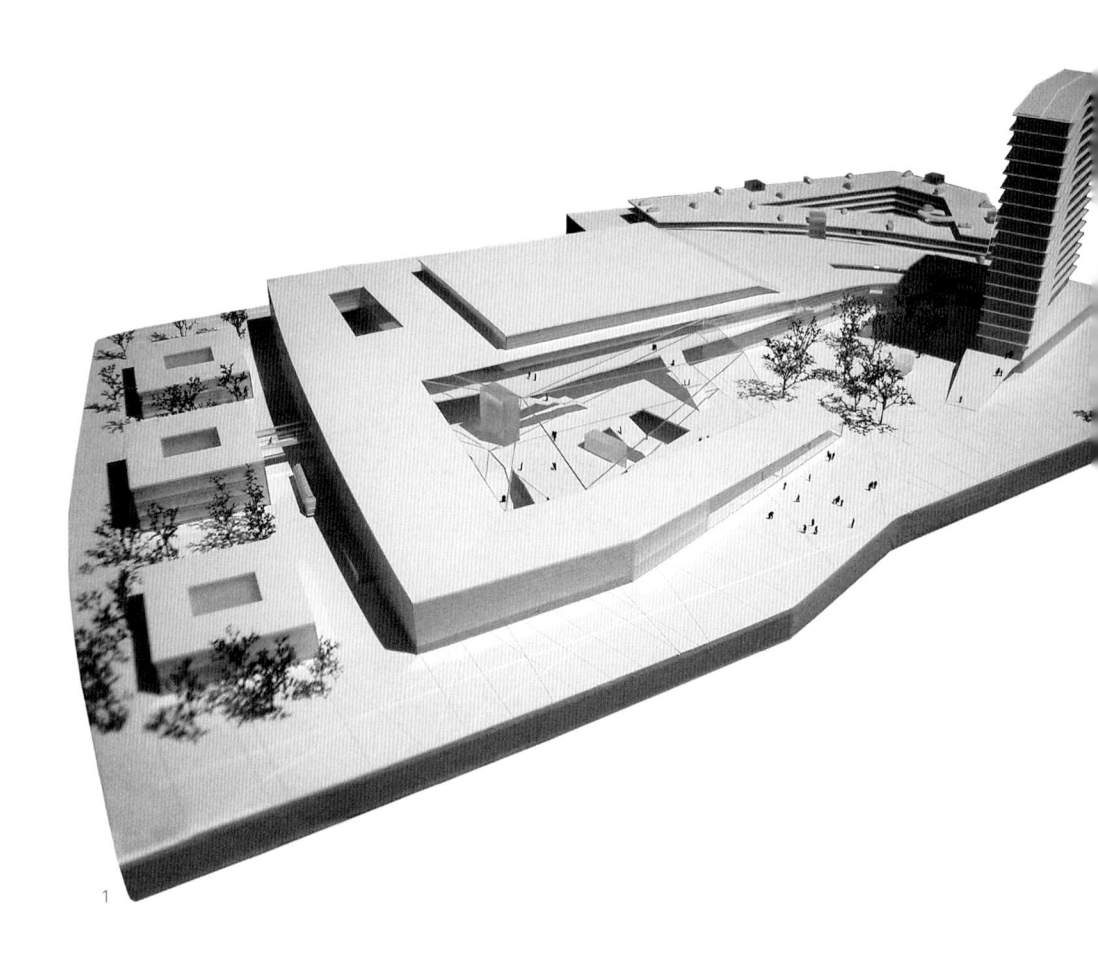

Der ehemalige Bundestag und der neue Plenarsaal bilden die Hauptachse des neuen Kongresszentrums. Zwischen ihnen spannen sich ein repräsentativer städtischer Vorplatz als Haupteingang zu den Zentren und die neue große gläserne Halle, die alle Kongresseinheiten übersichtlich miteinander verbindet und sich zum angrenzenden Park erweitert. Das Gesamtgefüge wird dezent in die Landschaft eingebettet und das Dach ergibt eine gefaltete Landschaft, welche die Massen des WCCB im richtigen Maßstab in Bezug zur alten Bebauung erscheinen lässt. Als einziger hoher Akzent im Stadtgefüge fungiert das 5-Sterne-Hotel, welches weithin sichtbar das Kennzeichen für das WCCB in der Stadt sein wird. Von der großen Haupteingangshalle des Kongresszentrums aus gibt es direkte Zugänge zu allen angegliederten Funktionen und Direktbezug zu Verwaltung, Presse, VIP-Lounges, Kongress-Hotel, Büros und Einkaufsmöglichkeiten. Diese übersichtliche Anordnung ermöglicht eine einfache Orientierung.

The former Bundestag building and the new Plenary Chamber form the end points of the new congress center's main axis. Between them is the urban square, which forms the main access area, and the large new glass hall, which interconnects the various buildings of the congress center and opens to the adjoining park. This hall is inconspicuously embedded in the surroundings, and its roof forms a folded landscape, which makes the WCCB building mass appear at the right scale in relation to the existing buildings. The only conspicuous element is the tall five-star hotel, which will be visible from afar as the WCCB landmark in the city. All of the functional areas—administration, rooms for the press and other media, VIP lounges, congress hotel, offices, and shops—are accessed directly via the main entrance hall of the congress center. This facilitates orientation inside the complex.

1   Modell der Gesamtanlage
    Model of the complex
2 – 3 Blicke in das gläserne Atrium
    Views into the glass hall

Barkow Leibinger Architekten
Berlin

Partner Partners
Frank Barkow
*1957 in Kansas City
Regine Leibinger
*1963 in Stuttgart

Gründung Established
1993 in Berlin

Mitarbeiter Assistants
45

Kontakt Contact
Schillerstrasse 94
10625 Berlin
Deutschland Germany

Tel +49 (0)30 31 57 12 0
Fax +49 (0)30 31 57 12 29

info@barkowleibinger.com
www.barkowleibinger.com

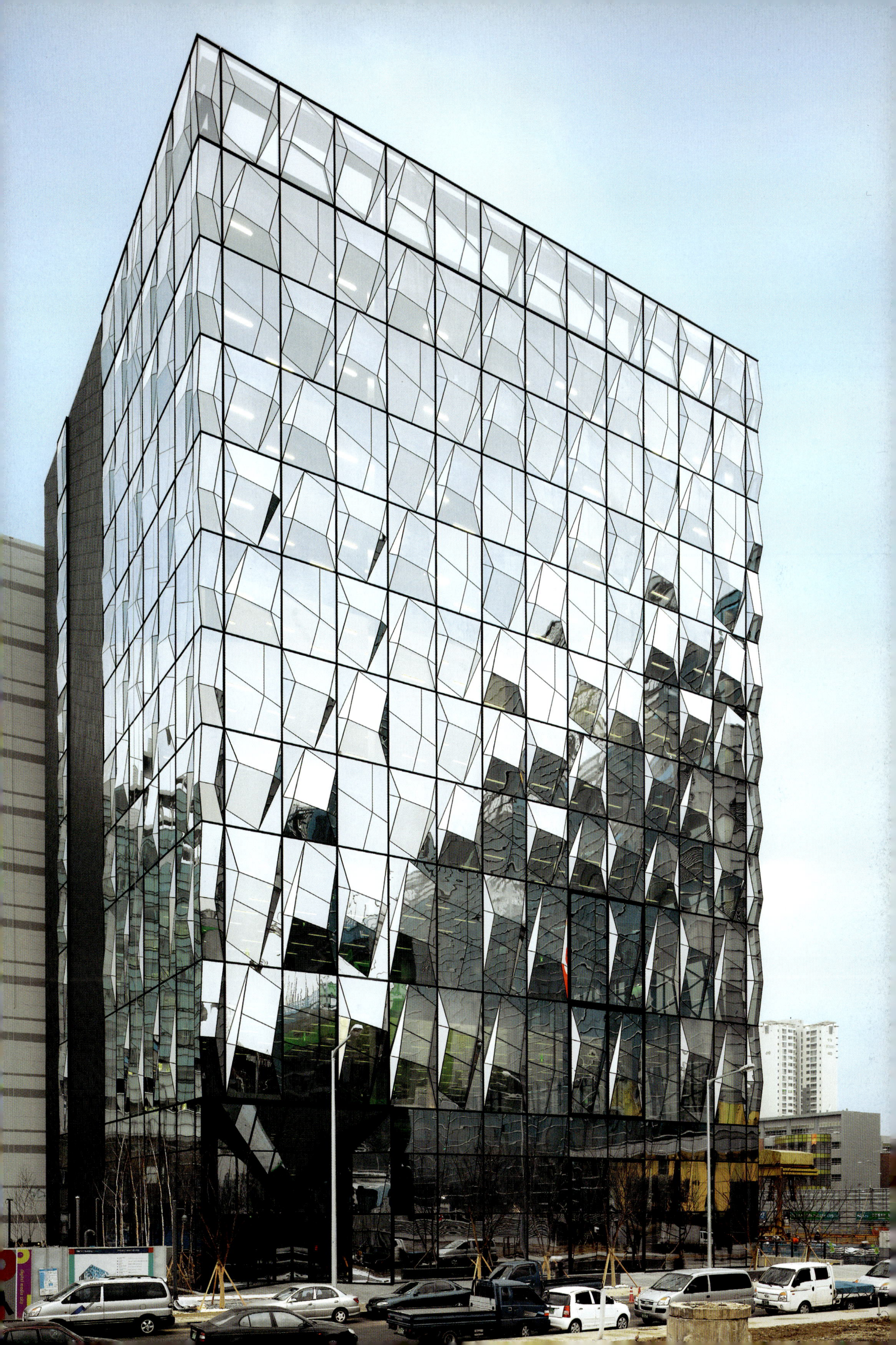

TRUTEC Building
TRUTEC Building
Auslandsprojekt Foreign project

Architekten Architects
Barkow Leibinger Architekten, Berlin
Frank Barkow, Regine Leibinger
Martina Bauer, Matthias Graf von Ballestrem,
Jan-Oliver Kunze, Michael Schmidt, Elke Sparmann

Partner Partners
Chang-Jo Architects, Seoul

Ingenieure Engineers
Schlaich Bergermann und Partner, Stuttgart
Jeon and Lee Partners, Seoul
Arup Facade Engineering, Berlin / Hong Kong
Alutek Ltd., Seoul

Bauherr Client
TKR Sang-Am Ltd., Seoul

Typologie Type
Verwaltungsbau Administration building

Standort Location
Seoul, Südkorea South Korea

Beginn Start
Juli July 2005

Fertigstellung Completion
Dezember December 2006

Brutto-Grundfläche Gross floor area
20 000 m²

Das knapp 55 Meter hohe TRUTEC Building, das im neuen Stadtviertel »Digital Media City« steht, besitzt elf Obergeschosse für Showrooms und Büros. Die auffällige Fassade besteht aus kristallinen Glaselementen, welche den Raum um über 20 Zentimeter erweitern. Die dreidimensional gefaltete Hülle, die Licht zugleich reflektiert und bricht, wird so zu einer abstrakten Oberfläche. Die umgebende Bebauung – welche bei der Planung noch nicht vorhersehbar war – wird auf dieser Projektionsfläche in Pixel zerlegt. Umgekehrt, von innen, bieten die großflächigen Öffnungen weite, von opaken Flächen eingefasste Blicke nach draußen. Der nicht mittig angeordnete Erschließungskern in einer dunklen Gebäudeecke schafft eine für Hochhäuser ungewöhnliche Grundrisskonfiguration und erlaubt es, in den Obergeschossen großflächig zusammenhängende und flexibel nutzbare Büroflächen unterzubringen. Das Erdgeschoss nimmt neben einem stützenfreien Showroom auch eine repräsentative Lobby mit Galerie auf.

The just under 55-meter-high TRUTEC Building in the new Digital Media City contains eleven stories of showrooms and offices aboveground. Its striking façade consists of crystalline glass elements that extend the interior by more than 20 centimeters beyond the building's footprint. As this glass skin is folded, it not only refracts and reflects sunlight, but also mirrors the surrounding buildings (which were not yet envisaged at the time of planning the tower), fragmenting their reflections into pixels. Large clear-glass windows afford views of the surroundings framed by opaque glass elements. The vertical circulation core, off-center in a dark corner of the building, generated a floor space configuration unusual for high-rise buildings and made it possible to create large, flexible, open-plan offices on the upper floors.

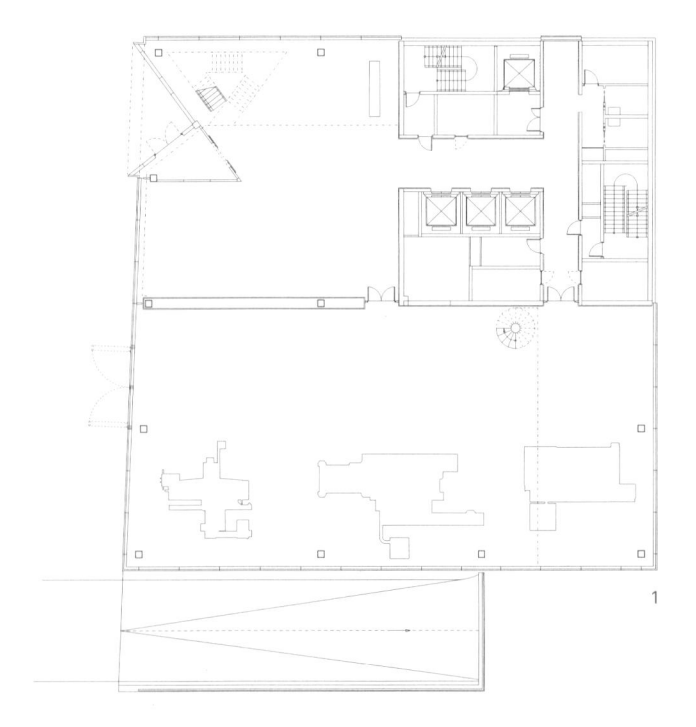

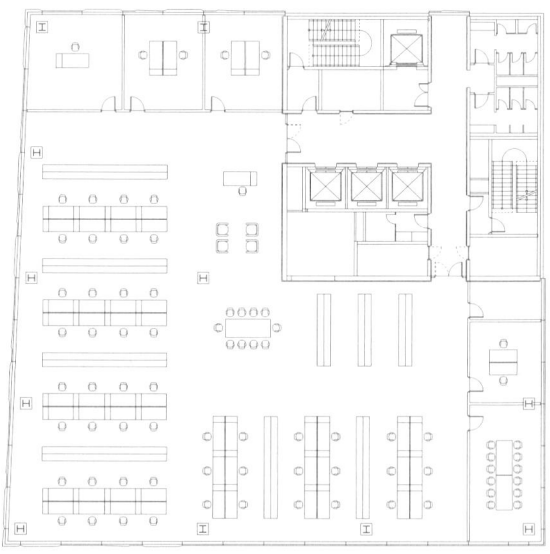

1
2

1 Grundriss Erdgeschoss
  Ground floor plan
2 Grundriss Büroetage
  Office level floor plan
3 Fassade
  Façade
4 Blick in eine Büroetage
  View into an office level
5 Treppenhaus
  Staircase
6 Eingang
  Entrance

Hauptpforte
Main Gate
Inlandsprojekt Domestic project

Architekten Architects
Barkow Leibinger Architekten, Berlin
Frank Barkow, Regine Leibinger
Caspar Hoesch, Carsten Krafft, Meredith Atkinson

Ingenieure Engineers
Werner Sobek, Stuttgart
Arup GmbH, Berlin

Bauherr Client
Trumpf GmbH & Co. KG, Ditzingen

Typologie Type
Verkehrsgebäude Traffic building

Standort Location
Stuttgart

Beginn Start
März March 2006

Fertigstellung Completion
Juli July 2007

Nutzfläche Effective area
130 m²

1 Grundriss
 Floor plan
2–3 Außenansichten
 Exterior views
4 Eingang
 Entrance

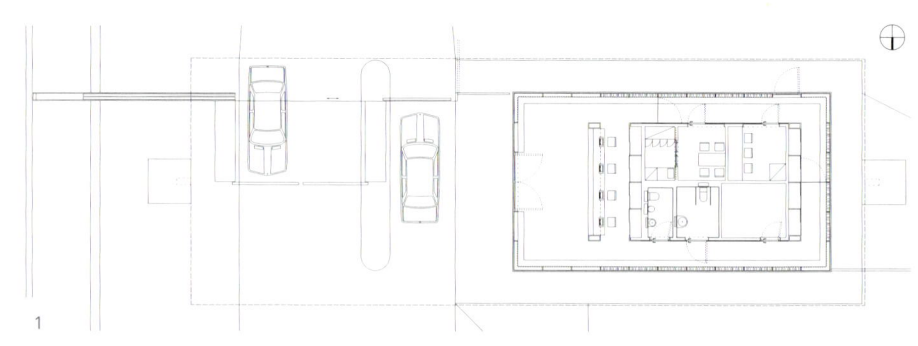

Der Entwurf für das neue Pförtnerhaus des Trumpf-Hauptsitzes war bestimmt von der Idee, das Gebäude mit Hilfe der Laser- und Metallverarbeitungstechnologie des Bauherrn zu entwickeln und auch zu realisieren. Ausgehend von einem gläsernen Baukörper kragt ein schlankes und 32 Meter langes Dach auf einer Länge von 20 Metern aus. Die Dachkonstruktion ist eine knapp 60 Zentimeter hohe, geschweißte Wabenstruktur aus Stahl, in der sich die wechselnden statischen Anforderungen durch unterschiedliche Dichte und Materialstärke abbilden. Der 130 Quadratmeter große Funktionskern beinhaltet neben einer Empfangs- und Wartezone Räume für die Mitarbeiter sowie die Haustechnik. Seine gläserne Hülle besteht aus einer äußeren und einer inneren Fassadenebene, die in einem Abstand von 20 Zentimetern zueinander stehen. Im Bereich des Funktionskerns sind zwischen diesen Ebenen unterschiedlich große Acrylglasröhren aufeinander gestapelt, über die sich die klare innere Struktur des festen Körpers weich nach außen abzeichnet.

The design for the new gatehouse of the Trumpf corporate headquarters was determined by the decision to develop and erect the building using the laser and metalworking technology produced by the client. The glass volume is covered by a filigree roof, 32 meters long and projecting outward over a length of 20 meters. The roof structure is a welded steel honeycomb, just under 60 centimeters thick, which expresses the various load-bearing requirements for the roof sections in varying degrees of material density and thickness. In addition to a reception and waiting area, the 130-square-meter interior accommodates staff and technical service rooms. The gatehouse has a cavity-wall glass façade, with the inner glass wall spaced at 20 centimeters from the outer one. Acrylic tubes of different lengths are stacked inside this cavity wall around the functional core of the gatehouse so that, seen from outside, the clear structure of the core appears as a nebulous mass.

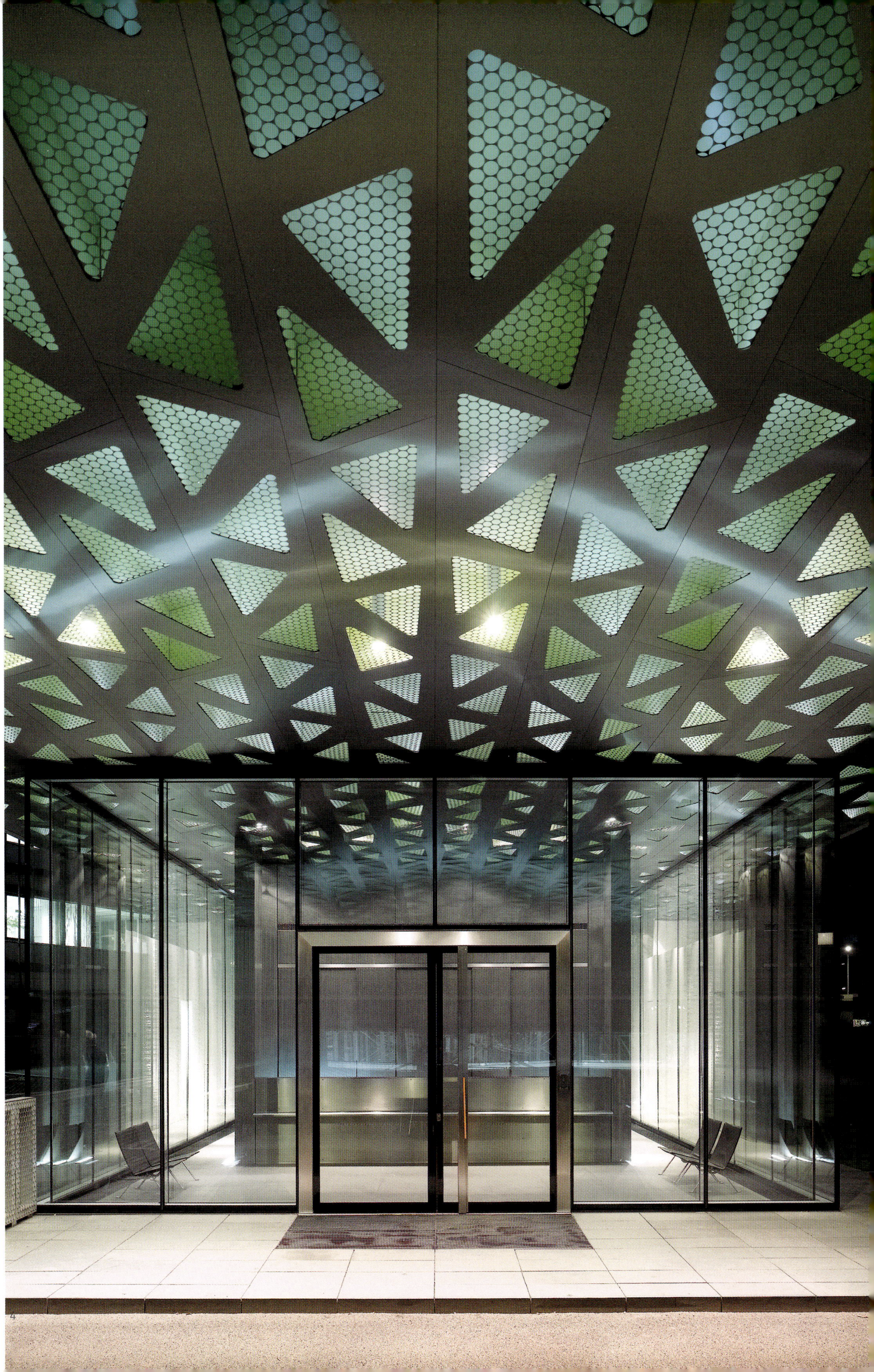

4

Behnisch Architekten
Stuttgart

Partner Partners
Stefan Behnisch
*1957 in Stuttgart
David Cook
*1966 in Manchester
Martin Haas
*1967 in Waldshut

Gründung Established
1989 in Stuttgart

Mitarbeiter Assistants
80

Kontakt Contact
Rotebühlstrasse 163A
70197 Stuttgart
Deutschland Germany

Tel +49 (0)711 60 77 20
Fax +49 (0)711 60 77 29 9

buero@behnisch.com
www.behnisch.com

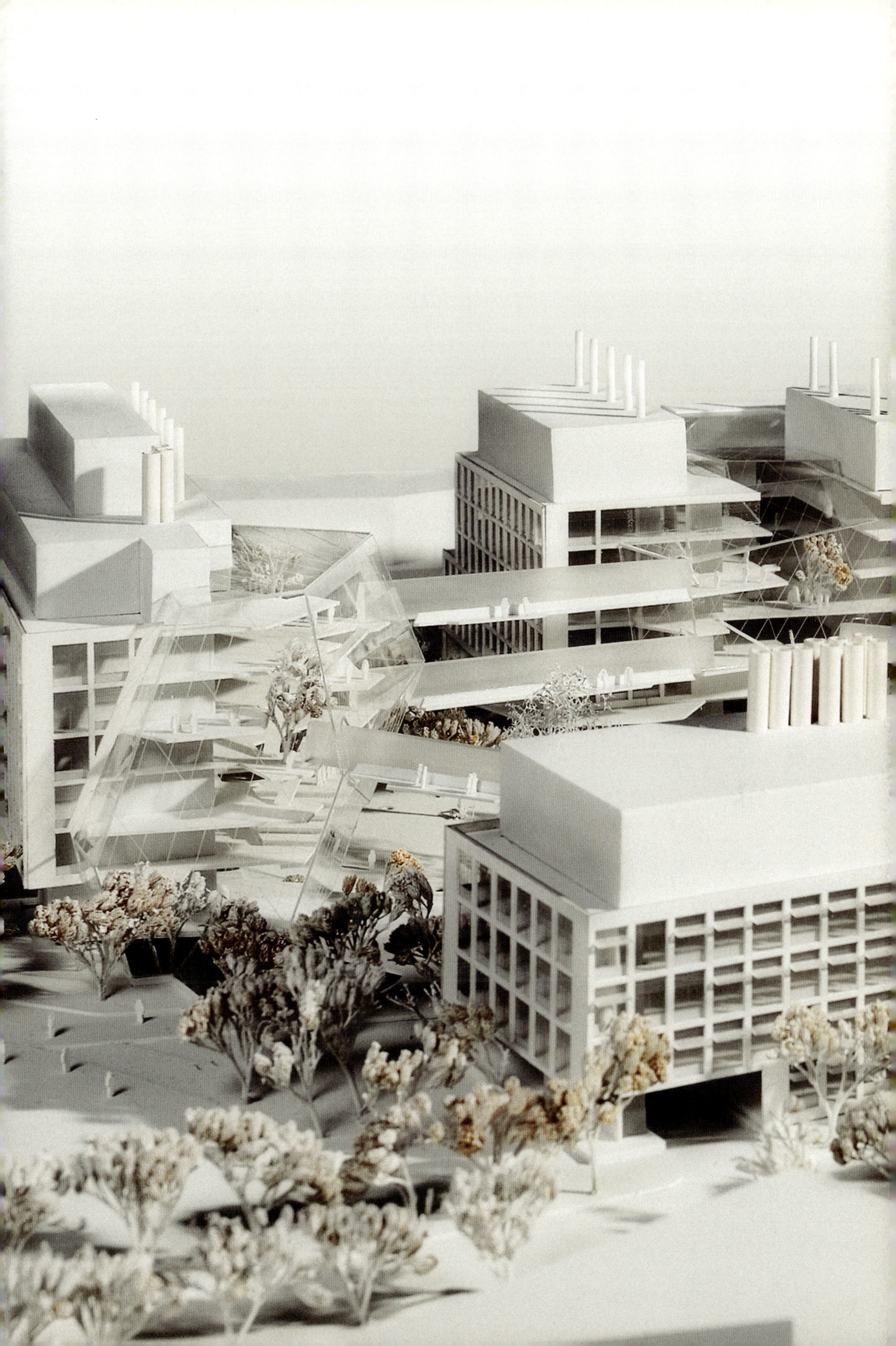

Harvard's Allston Science Complex
Harvard's Allston Science Complex
Auslandsprojekt Foreign project

Architekten Architects
Behnisch Architekten, Stuttgart
Stefan Behnisch, David Cook, Martin Haas
für for
Behnisch Studio East Inc., Boston
Stefan Behnisch, Christof Jantzen

Projektpartner Project Partner
Stefan Rappold

Partner Partners
Payette Associates Inc., Boston

Ingenieure Engineers
Buro Happold Consulting Engineers, Los Angeles / New York
Transsolar KlimaEngineering, Stuttgart
LichtLabor Bartenbach, Aldrans
Vanderweil Engineers LLP, Boston

Bauherr Client
Allston Development Group, Boston

Typologie Type
Hochschulbau University building

Standort Location
Boston (MA), USA

Wettbewerb Competition
2006

Fertigstellung Completion
2011

Brutto-Grundfläche Gross floor area
110 000 m²

Ziel der Universität Harvard ist die Schaffung eines nachhaltigen Campus mit exzellenten Bedingungen für die interdisziplinäre Forschung und Lehre. Der neue Science-Complex ist der erste Schritt eines Umwandlungsprozesses kaum noch genutzter Industriegebiete in einen lebendigen Campus in Allston. Die Anlage des Komplexes hat starke Bezüge zum traditionellen Harvard-Campus mit seiner Abfolge von grünen Höfen, den sogenannten Yards, Rasenflächen, Plätzen und Parks, jedoch in zeitgemäßer Interpretation. Gebäude 1 ist als zentrale Schnittstelle für das Forschungspersonal, Fakultätsmitarbeiter, Studenten und Anwohner konzipiert. Wintergärten mit öffentlichen Bereichen übernehmen wichtige Funktionen im Rahmen des Klimakonzepts und bieten ein innovatives Umfeld, das von Harvards Tradition als Stätte des Wissens, der Forschung auf höchstem Niveau und seinen besonderen Höfen geprägt wird. Während Harvard von Ziegelmauern oder Zäunen mit Pforten umschlossen ist, wird die Einfassung des neuen Komplexes durchlässiger, um die Verbindung zum Stadtteil Allston zu stärken.

Harvard University intended to create a sustainable campus that would offer excellent conditions for interdisciplinary academic research and teaching. The new science complex represents the first step toward this goal, to be achieved by transforming an underused industrial estate in Allston into a vibrant university campus. The design of the complex shows strong references to the traditional Harvard campus, with its series of green quadrangles called yards, lawns, squares, and parks, but in an up-to-date interpretation. Building 1 has been conceived as the central interface for research staff, faculty members, students, and residents. Conservatories containing public spaces play an important role in the air-conditioning concept for the complex and form an innovative environment marked by the yards and the university's traditional reputation as a place of academic learning and research at the highest level.

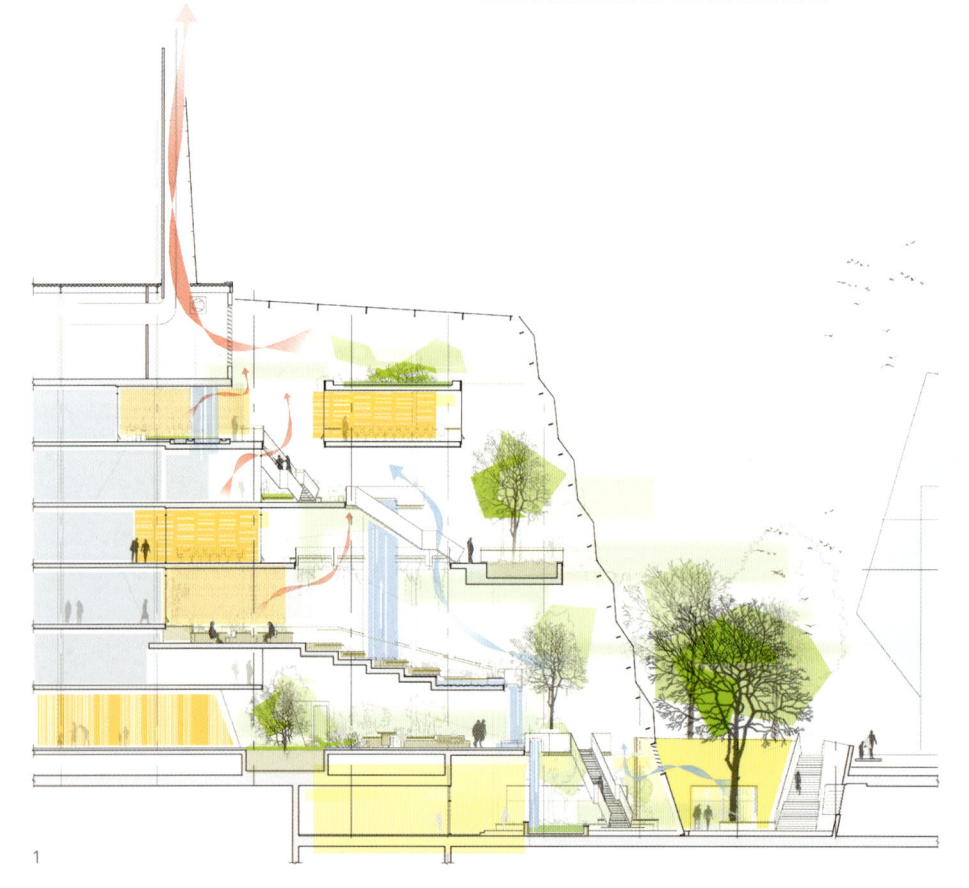

1 Schnitt Wintergarten
  Winter garden section
2 Ansicht Stadium Way
  Stadium Way elevation
3 Grundriss Ebene 1
  Level 1 floor plan

2

3

»Haus im Haus« der Handelskammer Hamburg
"House within a House" of the Hamburg Chamber of Commerce
Inlandsprojekt Domestic project

Architekten Architects
Behnisch Architekten, Stuttgart
(bis until 2005 Behnisch, Behnisch & Partner)
Stefan Behnisch, Martin Haas, David Cook,
Katja Knaus

Ingenieure Engineers
Wetzel & von Seht, Hamburg
TPlan, Berlin
Nimbus Design, Stuttgart
Brandi Licht, Hamburg

Bauherr Client
Handelskammer Hamburg
Hamburg Chamber of Commerce

Typologie Type
Innenausbau
Interior construction

Standort Location
Hamburg

Wettbewerb Competition
2003

Fertigstellung Completion
März March 2007

Nutzfläche Effective area
1 000 m²

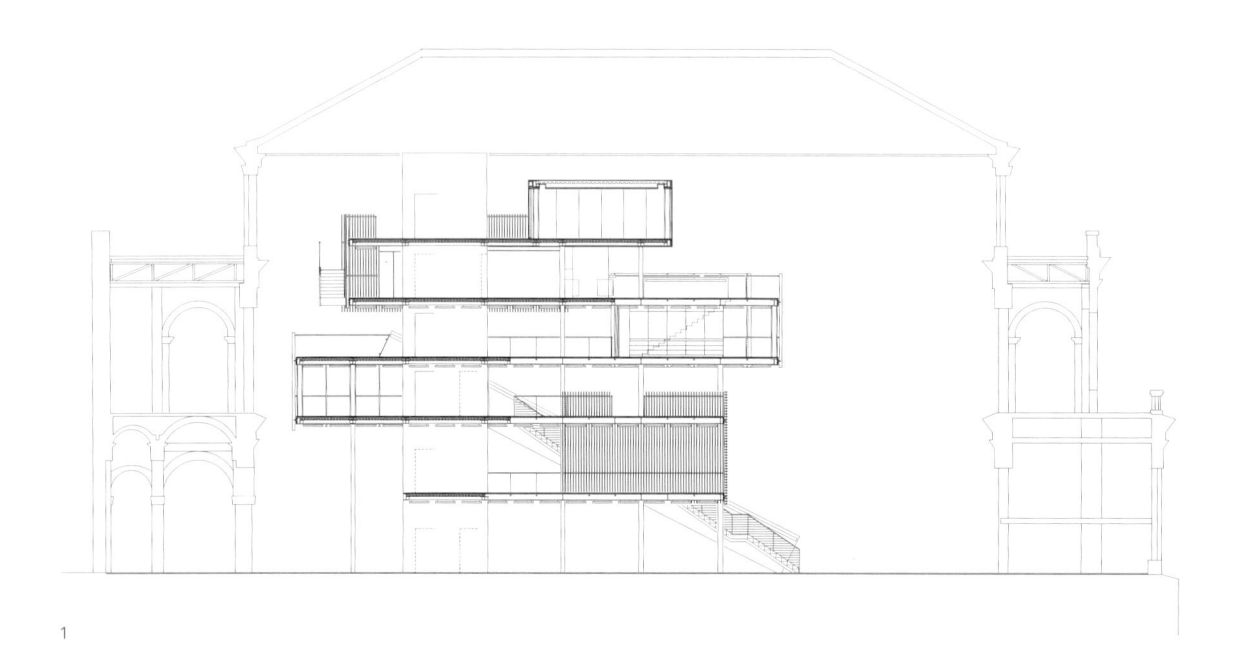

1

In die nicht mehr genutzte ehemalige Börsenhalle der Handelskammer Hamburg wurde unter Beachtung des Denkmalschutzes und der vorhandenen Bausubstanz ein neuer Baukörper als »Haus im Haus« eingefügt, der, über fünf Etagen verteilt, neue Nutzungen beherbergt und den Charakter des Gebäudes als Treffpunkt der Hamburger Wirtschaft in zeitgemäßer Form zum Ausdruck bringt. Immateriell entwickelt sich die neue Struktur in Scheiben und Ebenen, bewusst mit dem steinernen, schweren Erscheinungsbild der alten Halle kontrastierend. Transluzente Bauteile und Spiegellamellen schaffen Trompe-l'Œil-Effekte, ungewohnte Dimensionen und teils unwirklich wirkende, flirrende Eindrücke. Der leichte Charakter der neuen Struktur wird betont und gefördert durch das speziell entwickelte LED-Leuchtsystem. Das Licht passt sich den Arbeits- und Nutzungsanforderungen an und kann so eingestellt werden, dass es die Räume wie gleitende Wolken in gedämpftes Licht taucht oder umgekehrt zum Strahlen bringt.

In compliance with the requirements of monument conservation and respecting the structure and architecture of the Hamburg Chamber of Commerce's disused former stock exchange hall, a new five-story building was built into the old hall. The new structure accommodates new functions and expresses the role and character of this meeting place of Hamburg's business and industrial world in contemporary form. The walls and floor slabs of the new structure appear filigree, almost immaterial, in stark contrast to the massive stone walls of the historical hall. Translucent components and polished, reflecting segments create trompe l'oeil effects so that the spaces seem to have unusual dimensions and appear in a kind of glimmering surreality. The lightness of the new "house within a house" is enhanced by the custom-designed LED lighting system, which adapts light intensities to various requirements, so that rooms can be dimly lit—as if through clouds—or brightly, as if under a brilliant sun.

1 Schnitt
  Section
2 Innenraum
  Interior space
3 Restaurant Ebene 4
  Restaurant level 4
4 Gesamtansicht
  General view
5 Ebene 1
  Level 1

115

BeL
Köln Cologne

Partner Partners
Anne-Julchen Bernhardt
*1971 in Köln
Jörg Leeser
*1967 in Essen

Gründung Established
2000 in Köln

Mitarbeiter Assistants
3

Kontakt Contact
Kaiser-Wilhelm-Ring 2–4
50672 Köln
Deutschland Germany

Tel   +49 (0)221 13 05 65 60
Fax   +49 (0)221 13 05 65 62

info@bel.cx
www.bel.cx

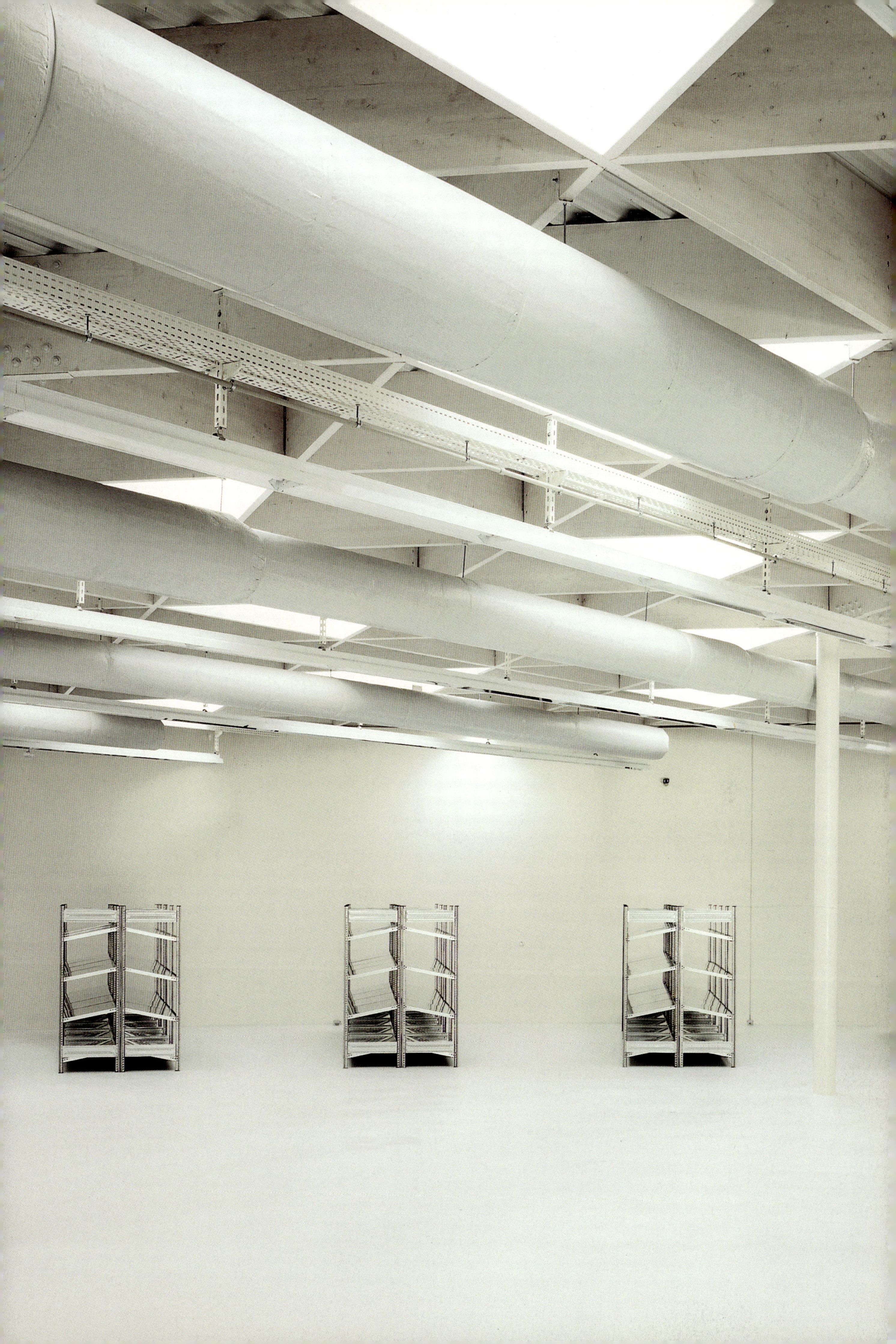

FRABA Produktionshalle
FRABA Production Hall
Auslandsprojekt Foreign project

Architekten Architects
BeL, Köln Cologne
Anne-Julchen Bernhardt, Jörg Leeser
Eveline Jürgens

Partner Partners
A.W. Polak, Gliwice

Ingenieure Engineers
Arup, Warschau Warsaw

Bauherr Client
FRABA AG, Conistics, Köln Cologne / Słubice

Typologie Type
Industriebau Industrial building

Standort Location
Słubice, Polen Poland

Beginn Start
Januar January 2005

Fertigstellung Completion
Oktober October 2006

Brutto-Grundfläche Gross floor area
2 100 m²

Die Produktionshalle für die Kölner Firma FRABA, ein Hersteller von Sensoren für die Automatisierungsindustrie, stellt einen Prototyp für maximal einhundert Mitarbeiter dar. Es ging neben dem Entwurf des Gebäudes auch darum, die Grundlagen des architektonischen Erscheinungsbildes der Firma zu definieren. Das Entwurfskonzept setzt die Unternehmensprinzipien – flache Hierarchien, Transparenz und Flexibilität – konsequent um. Der kreisförmige Grundriss und das dreieckige Stützenraster erlauben unterschiedliche Konfigurationen für die Montage, welche nur auf Tischen, Regalen und Rollwagen stattfindet. Über vorgefertigte Lichtkuppeln aus Polycarbonat, die 14 Prozent der Dachfläche ausmachen, wird die Halle gleichmäßig mit Tageslicht versorgt. Die einzigen Räume, die abgetrennt sein müssen – Duschen, WCs, Stillraum – sind als Zylinder eingestellt. Nur die Farbigkeit der Fassade, welche mit aluminiumkaschierten Bitumenbahnen verkleidet wurde, weicht vom reinen Weiß des Innenraums ab.

The production hall for FRABA, a Cologne manufacturer of sensors for industrial automation systems, is a prototype designed for a maximum of one hundred workers. The brief called for the design not only of a building, but also of the manufacturer's architectural corporate identity. The design consistently translated the company's operational principles—flat hierarchies, transparency, and flexibility—into architectural structure. The circular floor plan and triangular column grid make it possible to create differently configured areas for the assembly of the sensors, which is carried out exclusively at tables, on shelves, and on trolleys. The hall is evenly and naturally lit via prefabricated polycarbonate skylight domes, which cover 14 percent of the total roof surface. The only rooms that had to be enclosed—showers, toilets, and a room for breast-feeding—were inserted as cylinders. Only the color of the façade, which was clad with aluminum sheeting over bituminous felting, is differentiated from the purely white interior.

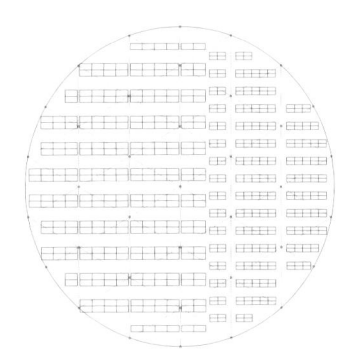

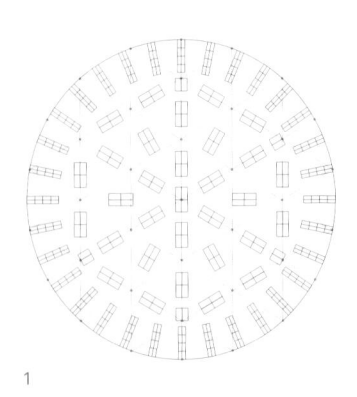

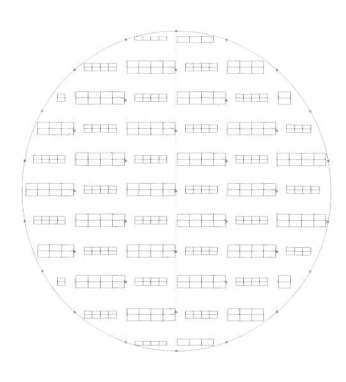

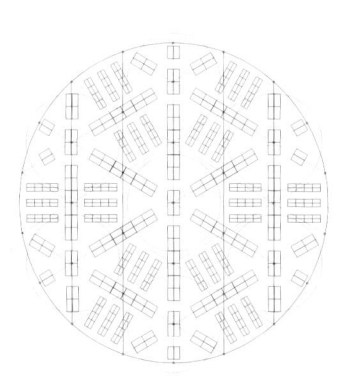

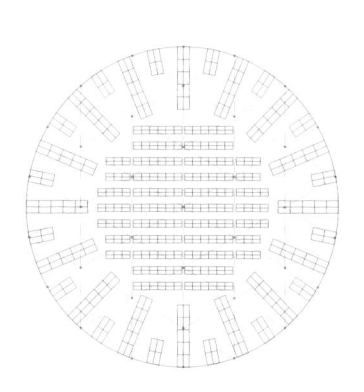

1

1 Layoutvarianten
  Layout variations
2 Außenansicht
  Exterior view
3 Blick durch das einzige Fenster
  in den Innenraum
  View through the only window
  into the interior space
4 Zylinder
  Cylinder
5–6 Produktionsraum
  Production space

119

Kaufhaus Breuer
Breuer Department Store
Inlandsprojekt Domestic project

Architekten Architects
BeL, Köln Cologne
Anne-Julchen Bernhardt, Jörg Leeser
Eveline Jürgens, Thomas Schneider

Ingenieure Engineers
Jürgen Bernhardt, Köln Cologne
energieplan, Köln Cologne

Bauherren Clients
Anna Maria und and Andrea Breuer

Typologie Type
Geschäfts- und Wohnungsbau
Residential and commercial building

Standort Location
Eschweiler

Beginn Start
April 2005

Fertigstellung Completion
Mai May 2006

Nutzfläche Effective area
1 465 m²

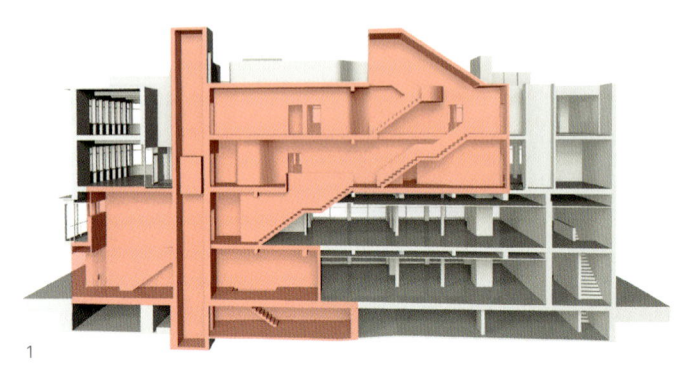

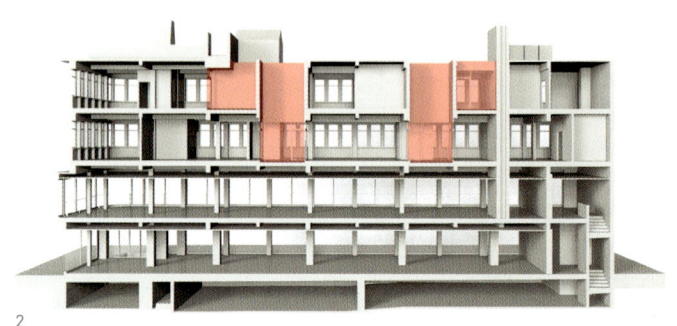

Nach dem Umbau des 1950er-Jahre-Kaufhauses in ein modernes Wohn- und Geschäftshaus befinden sich nur noch im Erdgeschoss Einzelhandelsflächen. Im ersten Obergeschoss liegt ein öffentlicher Aufenthaltsraum für die Betreuung von Kindern einkaufender Eltern durch Senioren, der auch als Büro- oder Praxisfläche umgenutzt werden kann. Die Zielgruppe für die zwei Wohngeschosse sind ältere und gehbehinderte Menschen, die in der Stadt leben und die Vorteile des barrierefreien Wohnens ohne fremde Hilfe genießen wollen. Im zweiten und dritten Obergeschoss haben acht Wohnungen Platz, die als Wohngemeinschaft oder einzeln genutzt werden können. Um die Offenheit des ehemaligen Kaufhauses zu erhalten, sind die Grundrisse nur durch einen eingestellten Sanitärkern und bewegliche Wandelemente gegliedert. Jede Wohnung hat einen eigenen, vollverglasten Innenhof. Das energetisch notwendige Wärmedämmverbundsystem beinhaltet einen neu entwickelten Lichtputz, der mit Hilfe von Glasperlen auf Sonnenlicht reagiert.

After the conversion of the 1950s department store into a modern apartment and commercial building, only the ground floor is still occupied by retail spaces. On the second floor, there is a public lounge where elderly people look after small children while their parents go shopping. This can also be converted into an office suite or a doctor's or dentist's office. The target group for the two residential floors is elderly people and people with walking disabilities who already live in the city and wish to enjoy the advantages of living "barrier free" without the help of strangers. The third and fourth floors accommodate eight apartments, which may be used by single people or shared by several tenants. To preserve the open-plan organization of the former department store, the apartment floor plans were subdivided only by means of sanitary cores and movable partitions. Every flat has its own fully glazed little patio. The composite façade system, required for reasons of thermal insulation, includes a newly developed plaster that reflects sunlight due to a glass-bead aggregate.

1 Schnitt durch das Treppenhaus
  Section through the staircase
2 Schnitt durch die Innenhöfe
  Section through the patios
3 Wohnraum mit gerundeter Ecke
  Living room with rounded corner
4 Außenansicht
  Exterior view
5 Treppenhaus
  Staircase
6 Wohnraum mit privatem Patio
  Living room with private patio

Carsten Roth Architekt
Hamburg

Inhaber Owner
Carsten Roth
*1958 in Hamburg

Gründung Established
1987 in Hamburg

Mitarbeiter Assistants
26

Kontakt Contact
Rentzelstrasse 10 B
20146 Hamburg
Deutschland Germany

Tel +49 (0)40 41 17 03 0
Fax +49 (0)40 41 17 03 30

info@carstenroth.com
www.carstenroth.com

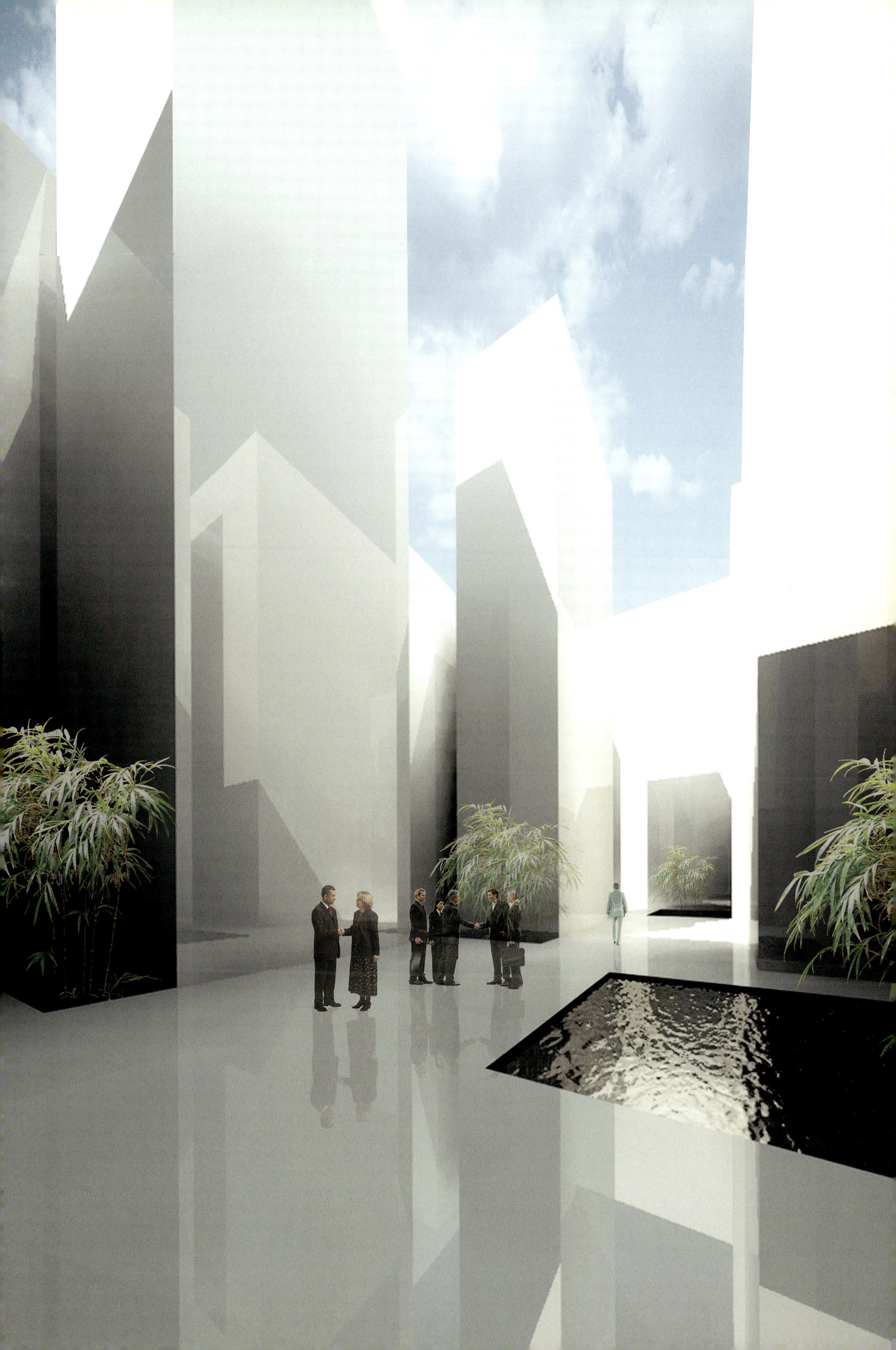

Hauptsitz Volksbank AG-Gruppe
Volksbank AG Group Headquarters
Auslandsprojekt Foreign project

Architekten Architects
Carsten Roth International GmbH, Hamburg
Carsten Roth
Christine Andreae, Jens Brockmann, Claudia Eckl, Carsten Gaebler, Tim Kettler, Markus Lager, Antje Lange, Thomas Maiß, Cord Marquardt, Mark Schiebler, Marie-Louise Seifert

Ingenieure Engineers
Bollinger + Grohmann, Frankfurt am Main
Arup GmbH, Berlin
RMN Ridder Meyn Nuckel, Norderstedt
Dipl.-Ing. Walter Prause, Wien

Bauherr Client
Volksbank AG-Gruppe, Wien Vienna

Typologie Type
Verwaltungsbau Administration building

Standort Location
Wien, Österreich Vienna, Austria

Beginn Start
2006

Fertigstellung Completion
2009/10

Brutto-Grundfläche Gross floor area
25 000 m²

Der Neubau des Hauptsitzes der Volksbank AG-Gruppe liegt in der Wiener Altstadt und bewegt sich daher im Spannungsfeld zwischen dem bewahrenden Anspruch des Weltkulturerbes und dem Selbstverständnis einer erfolgreichen Volksbank. Nach außen wird diskrete Zurückhaltung geübt, während sich im Inneren die moderne Bank zeigt. Zwei u-förmige Baukörper – Alt- und Neubau sind durch eine Fuge getrennt – umschließen in ihrer Mitte einen großzügigen Luftraum. Die beiden Baukörper werden im Dachgeschoss vereint, das tagsüber fast unsichtbar ist, jedoch bei Nacht als heller Ring über dem Gebäude zu schweben scheint. Während der Eingang über einen Sockel ins Erdgeschoss mit Kassenraum und Konferenzbereich führt, befindet sich darüber ein Innenhof. Er ist mit mehreren Türmen, einer Skyline ähnlich, gestaltet und bietet Raum für Versammlungen oder Kulturereignisse. Um dieses Atrium werden fast ausschließlich einhüftige Büros angeordnet, zwischen denen die turmartigen Konferenz- und sonstigen Serviceräume sowie Treppenhäuser und Aufzüge liegen.

The new headquarters of the Volksbank AG Group is located in Vienna's historic city center and therefore had to strike a balance between the contradicting interests of respecting a World Heritage site and expressing the self-concept of a successful people's bank. On the outside, the building exercises modest restraint, while inside it presents itself as a modern bank. The two U-shaped building volumes (i.e., the old and the new buildings, separated by a joint) surround a large airspace. The two buildings are joined by the new top floor, which by day is almost invisible, but by night seems to float above the building like a shining wreath. The entrance area raised on a plinth leads to the ground-floor counter hall and conference rooms. An atrium was created on top of these spaces. It is filled with a number of towering structures, similar to a city skyline, and offers space for meetings or cultural functions. The offices, to one side of a corridor, have been arranged around the atrium. Tower-like conference and other service rooms, as well as the stairwells and elevators, are set in between.

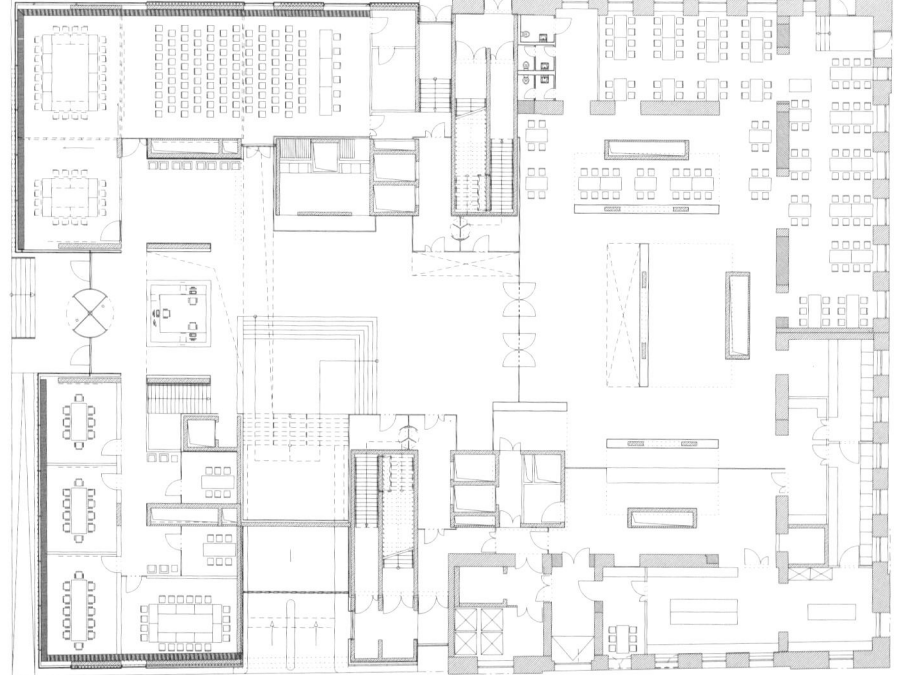

1 Grundriss Erdgeschoss
  Ground floor plan
2 Haupteingang
  Main entrance
3 Prinzipschnitt
  Basic section
4 Außenansicht
  Exterior view

Firmensitz Norddeutsche Vermögen Rolandsbrücke
Corporate Head Office Norddeutsche Vermögen Rolandsbrücke
Inlandsprojekt Domestic project

Architekten Architects
Carsten Roth Architekt, Hamburg
Carsten Roth
Christine Andreae, Julian Hillenkamp, Antje Lange,
Katja Ossmann, Bernd Rickert, Christoph Roselius,
Bengt Stiller

Ingenieure Engineers
Bollinger + Grohmann, Frankfurt am Main
RMN Ridder Meyn Nuckel, Norderstedt
BBI, Hamburg
Taubert und Ruhe, Halstenbek

Bauherr Client
Bernd Kortüm, Hamburg

Typologie Type
Verwaltungsbau
Administration building

Standort Location
Hamburg

Beginn Start
Februar February 2002

Fertigstellung Completion
März March 2005

Brutto-Grundfläche Gross floor area
4 500 m²

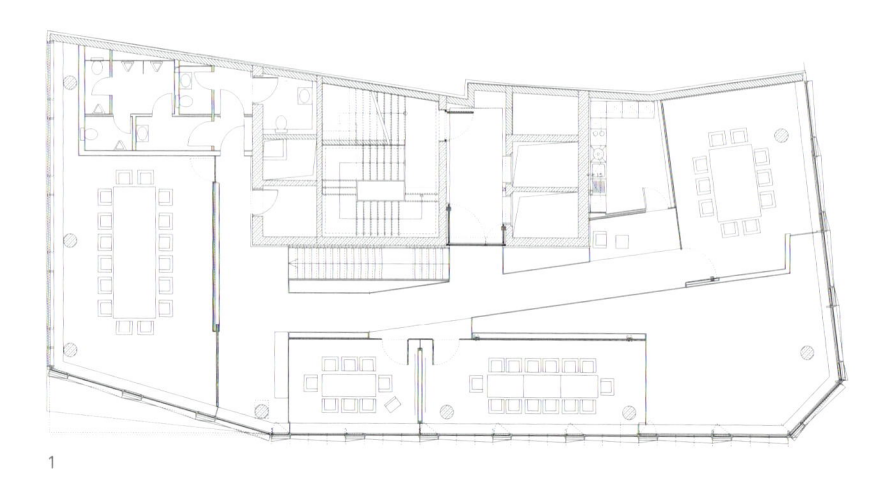

1 Grundriss 1. Obergeschoss
  Second floor plan
2 Fassade
  Façade
3 Foyer
  Foyer
4 Außenansicht
  Exterior view

Der Neubau des Firmensitzes der Norddeutschen Vermögen musste mit den unterschiedlichen angrenzenden Baumassen, den divergierenden Höhen und heterogenen Baustilen seines Umfeldes umgehen. Das Gebäude erreicht dies durch seine Höhenentwicklung und die ganz eigene skulpturale Form und Fassade. Vor- und Rücksprünge, die Ausformung der Obergeschosse und Zitate der horizontalen und vertikalen Linien der Nachbarbebauung fügen den Baukörper in die Umgebung ein. Trotz ihrer eindeutig modernen Grundhaltung greift die Fassade durch ihre Komplexität und Plastizität Aspekte gründerzeitlicher Fassaden auf und wirkt so in dem heterogenen Umfeld vermittelnd. Die Lobby ist das Bindeglied zwischen Außen- und Innenraum, indem sie sich großzügig zum Straßenraum öffnet und durch Lufträume vertikale Sichtbezüge in das erste Obergeschoss herstellt. Die Vertikalität des Gebäudes wird somit auch im Inneren spürbar. Es entstehen großzügige und sich immer wieder verändernde Raumsituationen.

The new head office for Norddeutsche Vermögen had to mediate between the neighboring buildings of different heights and heterogeneous design styles. This was achieved by staggering the building mass in terms of height and by giving it an original sculptural form and façade. Stepped-back and projecting sections, the configuration of the upper stories and quotes from the horizontal and vertical lines integrate the new structure into its surroundings. Despite its clearly modern design, due to its complex sculptural quality, the façade is reminiscent of turn-of-the-century façades and thus refers to neighboring buildings. The lobby forms the link between exterior and interior as it opens wide to the street and is visually linked to the second floor by its void. This makes the verticality of the building perceivable inside as well. Walking through the spacious interiors, one experiences constantly changing spatial situations.

Repräsentative
Büroflächen
zu vermieten

Telefon
480 580

Gerber Architekten
Dortmund / Hamburg

Inhaber Owner
Eckhard Gerber
*1938 in Oberhain

Gründung Established
1966 in Deutschland Germany

Mitarbeiter Assistants
55

Kontakt Contact
Tönnishof
44149 Dortmund
Deutschland Germany

Tel +49 (0)231 90 65 0
Fax +49 (0)231 90 65 11 1

kontakt@gerberarchitekten.de
www.gerberarchitekten.de

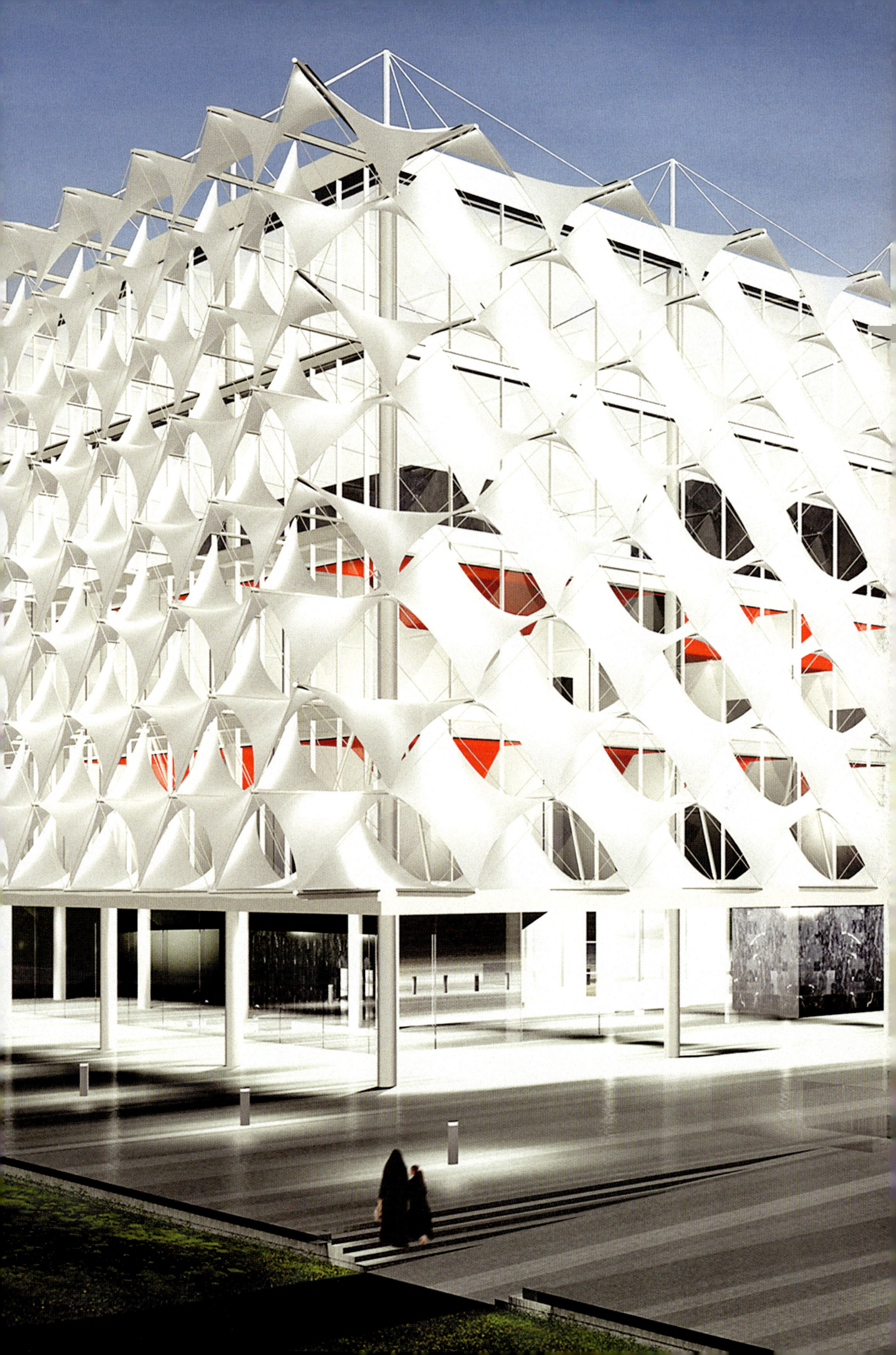

King Fahad Nationalbibliothek
King Fahad National Library
Auslandsprojekt Foreign project

Architekten Architects
Gerber Architekten, Dortmund
Eckhard Gerber
Britta Alker, Caroline Balkenhol, Olaf Ballerstedt, Sabine Diegritz, Simone Drechsler, Tiran K. Driver, Nicola Gerber, Markus Görtz, Thomas Helms, René Koblank, Nils Kummer, Marita Langen, Stefan Lemke, Thomas Lücking, Beate Mack, Till Müller, Ulrich Scheinhardt, Michael Schlegel, Henrike Schlinke, Jörg Schoeneweiß, Kerstin Tulke

Ingenieure Engineers
Bollinger+Grohmann, Frankfurt am Main
DS-Plan, Stuttgart
Saudi Consulting Services, Riad
Graner + Partner Ingenieure, Bergisch-Gladbach
Wacker Ingenieure, Birkenfeld

Bauherr Client
Königreich Saudi-Arabien,
 vertreten durch represented by
Arriyadh Development Authority

Typologie Type
Kulturbau Cultural building

Standort Location
Riad, Saudi-Arabien Riyadh, Saudi Arabia

Wettbewerb Competition
2002

Fertigstellung Completion
2009

Brutto-Grundfläche Gross floor area
68 500 m²

Der Neubau der King Fahad Nationalbibliothek umhüllt die bestehende Siebzigerjahre-Bibliothek und hebt sich deutlich von der heterogenen Stadtlandschaft Riads ab. Inmitten eines urbanen Parks erscheint die neue Bibliothek offen und transparent und ist trotz ihrer Größe auf grazile Art mit dem Stadtraum verwoben. Auf dem Flachdach des Altbaus befindet sich der Lesesaal, im Inneren liegen die Büchermagazine. Die vorhandene Kuppel wird aus Stahl und Glas neu gestaltet und überragt das neue Dach, welches die Innenhöfe und den Lesesaal überdeckt. Eine unterhalb des Daches gespannte weiße Membran filtert das Tageslicht und versorgt alle Räume gleichmäßig mit blendfreiem Licht. Von den übrigen Nutzungen getrennt und separat zugänglich ist die Bibliothek der Frauen im ersten Obergeschoss des neuen Südwestflügels untergebracht. Die weißen Membranflächen vor den Obergeschossfassaden dienen als Sonnenschutz und interpretieren die arabische Tradition der Zeltstrukturen auf moderne Art und Weise.

The new King Fahad National Library encloses the old library building built in the 1970s and stands out clearly from Riyadh's heterogeneous urban fabric. Surrounded by a park, the new library appears open and transparent. Despite its size, it is not overbearing, but forms an integral part of the city. The reading room is housed on top of the flat roof of the old building, which contains the closed stack. The old roof dome was redesigned in steel and glass. It towers over the new, flat roof, which covers a number of interior courtyards and the new reading room. White membranes—put up in front of the upper-floor façades and underneath the flat roof—filter the bright sunlight so that all the interior spaces are lit evenly and are free of glare. Not only do they serve as sun blinds, they also represent a contemporary reinterpretation of the traditional Arabic tent. The women's library on the second floor of the new southwest wing is separated from the rest of the library and also has a separate entrance.

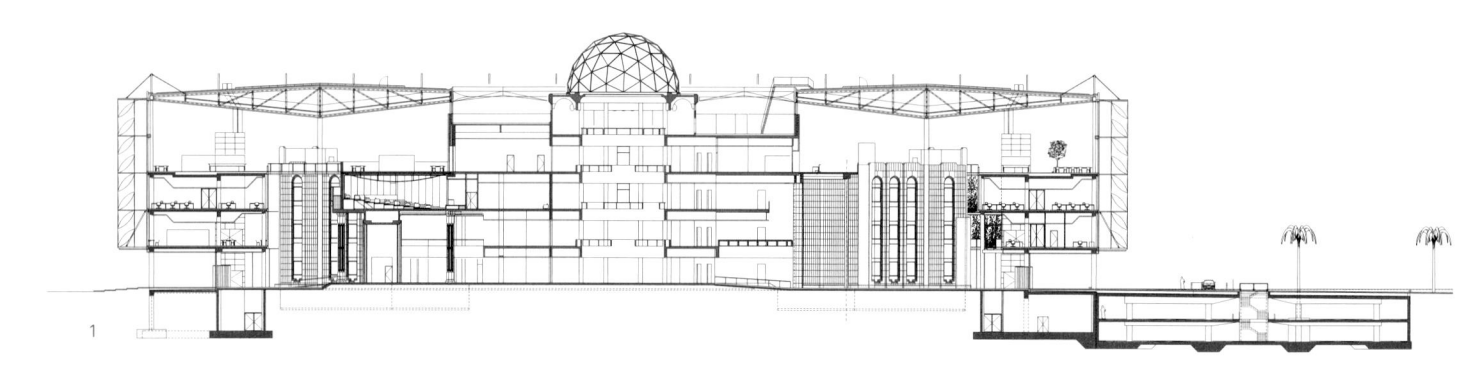

1

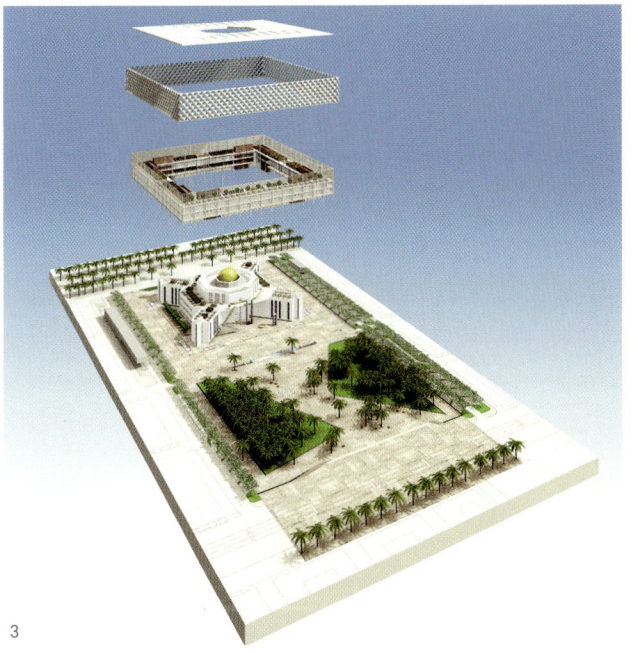

1	Schnitt
	Section
2	Außenansicht
	Exterior view
3	Explosionszeichnung
	Exploded view
4	Foyer
	Foyer
5	Modell
	Model

RWE Tower
RWE Tower
Inlandsprojekt Domestic project

Architekten Architects
Gerber Architekten, Dortmund
Prof. Eckhard Gerber
Jens Haake, Rolf Knie, Hans-Christoph Bittner, Andrzej Bleszynski, Juana Grunwald, Birgit Hassenteufel, Holger Heltewig, Susanne Kreimeyer, Nils Kummer, Petra Luis, Markus Petry, Simone Saul, Jörg Schoeneweiß, Keith Stoltenfeldt, Martin Timmermann

Ingenieure Engineers
Prof. Pfeifer und Partner, Darmstadt
Ingenieurbüro Düffel, Dortmund

Bauherr Client
DIAG GmbH & Co. KG II, Dortmund

Typologie Type
Verwaltungsbau
Administration building

Standort Location
Dortmund

Beginn Start
Januar January 2003

Fertigstellung Completion
Juni June 2005

Brutto-Grundfläche Gross floor area
27 300 m²

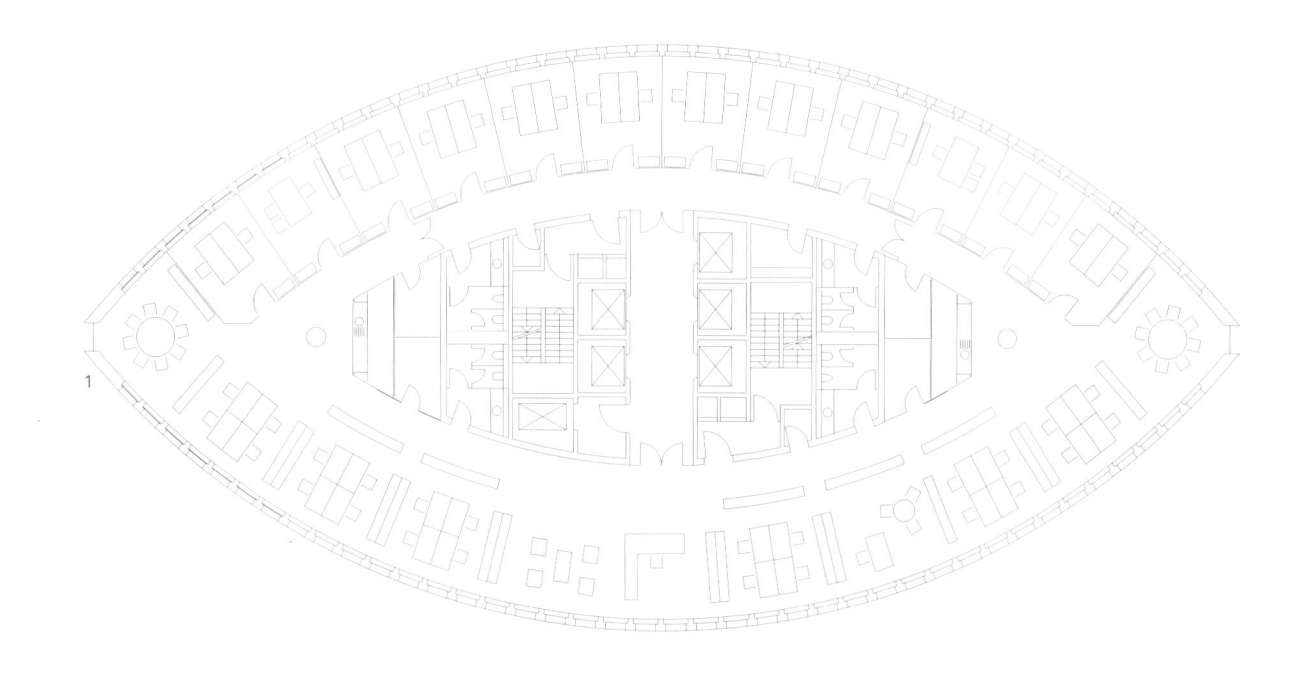

Der 22-geschossige RWE Tower im Zentrum Dortmunds trägt mit den beiden bereits vorhandenen Hochhäusern zur Verdichtung und Belebung des Umfeldes zwischen Hauptbahnhof und Innenstadt bei. Der linsenförmige Grundriss und seine Lage auf dem Grundstück stärken das bestehende Wegenetz, sodass interessante stadträumliche Beziehungen entstehen. Aus der Linsenform herausgedreht entwickelt sich im Erdgeschoss eine um das Hochhaus herumführende, eingeschossige Bebauung. Aufgrund des mittig angeordneten Betonkerns, der alle vertikalen Erschließungselemente und Nebenräume beinhaltet, liegen alle Büroräume stützenfrei an den Fassaden und werden natürlich belichtet. Statt einer Ganzglasfassade sorgen Einzelfenster, die sich in allen Büros öffnen lassen, für ein angenehmes Innenklima und große Transparenz. Den Abschluss des Hochhauses bildet ein asymmetrischer Keilausschnitt mit zwei Pultdachflächen, von denen die höhere und stärker geneigte als Glasdach über dem Bistro ausgebildet ist.

Together with two existing high-rises, the twenty-two-story RWE Tower in Dortmund contributes to consolidating and revitalizing the area between the main train station and the city center. Its lozenge-shaped plan and its position on the available plot have strengthened the city's network of roads and paths and are responsible for the building's interesting contextual relationships. The ground floor of the lozenge shape extends into a single-story structure, which surrounds the high-rise. On account of the central concrete core containing the staircases, elevators, and ancillary spaces, the column-free offices are all arranged along the façades and are thus naturally lit. Instead of fully glazed façades, the building was fitted with large, openable windows to create pleasant interior climates and transparency. The asymmetrical wedge structure on top of the building has a two-part pent roof, of which the higher and steeper section consists of glass and covers the bistro.

1 Grundriss Büroetage
  Office level floor plan
2 Bistro im obersten Geschoss
  Bistro on the top floor
3 Eingang
  Entrance
4 Außenansicht
  Exterior view
5 Foyer
  Foyer

GKK + Architekten
Berlin

Partner Partners
Swantje Kühn
*1964 in München Munich
Oliver Kühn
*1962 in Regensburg

Gründung Established
1991 in Berlin

Mitarbeiter Assistants
25

Kontakt Contact
Pariser Straße 1
10719 Berlin
Deutschland Germany

Tel   +49 (0)30 28 30 82 0
Fax   +49 (0)30 28 30 82 53

info@gkk-architekten.de
www.gkk-architekten.de

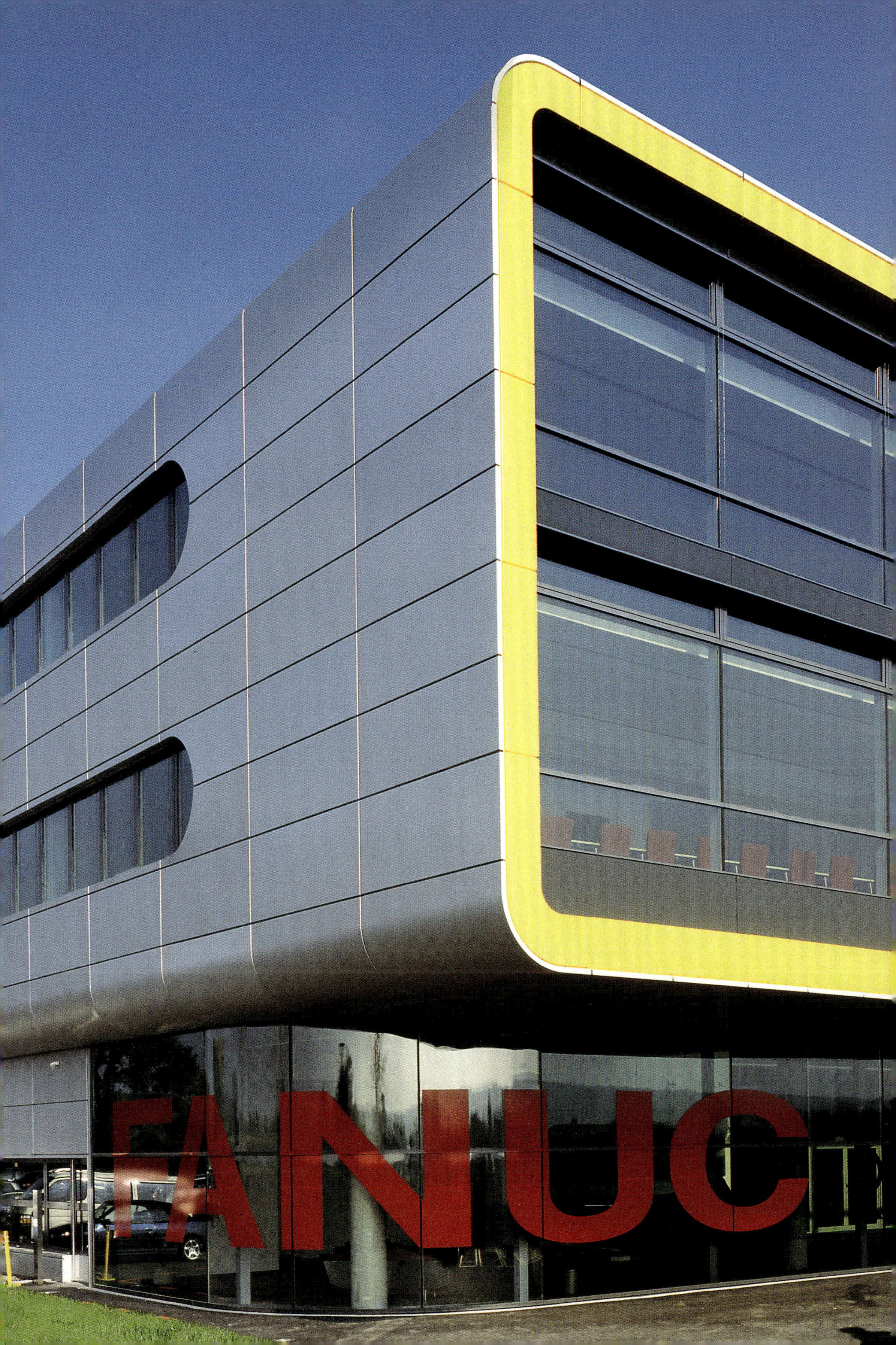
FANUC

FANUC Robotics France
FANUC Robotics France
Auslandsprojekt Foreign project

Architekten Architects
GKK + Architekten, Berlin
Georg Gewers, Swantje Kühn, Oliver Kühn
Diana Hermann, Volker Ruof, Marlene Schwabe,
Frederic Treheux

Ingenieure Engineers
Schlaich Bergermann und Partner, Stuttgart
Terrel Rooke Associés, Boulogne-Billancourt
EB Ebert Ingenieure, Berlin
Inex Bet, Paris

Bauherr Client
FANUC Robotics France S.A.R.L., Lisses / Évry

Typologie Type
Verwaltungs- und Industriebau
Administration and industrial building

Standort Location
Lisses, Frankreich France

Beginn Start
2005

Fertigstellung Completion
2007

Brutto-Grundfläche Gross floor area
6 970 m²

Die neue Hauptverwaltung für FANUC Robotics France wurde entworfen, um weltweiten Standards zu entsprechen, da das japanische Unternehmen, ein Marktführer im Feld der Automation, mehr als nur ein neues Gebäude gefordert hatte. Das Konzept folgt der Geschäftsphilosophie der »andauernden Bewegung« und ermöglicht eine Variation im Maßstab, den jeweiligen lokalen Bedürfnissen entsprechend. Der architektonische Entwurf übersetzt das Firmenimage – Modernität, Funktionalität und Offenheit –, die Planung basiert auf der Idee von drei Baukörpern variabler Höhe und Länge: Der südliche beinhaltet Präsentations- und Entwicklungseinrichtungen; mehrgeschossige Lagerräume, Ausbildungs- und Verwaltungsbereiche befinden sich im nördlichen Teil. Der letzte Baukörper, welcher von Ost nach West verläuft, verbindet die beiden anderen. Mit seiner schimmernden silbernen Aluminiumhaut, großflächigen Verglasungen und seiner gelben Farbe ist das Gebäude von fern sichtbar.

The new main administration building of FANUC Robotics France was designed to meet international standards, as the Japanese parent corporation—a leading manufacturer of industrial automation technology—wanted more than just a new building. The design expresses the corporate philosophy of "permanent movement" and can be implemented on varying scales, depending on local requirements. The architectural design translates FANUC Robotics' corporate claims—modernity, functionality, and openness—into three buildings of different heights and lengths. The southernmost building contains showrooms and the development department, while multistory stores, training facilities, and offices occupy the northernmost building. The third structure—oriented east-west—links the two others. With its shining aluminium skin, large glazings, and yellow façade sections, the building is visible from afar.

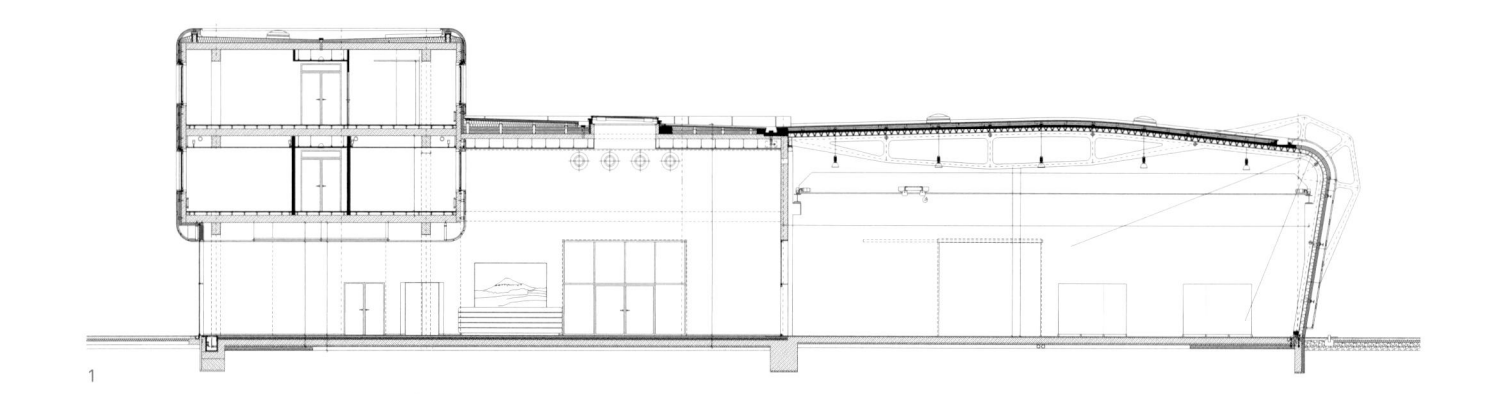

1

1 Querschnitt
  Cross section
2 Außenansicht: Haupteingang
  Exterior view: main entrance
3 Außenansicht mit Dachterasse
  Exterior view with roof terrace
4 Seitenansicht
  Side view

Admiralspalast
Admiralspalast
Inlandsprojekt Domestic project

Architekten Architects
GKK + Architekten, Berlin
Georg Gewers, Swantje Kühn, Oliver Kühn
Charly Deda, Uwe Karl, Bettina Ludwig, Alexander
Mayrhofer, Dirk Müller, Michael Spieler

Ingenieure Engineers
Andreas Leipold, Berlin
Jockwer & Partner, Berlin
GPC Ingenieure, Berlin
Lüttgens Loose, Berlin

Bauherr Client
Admiralspalast GmbH & Co. KG
vertreten durch represented by
Falk Walter, Berlin

Typologie Type
Kulturbau Cultural building

Standort Location
Berlin

Beginn Start
November 2005

Fertigstellung Completion
Januar January 2007

Brutto-Grundfläche Gross floor area
20 600 m²

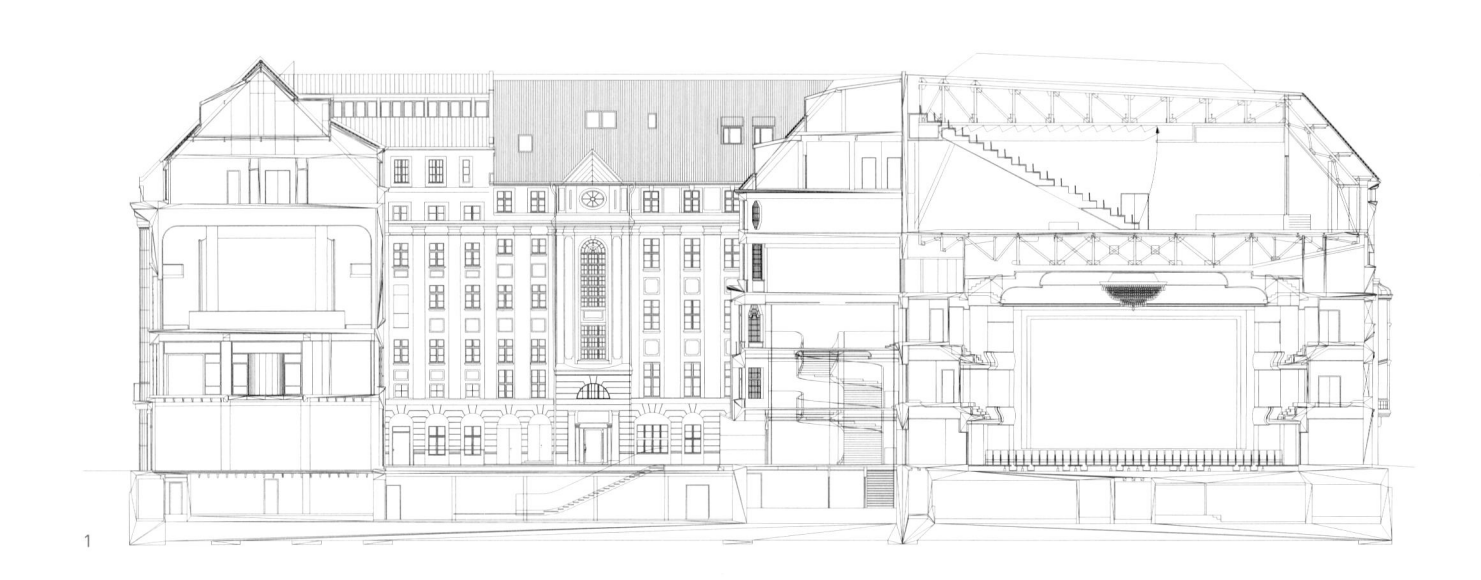

Der Umbau des Admiralspalasts in eine moderne Spielstätte behandelt den geschichtsträchtigen Altbau mit Respekt und erhält dessen Patina. Es galt, das Neue klar auszusprechen und unvermischt neben das Alte zu stellen. Die Hauptrolle unter den unterschiedlichen Veranstaltungsorten spielt der multifunktionale Große Saal mit 1 700 Plätzen auf drei Rängen, der in Abstimmung mit der Denkmalpflege wiederhergestellt wurde. Wichtigste Eingriffe sind hier die verschiebbaren Sitzreihen und der Teilrückbau der ehemaligen »Führerloge« von 1941. Für die Erschließung des Saals wurde eine neue monolithische Treppenskulptur frei in das Foyerhaus eingestellt. Ebenso erhielten die Umgänge eine neue Gestaltung, welche sich am Motiv des Saals als Klangkörper orientierte, der die gebogenen Wände des Umgangs in Schwingungen versetzt. Hinzu kommen eine flexible Studiobühne, ein Club sowie ein kleiner Veranstaltungsbereich und das Grand-Café.

The conversion and extension of the old Admiralspalast theater has treated the historic building with respect and preserved its patina. The idea was to make the new extension clearly identifiable and juxtapose it with the historic structure, without making any compromises. The Grand Hall (which seats 1,700 people on three levels) plays the leading part among the various entertainment venues in the palace. It was restored in coordination with Berlin's monument conservation authority. The most important measures were the installation of movable tiers and the elimination of Hitler's 1941 "Führer's Box." A new, freestanding, monolithic stairway sculpture was constructed inside the foyer building. The foyers and corridors surrounding the hall were redesigned, based on the fact that the hall is considered a "sound box," which makes the foyer's curving walls vibrate. New spaces were added: a variable studio theater, a club, a small events area, and the Grand Café.

1 Schnitt
  Section
2 Treppe
  Staircase
3 Umgang
  Corridor
3 Großer Saal
  Grand Hall

Ingenhoven Architekten
Düsseldorf

Inhaber Owner
Christoph Ingenhoven
*1960 in Düsseldorf

Gründung Established
1985 in Düsseldorf

Mitarbeiter Assistants
105

Kontakt Contact
Plange Mühle 1
40221 Düsseldorf
Deutschland Germany

Tel   +49 (0)211 30 10 10 1
Fax   +49 (0)211 30 10 3 1

info@ingenhovenarchitects.eu
www.ingenhovenarchitects.eu

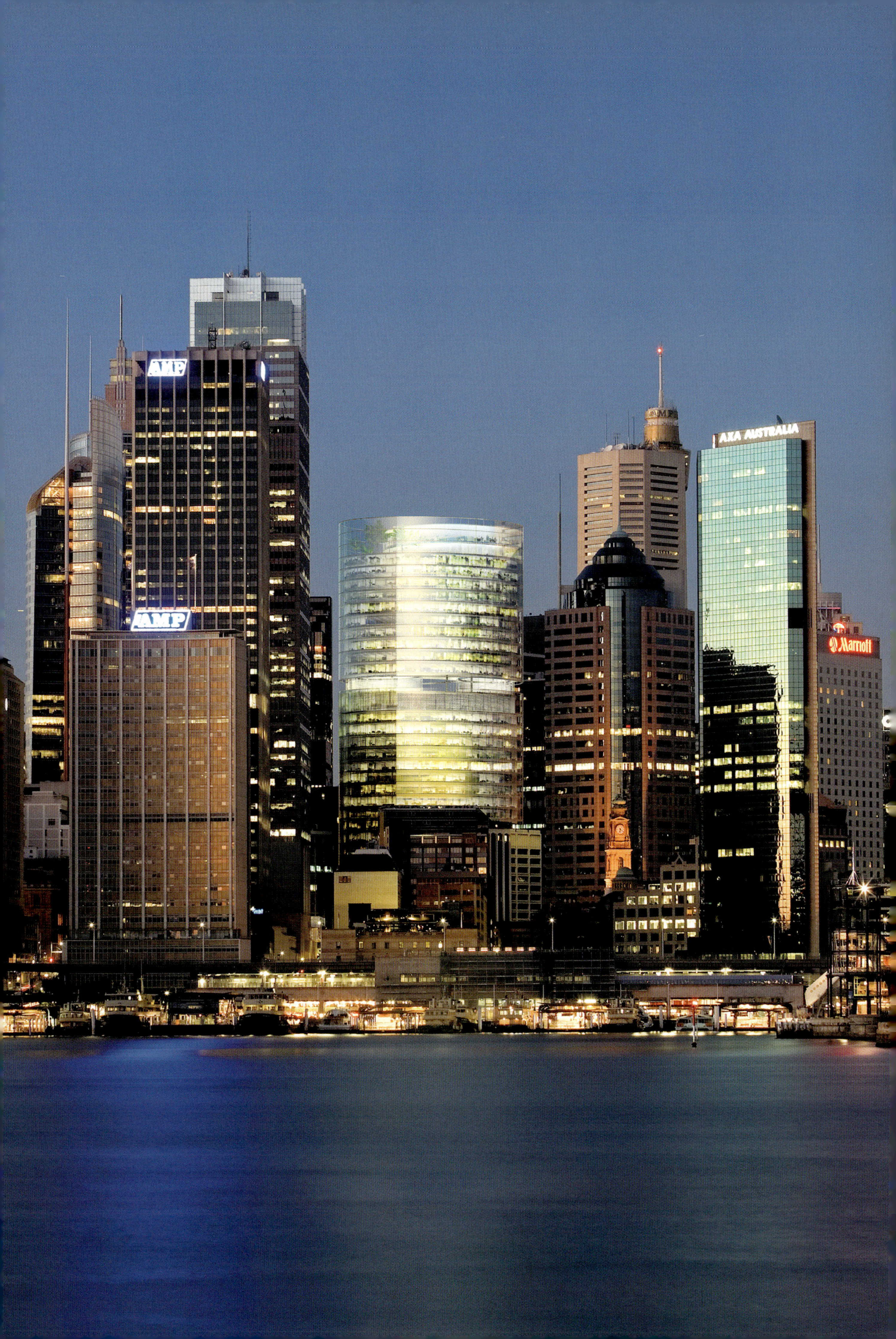
AMP
AMP
AXA AUSTRALIA
Marriott

1 Bligh Street
1 Bligh Street
Auslandsprojekt Foreign project

Architekten Architects
Ingenhoven Architekten, Düsseldorf
Christoph Ingenhoven
Martin Reuter, Felix Winter, Andre Barton, Jörg Bredenbröcker, Elisabeth Broermann, Darko Cvetuljski, Matthias Giesel, Christian Kob, Andrea König, Peter Pistorius, Mario Reale, Alexander Schmitz, Hinrich Schumacher, Thomas Weber

Partner Partners
architectus, Sydney

Ingenieure Engineers
enstruct, Milsons Point

Bauherr Client
DB RREEF, Sydney

Typologie Type
Verwaltungsbau Administration building

Standort Location
Sydney, Australien Australia

Beginn Start
2008

Fertigstellung Completion
2011

Brutto-Grundfläche Gross floor area
45 000 m²

Durch die kompakte Geometrie und eine Drehung des 139 Meter hohen Büroturms auf dem Grundstück an der Bligh Street im Norden von Sydney profitieren alle Büroflächen von einem unverbaubaren Blick auf den Hafen. Hierzu wurde auch die Erdgeschosszone zugunsten eines öffentlichen Platzes angehoben. Das Hochhaus wird so zu einem signifikanten Gebäude in der Skyline von Sydney. Neben der hohen Flächeneffizienz überzeugte den Bauherrn vor allem das ökologische Gesamtkonzept des Hochhauses, das in dieser Form einmalig für Sydney und den australischen Kontinent ist. Das vollständig verglaste Hochhaus erhält eine zweischalige Fassade und wird über ein gebäudehohes Atrium durchlüftet.

Due to the compact geometry of the 139-meter-high office tower and its position at an angle on the Bligh Street site in the northern part of Sydney, all of the offices benefit from unobstructed views (which will remain unobstructed) of Sydney's skyline. The client appreciated not only the efficient use of available floor space, but above all the optimal ecological design for the high-rise, unequalled in Sydney and Australia as a whole in this form. The tower's façades are cavity walls made entirely of glass, and the interior is aerated via a top-to-bottom atrium.

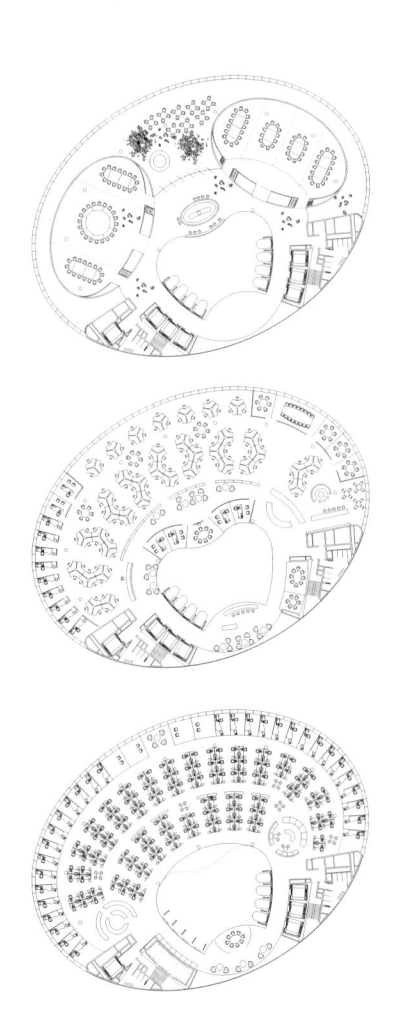

1 Grundrissvarianten
   Floor variations
2 Schnitt
   Section
3 Außenansicht
   Exterior view

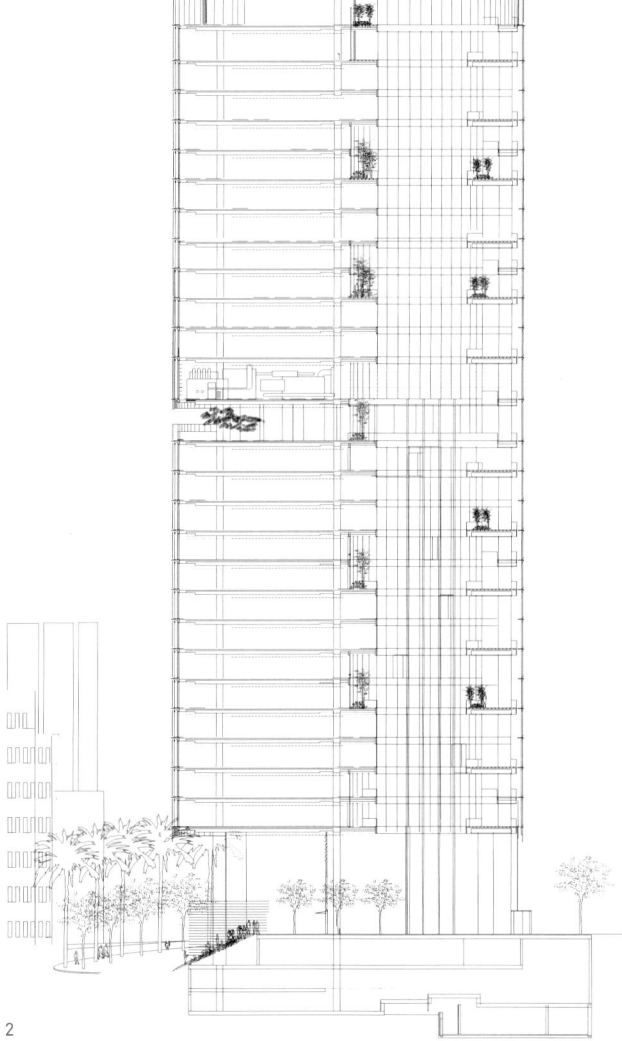

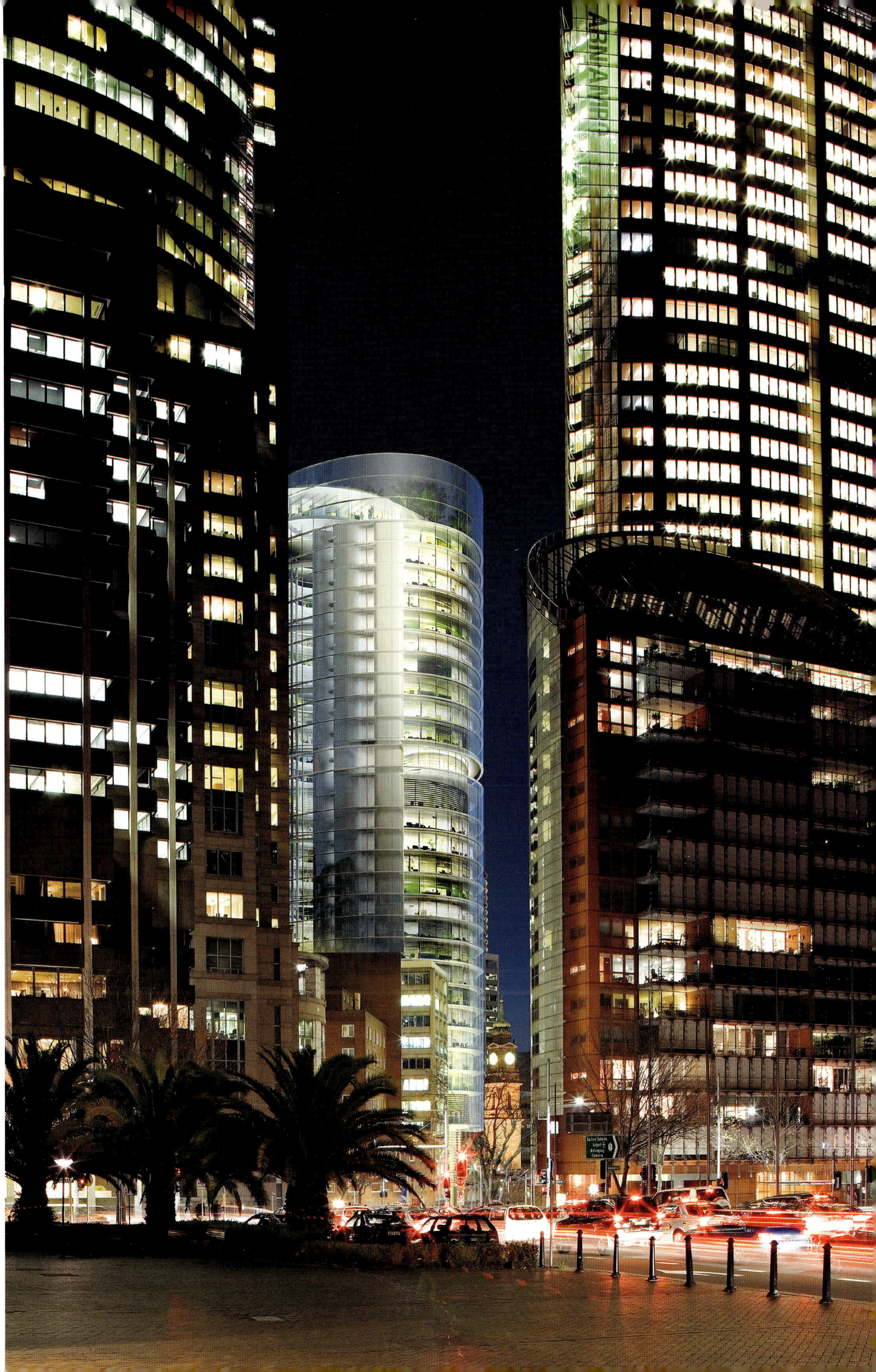

Lufthansa Aviation Center
Lufthansa Aviation Center
Inlandsprojekt Domestic project

Architekten Architects
Ingenhoven Architekten, Düsseldorf
Christoph Ingenhoven
Klaus Frankenheim, Thomas Höxtermann, Götz-Peter Kaiser, Prof. Dieter Henze, Christel Bauscher, Rainer Binnig, Marc Böhnke, Tina Brinkmeier, Lutz Büsing, André Burkhard, Ortwin Burkheiser, Ralf Dorsch-Rüter, Meike Dreger, Denis Donat, Uwe Eiffert, Marco Glashagen, Roman Gohlke, Holger Gravius, Xiao Ping Guo, Imre Halmai, Martin Herbrand, Dirk Hümpfner, Manfred Junghans, Marcus Kraemer, Andreas Kramer, Christiane Luiz, Anja Merz, Kirsten Opitz, Klaus J. Osterburg, Peter-Jan van Ouwerkerk, Jan Quadbeck, Peter Pistorius, Michael Reiß, Udo Rex, Stefan Rhein, Manuel Ruf, Ulla Schoemakers, Hendrik Schumacher, Hinrich Schumacher, Robert Schwalm, Andrea Timmermanns, Peter Jan Vanek, Maximo Victoria, Herbert Voss, Harald Wennemar, Regina Wuff

Ingenieure Engineers
Werner Sobek Ingenieure, Stuttgart
HL-Technik AG Beratende Ingenieure, Frankfurt am Main
DS-Plan, Stuttgart

Bauherr Client
Deutsche Lufthansa AG, Frankfurt am Main

Typologie Type
Verwaltungsbau
Administration building

Standort Location
Frankfurt am Main

Wettbewerb Competition
1999

Fertigstellung Completion
2006

Brutto-Grundfläche Gross floor area
124 800 m²

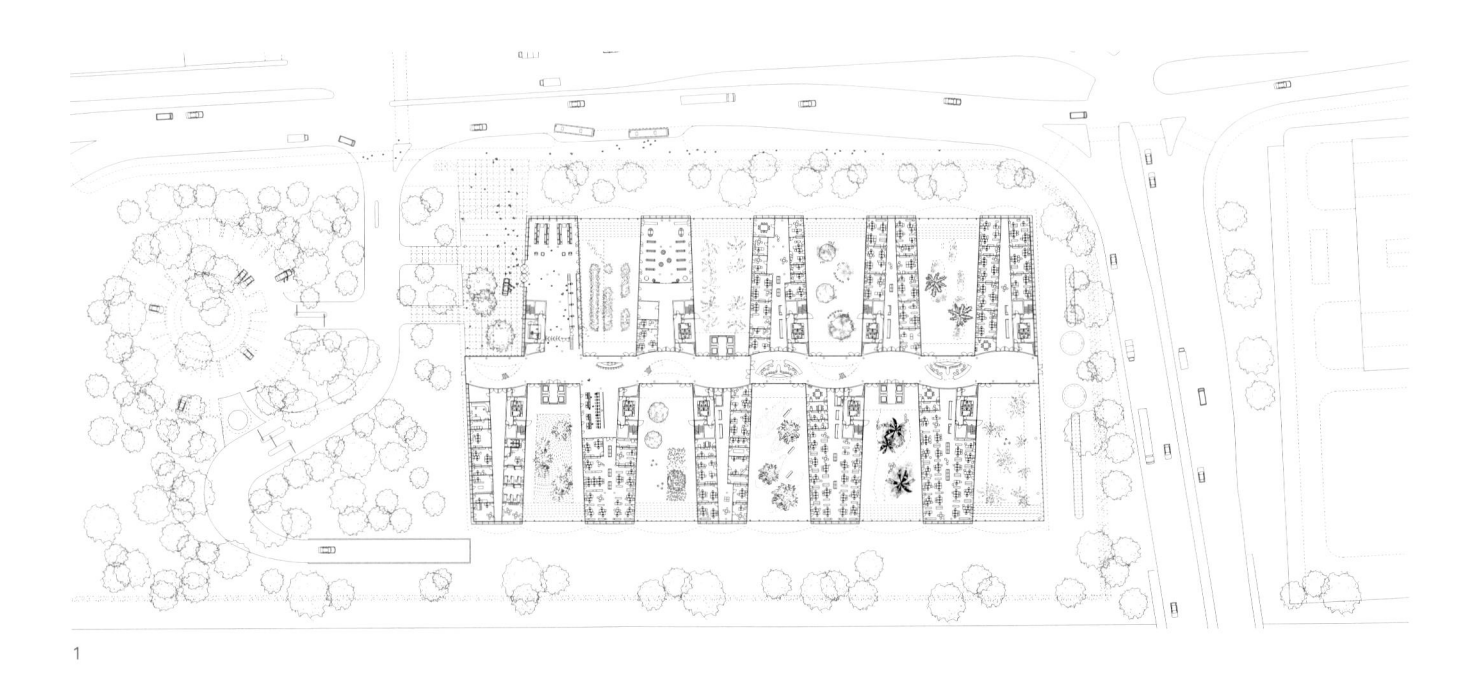

1

Das neue Lufthansa Aviation Center befindet sich an einem der verkehrstechnisch besterschlossenen Standorte Europas, zwischen dem Frankfurter Flughafen, der Autobahn und der ICE-Hochgeschwindigkeitsstrecke. Unter einem Dach, welches einem Gleitschirm ähnelt, liegen zehn Gärten, die von flügelförmigen Segmenten, sogenannten Büroheimatbereichen, umfasst werden. Diese sind mit ihren flexiblen Bürostrukturen wie Häuser an einer Straße entlang einer inneren Passage aufgereiht. Die Passage verbindet alle vertikalen und horizontalen Wege im Haus. Insgesamt 1 850 Büroarbeitsplätze orientieren sich zu den verglasten Gärten und können natürlich be- und entlüftet werden. Die Bepflanzungen der Gärten sind den gemäßigten Klimazonen der Kontinente entlehnt. Sie ermöglichen ein ökologisches Klimakonzept und gesundes Arbeiten. Sie dienen als Kälte-, Wärme- und Lärmpuffer und sorgen im Wesentlichen für eine hervorragende Klimabilanz und baubiologische Leistung.

The new Lufthansa Aviation Center was built in one of Europe's best-connected locations, between Frankfurt International Airport, a highway, and the ICE high-speed railway line. The roof resembles a paraglider and covers ten different gardens, which alternate with wedge-shaped structures containing the offices, called "office homes." These gardens and buildings line a central interior passage, similar to a street, which interconnects all the vertical and horizontal circulation routes inside the center. A total of 1,850 office workplaces overlook the glazed gardens and are ventilated naturally. The garden plants originate from the temperate climatic zones of the different continents. As an integral part of the overall climatizing concept, they provide healthy working atmospheres, serve as insulating and noise buffers, and make a substantial contribution to the excellent energy balance and ecological performance of the structure.

1 Grundriss Erdgeschoss
  Ground floor plan
2 Bürobereich
  Office zone
3 Garten
  Garden
4 Luftraum in der Passage
  Void in the passage
5 Außenansicht
  Exterior view

145

J. Mayer H.
Berlin

Inhaber Owner
Jürgen Mayer H.
*1965 in Stuttgart

Gründung Established
1996 in Berlin

Mitarbeiter Assistants
15

Kontakt Contact
Bleibtreustrasse 54
10623 Berlin
Deutschland Germany

Tel +49 (0)30 31 50 61 17
Fax +49 (0)30 31 50 61 18

contact@jmayerh.de
www.jmayerh.de

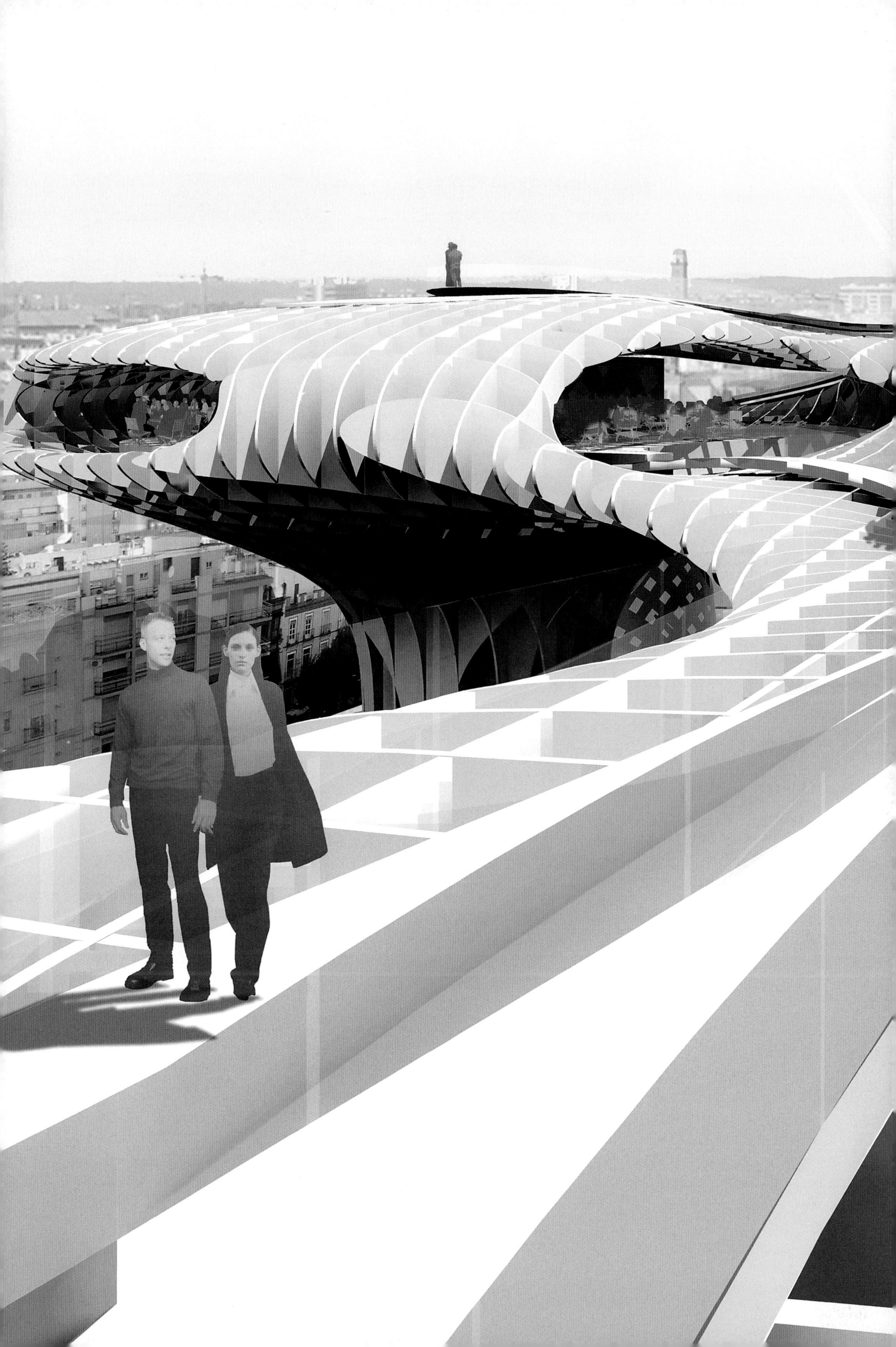

Metropol Parasol
Metropol Parasol
Auslandsprojekt Foreign project

Architekten Architects
J. Mayer H., Berlin
Jürgen Mayer H.
Ana Alonso de la Varga, Paul Angelier, Thorsten Blatter, Marcus Blum, Sebastian Finckh, Wilko Hoffmann, Olivier Jacques, Klaus Küppers, Claudia Marcinowski, Julia Neitzel, Marta Ramírez Iglesias, Alessandra Raponi, Andre Santer, Ingmar Schmidt, Georg Schmidthals, Hans Schneider, Dominik Schwarzer, Jan-Christoph Stockebrand, Daria Trovato, Nai Huei Wang

Ingenieure Engineers
Arup GmbH Berlin / Madrid

Bauherren Clients
Ayuntamiento de Sevilla und and SACYR

Typologie Type
Kultur- und Geschäftsbau
Cultural and commercial building

Standort Location
Sevilla, Spanien Seville, Spain

Wettbewerb Competition
2004

Fertigstellung Completion
2009

Brutto-Grundfläche Gross floor area
12 670 m²

Der Metropol Parasol ist das neue Wahrzeichen von Sevilla – ein Ort der Identifikation, welcher das kulturelle Leben der Stadt präsentiert. Er hat das Potenzial, die Plaza de la Encarnación zu einem neuen zeitgenössischen, urbanen Zentrum zu machen, und eine dynamische Entwicklung für kulturelle und kommerzielle Einrichtungen zu initiieren. Dieser einzigartige Ort im Zentrum der dichten Struktur der mittelalterlichen Altstadt bietet Raum für Aktivitäten aus unterschiedlichen Bereichen – Kultur, Freizeit und Kommerz. In den großen schirmartigen Strukturen befinden sich mehrere Ebenen, mit einem archäologischen Museum im Untergeschoss und einer Markthalle im Erdgeschoss. Die angehobene Plaza ist speziell für Events gedacht, in den Schirmen liegen das Skycafé und ein Restaurant. Von hier beginnt auch ein Panoramarundgang auf den Parasols. Die mit Polyurethan beschichtete Holzstruktur wächst aus der Ebene der archäologischen Ausgrabung heraus und wird so zu einem Signet für die ganze Stadt.

The Metropol Parasol is Seville's new landmark—a place of identification that spotlights the cultural life of the city. It has the potential to make an urban focus of the Plaza de la Encarnación and to trigger the dynamic development of other cultural and commercial facilities. This unique place at the heart of the densely built-up medieval city center offers space and scope for various activities in the fields of culture, leisure, and commerce. Its huge, umbrella-shaped volumes contain an archaeological museum in the basement and a market hall on the ground floor. The elevated plaza was devised for events; the Skycafé and a restaurant are located inside the umbrellas. This floor is also the starting point for a panorama tour of the parasols. These polyurethane-coated wooden structures rise up from the basement archaeological excavation site and form signature elements of the entire city of Seville.

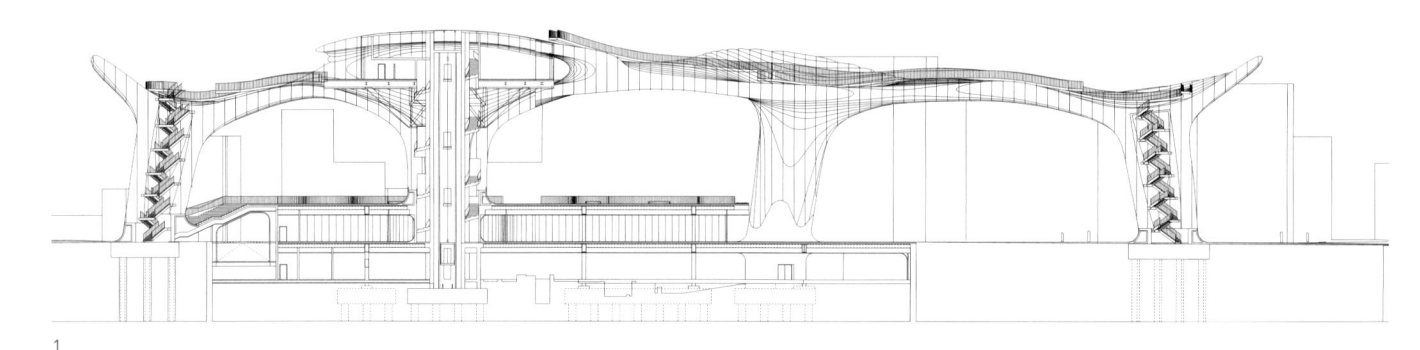

1

2

1 Längsschnitt
  Longitudinal section
2 Dachaufsicht
  Rooftop view
3 Lage auf der Plaza
  Site on the plaza
4 Blick in die Markthalle
  View into the market hall

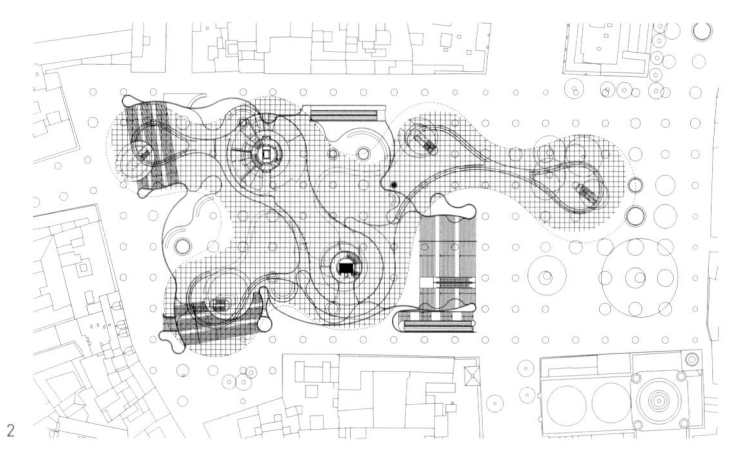

148

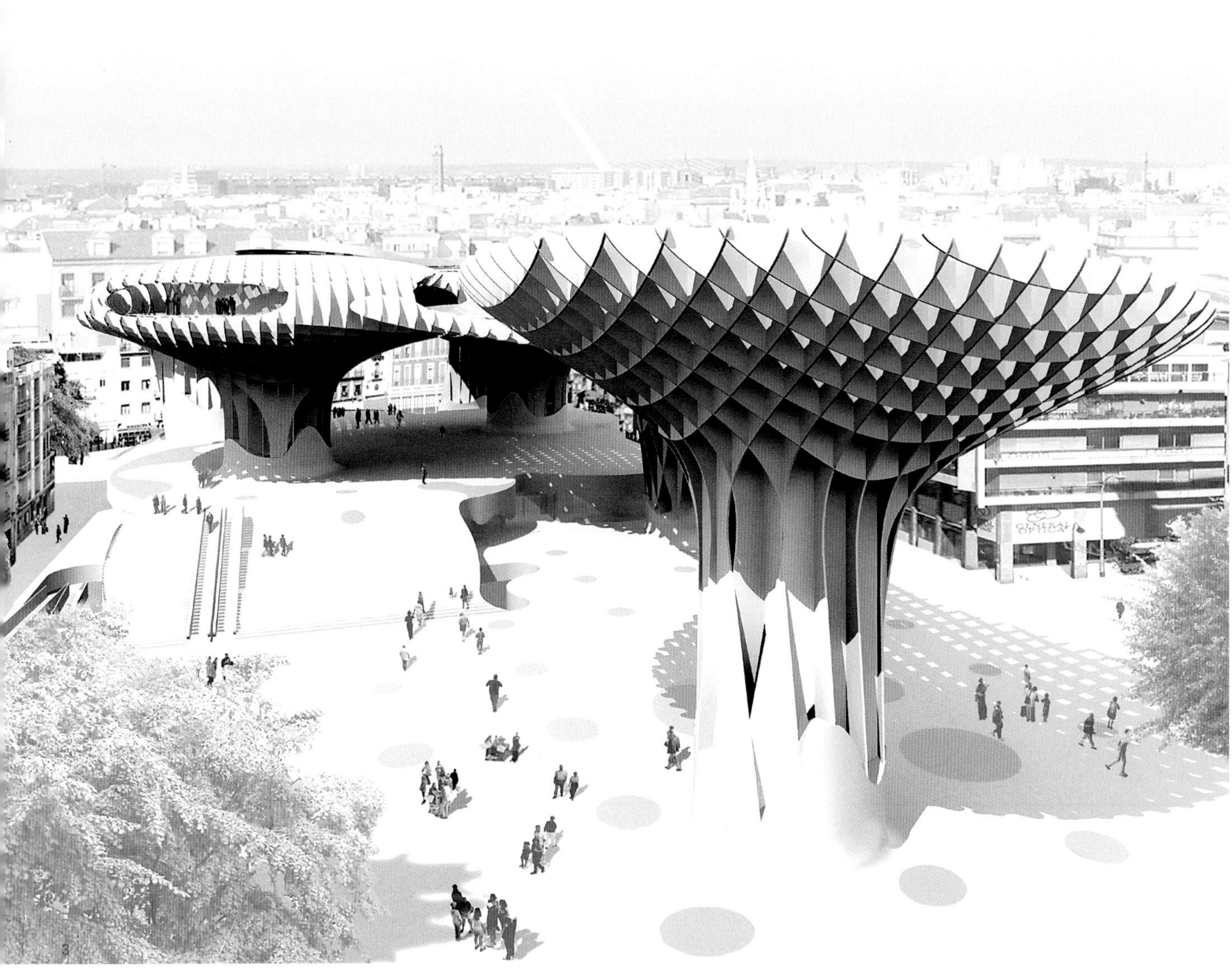

3

4

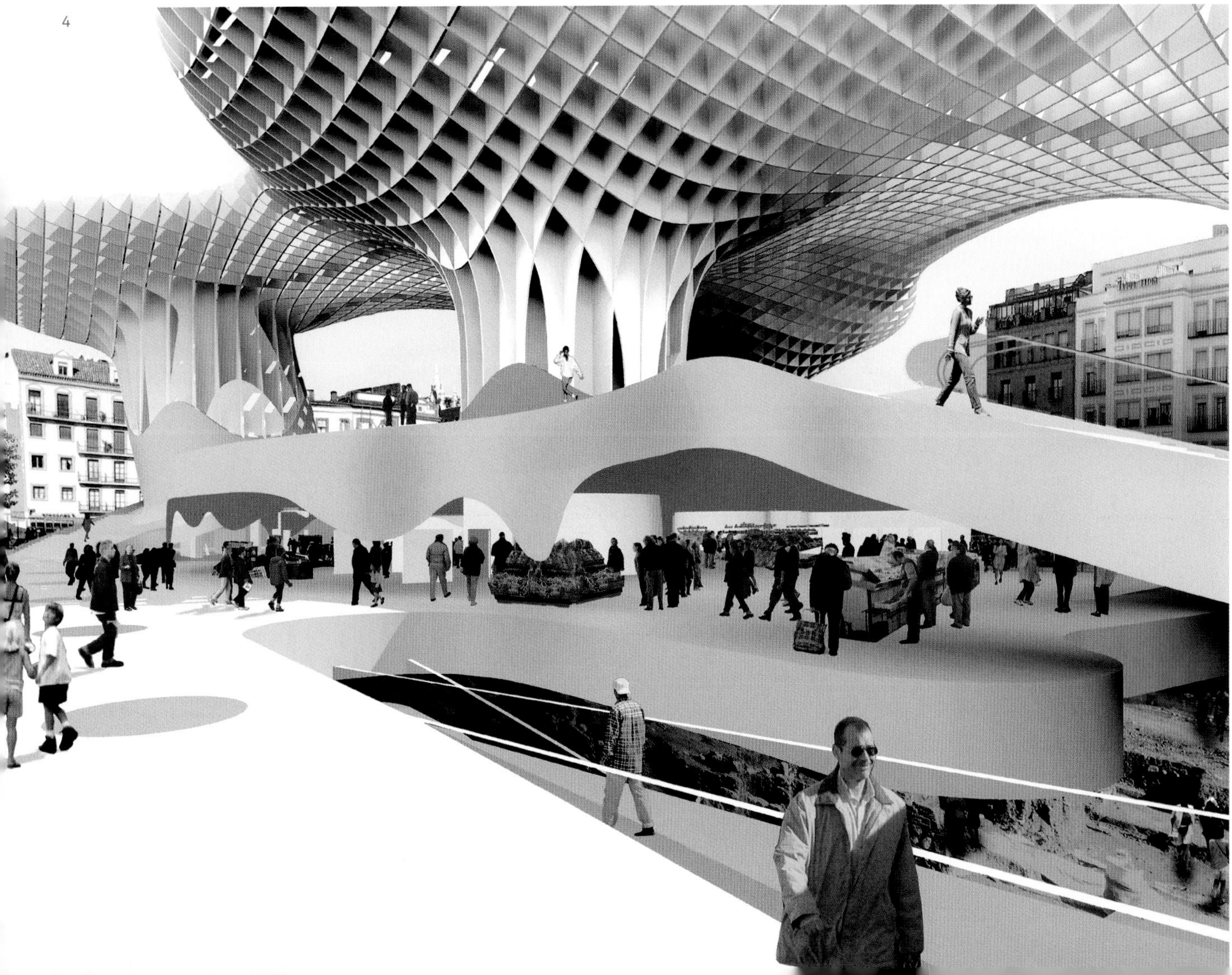

Mensa Karlsruhe
Mensa Karlsruhe
Inlandsprojekt Domestic project

Architekten Architects
J. Mayer H., Berlin
Jürgen Mayer H.
Andre Santer, Julia Neitzel, Sebastian Finckh, Wilko Hoffmann, Ingmar Schmidt, Dominik Schwarzer, Daria Trovato

Ingenieure Engineers
Arup GmbH, Berlin
Martin Scherer, Darmstadt
Dr. Schäcke und Bayer, Waiblingen-Hegnach

Bauherr Client
Land Baden-Württemberg, vertreten durch represented by
Vermögen und Bau Baden-Württemberg, Amt Karlsruhe

Typologie Type
Hochschulbau University building

Standort Location
Karlsruhe

Wettbewerb Competition
2004

Fertigstellung Completion
2007

Brutto-Grundfläche Gross floor area
3 500 m²

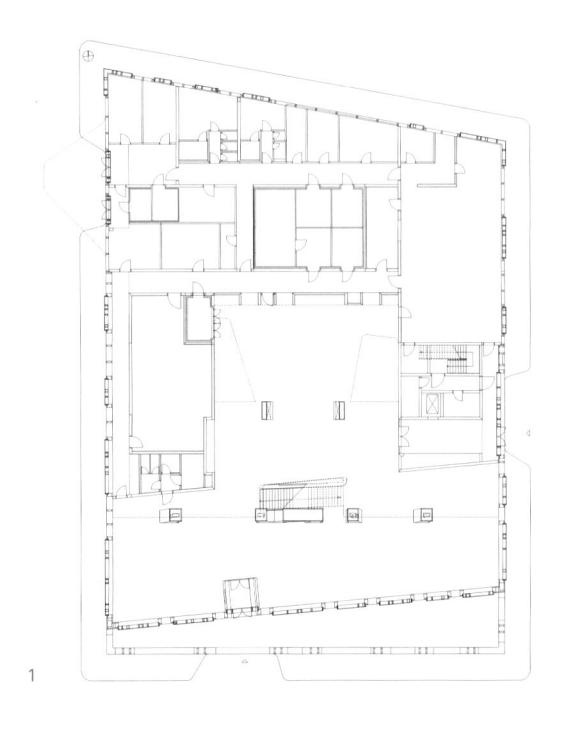

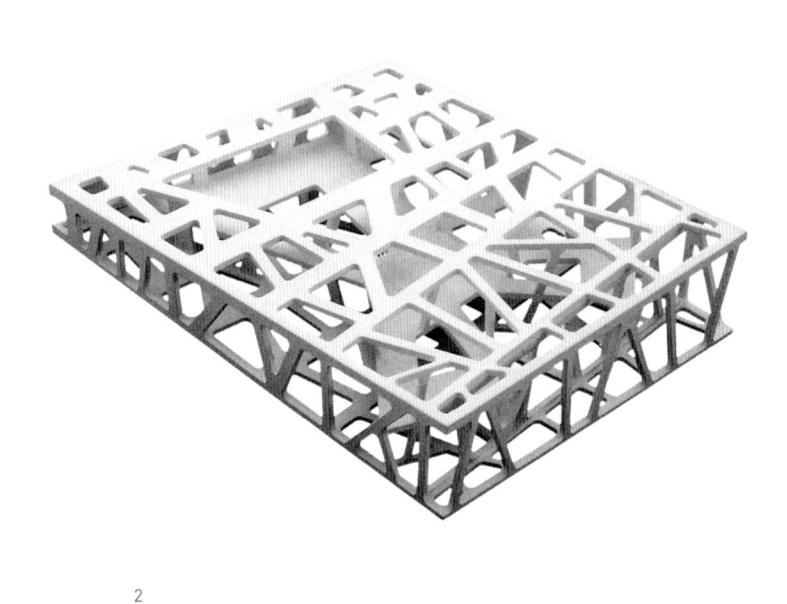

1

2

Die Mensa Karlsruhe befindet sich im Zentrum des Universitätscampus (Fachhochschule, Pädagogische Hochschule und Kunstakademie), zwischen einer städtischen Bebauung im Süden und den naturnahen Freiräumen des Hardtwaldes im Norden. Das Gebäude orientiert sich mit großzügig verglasten Öffnungen zu den Hochschulen und zum urbanen Leben. Die Auflösung des Baukörpers in »stammartige« Strukturen zeigt eine assoziative Verwandtschaft mit dem nahe gelegenen Baumbestand und leitet damit atmosphärisch von den dichten baulichen Strukturen der Stadt zu den schattigen gewachsenen des Waldes über. Das Mensagebäude selbst unterteilt sich in einen großzügig angelegten, lichten Speiseraum mit einer Galerie nach Süden und einen kompakten Funktionsbereich nach Norden, unter anderem für Lager und Küche. Der Speisesaal verschränkt sich, mit Hilfe einer Veranda und einer windgeschützten Terrasse, mit dem Außenraum und bietet so wetterbedingt flexible Nutzungsmöglichkeiten an. Auf diese Weise ist die neue Mensa ein wesentlicher Baustein für die Identität des Hochschulgeländes.

The *mensa* (university cafeteria) in Karlsruhe lies right in the middle of the campus (which includes the University of Applied Sciences, the Teacher Training College, and the Academy of Art), between an urban development to the south and the countryside of the Hardtwald forest to the north. The cafeteria's large windows offer a view of the surrounding institutional buildings and urban life. The division of the building mass into trunk-like sections refers to the nearby forest and thus illustrates the transition from the densely built-up city to the natural environment. The cafeteria proper consists of a spacious, south-facing, light-flooded dining hall with a gallery and a compact functional area (kitchens, storerooms, etc.) to the north. The dining hall is interlocked with the exterior by means of a veranda and a wind-screened terrace for al fresco meals, weather permitting. The cafeteria has thus become an essential building block for the identity of the university campus.

1 Erdgeschoss
  Ground floor plan
2 Konzeptmodell
  Concept model
3 Veranda bei Nacht
  Veranda at night
4 Außenansicht
  Exterior view
5 Speisesaal im Erdgeschoss
  Dining hall on the ground floor
6 Treppe
  Stair
7 Auf der Galerie
  On the gallery

151

Kirsten Schemel Architekten
Berlin

Inhaber Owner
Kirsten Schemel
*1965 in Bad Oeynhausen

Gründung Established
1998 in Berlin

Mitarbeiter Assistants
3

Kontakt Contact
Kurfürstendamm 11
10719 Berlin
Deutschland Germany

Tel +49 (0)30 88 72 49 56
Fax +49 (0)30 88 72 49 58

ks@k-s-architekten.de
www.k-s-architekten.de

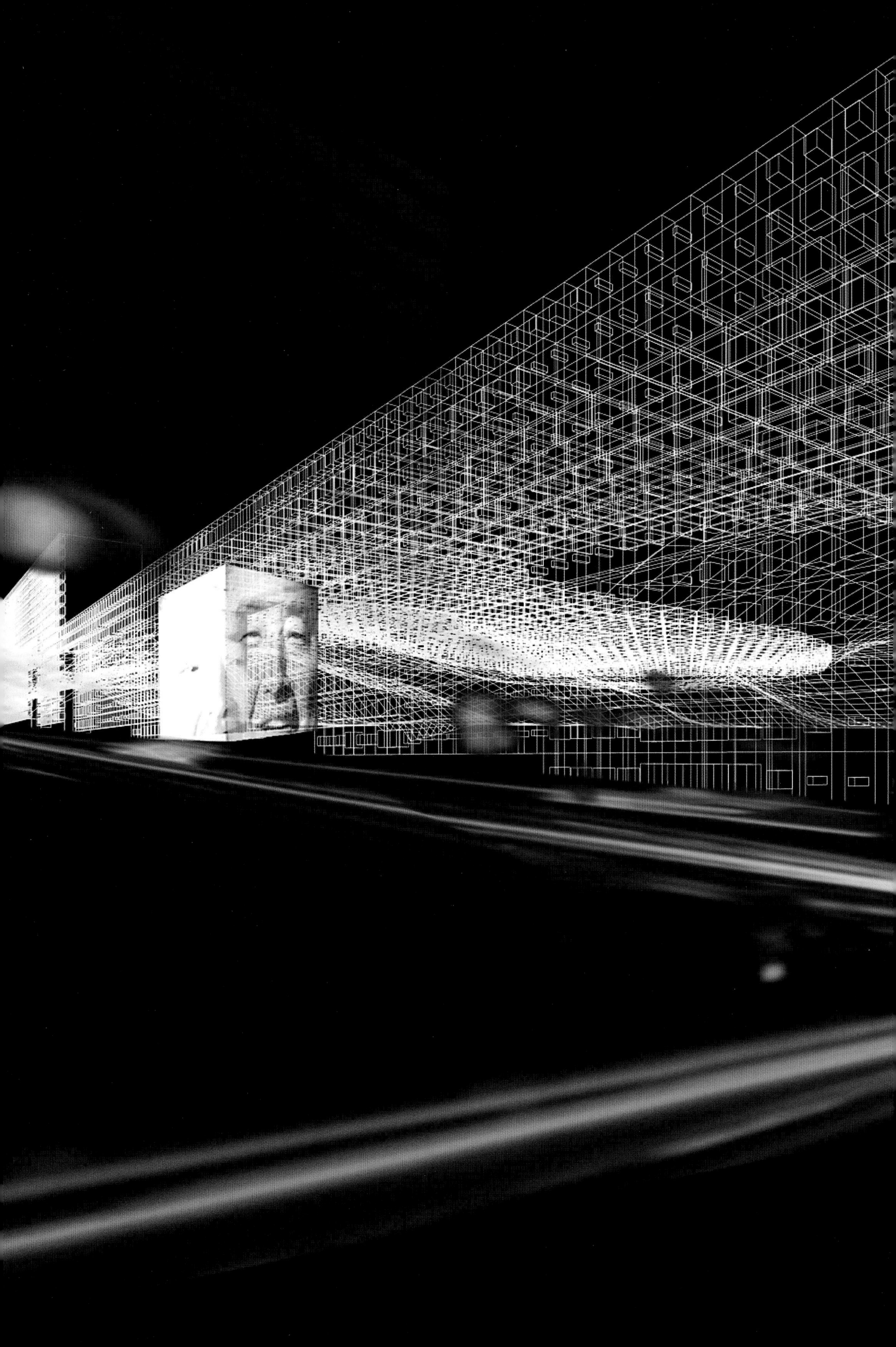

Nam-June-Paik-Museum
Nam June Paik Museum
Auslandsprojekt Foreign project

Architekten Architects
Kirsten Schemel Architekten, Berlin
(Wettbewerb Competition)
Kirsten Schemel
Matthias Anegg, Heiko Kampherbeek, Marc Matzken
KSMS Schemel Stankovic Gesellschaft von Architekten mbH, Berlin
(Projekt Project)
Kirsten Schemel, Marina Stankovic
Etienne Fuchs, Nicole Hoffmann, Tobias Jortzick, Anna Krüger, Chan-Ik Park, Sven Pfeiffer, Christine von der Schulenburg

Partner Partners
Chang-Jo Architects Inc., Seoul

Ingenieure Engineers
Schlaich Bergermann und Partner, Stuttgart
Jeon Architects, Seoul
HL-Technik & Partner, München
HIMEC, Seoul
Emmer Pfenninger Partner AG, Basel
George Sexton Associates Lighting Design, Washington DC

Bauherr Client
Gyeonggi Cultural Foundation, Suwon

Typologie Type
Kulturbau Cultural building

Standort Location
Yong-In, Südkorea South Korea

Wettbewerb Competition
2003

Fertigstellung Completion
2008

Brutto-Grundfläche Gross floor area
5 500 m²

Nach dem Gewinn des Wettbewerbs und einer weiteren Entwurfsphase wurde in enger Kooperation mit dem Bauherrn, dem Nam-June-Paik-Studio in New York und einem internationalen Fachplanerteam ein Museumsbau geplant, der sich in die Topografie des Sangkal-Parks einfügt und sich entlang der Erschließungsstraße entwickelt. Im Außenraum entsteht zwischen dem Gebäude und der Parklandschaft eine zum Teil begehbare, gekrümmte Fläche. In diese topografische Schale wird der zweigeschossige Ausstellungsbau, der in seiner Form an einen Konzertflügel erinnert, »eingestanzt« und von einer gläsernen, dunkel eingefärbten Haut umhüllt. Diese Filterschicht, in der sich reflektierende und bedruckte Gläser überlagern, verwischt die Grenze zwischen Objekt und Umgebung durch Spiegelung und Abstraktion. So setzt sich das Projekt mit den Gegebenheiten des Vorgefundenen auseinander, analog zur Kunst von Nam June Paik. Die ausgewählten Materialien entsprechen der Idee des Readymade und werden ohne weitere Veredelung als Rohbaustoffe eingesetzt.

Following the competition win and the ensuing second design phase, the architects closely cooperated with the client, the Nam June Paik Studio in New York, and an international team of expert planners to design a museum that inserts itself naturally into the Sangkal Park and develops along the access road. A partly walk-on concave surface sets off the museum from the parkland. The two-story exhibition building (whose form resembles a grand piano) is "pressed" into this topographical bowl and clad with a skin of dark-colored glass, in places reflecting, in others screen-printed. This acts as a filter and, through light reflection and abstraction, dissolves the line between the building and its surroundings. The project thus responds to the conditions of the site, in analogy to Nam June Paik's art. The materials were chosen according to the ready-made concept and were used without further finishing as "raw materials."

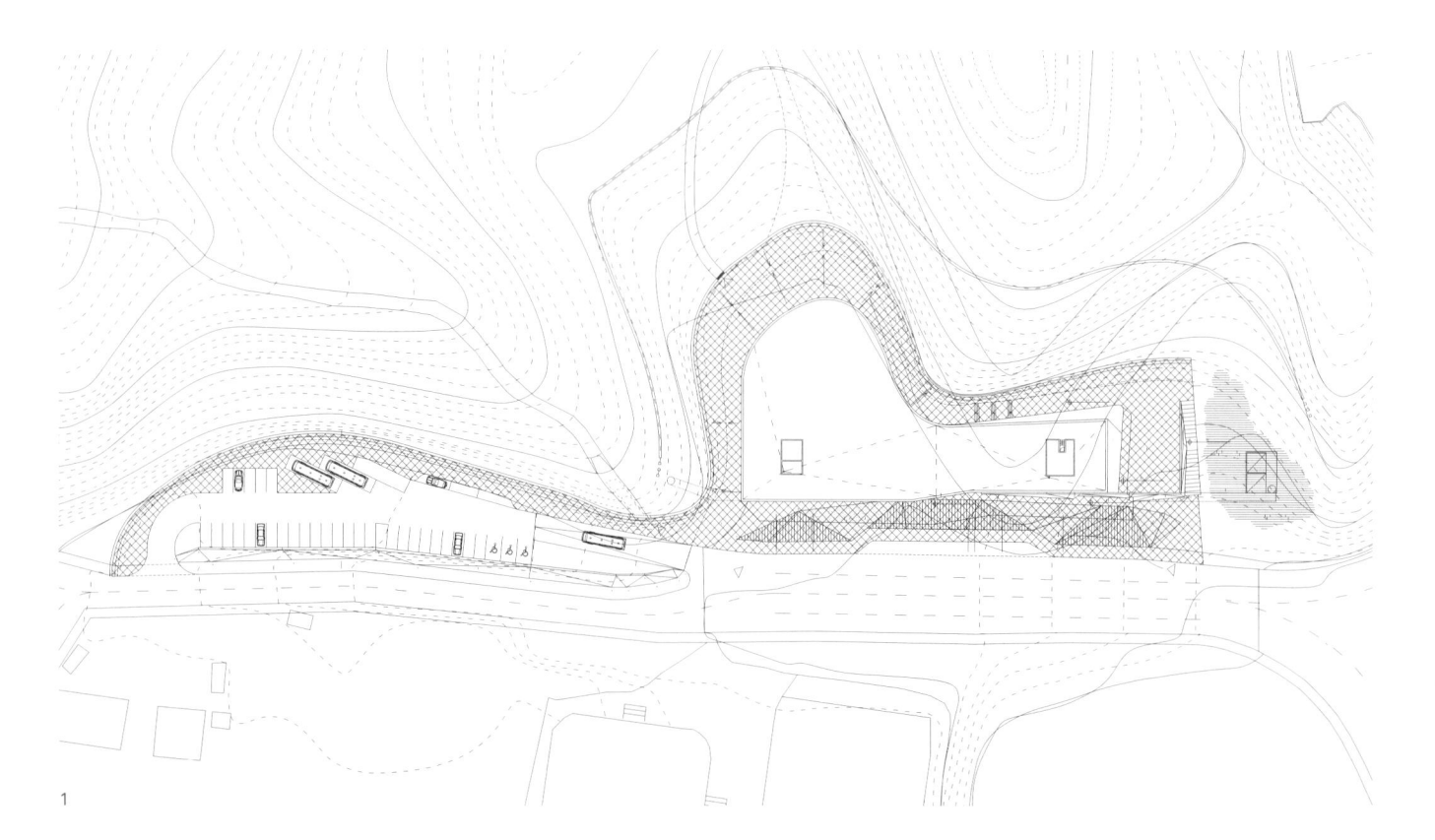

1

1 Lageplan
  Site plan
2 Innenraum Schemaentwurf
  Interior space schematic design
3 »See des Lichts«
  "Lake of light"
4 Schnitt Schemaentwurf
  Schematic design section
5 »Räume des Schattens«
  "Shadow spaces"

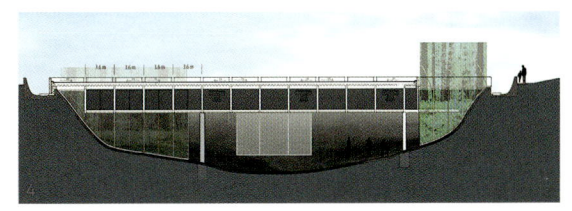

Umbau Arne-Jacobsen-Haus
Conversion Arne Jacobsen House
Inlandsprojekt Domestic project

Architekten Architects
Kirsten Schemel Architekten, Berlin
Kirsten Schemel
Nina Sommer

Projektpartner Project partner
Henning von Wedemeyer

Ingenieure Engineers
Pichler Ingenieure GmbH, Berlin

Bauherr Client
Privat Private

Typologie Type
Wohnungsbau Residential building

Standort Location
Berlin

Beginn Start
2004

Fertigstellung Completion
2005

Nutzfläche Effective area
137 m²

1 Grundriss
  Floor plan
2 Außenansicht
  Exterior view
3 Kammer
  Cubicle
4 Wohnraum
  Living room

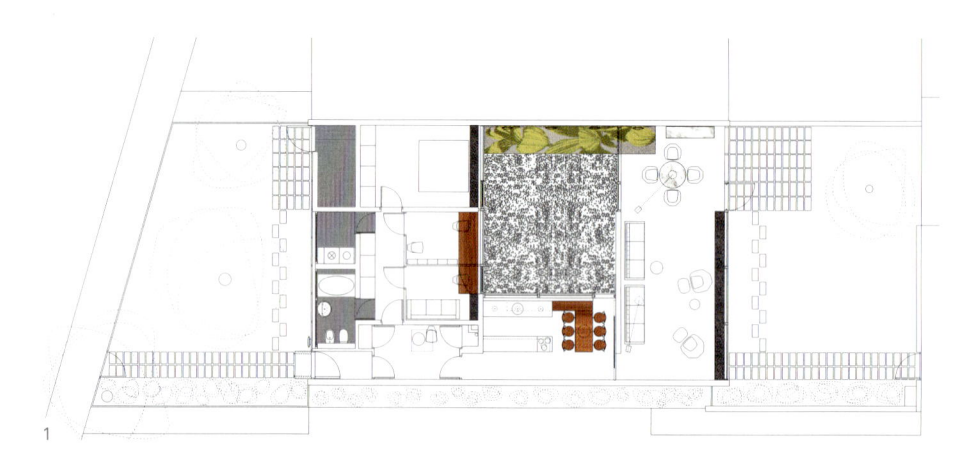

Die Siedlung des Architekten Arne Jacobsen im Berliner Hansa-Viertel (Interbau-Ausstellung 1957) überrascht durch einfache, aber besondere Materialien, deren Verbindungen und Details sowie deren besondere Farbigkeit. Das Arne-Jacobsen-Haus wurde bis auf die tragenden Teile fast gänzlich rückgebaut und wieder neu aufgebaut. In Form, Material und Detailqualität versuchen alle neuen Eingriffe und Modernisierungen den ursprünglichen Charakter des Einfachen und Leichten zu stärken. So wurden das Bad und die Gärten neu gestaltet, für den Innenhof wurde ein beweglicher textiler Sonnenschutz eingesetzt. Die größte gestalterische Herausforderung waren die Rekonstruktion und Interpretation der pflanzlichen, stofflichen, haptischen oder farblichen Erscheinung der Einzelteile und Flächen.

The courtyard houses built by Danish architect Arne Jacobsen as part of the Hansaviertel, Berlin (1957 International Building Exhibition) are unusual for their simple but unique materials and the way these are joined together, and for their details and colors. The Arne Jacobsen House was almost entirely dismantled, except for the structural members, and reconstructed anew. In terms of form, material, and quality of details, the reconstruction and modernization of the house was geared to strengthen its original aspect of simplicity and lightness. The bathroom and the gardens were redesigned and the interior courtyard fitted with a retractable textile awning. Reconstructing, restoring, and reinterpreting the planting, fabrics, textures, and colors of individual details and surfaces represented the biggest challenge.

Umbau Johannes-Krahn-Haus
Conversion Johannes Krahn House
Inlandsprojekt Domestic project

Architekten Architects
Kirsten Schemel Architekten, Berlin
Kirsten Schemel
Nina Sommer

Projektpartner Project partner
Henning von Wedemeyer

Ingenieure Engineers
Pichler Ingenieure GmbH, Berlin

Bauherr Client
Privat Private

Typologie Type
Wohnungsbau Residential building

Standort Location
Berlin

Beginn Start
2004

Fertigstellung Completion
2005

Nutzfläche Effective area
185 m²

1 Grundriss
  Floor plan
2 Küche
  Kitchen
3 Bibliothek
  Library
4 Blick in den Innenhof
  View into the atrium

Die Bebauung des Architekten Johannes Krahn im Berliner Hansa-Viertel (Interbau-Ausstellung 1957) interpretiert das traditionelle städtische Atriumhaus und dessen besondere Raumqualitäten von Offenheit und Umschließung. Der Umbau des Johannes-Krahn-Hauses modifiziert die kleinteilige Struktur zugunsten eines neuen großzügigeren Maßstabs. Die maßgebliche Innovation liegt dabei in der Umnutzung der Außenräume, die als erweiterte Zimmer begriffen werden. Alle Böden des Hauses und des Innenhofs sind daher durchgängig mit einem dunklen, glänzenden Holz belegt, aus dem auch die Schrankobjekte im Innenraum und die Pflanzinseln im Außenraum gestaltet sind. Die Fassade wird durch respektvolle Eingriffe mit großformatigen Fensterelementen geöffnet. Eine leichte Membran aus Bambus- und Holzjalousien dient der Verschattung und komplettiert mit der neuen Beleuchtung eine fernöstlich inspirierte Raumwirkung.

With his buildings in the Hansaviertel, Berlin (1957 International Building Exhibition), architect Johannes Krahn interpreted the traditional urban courtyard house with its particular spatial contrasts of openness and enclosure. The restructuring process modified this small-scale structure to obtain spaces of more generous dimensions. The main innovation consisted in converting the exterior spaces into outdoor living rooms. This is why the floors of both the interior rooms and the courtyard were covered with the same dark, shimmering wooden flooring, which was also used for the built-in cupboards and storage units inside, and for bordering the flower beds outdoors. The façades were opened up with larger windows, respecting the original design. A bamboo screen and wooden sun blinds shade the windows. Together with the new luminaries, they create an effect inspired by the Far East.

KSP Engel und Zimmermann
Braunschweig / Berlin / Frankfurt am Main /
Köln Cologne / München Munich

Partner Partners
Jürgen Engel
*1954 in Düsseldorf
Michael Zimmermann
*1956 in Paderborn

Gründung Established
1998 in Deutschland Germany

Mitarbeiter Assistants
250

Kontakt Contact
Hanauer Landstrasse 287–289
60314 Frankfurt
Deutschland Germany

Tel   +49 (0)69 94 43 94 0
Fax +49 (0)69 94 43 94 38

info@ksp-architekten.de
www.ksp-architekten.de

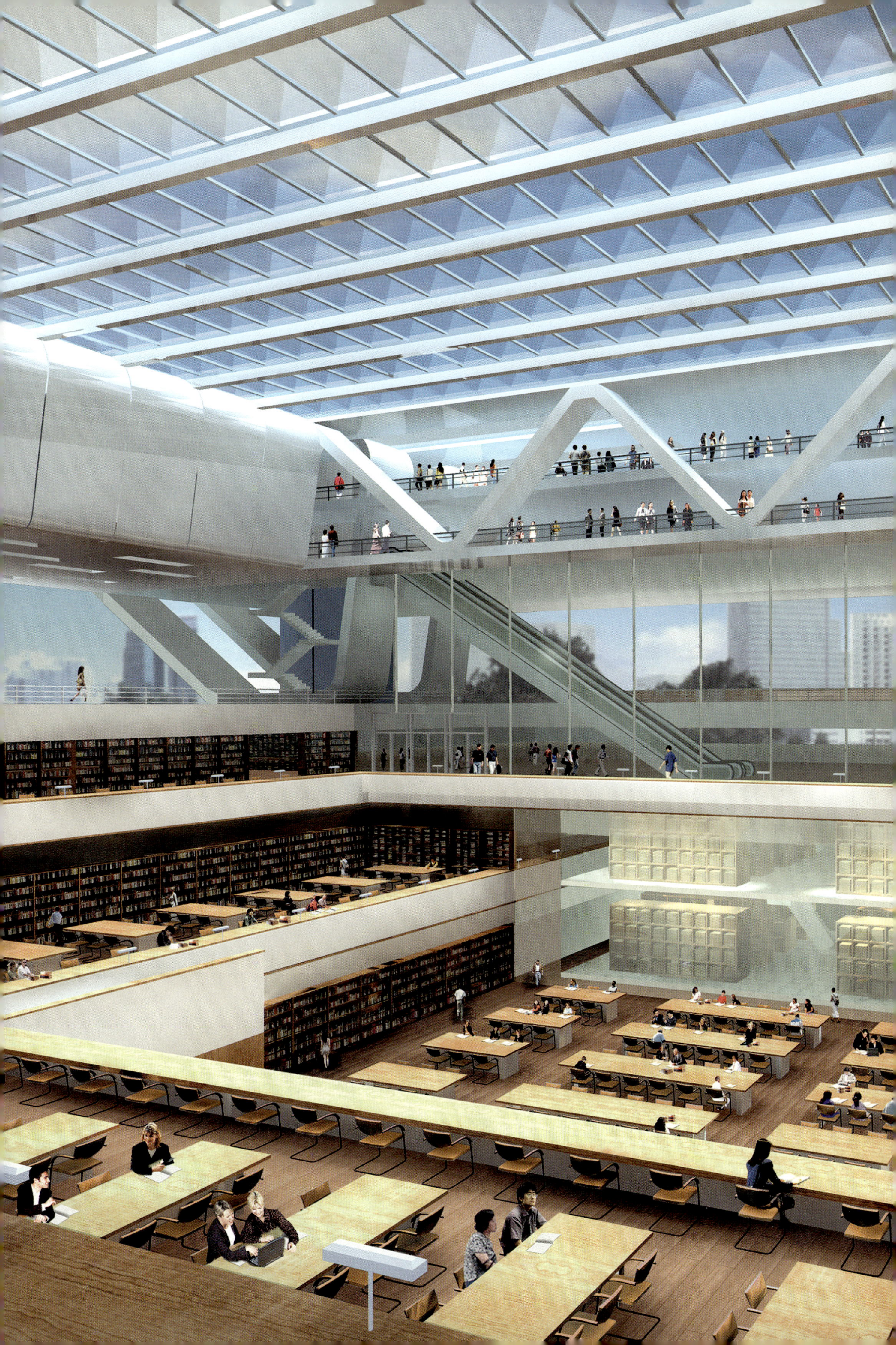

Chinesische Nationalbibliothek
Chinese National Library
Auslandsprojekt Foreign project

Architekten Architects
KSP Engel und Zimmermann,
Berlin / Frankfurt am Main
Jürgen Engel, Michael Zimmermann
Diether Mehlo, Johannes Reinsch, Jorge Veiga,
Mirela Bosnjak, Marco Callegaro, Philip Englert,
Thomas Freiwald, Sandra Horesch, Valentin Schmitz,
Sebastian Seibold, Chen Weng, Liao Xin, Zhou Yue

Partner Partners
ECADI Shanghai, China

Ingenieure Engineers
WHP Weischede, Herrmann und Partner, Stuttgart
Lemon Consult, Zürich Zurich

Bauherr Client
Chinesische Nationalbibliothek, Peking
Chinese National Library, Beijing

Typologie Type
Kulturbau

Standort Location
Peking Beijing, China

Wettbewerb Competition
2003

Fertigstellung Completion
2008

Brutto-Grundfläche Gross floor area
77 687 m²

Der Entwurf der Chinesischen Nationalbibliothek baut auf der Sammlung Si Ku Quan Shu des Kaisers Quianlong (1736–1795) auf, die im Sockel des Gebäudes untergebracht und stets sichtbar ist. Um diese herum liegt auf mehreren Ebenen der große Raum der zeitgenössischen Bibliothek. Im »schwebenden« Dach befindet sich die digitale Bibliothek. Der Neubau verknüpft so symbolisch Vergangenheit, Gegenwart und Zukunft. Der Eingang führt über eine breite Freitreppe in die zweite Etage. Von hier aus überblickt man die gesamte Bibliothek mit der weit gespannten Stahlkonstruktion des Dachs. Von außen betrachtet wirken die obersten beiden Ebenen wie ein liegendes Buch, das von schrägen Stützen gehalten wird. Der erhöhte Sockel, die Säulen und das Dach sind in der chinesischen Baugeschichte stilistische Elemente, die den bedeutenden, meist öffentlichen Bauten vorbehalten waren. In einer zeitgenössischen Interpretation greift der Entwurf diese Elemente auf.

The design for the Chinese National Library literally builds on the most important section of its collections, the Collection Si Ku Quan Shu of Emperor Quianlong (1736–95), which is permanently on show in the base of the building. It is surrounded by the large multistory hall of the modern library, while the digital library occupies the top floor under the "floating" roof. Thus the new building combines and symbolizes China's past, present, and future. A wide front stairway leads to the entrance on the second upper level. From here one overlooks the entire library interior, covered by the wide-span steel structure of the roof. Seen from outside, the top two floors look like a book lying on slanted supports. In Chinese architectural history, the raised base, the columns, and the roof are the stylistic elements reserved for prestigious, mostly public buildings. The current project has interpreted these elements in a contemporary way.

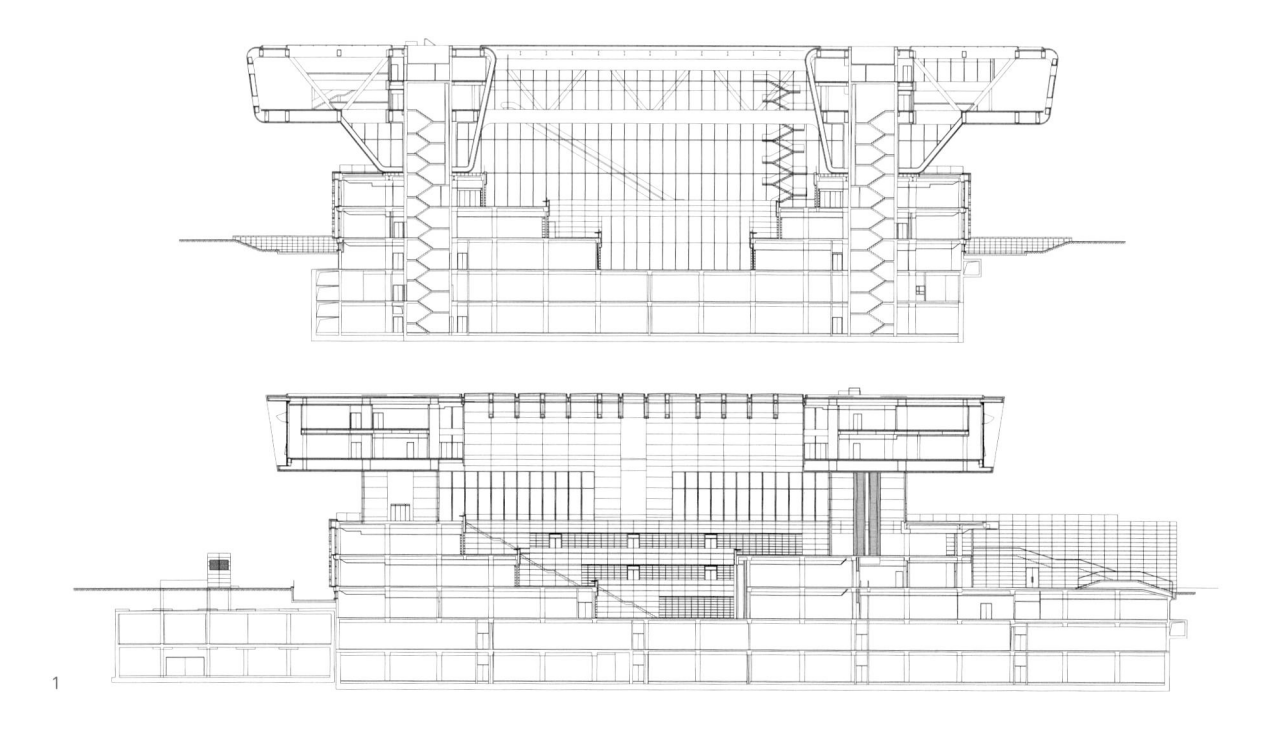

1

1 Schnitte
  Sections
2 Vogelperspektive bei Nacht
  Bird's-eye view at night
3 Außenansicht
  Exterior view
4 Richtfest
  Topping-out ceremony

161

WestendDuo
WestendDuo
Inlandsprojekt Domestic project

Architekten Architects
KSP Engel und Zimmermann, Frankfurt am Main
Jürgen Engel, Michael Zimmermann
Martina Lasse, Uwe Mehring, Ulf Gatzke-Yu,
Daniel Arfeller, Oliver Burk, Thomas Busse, Zlatka
Damjanova, Johannes Eichelberger, Marc Höricht,
Pagorn Potiwihok, Vitoria Vasquez-Roiz, Anke
Wünschmann, Jong-A Yu

Ingenieure Engineers
WHP Weischede, Herrmann und Partner, Stuttgart
Lemon Consult, Zürich
Reuter + Rührgartner, Rosbach
AMP Albrecht Memmert & Partner GBR, Neuss
Sommerlad Haase Kuhli, Gießen
Lüsebrink Ingenieure, Hamburg
Pabst und Partner Ingenieure, Bonn

Bauherr Client
Hochtief Projektentwicklung GmbH

Typologie Type
Verwaltungsbau Office building

Standort Location
Frankfurt am Main

Wettbewerb Competition
2001

Fertigstellung Completion
2006

Brutto-Grundfläche Gross floor area
32 700 m²

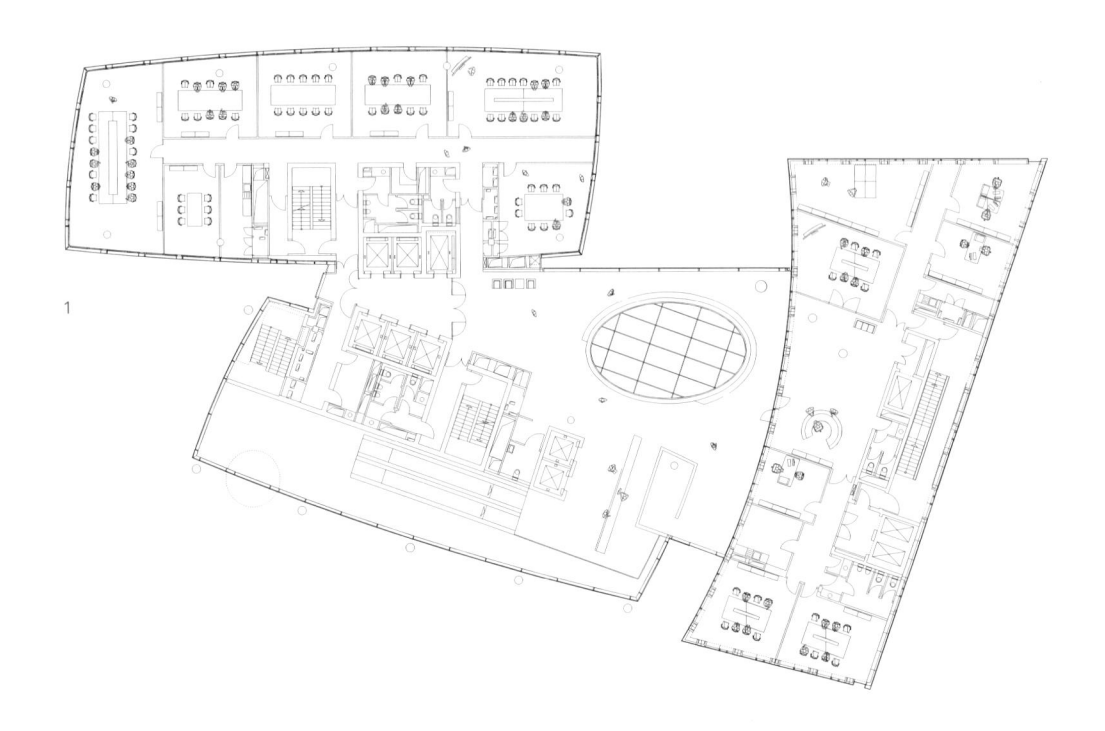

Das Doppelhochhaus WestendDuo liegt im Frankfurter Stadtteil Westend in der Nähe der Alten Oper und ist mit 96 Metern Höhe eines der kleineren Hochhäuser Frankfurts. Selbstbewusst und spannungsreich nehmen die beiden schlanken Türme die unterschiedlichen Stadtraster auf. Während sich der Südturm parallel zur Bockenheimer Landstraße stellt, steht der Nordturm orthogonal zum Stadtraster des Westends. Durch die Verdrehung der Türme zueinander entsteht eine sich öffnende Geste zur Alten Oper. Zum Wohngebiet hin verbergen die Türme ihre tatsächliche Dimension. Durch die leicht gebogenen zweigeschossigen Fassaden entsteht eine dynamische Wirkung. Der Blick gleitet von den Fassaden zu den Ecken, was perspektivisch den Umfang des Baus verkürzt. Das Zusammenfassen von zwei Geschossen betont zusätzlich die schlanke Eleganz. Der Neubau ist für verschiedene Mietkonstellationen flexibel konzipiert worden. Gefaltete Betondecken ermöglichen eine stützenfreie Raumdisposition und minimieren die Bauhöhe.

The twin towers called WestendDuo are located in Frankfurt's Westend area, near the Old Opera House. They are 96 meters high and therefore two of the smaller high-rises in Frankfurt. Assertive and dynamic, the two slender towers follow different lines of the urban grid. While the south tower was placed parallel to Bockenheimer Landstrasse, the north tower was placed at right angles to the Westend street grid. As the towers stand at angles to each other, they form an opening gesture toward the Old Opera House. The real dimensions of the twin towers, however, are not visible from the residential area. The slightly curving two-story façade modules create a dynamic effect that, seen in perspective, seems to shorten the length of the façades. Their double-story articulation enhances the towers' elegant slenderness. The floor areas were designed to allow for flexible uses by different tenants. Folded concrete ceilings made it possible to create large column-free spaces and to minimize the height.

1 Grundriss 1. Obergeschoss
  Second floor plan
2 Lage in der Stadt
  Site within the city
3 Fassade
  Façade
4 Außenansicht
  Exterior view
5 Foyer im 1. Obergeschoss
  Foyer on the second floor

KSV Krüger Schuberth Vandreike
Berlin

Partner Partners
Torsten Krüger
*1963 in Berlin
Christiane Schuberth
*1962 in Thale
Bertram Vandreike
*1961 in Eisenach

Gründung Established
1990 in Berlin

Mitarbeiter Assistants
29

Kontakt Contact
Brunnenstrasse 196
10119 Berlin
Deutschland Germany

Tel   +49 (0)30 28 30 31 0
Fax   +49 (0)30 28 30 31 10

ksv@ksv-network.de
www.ksv-network.de

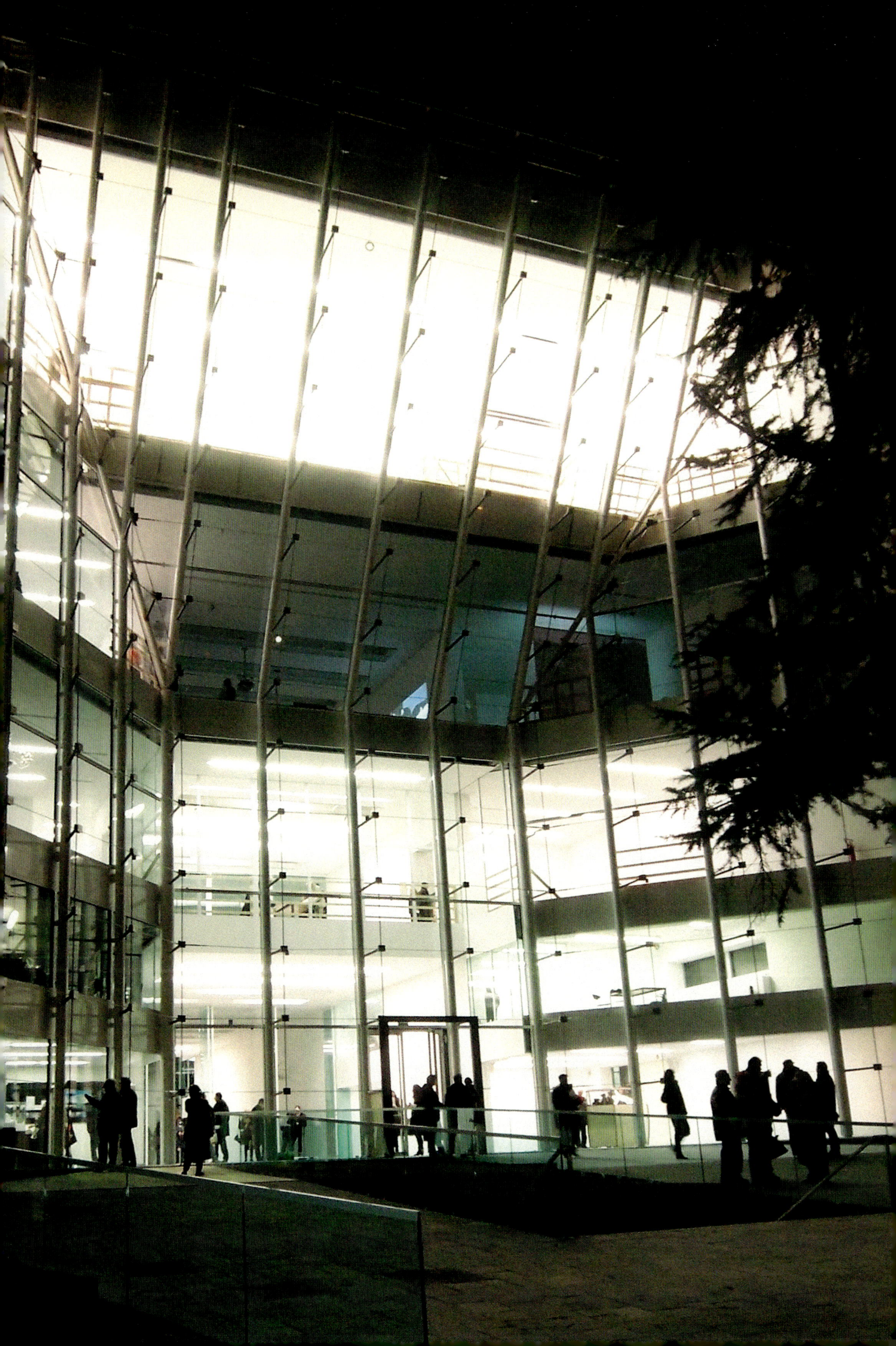

Museion
Museion
Auslandsprojekt Foreign project

Architekten Architects
KSV Krüger Schuberth Vandreike, Berlin
Torsten Krüger, Christiane Schuberth, Bertram Vandreike
Markus Reinhardt, Annemike Banniza, Jana Eckhoff, Markus Fiegl, Karena Filter, Moritz Hanke, Daniel Kohler, Jan Kunze

Ingenieure Engineers
Ingenieurbüro Pohl, Latsch
Ingenieurbüro Starke, Bozen
Ingenieurbüro Krone, Berlin
Lichtvision, Berlin
Thermostudio, Meran
Studio I. M., Klausen
Ingenieurbüro Schmidt-Olufsen, Berlin
Ingenieurbüro Rahn, Berlin
Ingenieurbüro Wagner, Berlin

Bauherr Client
Provinz Bozen-Südtirol, Amt für Hochbau, Bozen

Typologie Type
Kulturbau Cultural building

Standort Location
Bozen, Italien Italy

Wettbewerb Competition
2001

Fertigstellung Completion
2008

Brutto-Grundfläche Gross floor area
8 370 m²

Der Neubau des Kunstmuseums Museion ist ein expressives Symbol der Stadt und Provinz Bozen: Zum Fluss und zur Altstadt hin öffnet sich der Baukörper und lädt das Publikum ein, beim Durchwandern des Museums die Grenzen zwischen Stadt und Landschaft zu überwinden. Die beiden Stirnseiten fungieren als Schaufenster oder Projektionsflächen und unterscheiden sich in ihrer Transparenz von den mit profilierten Aluminiumplatten verkleideten Längsseiten. Der Kubus nimmt auf vier Ebenen den Großteil der geforderten Flächen auf, ergänzt durch ein weiteres Gebäude im Nordteil des Grundstücks. Der Vorplatz zwischen den beiden Gebäuden ist ebenfalls für Ausstellungen und Veranstaltungen bespielbar. Das Mittelschiff des Kubus, das den Ausstellungen vorbehalten ist, lässt eine große räumliche Vielfalt zu. In den Seitenflügeln sind die Erschließung und weitere Funktionen untergebracht. So entsteht ein räumliches Konzept, das die Flexibilität und Offenheit einer Werkstätte mit den Ausstellungsqualitäten einer klassischen Galerie verbindet.

The new Museion art museum is an expressive symbol of the city and region of Bolzano. The building opens toward the river and the historic city center and invites the public to negotiate the borderline between the city and the countryside while going through the museum. The two end walls form shop-window or projection screens and are in stark contrast to the long, massive, aluminum-clad side façades. The box-shaped museum accommodates a major part of the program on four levels and is supplemented by a secondary building on the northern site section. The open area between the two can be used for outdoor exhibitions and events. The central aisle of the main building is reserved for exhibitions and offers great spatial variety. The side tracts contain the circulation areas and other functions. Altogether, the new museum's spatial concept has combined the flexibility and openness of a workshop with the qualities of a classical exhibition gallery.

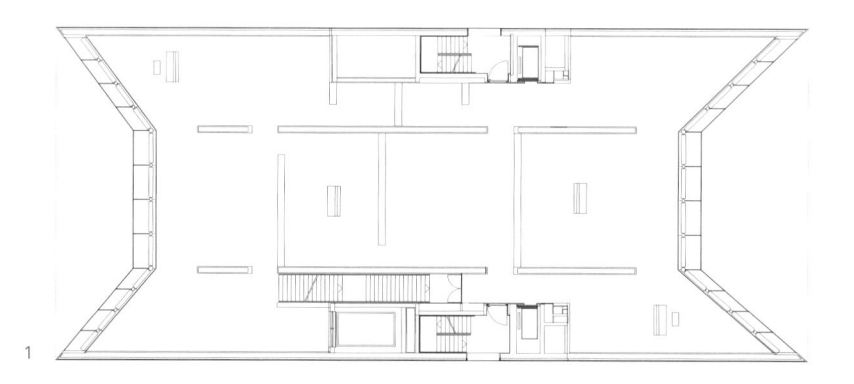

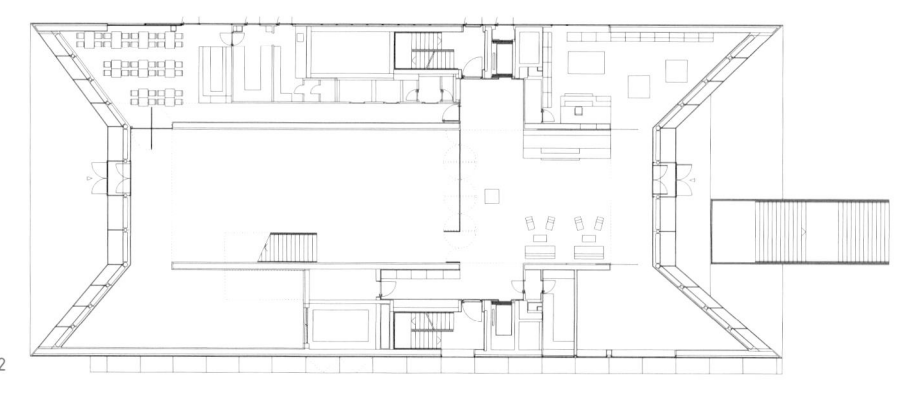

1 Grundriss 3. Obergeschoss
  Fourth floor plan
2 Grundriss Erdgeschoss
  Ground floor plan
3 Blick in den Eingangsbereich
  View into the entrance area
4 Aluminiumfassade
  Aluminum façade
5 Museion und Talferbrücke
  Museion and Talfer bridge
6 Ausstellungsraum
  Exhibition space

167

Erweiterung Institut für Ostseeforschung
Extension Institute for Baltic Sea Research
Inlandsprojekt Domestic project

Architekten Architects
KSV Krüger Schuberth Vandreike, Berlin
Torsten Krüger, Christiane Schuberth, Bertram Vandreike
Annemike Banniza, Hans Öchsner, Markus Pfeil, Thomas Reichold, Thomas Uhlig

Ingenieure Engineers
Wetzel & von Seht, Hamburg / Berlin
Arge Planung Haustechnik IOW, Elmenhorst-Lichtenhagen
Ingenieurbüro Widell, Berlin

Bauherr Client
Betrieb für Bau und Liegenschaften Mecklenburg-Vorpommern, Geschäftsbereich Rostock

Typologie Type
Forschungs- und Verwaltungsbau
Research and administration building

Standort Location
Warnemünde

Wettbewerb Competition
2004

Fertigstellung Completion
2007

Brutto-Grundfläche Gross floor area
3 430 m²

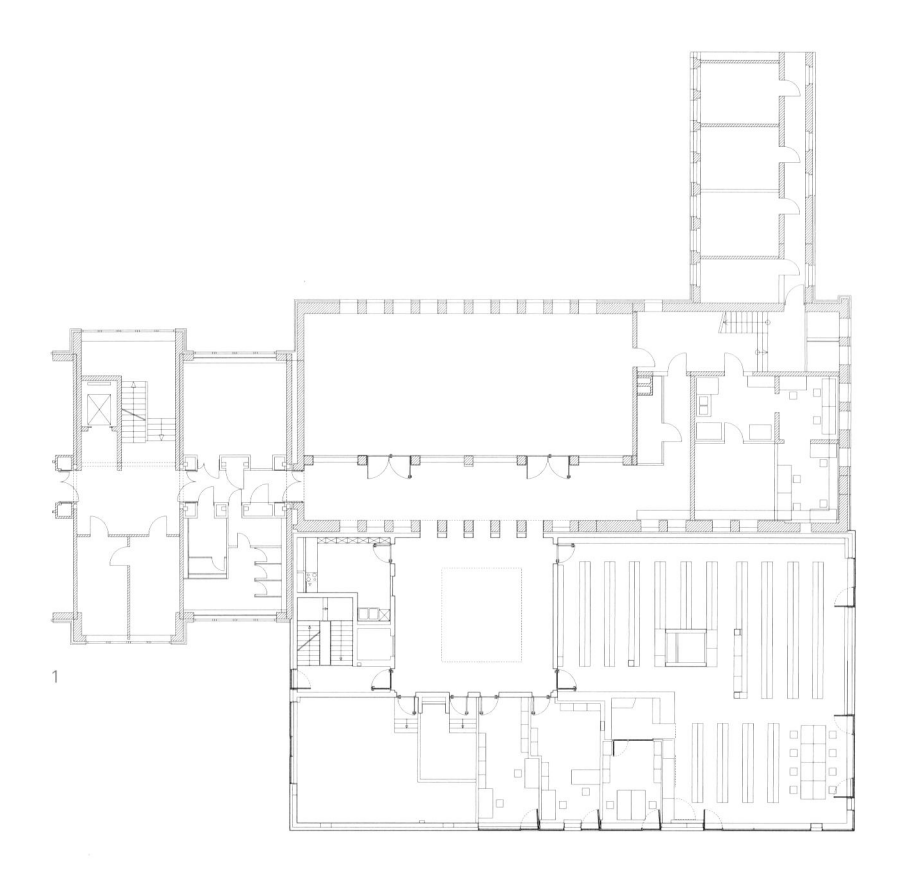

Das neue Institutsgebäude positioniert sich städtebaulich selbstbewusst als Baukörper am Kurpark des Ostseebads. Es bildet eine klare Kante zur bestehenden Villenstruktur der Uferpromenade und schafft mit dieser räumlichen Ordnung den nördlichen Abschluss des Parks. Durch die Konzentration der Baumaßnahmen in einem Kubus wurde ein hohes Maß an Flexibilität gewonnen. Alt- und Neubau sind ab dem ersten Obergeschoss räumlich-funktionell miteinander verwoben. Die materialbündige Ausbildung der Fassade in dunklem Putz, hellem Stein und Glas unterstützt die kompakte Form, einzelne Laborbereiche und Raummassen sind durch unterschiedliche Fensterbandlängen ablesbar. Für die Nutzung des Erweiterungsbaus sind Labore, Büros und eine Bibliothek vorgesehen. Der Forschungsbereich des Instituts umfasst die marine Ökosystemforschung in Küsten- und Randmeeren sowie das Monitoring für die Bundesrepublik Deutschland im Auftrag des Bundesamtes für Seeschifffahrt und Hydrographie.

The new building asserts itself as an urban element overlooking the park of the spa town of Warnemünde on the Baltic Sea. It forms a clear urban edge toward the residential neighborhood of the coastal promenade as well as the northern border of the park. Concentrating the program within a building cube offered a high degree of flexibility. From the second floor upward, the old and the new structures were interlocked in terms of both space and function. The smooth façade of dark plaster, pale stone, and glass enhances the building's compact shape. Individual laboratory and other interior spaces are indicated on the façade by window bands of different lengths. The extension is to accommodate laboratories, offices, and a library. The research department specializes in marine ecology in coastal and epicontinental seas. The institute also assumes sea-monitoring tasks on behalf of the Federal Republic of Germany, represented by the Federal Office for Maritime Traffic and Hydrography.

1 Grundriss 1. Obergeschoss
  Second floor plan
2 – 4 Innenhof
  Atrium
5 Außenansicht
  Exterior view

Pysall Ruge Architekten
Berlin

Partner Partners
Justus Pysall
*1961 in Braunschweig
Peter Ruge
*1959 in Düsseldorf

Gründung Established
1993 in Berlin

Mitarbeiter Assistants
18

Kontakt Contact
Zossener Strasse 56 – 58
10961 Berlin
Deutschland Germany

Tel   +49 (0)30 69 81 08 0
Fax   +49 (0)30 69 81 08 11

info@pysall-ruge.de
www.pysall-ruge.de

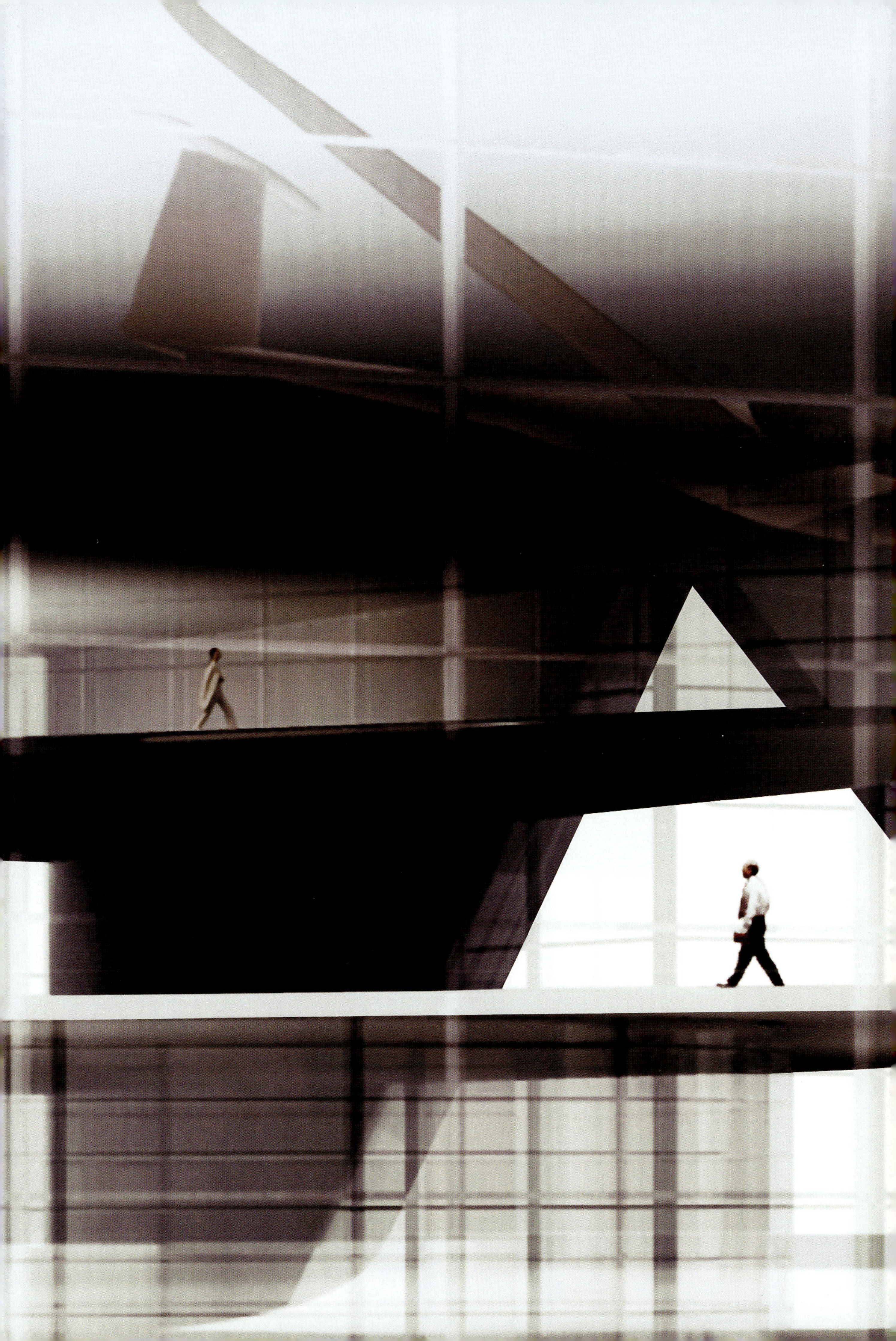

Muzeum Lotnictwa Polskiego
Muzeum Lotnictwa Polskiego
Auslandsprojekt Foreign project

Architekten Architects
Pysall Ruge Architekten, Berlin
mit with Bartlomiej Kisielewski
Justus Pysall, Peter Ruge
Mateusz Rataj, Katarzyna Ratajczak

Ingenieure Engineers
Arup GmbH, Krakau Krakow

Bauherr Client
Muzeum Lotnictwa Polskiego, Krakau Krakow

Typologie Type
Kulturbau Cultural building

Standort Location
Krakau, Polen Krakow, Poland

Wettbewerb Competition
2005

Fertigstellung Completion
2009

Brutto-Grundfläche Gross floor area
4 504 m²

Der Neubau des Museums für Luftfahrt greift alle topologischen und gedanklichen Bezüge zur Umgebung auf und verdichtet sie in einem zeichenhaften Bauwerk. Das Empfangs-, Ausstellungs- und Verwaltungsgebäude reiht sich als eines der baulichen Elemente ganz logisch und ungezwungen in das vorhandene Ensemble der Hallen und Dienstgebäude ein. Die alten Hangars lieferten das Modulmaß der quadratischen Grundplatte und die Firstlinie des Neubaus. Eingeschnitten und gefalzt wie beim Falten eines Papierflugzeugs entsteht die Großform: ein Flügeldreieck, in Beton gegossen und dennoch leicht wie ein Windrad oder ein Propeller. Die Räume öffnen sich großflächig verglast in alle Himmelsrichtungen. Die Ausstellung verbindet sich optisch mit den Freiflächen und bietet einen Ausblick auf das Flugfeld mit den im Freien aufgestellten Maschinen. Die Flugzeuge im Nordflügel erscheinen nicht wie eingeschlossen, sondern nur untergestellt, jederzeit bereit, zur Startbahn zu rollen. Auf drei Ebenen befinden sich die Museumsräume und die Verwaltung.

The design of Poland's new museum for aviation responds to the topography and "immaterial substance" of its environment and translates these into an emblematic building. The reception, exhibition, and administration building inserts itself logically and naturally into the existing complex of exhibition pavilions and service buildings. The old hangars provided the modular grid for the new building's square foundation raft and ridgelines. Though cast in concrete, the large building mass on a three-wing pinwheel plan appears as light as a cut and folded paper aircraft or propeller. Large glazed façade sections open the interior galleries to the outdoors in all directions and thus visually link the interior and the aircraft exhibited on the airfield. The aircraft shown in the north wing do not appear locked in, but rather seem to stand in the open hangar ready to roll out onto the runway. The museum building contains three levels of exhibition galleries and administration offices.

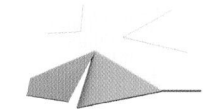

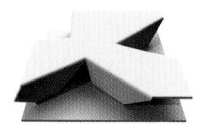

1 Faltmodell
  Folded model
2 Grundriss Erdgeschoss
  Ground floor plan
3 Grundriss 1. Obergeschoss
  Second floor plan
4 Grundriss 2. Obergeschoss
  Third floor plan
5–6 Außenansichten
  Exterior views

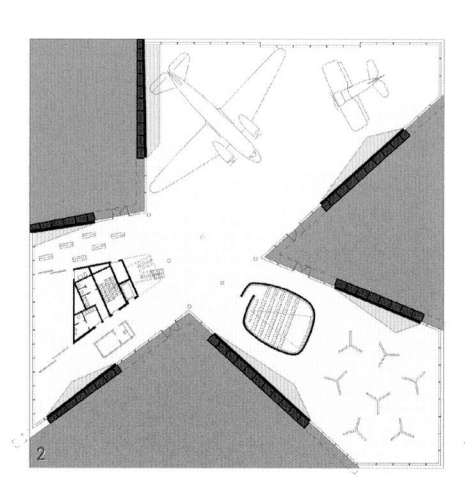

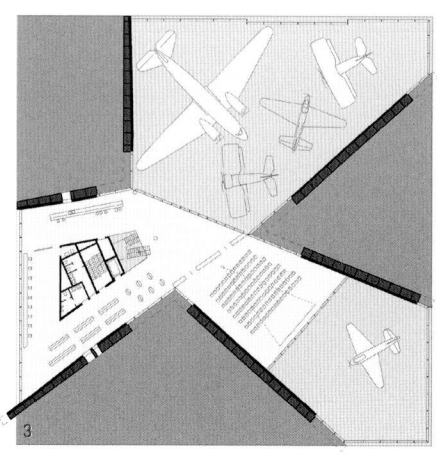

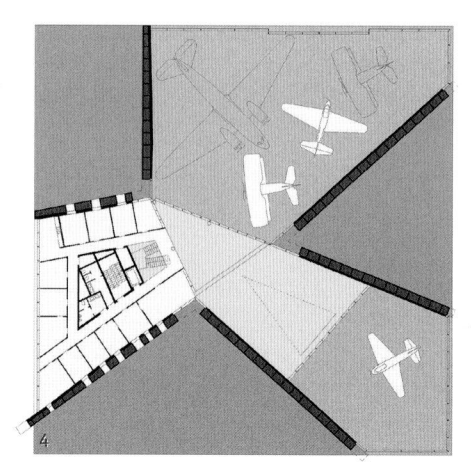

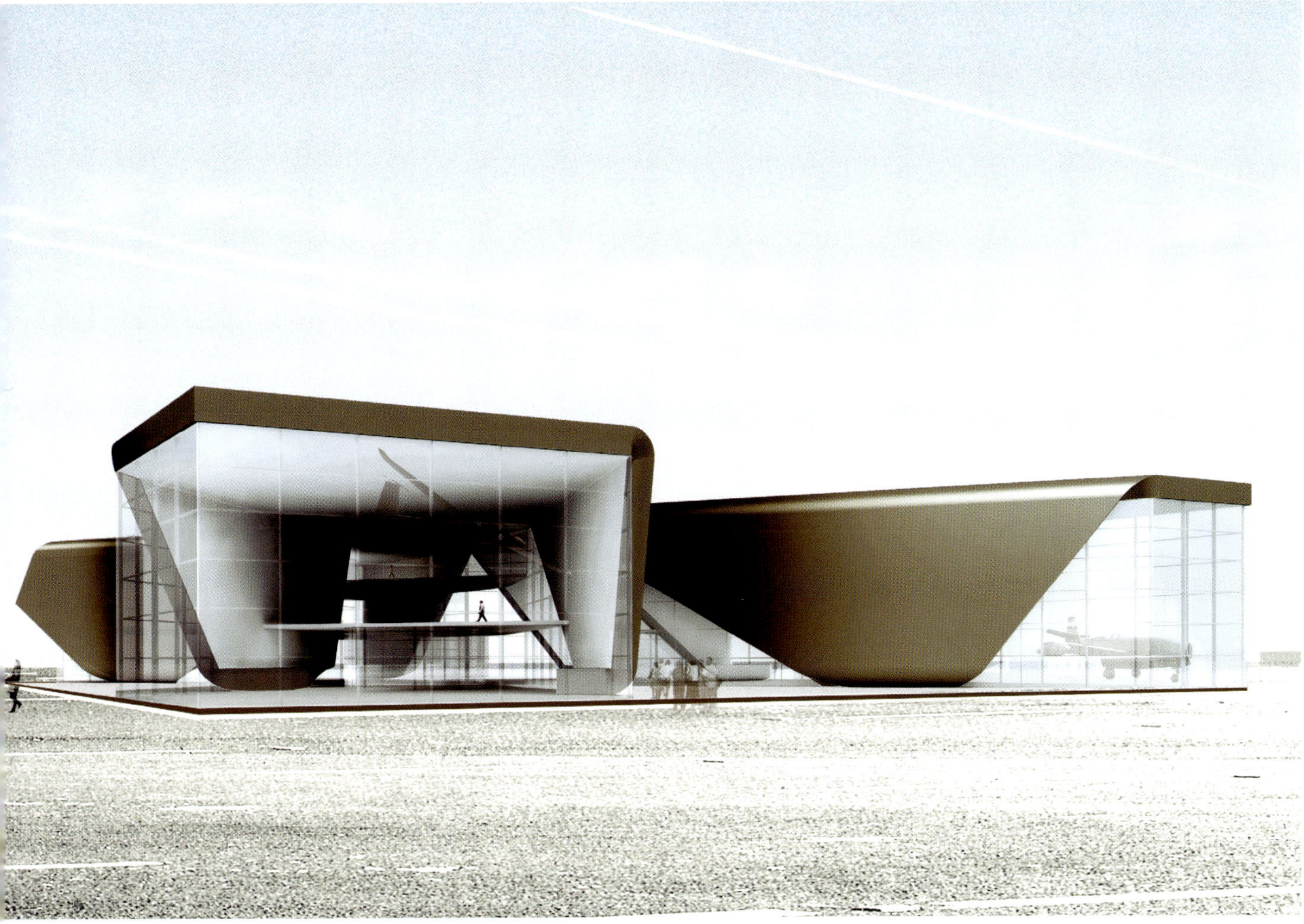

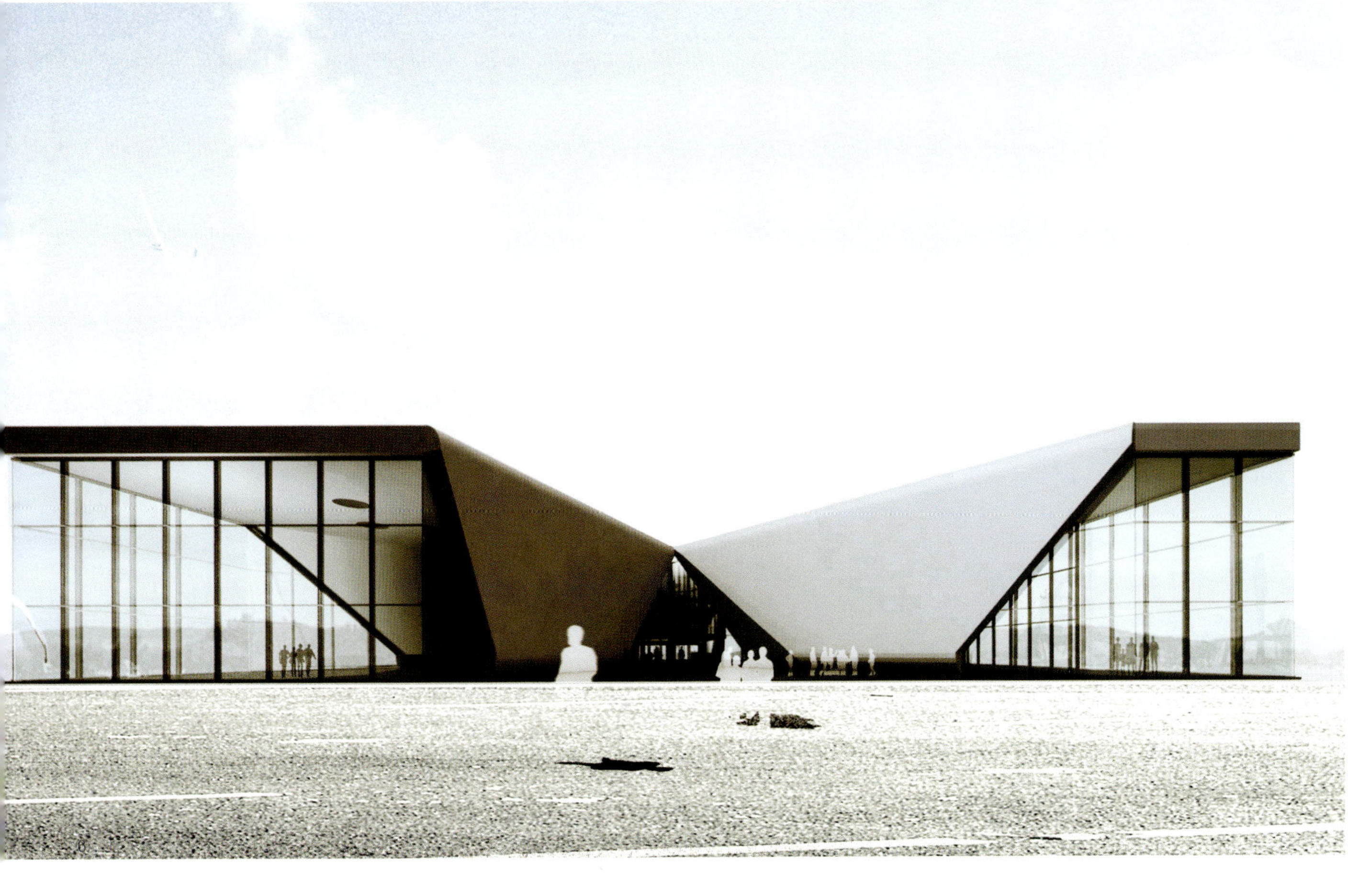

LTD_1 Lübeckertordamm
LTD_1 Lübeckertordamm
Inlandsprojekt Domestic project

Architekten Architects
Pysall Ruge Architekten, Berlin
Justus Pysall, Peter Ruge
Tobias Ahlers, Maha Alusi, Bartlomiej Kisielewski, Nicole Kubath, Matthias Matschewski, Philipp von Matt, Jan-Michael Strauch, Yolanda Yuste

Ingenieure Engineers
Lichtenau Himburg Tebarth Bauingenieure GmbH, Berlin
Reese Beratende Ingenieure VDI, Hamburg

Bauherr Client
L.T.D. Lübeckertordamm Entwicklungs-GmbH, c/o Versicherungskammer Bayern, München Munich

Typologie Type
Verwaltungsbau
Administration building

Standort Location
Hamburg

Wettbewerb Competition
2003

Fertigstellung Completion
2007

Brutto-Grundfläche Gross floor area
26 643 m²

1 1.–3. Obergeschoss
   Second–fourth floor plan
2 4.–6. Obergeschoss
   Fifth–seventh floor plan
3 Außenansicht
   Exterior view
4 Innenhof
   Inner courtyard

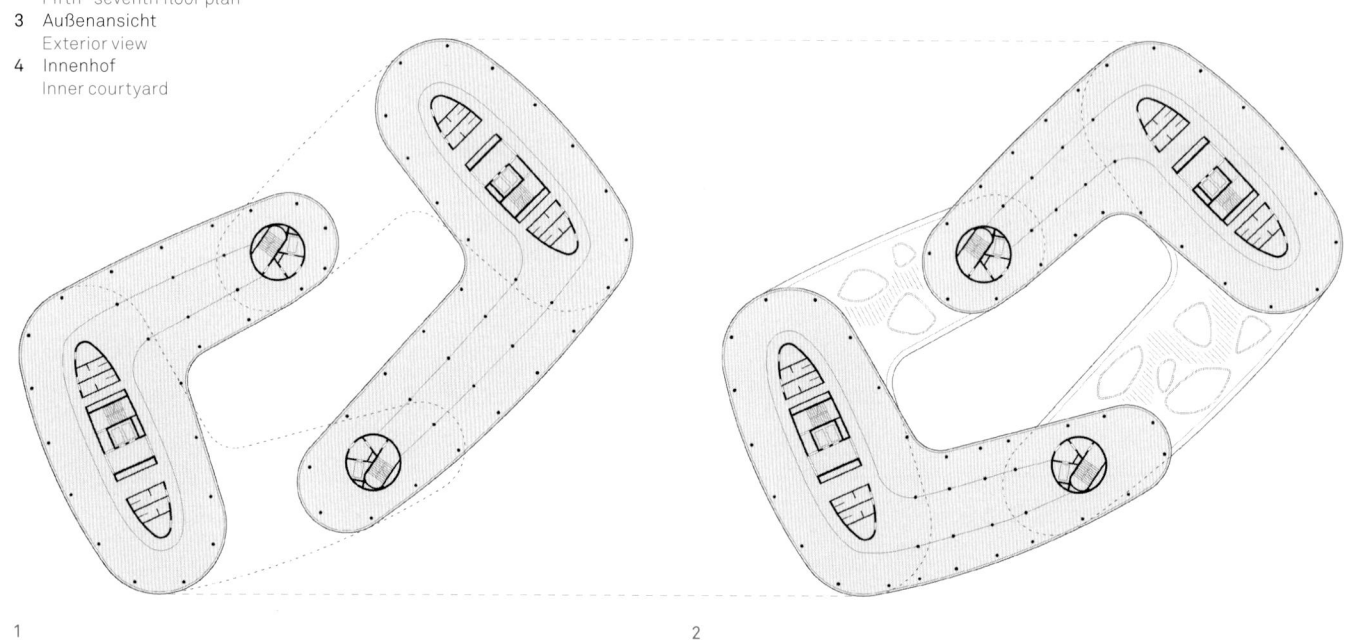

Auf einer Teilfläche des Krankenhauses St. Georg am Lübeckertordamm liegt das neue Büro- und Gesundheitszentrum. Den Kopf der Bebauung bildet das freistehende Bürohaus, welches in dynamischem Schwung, den Verkehrsfluss aufnehmend, die Topografie der einstigen Wallanlage nachzeichnet. Durch die Figuration der vier bumerangförmigen Bauteile ergeben sich ein repräsentativer Eingang, ein begrünter Innenhof sowie ein ungehinderter Blick aus allen Büroräumen. Die Farbe der Fassadenrahmungen vermittelt beim Passieren des Gebäudes ein bewegtes Spiel, das zur Markenbildung des Bauwerks beiträgt. Helle, natürlich belüftete Büros, nachhaltige Materialien und die Ausrichtung nach der Lehre des Feng Shui entsprechen den Anforderungen präventiver Gesundheitsvorsorge, einer gesunden Arbeitswelt und fernöstlicher Harmonie. Der Energie- und Klimahaushalt erreicht fast den Standard eines Passivhauses.

The new office and health-care center was built on the site of the St. Georg hospital complex on Lübeckertordamm. The new freestanding office block forms the head building of the complex and seems to emulate the shape of the former city ramparts with its dynamic curves. The four boomerang-shaped building sections—two stacked at angles on top of the other two—form an impressive entrance hall and enclose a spacious courtyard. All of the offices either overlook the courtyard or afford views of the surroundings. The color of the window frames contributes to the dynamic play of the various façade surfaces, which unfold as one walks past them and contribute to the branding of the building. Brightly lit and naturally ventilated offices, materials from sustainable resources, and interior designs based on feng shui principles comply with the demand for preventive health care, healthy working environments, and Far Eastern–type harmony. Heating and air-conditioning consume a minimum of energy, almost as little as a standard passive house.

3

4

Sauerbruch Hutton
Berlin

Partner Partners
Matthias Sauerbruch
*1955 in Konstanz
Louisa Hutton
*1957 in Norwich
Juan Lucas Young
*1963 in Buenos Aires

Gründung Established
1989 in London
1993 in Berlin

Mitarbeiter Assistants
105

Kontakt Contact
Lehrter Strasse 57
10557 Berlin
Deutschland Germany

Tel   +49 (0)30 39 78 21 0
Fax +49 (0)30 39 78 21 30

mail@sauerbruchhutton.com
www.sauerbruchhutton.com

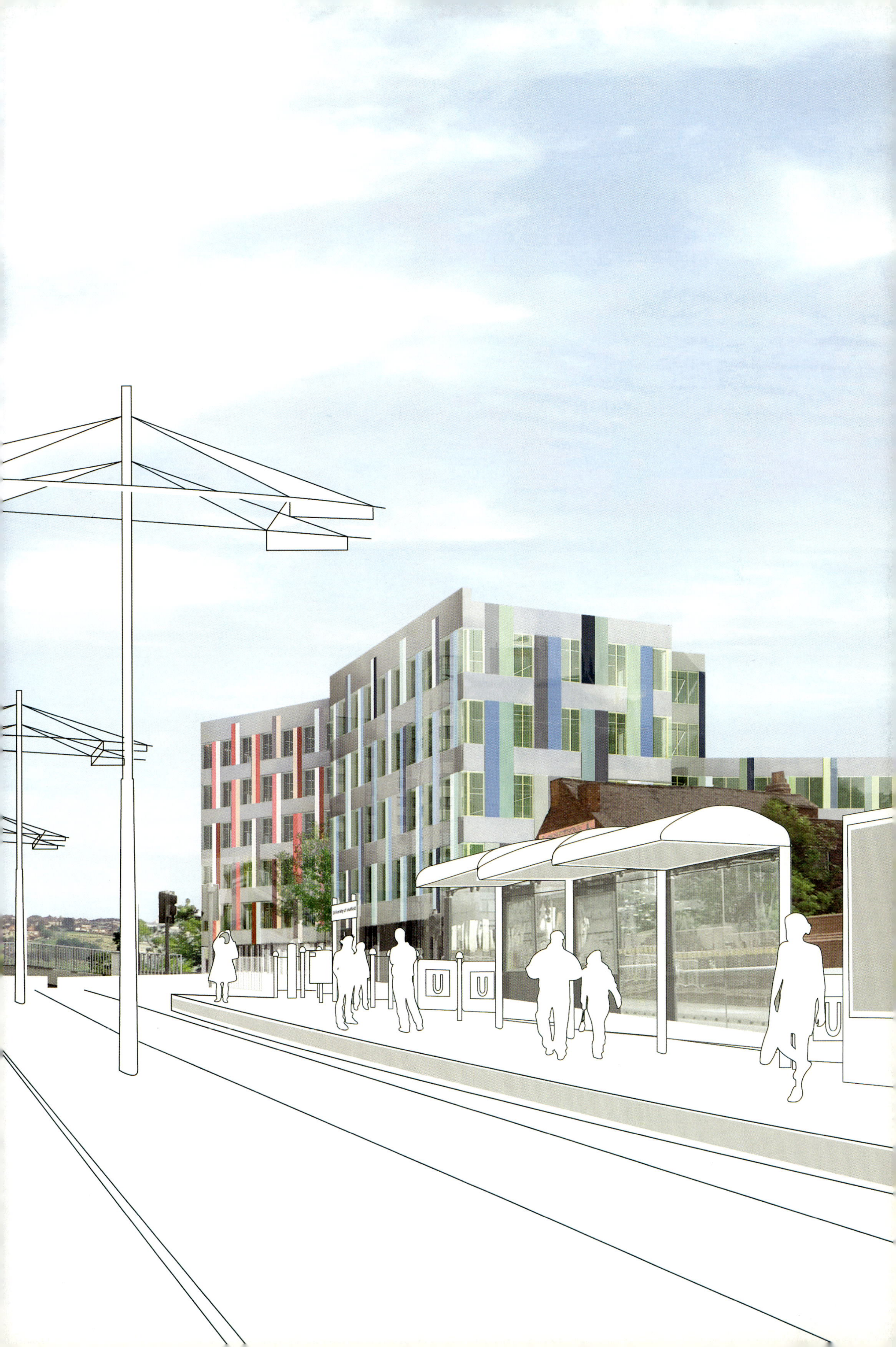

University of sheffield
U
U
U

Jessop West
Jessop West
Auslandsprojekt Foreign project

Architekten Architects
Sauerbruch Hutton, Berlin
Matthias Sauerbruch, Louisa Hutton, Juan Lucas Young, Jens Ludloff
Zachary Hinchliffe, Lina Lahiri, Stephanie Heese, Mareike Lamm, Ilja Leda, Tom Mival, Claus Nannen, Florian Öttl

Partner Partners
rmjm, Cambridge

Ingenieure Engineers
Arup GmbH, London
Gleeds, Cambridge

Bauherr Client
The University of Sheffield

Typologie Type
Hochschulbau University building

Standort Location
Sheffield, Großbritanien UK

Wettbewerb Competition
2005

Fertigstellung Completion
2008

Brutto-Grundfläche Gross floor area
5 900 m²

Der Masterplan zu Umbau und Umnutzung eines ehemaligen Krankenhausgeländes beinhaltet die Gestaltung einer neuen Mitte für die Universität von Sheffield und die Einrichtung eines neuen öffentlichen Außenraums für die Stadt. Neben der Gesamtplanung wird das Gebäude Jessop West für die Institute Recht, Geschichte und Englisch gebaut. Die drei unterschiedlich hohen Bauteile beherbergen die drei Fakultäten. Jeweils zwei Flügel bilden unterschiedliche Eingangssituationen, wobei der Haupteingang an der Leavy Greave Road liegt. Der Bau ist als einfache, robuste Struktur konzipiert, die aus diversen Überlegungen zur Nachhaltigkeit entstanden ist. Das Gebäude ist natürlich belüftet und seine Betondecken bleiben unverkleidet, um die Speichermasse zur Nachtkühlung zu nutzen. Das Tragwerk ist auf ein Minimum reduziert, mit ebenfalls rohen Stützen und Wänden. Die Fassade besteht aus einer Edelstahlverkleidung und farbigem Glas, mit jeweils eigenen Farben für jeden Flügel.

The master plan for restructuring and reusing a former hospital complex also entailed designing a new center and focus for Sheffield University and a new public area for the city. In addition to the master plan, the architects designed the Jessop West Building, with a wing each for the university's law, history, and English departments. The wings have different heights and are accessed via entrances in the three corners, each formed by two wings, with the main entrance from Leavy Greave Road. The building was conceived to be simple, robust, and ecologically sustainable. It is ventilated naturally, and its concrete floor slabs were left exposed to utilize their mass for night storage cooling. The structure was reduced to a minimum and consists of largely exposed concrete supports and walls. The façades were clad with stainless steel sheeting and colored glass, with a different color scheme for each wing.

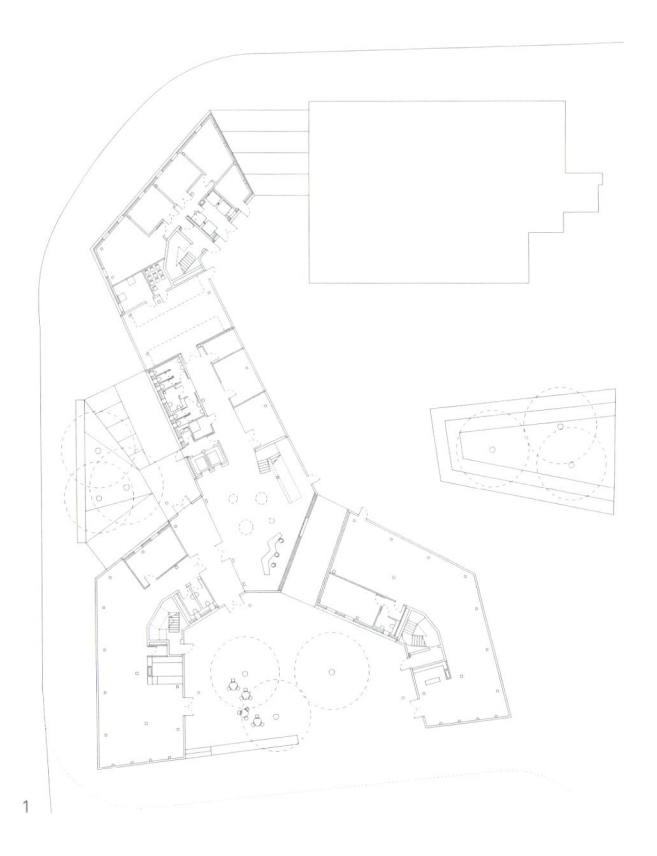

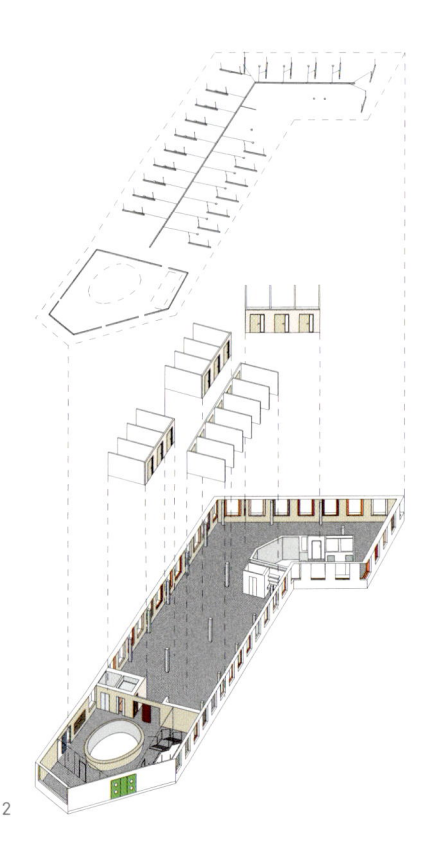

1

2

1 Grundriss Erdgeschoss
  Ground floor plan
2 Explosionszeichnung
  Exploded view
3 Modell
  Model

Umweltbundesamt
Federal Environment Agency
Inlandsprojekt Domestic project

Architekten Architects
Sauerbruch Hutton, Berlin
Matthias Sauerbruch, Louisa Hutton, Juan Lucas Young, Jens Ludloff
Andrew Kiel, René Lotz, Nicole Berganski, Denise Dih, Andrea Frensch, Matthias Fuchs, Frauke Gerstenberg, Andreas Herschel, Rasmus Joergensen, Agnieszka Kociemska, Mareike Lamm, Jan Laeufer, Jan Liesegang, René Lotz, Ian McMillan, Julia Neubauer, Konrad Opitz, Olaf Pfeifer, Jakob Schemel, David Wegener, Nicole Winge

Ingenieure Engineers
Krebs und Kiefer, Berlin
Zibell Willner & Partner, Köln Cologne / Berlin
Harms & Partner, Hannover

Bauherr Client
Die Bundesrepublik Deutschland, vertreten durch das BMVBW Bundesministerium für Verkehr, Bau- und Wohnwesen, vertreten durch LBB Sachsen-Anhalt Hauptniederlassung, Magdeburg, letztendlich vertreten durch Landesbetrieb Bau Niederlassung Ost, Dessau
The Federal Republic of Germany, represented by the BMVBW Bundesministerium für Verkehr, Bau- und Wohnwesen, represented by LBB Sachsen-Anhalt Hauptniederlassung, Magdeburg, finally represented by Landesbetrieb Bau Niederlassung Ost, Dessau

Typologie Type
Verwaltungsbau
Administration building

Standort Location
Dessau

Wettbewerb Competition
1998

Fertigstellung Completion
2006

Brutto-Grundfläche Gross floor area
39 800 m²

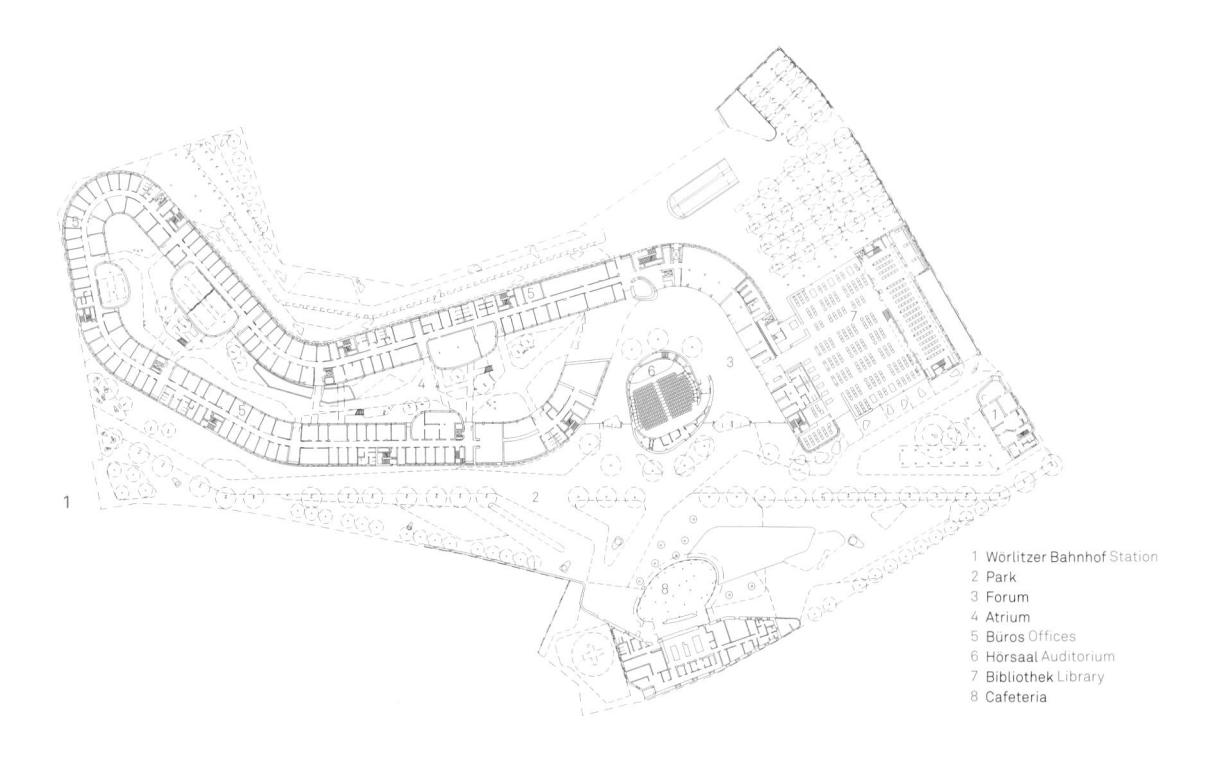

1 Wörlitzer Bahnhof Station
2 Park
3 Forum
4 Atrium
5 Büros Offices
6 Hörsaal Auditorium
7 Bibliothek Library
8 Cafeteria

Das Umweltbundesamt ist als beispielhaftes Projekt ökologischen Bauens geplant worden. Aktive und passive Maßnahmen zur Einschränkung von Energieverbrauch und CO2-Ausstoß werden mit einer Architektur kombiniert, die eine räumliche und materielle Ökonomie mit einer ansprechenden Sinnlichkeit verbindet. Der Standort, die Brache des Gasviertels, ist unter dem Gesichtspunkt des nachhaltigen Städtebaus ausgewählt worden. Kontaminierte Flächen wurden saniert, zwei bestehende Bauten in den Komplex integriert. Die Form des Neubaus wurde so gewählt, dass ein Großteil des Grundstücks der Öffentlichkeit als Park zur Verfügung steht. Vom Eingang, dem Forum, werden die öffentlichen Bereiche des Amtes, wie beispielsweise die Bibliothek und der Hörsaal, erschlossen; durch das überdachte Atrium wird der Rest des Komplexes betreten. Das Gebäude verbindet eine kompakte Gesamtform und hohe Wärmedämmung mit intelligenter Haustechnik und dem Einsatz erneuerbarer Energien. Die Materialien wurden aus ökologischen Gründen ausgesucht.

The Federal Environment Agency building was planned as an exemplary piece of ecological architecture. Active and passive measures to reduce energy consumption and CO2 emissions were integrated into an architectural configuration that combined spatial and material economy with aesthetic and sensual appeal. The site—an industrial waste of the gasworks area—was chosen with a view to redeveloping it in a sustainable way. Areas of contaminated soil were rehabilitated, and two existing structures were integrated into the new building. It was shaped to create a public park on a major section of the site. The public areas such as the library and the auditorium are accessed directly from the entrance hall—the forum—while the atrium leads to the other areas of the complex. The architecture combines a compact outer form and highly efficient heat insulation with intelligent service technology and the use of renewable energy supplies. The choice of materials followed ecological criteria.

1 Grundriss Erdgeschoss
  Ground floor plan
2 Zugang vom Bahnhof
  Entrance from the station
3 Bibliothek
  Library
4 Atrium
  Atrium

Staab Architekten
Berlin

Partner Partners
Volker Staab
*1957 in Heidelberg
Alfred Nieuwenhuizen
*1953 in Bocholt

Gründung Established
1991 in Berlin

Mitarbeiter Assistants
50

Kontakt Contact
Schlesische Strasse 20
10997 Berlin
Deutschland Germany

Tel +49 (0)30 61 79 14 0
Fax +49 (0)30 61 79 14 11

info@staab-architekten.com
www.staab-architekten.com

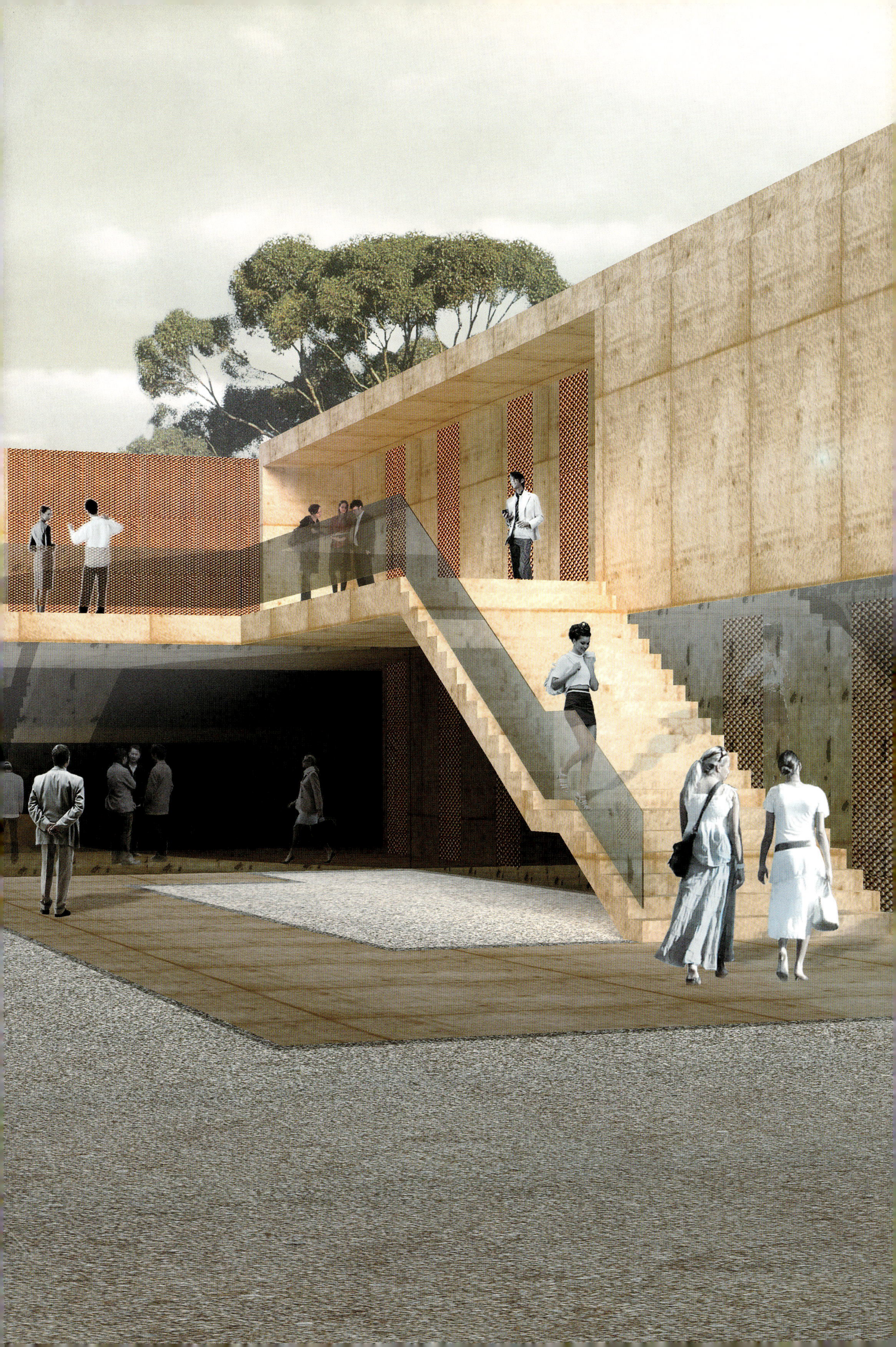

German International School
German International School
Auslandsprojekt Foreign project

Architekten Architects
Staab Architekten, Berlin
Volker Staab, Alfred Nieuwenhuizen
Birgit Decker, Stefan Brodmann, Sebastian Haufe, Ayse Hicsasmaz, Johannes Löbbert, Daniel Verhülsdonk, Petra Wäldle

Partner Partners
Cracknell Lonergan Architects mit Atelier 21, Sydney

Ingenieure Engineers
Scientists Engineers Managers & Facilitators, Sydney

Landschaftsplaner Landscape designers
Paul Scrivener, Sydney

Bauherr Client
German International School Sydney,
Johannes Gutenberg Limited by Guarantee

Zuwendungsgeber Financial backer
Bundesministerium der Finanzen BMF vertreten durch das Auswärtige Amt vertreten durch das Bundesamt für Bauwesen und Raumordnung BBR, Referat IV
Federal Ministry of Finance BMF, represented by the Federal Foreign Office, represented by the Federal Office for Building and Regional Planning BBR, Department IV

Typologie Type
Schulbau School building

Standort Location
Sydney, Australien Australia

Wettbewerb Competition
August 2003

Fertigstellung Completion
Juli July 2008

Brutto-Grundfläche Gross floor area
4 475 m²

Die German International School ist ein kleines, aber räumlich komplexes und vielfältiges Schuldorf, das angemessene Orte für die unterschiedlichen Nutzungen zur Verfügung stellt. In die vorhandene Topografie wird ein Wegenetz für die Erschließung der Schule eingeschrieben, sodass sich eine modellierte Landschaft mit versetzten Freiflächen ergibt. Die Erschließungsräume werden formal als skulpturaler Teil der Freiflächen begriffen und in Form von überdachten Außenbereichen gestaltet. Die verschiedenen Gebäude werden daran angegliedert. Ein zentraler Schulhof, der direkt über die Vorfahrt erreicht wird, dient als Verteiler und als Haupteingang zur Anlage. Dort liegen ein kleines Foyer und die Verwaltungsräume sowie die allgemeinen Funktionen wie Bücherei und Pausenraum. Jeder Schulbereich – Kindergarten, Vorschule, Grundschule, Gymnasium – hat einen eigenen Gebäudetrakt und einen dazugehörigen Freibereich. Im Zentrum der Anlage liegen die Räume der Fachklassen und der Sportbereich.

The German International School in Sydney is a small, spatially complex, and varied school "village" that offers spaces suited to various school functions. The slightly sloping site was remodeled to create outside circulation areas and yards. The entrance forecourts were interpreted as "sculptured" parts of the open areas and designed as covered open passages adjoining and interconnecting the different buildings. The central school yard is directly accessed via the front drive and forms the main entrance area, with the entrance building containing a small foyer, offices, and central functional spaces such as the library and recreation hall. Every school section—kindergarten, preschool, primary and secondary schools—is housed in a separate building. The classrooms and sports facilities form the center of the grounds.

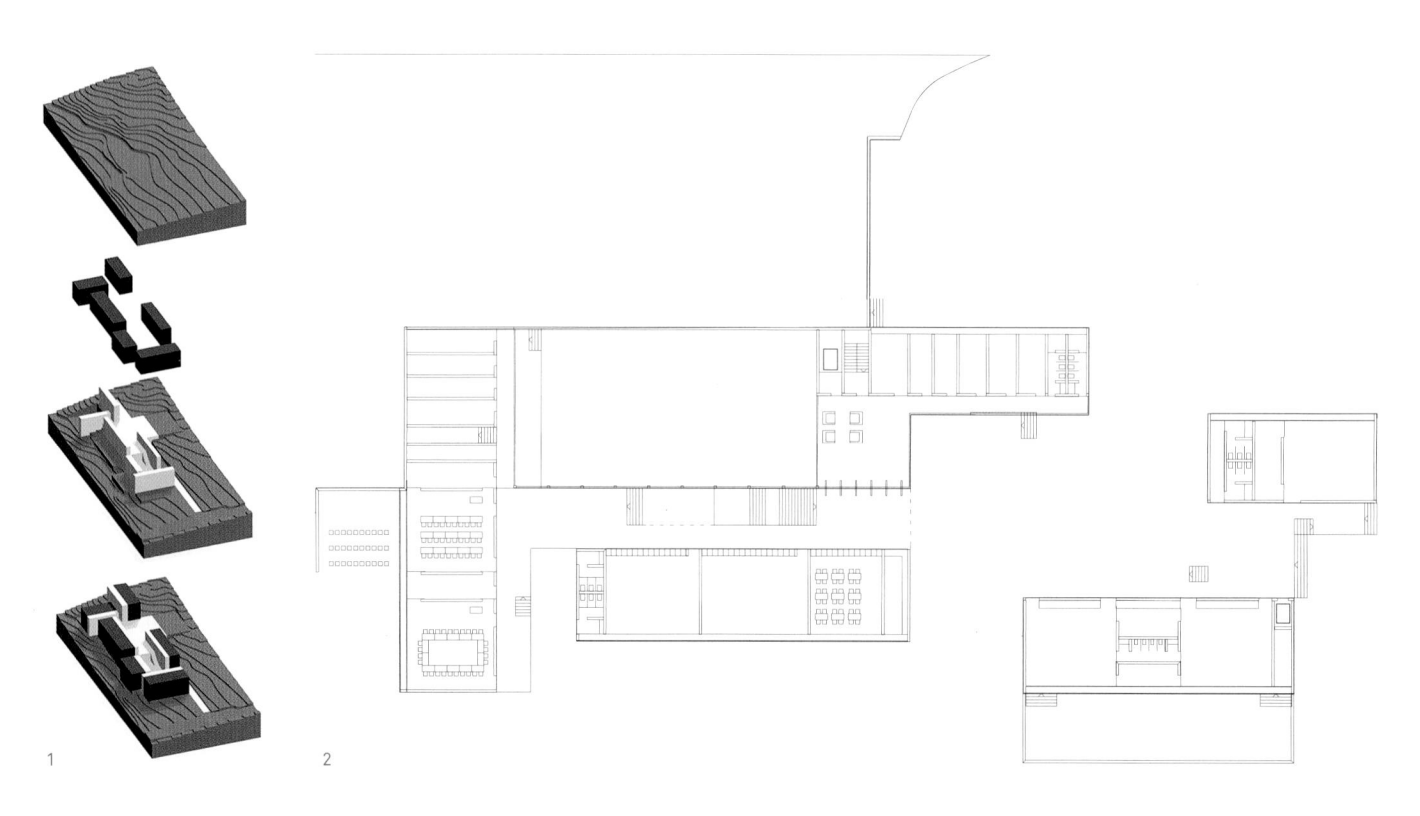

1   2

1 Konzeptmodell
  Concept model
2 Grundriss Ebene 0
  Level 0 floor plan
3 Zentraler Schulhof
  Central schoolyard
4 Eingang zum zentralen Schulhof
  Entrance to the central schoolyard

Bioquant
Bioquant
Inlandsprojekt Domestic project

Architekten Architects
Staab Architekten, Berlin
Volker Staab, Alfred Nieuwenhuizen
Birgit Decker, Birgit Knicker, Daniel Angly, Madina von Arnim, Alexander Böhme, Filiz Dogu, Sebastian Haufe, Corinna Moesges, Marion Rehn, Michael Schmid, Hanns Ziegler

Ingenieure Engineers
Krebs und Kiefer, Berlin
Winter Ingenieure, Berlin
LCI Labor Concept Ingenieurgesellschaft mbH, Lüneburg
Akustik-Ingenieurbüro Moll GmbH, Berlin

Landschaftsplaner Landscape designers
Levin Monsigny, Berlin

Bauherr Client
Land Baden-Württemberg vertreten durch Vermögen und Bau Baden-Württemberg, Universitätsbauamt Heidelberg
State of Baden-Württemberg represented by Vermögen und Bau Baden-Württemberg, Universitätsbauamt Heidelberg

Typologie Type
Hochschulbau University building

Standort Location
Heidelberg

Wettbewerb Competition
Oktober October 2002

Fertigstellung Completion
Februar February 2007

Brutto-Grundfläche Gross floor area
10 598 m²

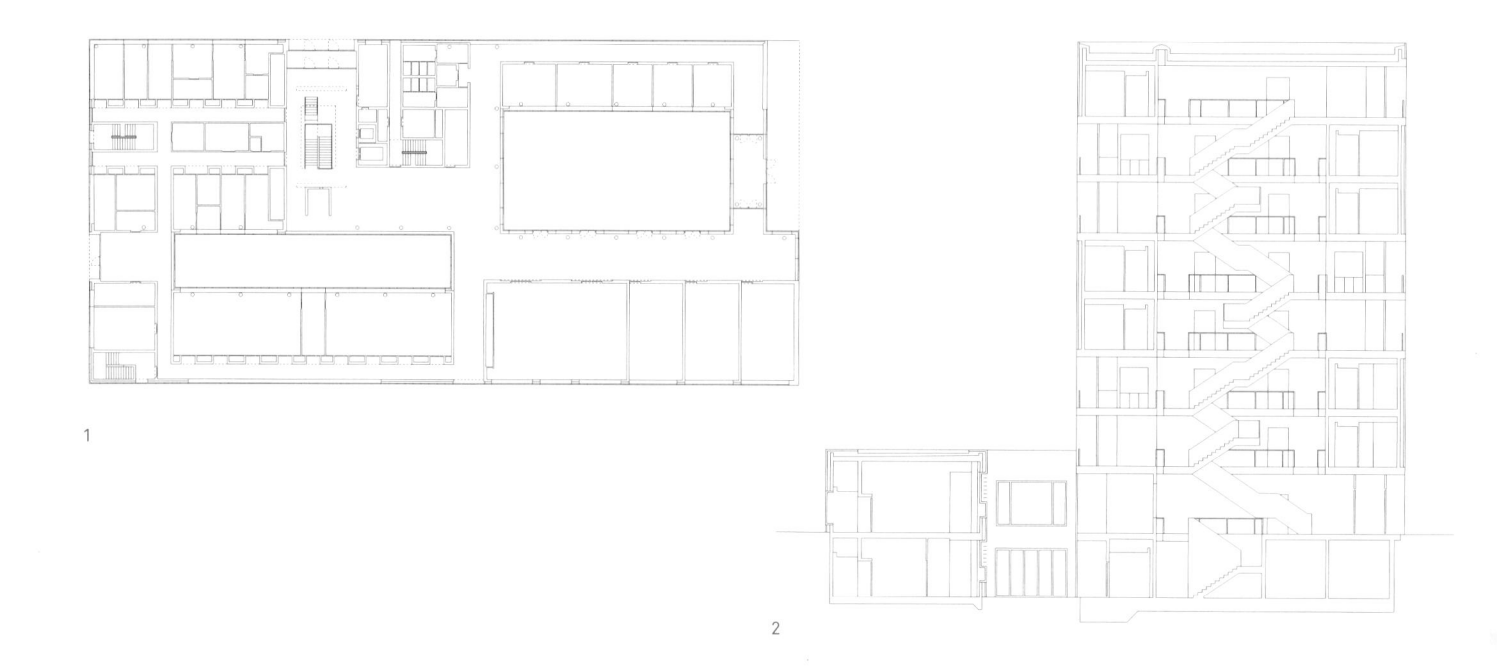

1

2

Der Neubau des Bioquant (Quantitative Analyse molekularer und zellulärer Biosysteme) für die Universität Heidelberg verbindet einen vertikalen Baukörper mit einem eingeschossigen Gebäude und reflektiert sowohl die funktionalen Anforderungen des Raumprogramms als auch den Kontext der benachbarten Bauten. Die öffentlichen Bereiche für Fortbildung und Kommunikation sind im einstöckigen Baukörper untergebracht, der von der räumlichen Dominanz der Bäume und des Grünraums bestimmt wird. Die integrierten Gartenräume und erweiterten Flurräume bieten hier eine angenehme Arbeitsatmosphäre und Orte der informellen Kommunikation. Im vertikalen Institutsbaukörper wird die fachübergreifende Zusammenarbeit von biowissenschaftlichem Forschungsbereich und dem Interdisziplinären Zentrum für Wissenschaftliches Rechnen architektonisch übersetzt. Die Laborbereiche und die Bereiche für das wissenschaftliche Rechnen sind zueinandergestellt und über den gemeinsamen Erschließungs- und Kommunikationsbereich miteinander verbunden.

Heidelberg University's new Bioquant center (destined for the quantitative analysis of molecular and cellular biological systems) combines a multistory block with a single-story wing, thus implementing the functional program and responding to the context. The low building contains public areas for training and communication and is surrounded by greenery and tall trees. Planted patios and wide corridors create a pleasant working atmosphere and offer scope for informal exchanges. The multistory institute building expresses in architectural terms the interdisciplinary character of the bio-scientific research and scientific quantification carried out here. Laboratories and computer rooms are juxtaposed and interconnected via shared circulation and communication areas.

1 Grundriss Erdgeschoss
  Ground floor plan
2 Schnitt
  Section
3 Foyer
  Foyer
4 Außenansicht
  Exterior view
5 Treppenhaus
  Staircase
6 Teeküche
  Kitchen area

187

Wandel Hoefer Lorch + Hirsch
Saarbrücken / Frankfurt am Main

Partner Partners
Andrea Wandel
*1963 in Saarbrücken
Rena Wandel-Hoefer
*1959 in Saarbrücken
Andreas Hoefer
*1959 in Hamburg
Wolfgang Lorch
*1959 in Nürtingen
Nikolaus Hirsch
*1964 in Karlsruh

Gründung Established
1992 in Saarbrücken

Mitarbeiter Assistants
21

Kontakt Contact
Dolomitenweg 19
66119 Saarbrücken
Deutschland Germany

Tel   +49 (0)68 19 26 55 88
Fax   +49 (0)68 19 26 55 95

Kettenhofweg 113
60325 Frankfurt
Deutschland Germany

Tel   +49 (0)69 74 90 29
Fax   +49 (0)69 74 90 24

mail@whlh.de

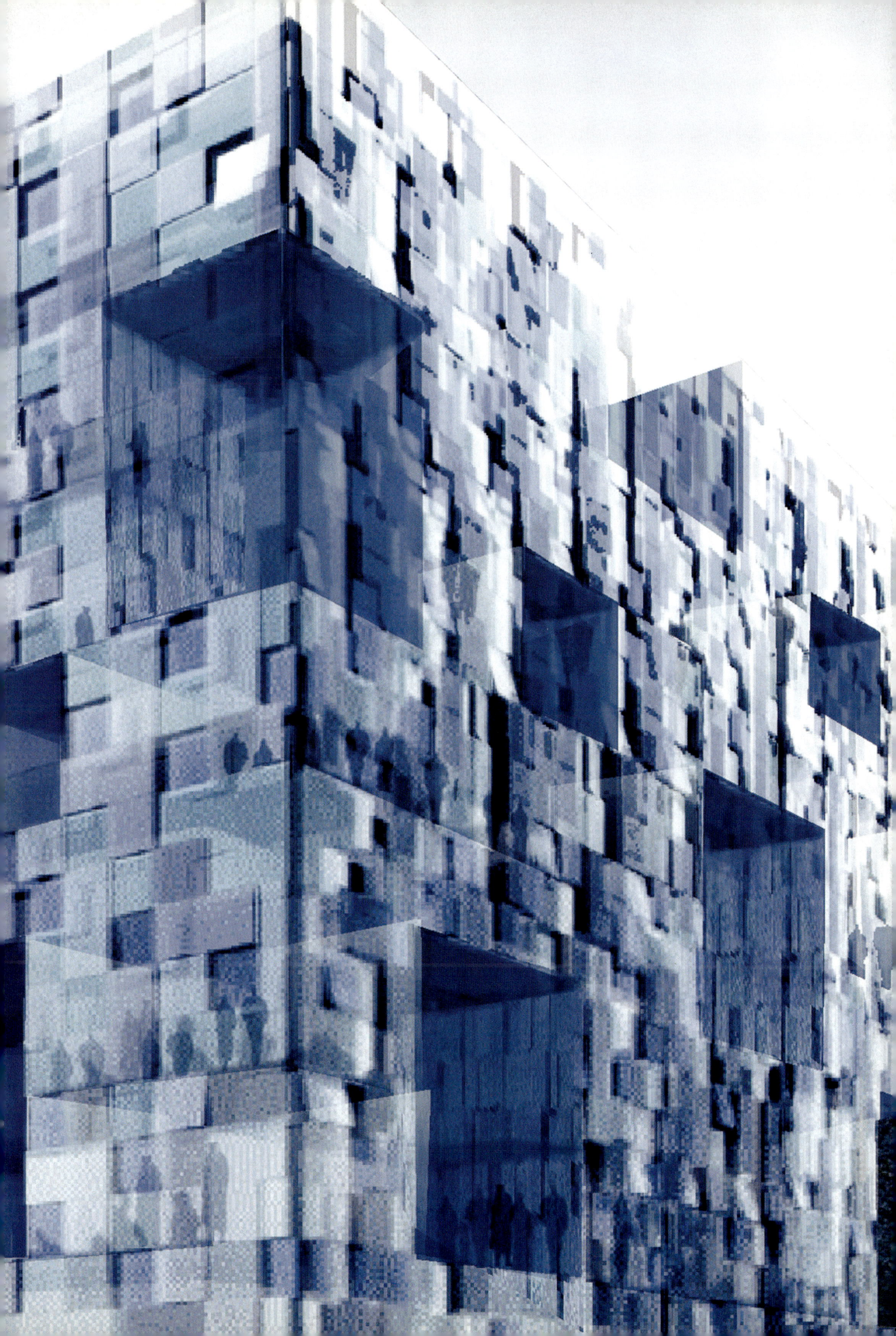

Hybrid Highrise Tbilisi
Hybrid High-rise Tbilisi
Auslandsprojekt Foreign project

Architekten Architects
Wandel Hoefer Lorch + Hirsch, Saarbrücken /
Frankfurt am Main
Wolfgang Lorch, Nikolaus Hirsch
Christine Biesel, Dirk Lang, Andreas Schmalz,
Johannes Thoma

Partner Partners
Bega Karsidze, Tiflis

Ingenieure Engineers
WPW Ingenieure, Saarbrücken

Bauherr Client
TIC, Tiflis

Typologie Type
Verwaltungs- und Geschäftsbau
Administration and commercial building

Standort Location
Tiflis, Georgien Georgia

Wettbewerb Competition
August 2005

Fertigstellung Completion
Dezember December 2008

Brutto-Grundfläche Gross floor area
35 000 m²

Das zehngeschossige Hybrid Highrise bildet in Größe und Form einen markanten Akzent im Stadtbild von Tiflis. Es handelt sich um einen kubischen, gläsernen Baukörper, dessen ausgeprägte Fassadenmodulation ein hohes Maß an Differenziertheit und Maßstäblichkeit herstellt. Die Fassade wird durch Vor- und Rücksprünge sowie großzügige Loggien und Dachgärten gegliedert, die das Volumen des Gebäudes rhythmisieren und gleichzeitig natürliches Licht in die Tiefe des Gebäudes bringen. Hochselektive Sonnenschutzgläser, die ein optimales Verhältnis von Lichttransmission und Gesamtenergiedurchlass ergeben, bestimmen in ihrer Tönung die Farbigkeit der Fassade. Funktional stellt das neue Gebäude eine komplexe Mischung aus Geschäfts-, Gastronomie-, Büro-, Konferenz- und Hotelnutzungen her, die den urbanen Kontext der Umgebung aktiviert. Der großzügige Hauptzugang dient den Geschäftsfunktionen, während ein weiterer Zugang die Büros erschließt. Der Supermarkt im Untergeschoss kann unabhängig erreicht werden.

In terms of mass and height, the ten-story "Hybrid High-rise" is prominent in the city of Tbilisi. The building is a glass cube with modulated and articulated façades that give it great variety, aesthetic appeal, and scale effects. The façade modulation and articulation take the form of recessed and projecting sections, spacious loggias, and roof gardens creating a rhythmical pattern and directing daylight into the depths of the building. Highly selective anti-sun glass panes with an optimal light-transmission-to-total-thermal-conduction ratio change color depending on weather conditions, and thus determine the color of the façade. In terms of function, the new building is a complex hybrid containing retail and catering outlets, offices, conference facilities, and a hotel. This variety of functions livens up the immediate environment. The generously dimensioned main entrance leads to the commercial areas, while a secondary entrance gives access to the office floors. The basement supermarket is accessed separately.

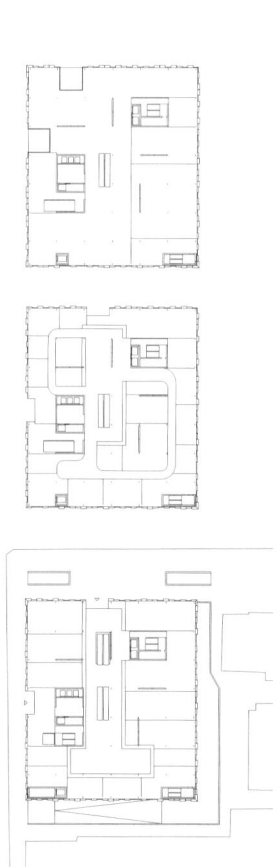

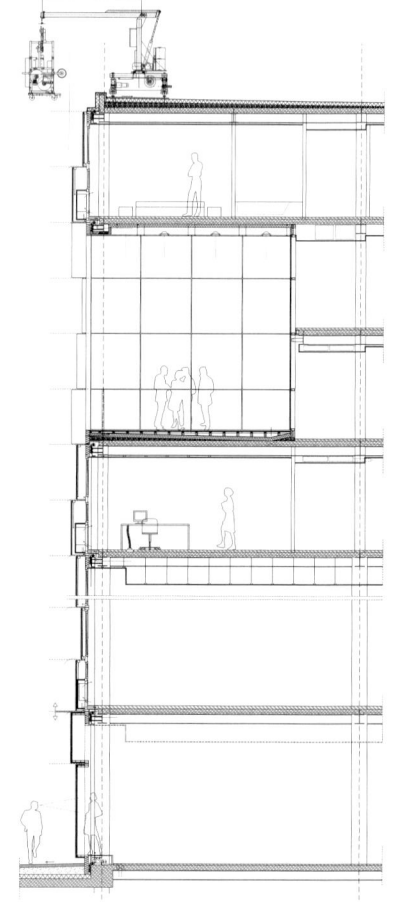

1 Grundrissvarianten
  Floor plan variations
2 Schnitt Detail
  Section detail
3 Fassadenausschnitt
  Façade mock-up
4 Außenansicht
  Exterior view
5 Fassade
  Façade

Dokumentationshaus Hinzert
Hinzert Document Center
Inlandsprojekt Domestic project

Architekten Architects
Wandel Hoefer Lorch + Hirsch, Saarbrücken / Frankfurt am Main
Andrea Wandel, Wolfgang Lorch, Nikolaus Hirsch
Christine Biesel, Alexander Keuper, Dirk Lang

Ingenieure Engineers
Schweitzer Ingenieure, Saarbrücken
Landesbetrieb LBB, Trier
IG Tech, Saarbrücken

Bauherr Client
Land Rheinland-Pfalz

Typologie Type
Kulturbau Cultural building

Standort Location
Hinzert

Wettbewerb Competition
2003

Fertigstellung Completion
2006

Brutto-Grundfläche Gross floor area
689 m²

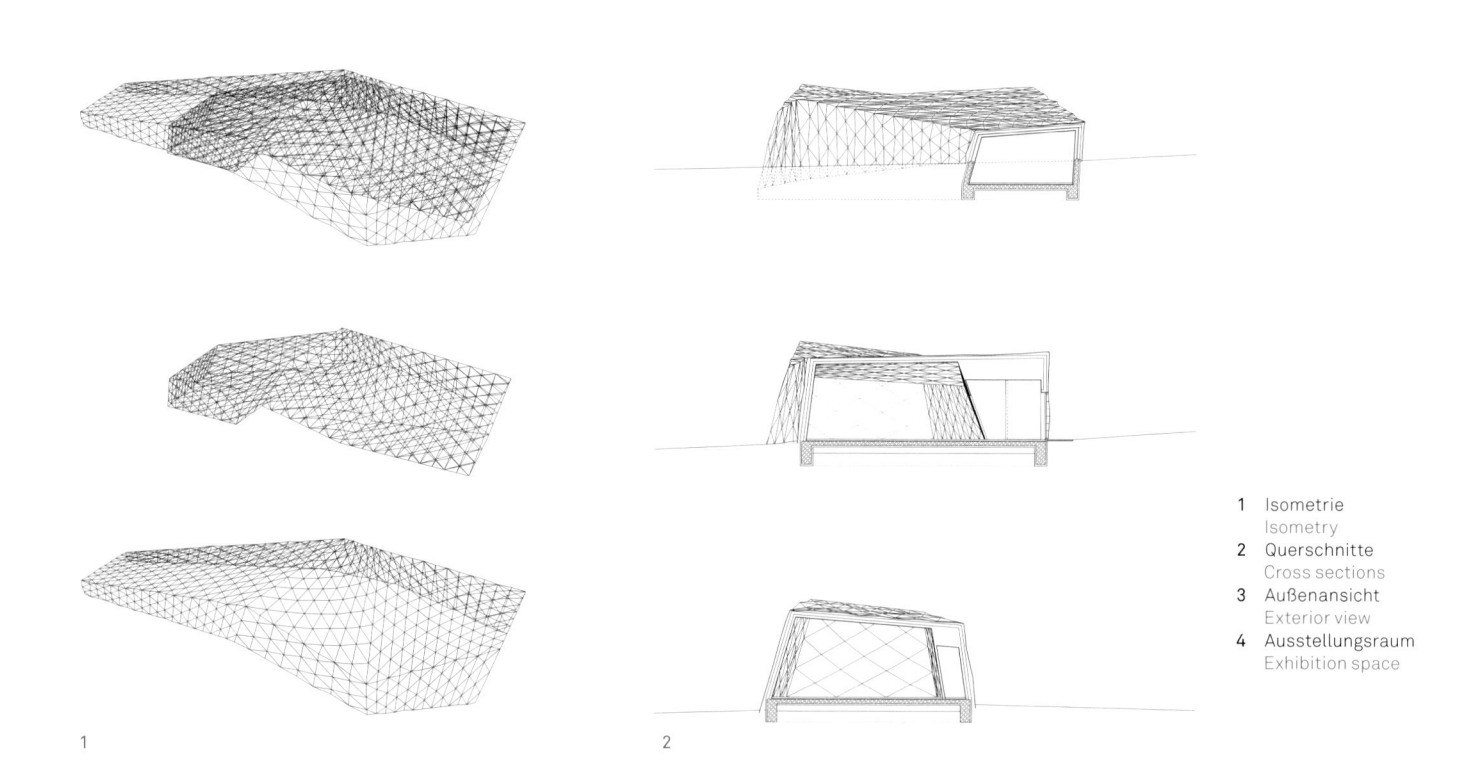

1 Isometrie
  Isometry
2 Querschnitte
  Cross sections
3 Außenansicht
  Exterior view
4 Ausstellungsraum
  Exhibition space

1

2

Die idylllische Landschaft um den Ort Hinzert wird von weichen Hügel und Feldern geprägt. Aus der Zeit von 1939 bis 1945, als sich hier ein Sonderlager für politische Gefangene befand, sind keine Spuren mehr zu sehen. Das eher unkonventionelle Dokumentationshaus, ein 43 Meter langes Gebilde, liegt auf einem leichten Hang und erhebt sich 2 bis 7 Meter in die Höhe. Das Tragwerk, Dach und Fassade in einem, besteht aus mehr als 3 000 verschiedenen dreieckigen Stücken aus 12 Millimeter dickem Corten-Stahl. Diese wurden in einer Werkstatt zu 12 Elementen geschweißt, die dann vor Ort zu einem Faltwerk zusammengesetzt wurden. Die rötlichbraune Haut umhüllt einen Ausstellungsraum, einen Seminarraum, eine Bibliothek, ein Archiv und Büros. Die innere Haut besteht aus dreieckigen Birkensperrholz-Tafeln, die mit Fotos und Texten bedruckt wurden. Das introvertierte Gebäude hat eine einzige Öffnung zum Tal, mit der Überblendung eines historischen Fotos vor dem heutigen Ausblick.

The idyllic, rolling countryside around the village of Hinzert is characterized by woods and fields. The concentration camp for political prisoners that existed here from 1939 to 1945 has left no visible traces. The unconventional Document Center— an irregular architectural object, 43 meters long and 2 to 7 meters high—was erected on a gently sloping hillside. The structure forms both roof and walls and consists of over 3,000 triangular pieces of 12-millimeter Corten steel, assembled on-site from 12 sections that had been welded together in a workshop to form a prismatic shell. This rust-colored shell encloses an exhibition gallery, a small lecture hall, a library, an archive, and offices. The interior walls were clad with triangular laminated birch panels printed with photo reproductions and texts. The building has only one glazed opening to the valley, screen-printed with a historical view of the camp.

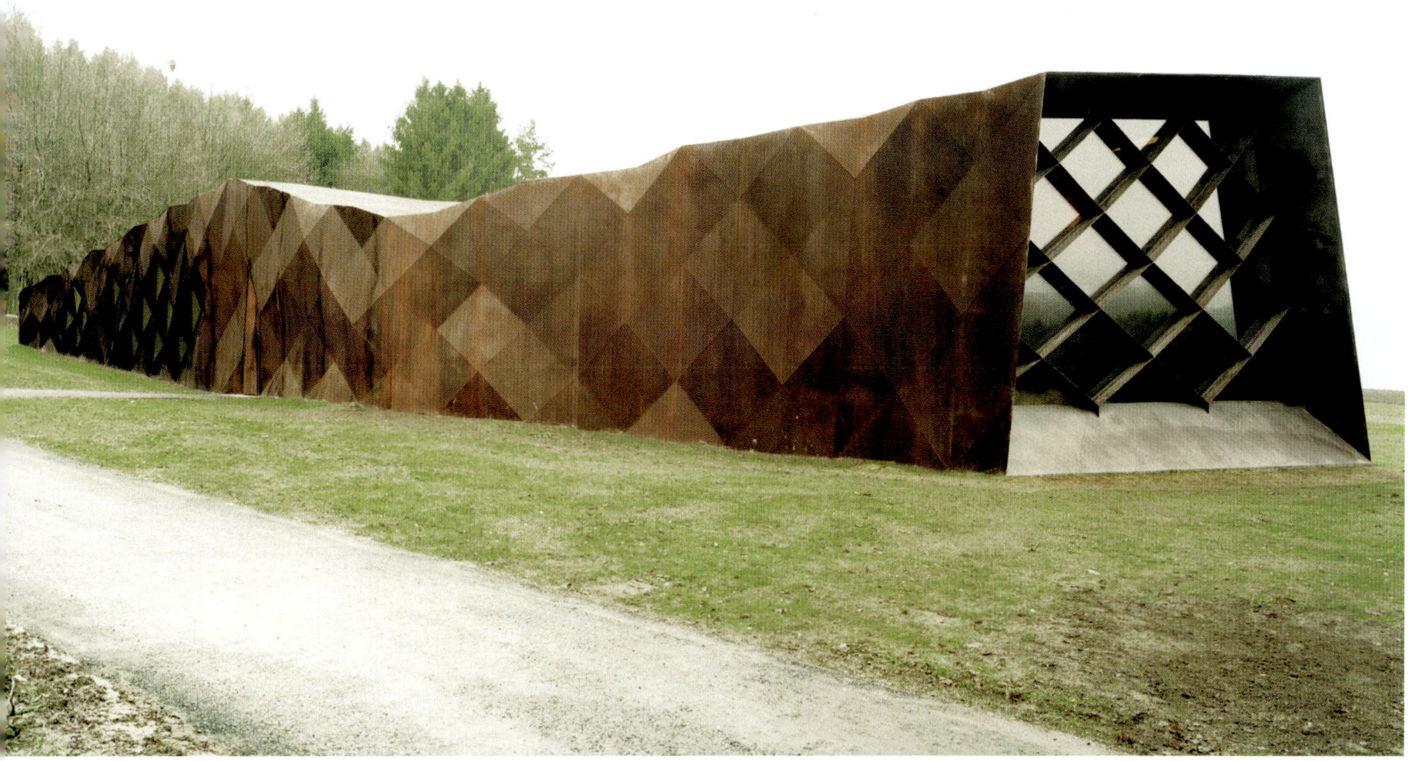

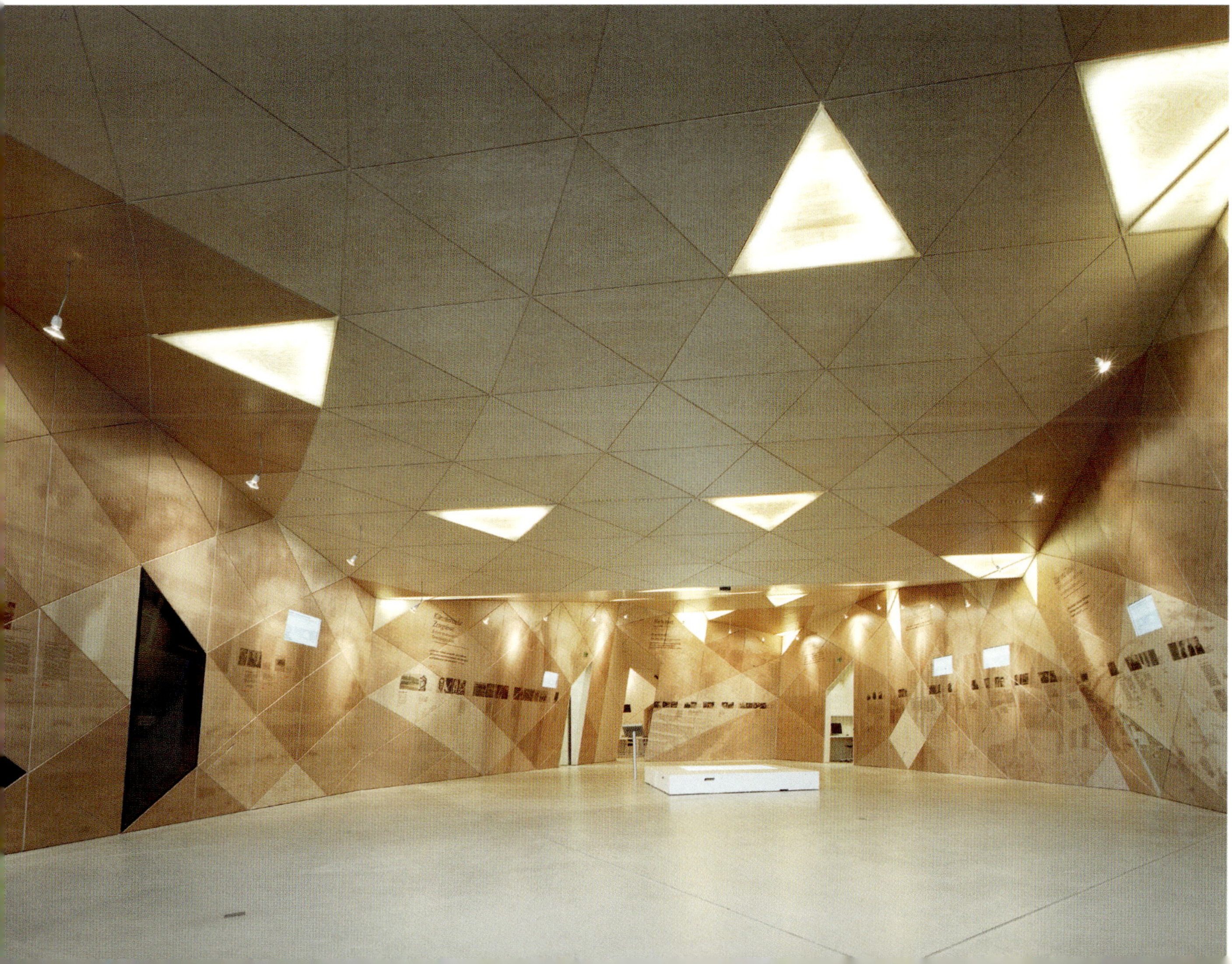

Parque de Wellness ELSE Club
Audi Terminal Velizy
Paris, França
Sala de Educação Física Hausburgviertel
Berlim, Alemanha
SchwabenGalerie
Stuttgart, Alemanha

195

Architekturexport:
Deutsche Planer auf der Architekturbiennale in São Paulo
Sally Below, Moritz Henning

Ready for Take-Off
auf der 7. BIA São Paulo 2007
Ready for Take-Off
at the 7th BIA São Paulo 2007

Jeder fünfte deutsche Arbeiter ist für den Export tätig, und deutsche Technologie ist international hoch angesehen. Auch die Leistungen der Ingenieure sind gefragt, und nicht wenige Architektur- und Ingenieurbüros in aller Welt haben Mitarbeiter – bis hinauf in die Führungsebene – in Deutschland rekrutiert. Deutsche Planungsbüros sind allerdings mit eigenem Auslandsengagement im Verhältnis zu anderen Branchen noch im Rückstand. Doch gibt es mittlerweile eine ganze Reihe von Aktivitäten, mit denen diesem Missstand abgeholfen werden soll – nicht zuletzt, da sich die Marktsituation für Planungsbüros in Deutschland alles andere als positiv darstellt. Beispiele für einen solchen »Architekturexport« zeigte auch der deutsche Beitrag *Ready for Take-Off* auf der Architekturbiennale in São Paulo. Das Bundesministerium für Verkehr, Bau und Stadtentwicklung beteiligte sich zum zweiten Mal an dieser Schau, die für Lateinamerika von großer Bedeutung ist. Nachdem 2005 die vorher bereits in Deutschland gezeigte Ausstellung *Neue deutsche Architektur,* kuratiert von Ullrich Schwarz, nach Brasilien geschickt wurde, hat das Deutsche Architekturmuseum diesmal im Auftrag des Bundes ein Konzept speziell für diesen Auftritt erarbeitet. São Paulo ist – man mag es kaum glauben – die größte »deutsche« Industriestadt, rund 1 000 deutschstämmige Unternehmen haben hier ihren Sitz. Am Vorabend der Biennale-Eröffnung fand sich neben anderen internationalen Gästen eine bunte Mischung dieser in São Paulo lebenden Deutschen zum Empfang für den deutschen Beitrag im Goethe-Institut ein.

Ein Schwerpunkt der Biennale 2007 war die Darstellung brasilianischer Architektur: Architekturbüros, einige Städte sowie Verbände zeigten den Stand ihrer Planungen in Brasilien. Dem Außenstehenden erschloss sich manches nicht gänzlich, eine klare Thematik war nur schwer zu erkennen. Die Biennale-Leitung hatte erst wenige Monate vor der Eröffnung das übergeordnete Thema »Architecture: The Public and the Private« bekannt gegeben, auf das die meisten internationalen Präsentationen wegen dieser kurzen Vorlaufzeit nicht mehr reagieren konnten. Nicht zuletzt waren die Erläuterungstexte vieler Beiträge ausschließlich auf Portugiesisch.

Ansonsten fand der Architekturinteressierte eine vielfältige Auswahl von Projektdarstellungen aus aller Welt versammelt: So hat Steven Holl beispielsweise ein paar Blätter aus dem Plotter laufen lassen, und das Berlage Institut hat sich mit der Weiterentwicklung von Brasilia beschäftigt. Neben Deutschland präsentierten sich noch zwölf weitere Länder mit eigenen Beiträgen auf der Biennale, darunter Dänemark, die Niederlande, Österreich, Portugal und die Schweiz.

Ready for Take-Off stellte den Besuchern fünfzehn aktuelle Auslandsprojekte deutscher Architekturbüros und vier Auslandsprojekte des Architekturbüros Deutschland mit ihren jeweiligen Ingenieurpartnern vor. Gezeigt wurden das jeweils erste zur Realisierung anstehende oder bereits realisierte Projekt im Ausland sowie ein aktuelles Projekt in Deutschland. Obwohl die deutsche Schau mit 300 Quadratmetern Grundfläche nur circa 1 Prozent der Fläche des vom brasilianischen Stararchitekten Oscar Niemeyer erbauten Biennale-Pavillons einnahm, war sie kaum zu übersehen. In riesigen Buchstaben prangten sogenannte deutsche Sekundärtugenden auf einer gigantischen deutschen Fahne, die sich als schwarz-rot-goldener Teppich vom Boden die Wand hinaufzog. Unter anderem »pünktlich«, »gründlich« oder »zuverlässig« war dort in Deutsch und Portugiesisch zu lesen. Nicht jeder Besucher, insbesondere aus dem deutschsprachigen Raum, konnte die plakative

Exporting Architecture:
Germany at the Architecture Biennial in São Paulo
Sally Below, Moritz Henning

In Germany, one worker in five is involved in the production of goods or services destined for export. German technology enjoys an excellent international reputation, and the services of German engineers are much in demand, with architecture and engineering offices throughout the world recruiting employees, right up to management level, in Germany. When it comes to pitching for business abroad themselves, however, German architectural and engineering offices tend to lag behind other sectors. But now, given a domestic market that is looking anything but rosy, there is a whole raft of initiatives aimed at actively remedying this situation. This upturn in architectural exports was demonstrated at the Architecture Biennial in São Paulo by Germany's *Ready for Take-Off* exhibition, which showcased the latest German architecture abroad. It was the second time that the Federal Ministry of Transport, Building and Urban Affairs had taken part in the Biennial, which is of major importance for Latin America. In 2005, Germany sent an existing exhibition—*New German Architecture,* curated by Ullrich Schwarz—to Brazil. But in 2007, at the invitation of the federal government, the Deutsches Architekturmuseum devised a concept especially for the Biennial. São Paulo, believe it or not, is actually the largest "German" industrial town outside Germany, with more than 1,000 companies owned by people of German origin. On the eve of the Biennial opening, a colorful mix of São Paulo's German émigrés and other international guests attended a reception for the German entry at the Goethe-Institut.

Brazilian architecture was a focal point of the 2007 Biennial. The country's latest designs and projects were presented by individual architectural firms, city authorities, and professional organizations. Not all of the material on display was readily accessible to outsiders, and it was difficult to discern any clear theme. The management of the Biennial had announced the general theme of "Architecture: The Public and the Private" only a few months before the opening. The limited amount of time allowed for preparation meant that most of the international participants were unable to respond adequately to this theme. In addition, the explanatory texts accompanying many contributions were offered only in Portuguese.

Apart from these difficulties, those interested in architecture generally found a rich selection of project presentations collected from around the world. For example, Steven Holl ran a few sheets through his plotter, and the Berlage Institute examined the further development of Brasília. In addition to Germany, twelve other countries, including Denmark, the Netherlands, Austria, Portugal, and Switzerland, made individual contributions to the Biennial.

Ready for Take-Off introduced visitors to fifteen projects currently being built abroad by German architects' offices, as well as four foreign projects by the Architekturbüro Deutschland and collaborating engineering firms. In each case, the first foreign project, either forthcoming or already realized abroad, was shown, along with a current project in Germany. Although the German show, with its 300-square-meter floor area, took up only about 1 percent of the area of the Biennial pavilion (designed by Brazilian star architect Oscar Niemeyer) it could hardly be overlooked. A gigantic German flag rose from the floor up the wall in the form of a black, red, and gold carpet resplendently adorned with huge letters spelling out the so-called secondary German virtues in German and Portuguese: among them, "punctual," "thorough," and "dependable." Admittedly, the tongue-in-cheek irony of these clichés was lost

Besucherandrang zur Eröffnung der 7. BIA
Crowd of visitors at the opening of the 7th BIA

Thomas Lücking (Gerber Architekten)
bei der Präsentation des Auslandsprojektes
King Fahad Nationalbibliothek
Thomas Lücking (Gerber Architekten)
presenting the foreign project
King Fahad National Library

Besucher des deutschen Beitrags
zur Eröffnung der 7. BIA
Visitors to the German stand
at the opening of the 7th BIA

und leicht ironische These nachvollziehen, die der Präsentation unterlag. Es sind zwar genau diese Eigenschaften, die oft zuerst genannt werden, wenn es um das Thema »Made in Germany« geht, und so wurden sie auch hier plakativ zur Schau gestellt. Die Projekte selbst, ansprechend präsentiert in sorgsam arrangierten, überdimensionalen Reisekoffern, zeigten jedoch eine weitere Dimension: Nicht immer sind deutsche Architekten nur »gründlich« und »zuverlässig« – oder auch schlichtweg »langweilig«, wie gern behauptet wird. Zumindest die vorgestellten Architekturbüros haben weitaus mehr zu bieten als nur »Sekundärtugenden«. Alle Architekten und Ingenieure können mit ihren Arbeiten auf dem internationalen Parkett bestehen und verdeutlichen damit, dass die »Sekundärtugenden« zwar hilfreich, aber eben nicht das einzig Ausschlaggebende sind, wenn es um den Erfolg von Architektur geht. Schmunzeln lässt dennoch die Tatsache, dass – während zwei Tage vor der Eröffnung von einem Großteil der sonstigen Arbeiten noch wenig zu sehen war und die Halle eher einer Werkstatt glich – der deutsche Beitrag schon lange fertig war, frisch gesaugt, poliert und mit Flatterband abgesperrt.

Die Präsentation der einzelnen Projekte, die aus den Koffern förmlich herausleuchteten, war sehr ansprechend und für den Besucher leicht zugänglich. In einer solchen Fülle von Beiträgen wie in der 25 000 Quadratmeter großen Halle war dieser Ansatz einer klaren und verständlichen Darstellung sinnvoll. Im Gegensatz zum diskursiven Anspruch der Biennale in Venedig war in der eher messeähnlichen Anmutung in São Paulo ein rasches Erfassen von Inhalten und Fakten hilfreich.

Diese Ausstellung demonstrierte denn auch, dass eine ganze Reihe von deutschen Planern *Ready for Take-Off* ist und Anerkennung im Ausland verdient hat. Sie in einem solch internationalen Kontext wie der Architekturbiennale in São Paulo zu zeigen, ist mit Sicherheit wichtige Grundlagenarbeit für die Wahrnehmung deutscher Architektur im Ausland. Nicht nur die vielen einheimischen Besucher, die zur Biennale jedes Mal erwartet werden – 2007 kamen circa 150 000 Interessierte – nehmen Eindrücke mit, sondern auch die internationalen Gäste und Teilnehmer aus anderen Ländern tragen zum Austausch bei. So wurde auch das deutsche Ausstellungskonzept mit den Kuratoren und den teilnehmenden deutschen Architekten, die zum Teil vor Ort waren, lebhaft und durchaus kontrovers diskutiert.

Vielleicht trägt *Ready for Take-Off* dazu bei, das Bild deutscher Architekten in Brasilien und in Lateinamerika zu stärken. Von einer ernsthaften Präsenz deutscher Architekten im lateinamerikanischen Raum kann bislang jedenfalls nicht gesprochen werden. Natürlich ist der Einstieg im Ausland schwer – nicht nur für Architekten. In Brasilien ist zudem die starke Orientierung der örtlichen Szene in Richtung Nordamerika für Europäer ein Hindernis. Umso wichtiger ist es, präsent zu sein, zu zeigen, was aktuell geplant und gebaut wird, denn nur so kann ein Austausch entstehen. Die nach São Paulo gekommenen deutschen Architekten jedenfalls waren begeistert. Neue Kontakte, interessante Gespräche mit Kollegen und ein kleines Rahmenprogramm mit einer »Pecha Kucha Night« an der Architekturfakultät der Universität von São Paulo machten den *Take-Off* nach Brasilien zu einer lohnenswerten Reise. Überlegenswert wäre es, zukünftig den Kontakt zu lokalen Akteuren zu intensivieren: In der größten »deutschen« Industriestadt könnte man einiges an Potenzial für deutsche Planer vermuten. Flankierende Treffen mit Wirtschaft, Verwaltung und Kultur gemeinsam mit den Architekten sowie die Einbindung in eine biennaleübergreifende Diskussion könnten helfen, Ideen auch hier zu Projekten werden zu lassen.

on some of the visitors, especially those from the German-speaking world. Yet these clichés are precisely the characteristics that are so often mentioned in connection with the words Made in Germany, which is why they were highlighted at the show. The projects themselves, appealingly presented in carefully arranged oversize suitcases, revealed a further dimension: contrary to popular belief, German architects are not always merely "thorough" and "dependable"—let alone downright "boring." Certainly, the architecture practices represented there have far more to offer than just secondary virtues. The works of all of the architects and engineers can easily hold their own in the international arena, demonstrating that the secondary virtues, useful as they may be, are not the sole factor in the pursuit of successful architecture. Even so, it was hard to suppress a smile at the fact that while, with just two days to go before the opening, the exhibition hall still looked like a workshop and there was little evidence of the other contributions, the German entry had long since been completed, freshly vacuumed, polished, and sealed off with barrier tape.

The presentation of the individual projects, which positively shone out of the suitcases, was highly attractive and easily legible. Given the wealth of contributions in the 25,000-square-meter hall, it made sense to use a clear, accessible presentation. In contrast to the discursive ambitions of the Biennale in Venice, São Paulo is organized more along the lines of a trade fair, so it is extremely helpful to be able to quickly grasp the facts and contents of a presentation.

This exhibition also demonstrated that there are many German architects, engineers, and planners who are indeed Ready for Take-Off and deserving of recognition abroad. Presenting them in an international context such as the São Paulo Biennial undoubtedly achieved important groundwork in showcasing German architecture abroad. The show is seen not only by the large Brazilian audience expected at each Biennial—the 2007 event attracted some 150,000 visitors—but also by the many international guests and participants who engage with the subject. In fact, the German curators and participating architects who attended found themselves involved in some lively and at times heated discussions about their exhibition concepts.

Perhaps Ready for Take-Off can help to boost the image of German architects in Brazil and throughout Latin America, where they do not yet have a high profile. Of course, gaining a foothold abroad can be difficult—not just for architects. In Brazil, the strong orientation of the local scene toward North America is an additional obstacle for Europeans. This makes it all the more important to be present locally and to show what is being currently planned and built; only in this way can a genuine exchange develop. The German architects who came to São Paulo were highly enthusiastic. New contacts, interesting discussions with colleagues, and a fringe program that included a "Pecha Kucha Night" at the architecture faculty of the University of São Paulo all made the take-off to Brazil truly worthwhile. Ways of strengthening local contacts in the future should be considered, for there is every reason to suppose that there is real potential for German architects and engineers to operate in this major "German" industrial city. Meetings between the architects and people from the worlds of business, administration, and culture to engage in discussions that go beyond the bounds of the Biennial could help to turn ideas into projects.

Das Inlandsprojekt Firmensitz Norddeutsche Vermögen Rolandsbrücke
von Carsten Roth Architekt
The domestic project Corporate Head Office Norddeutsche Vermögen Rolandsbrücke by Carsten Roth Architekt

Die deutschen Architekten
auf Stadtexkursion in São Paulo
German architects on a field trip in São Paulo

1 Der Biennale-Pavillon
  von Oscar Niemeyer
  The Biennial pavilion
  by Oscar Niemeyer
2 *Ready for Take-Off*
  auf der 7. BIA São Paulo 2007
  Ready for Take-Off
  at the 7th BIA São Paulo 2007
3 Besucher des deutschen Beitrags
  zur Eröffnung der 7. BIA
  Visitors to the German stand
  at the opening of the 7th BIA
4 Staatssekretär Engelbert Lütke
  Daldrup begutachtet die
  Ausstellungskoffer von Carsten
  Roth Architekt
  State Secretary Engelbert Lütke
  Daldrup examining the exhibition
  suitcase by Carsten Roth Architekt
5 *Ready for Take-Off*
  auf der 7. BIA São Paulo 2007
  Ready for Take-Off
  at the 7th BIA São Paulo 2007
6 Staatssekretär Engelbert Lütke
  Daldrup und José Serra,
  Gouverneur von São Paulo
  State Secretary Engelbert Lütke
  Daldrup and José Serra,
  governor of São Paulo
7 Die Ausstellungskoffer von
  Staab Architekten
  The exhibition suitcases for
  Staab Architekten
8 *Ready for Take-Off*
  auf der 7. BIA São Paulo 2007
  Ready for Take-Off
  at the 7th BIA São Paulo 2007
9 *Ready for Take-Off*
  auf der 7. BIA São Paulo 2007
  Ready for Take-Off
  at the 7th BIA São Paulo 2007
10 Der Kofferanhänger von
   Kirsten Schemel Architekten
   The luggage label for
   Kirsten Schemel Architekten
11 *Ready for Take-Off*
   auf der 7. BIA São Paulo 2007
   Ready for Take-Off
   at the 7th BIA São Paulo 2007
12 Der Kofferanhänger von
   schneider+schumacher
   The luggage label for
   schneider+schumacher
13 Der Generalkommissar Peter
   Cachola Schmal bei einer Führung
   General commissioner Peter
   Cachola Schmal doing a tour

200

201

Autoren und Interviewpartner
Authors and Interview Partners

Sally Below
*1965 in Hamburg. Inhaberin von Sally Below Cultural Affairs, Berlin. Initiiert und organisiert gemeinsam mit Architekten und Kuratoren Ausstellungen und Symposien zu aktuellen gesellschaftlichen Themen. Dozentin u. a. an der TU Braunschweig. Herausgeberin des Ratgebers *Wege in die Öffentlichkeit. Public Relations und Marketing für Architekten*. 2005 Gründung der Akademie für Architektur Kommunikation Perspektiven (AAKP) in Berlin mit Moritz Henning und Herausgeberin der Publikation *Wege in die Selbständigkeit. Existenzgründung und Positionierung für Architekten*.

Born 1965 in Hamburg. Head of Sally Below Cultural Affairs, Berlin. Together with architects and curators initiates and organizes exhibitions and symposia on current social themes. Lecturer at Braunschweig Technical University, among others. Editor of the guide *Wege in die Öffentlichkeit. Public Relations und Marketing für Architekten*. In 2005 founded, with Moritz Henning, the Academy of Architecture Communication Perspectives (AAKP) in Berlin. Co-editor of *Wege in die Selbständigkeit. Existenzgründung und Positionierung für Architekten*.

Kees Christiaanse
*1953 in Amsterdam. Bis 1988 Studium der Architektur an der Technischen Universität Delft. Sein Diplomprojekt »Kavel 25« wurde als Teil seines Städteplans für das Wohnungsbau-Festival in Den Haag umgesetzt und mit der Berlage Flag ausgezeichnet. 1980–1989 in Rem Koolhaas' Office for Metropolitan Architecture (OMA) in Rotterdam, dessen Partner er 1983 wurde. 1989 Gründung eines eigenen Büros Kees Christiaanse Architects & Planners in Rotterdam. 1990 Gründung von Astoc Architects & Planners in Köln. 1996–2003 Professor für Architektur und Stadtplanung an der TU Berlin. Seit 2003 Professor an der ETH Zürich. Wird 2006 Mitglied der kommunalen Gestaltungsbeiräte von Dublin und London. Regelmäßige Tätigkeit als Jurymitglied bei internationalen Wettbewerben. Autor verschiedener Publikationen über Architektur und Stadtplanung.

Born 1953 in Amsterdam, the Netherlands. Studied architecture at Delft University of Technology until 1988. Graduation project "Kavel 25" was realized as part of his urban plan for the housing festival in The Hague; awarded the Berlage Flag. 1980–1989 worked for the Office for Metropolitan Architecture (OMA) in Rotterdam. Partnership in 1983. 1989 started his own firm, Kees Christiaanse Architects & Planners, in Rotterdam. 1990 founded Astoc Architects & Planners in Cologne. 1996–2003 Professor of Architecture and Urban Design at the Berlin University of Technology. Since 2003 professor at ETH Zurich. Since 2006 member of Dublin's advisory board and of Design for London advisory board. Regularly acts as a jury member for international competitions. Author of several publications on architecture and urban design.

Spencer de Grey
Geschäftsführer und Leiter der Entwurfsabteilung von Foster + Partners. Studium der Architektur an der Cambridge University unter Leslie Martin. Seit 1973 bei Foster Associates, 1979 Eröffnung des Büros in Hongkong für den Bau der Hongkong und Shanghai Bank. 1981 Rückkehr nach London, Büropartner seit 1991. De Grey leitete ein umfassendes Spektrum an Projekten, darunter den Stansted Airport, den Umbau der Sackler Galleries in der Royal Academy of Arts, den Hauptsitz der Commerzbank in Frankfurt, den Great Court im British Museum, sieben neue City-Academy-Schulen in Großbritannien und Walbrook Square in London. In den USA betreute er Bauten wie das Boston Museum of Fine Arts und das neue Opernhaus in Dallas. Vorsitzender des Building Centre Trust und Mitglied des Londoner Gestaltungsbeirats. Erhielt im Sommer 1997 den Ritterorden Commander of the British Empire und wurde später Fellow der Royal Society of Arts. Umfassende Vortragstätigkeit.

Senior Executive and Head of Design for Foster + Partners. Studied architecture at Cambridge University under Sir Leslie Martin. Joined Foster Associates in 1973, setting up the Hong Kong office in 1979 to build the Hong Kong and Shanghai Bank. 1981 returned to London, director in charge of Stansted Airport. Worked on the Sackler Galleries at the Royal Academy of Arts in London. Partnership in 1991. Has overseen a wide range of projects, e.g., the Commerzbank Headquarters in Frankfurt, the Great Court at the British Museum, seven new City Academy schools in the UK, and Walbrook Square in London. Also responsible for projects in the United States, including the Boston Museum of Fine Arts and the new Opera House in Dallas. Chairman of the Building Centre Trust and

member of the Design for London Advisory Board. CBE since the Queen's Birthday Honours of 1997 and later Fellow of the Royal Society of Arts. Lectures widely.

Stefan Helming
*1954 in Beckum. Diplomvolkswirt, Absolvent des Deutschen Instituts für Entwicklungspolitik. Seit 1982 bei der Deutschen Gesellschaft für Technische Zusammenarbeit (GTZ). Längere Auslandseinsätze in Somalia (1982–1984), Simbabwe (1992–1997) und in Äthiopien (seit 2006). Im Inland verantwortlich für unterschiedliche Bereiche, u. a. Entwicklungspolitische Grundsätze, Nahost und Wasserpolitik.

Born 1954 in Beckum. Degree in economics, graduate of the German Institute of Development Policy. Has worked for Deutsche Gesellschaft für Technische Zusammenarbeit (GTZ) since 1982. Prolonged missions abroad in Somalia (1982–1984), Zimbabwe (1992–1997) and Ethiopia (since 2006). In Germany is responsible for various areas, including fundamentals of development policy, the Middle East, and water policy.

Moritz Henning
*1963 in Karlsruhe. Freier Architekt in Berlin, seit 1995 in verschiedenen Arbeitskonstellationen. Verantwortlich für unterschiedlichste Projekte vom kleinen Umbau bis zum Siebzig-Millionen-Euro-Projekt. Beschäftigt sich seit Jahren gemeinsam mit Sally Below mit Fragen zum Berufsbild des Architekten und zur Architekturvermittlung. 2005 Gründung der Akademie für Architektur Kommunikation Perspektiven (AAKP) in Berlin mit Sally Below und Herausgeber der Publikation *Wege in die Selbständigkeit. Existenzgründung und Positionierung für Architekten.*

Born 1963 in Karlsruhe. Freelance architect in Berlin, since 1995 in various work constellations. Responsible for a wide range of projects, from small conversions to large-budget projects. For many years has addressed, with Sally Below, the question of the job specification of architects and the conveying of architecture. In 2005 founded, with Below, the Academy of Architecture Communication Perspectives (AAKP) in Berlin. Co-editor of *Wege in die Selbständigkeit. Existenzgründung und Positionierung für Architekten.*

Anna Hesse
*1977 in Lahn-Gießen. 1997–2004 Architekturstudium an der TU Darmstadt und am Tec de Monterrey in Querétaro, Mexiko. Studentische Ausstellungen und Publikationen an der TU Darmstadt, Mitarbeit in verschiedenen Architekturbüros. 2005–2006 Volontärin am Deutschen Architekturmuseum, Frankfurt am Main; seit 2006 dort als freie Kuratorin tätig. Seit 2007 Presse- und Öffentlichkeitsarbeit für verschiedene Architekturbüros. Auswahl bisheriger Ausstellungen: *sichten6/ TUDimDAM, UN Studio. Entwicklung des Raums, Personen und Possen. Architektenporträts und Collagen von Manfred Sack, Verena Dietrich: Eine Architektin.* Zusammen mit Peter Cachola Schmal Kuratorin des deutschen Beitrags *Ready for Take-Off* auf der 7. BIA São Paulo 2007.

Born 1977 in Lahn-Giessen. 1997–2004 studied architecture at the Darmstadt University of Technology and the Tec de Monterrey in Querétaro, Mexico. 2004–05 worked in various architecture offices. 2005–06 trained at the Deutsches Architekturmuseum (DAM), Frankfurt; freelance curator there since 2006. Since 2007 press and public relations for various architecture offices. Previous exhibitions include *sichten6/ TUD at the DAM; UN Studio: Evolution of Space, People, and Pranks; Portraits of Architects and Collages by Manfred Sack;* and *Verena Dietrich: A Female Architect.* Curator, with Peter Cachola Schmal, of *Ready for Take-Off*, the German contribution to the 7th BIA São Paulo 2007.

Claus Käpplinger
*1963 in Alzey (Rheinhessen), freier Architekturkritiker in Berlin. Studium der Sozial- und Kunstgeschichte, Soziologie und Philosophie in Mainz, Perugia und Berlin. 1990–1996 Mitarbeit beim Deutschlandsender-Kultur, 1994–2001 beim *Tagesspiegel* Berlin. Kritiker u. a. für *Architektur Aktuell, DBZ* und *DB.* Leitete und moderierte verschiedene Initiativen junger Architekten, u. a. »Berlin und seine Zeit«, »La grande étagère« und den »Arbeitskreis Junger Architekten und Architektinnen« (AKJAA). Seit 1998 Organisator des interdisziplinären »Stadtsalons« in Berlin (seit 2007 »BDA-Stadtsalon«) zu den Themenfeldern Stadt, Gesellschaft und Wahrnehmung.

Born 1963 in Alzey (Rheinhessen). Freelance architecture critic in Berlin. Studied social and art history, sociology, and philosophy in Mainz, Perugia, and Berlin. 1990–1996 worked for Deutschlandsender Kultur, 1994–2001 for *Tagesspiegel* Berlin. Critic for, among other publications, *Architektur Aktuell, DBZ,* and *DB*. Organized and hosted various initiatives for young architects, including "Berlin und seine Zeit," "La grande étagère," and "Arbeitskreis Junger Architekten und Architektinnen" (AKJAA). Since 1998 organizer of the interdisciplinary Stadtsalon in Berlin (since 2007 BDA-Stadtsalon), addressing the topics of the city, society, and perception.

Dominique Perrault

*1953 in Clermont-Ferrand. Architekt und Stadtplaner, Inhaber von Dominique Perrault Architecture, Paris. Internationales Ansehen für den Entwurf der französischen Nationalbibliothek in Paris 1989, des Velodroms und des Schwimmbads in Berlin 1992. Bau des Hotel Industriel Jean-Baptiste Berlier in Paris, der Aplix-Fabrik in Nantes und der Multimediabibliothek in Vénissieux; weitere aktuelle Projekte in Lille, Boulogne-Billancourt und Rouen. Zu den europäischen Projekten zählen außerdem die Piazza Garibaldi in Neapel, zwei Hoteltürme an der Fiera di Milano (Mailänder Messe), ein Hotel auf der Nueva Diagonal in Barcelona und ein Konferenzzentrum in León. In Japan werden ein Noh-Theater in der Provinz Niigata und ein Bürogebäude in Osaka realisiert. Das Büro plant zurzeit große Projekte in der ganzen Welt, z. B. den Europäischen Gerichtshof in Luxemburg, das olympische Tenniszentrum in Madrid, die Gesamtkonzeption für das Zentrum der Donau-City mit zwei 200 Meter hohen Türmen in Wien, den neuen Zuschauerraum für das Mariinski-Theater in St. Petersburg und den Campus der EWHA Frauenuniversität in Seoul, Korea.

Born 1953 in Clermont-Ferrand, France. Architect and urban designer, head of Dominique Perrault Architecture, Paris. International reputation for designing the French National Library in Paris in 1989 and the Olympic Velodrome and Swimming Pool in Berlin in 1992. Built the Industrial Hotel Jean-Baptiste Berlier in Paris, the Aplix factory in Nantes, and a multimedia library in Vénissieux; other projects are in process in Lille, Boulogne-Billancourt, and Rouen. European projects include the Piazza Garibaldi in Naples; two hotel towers at the Fiera di Milano, the trade fair of Milan; a hotel on the Nueva Diagonal of Barcelona; and a conference center in León. Japanese projects include a Noh theater in the province of Niigata and an office building in Osaka. Currently working on large urban projects all over the world, including the European Court of Justice in Luxembourg; the Olympic Tennis Center in Madrid; the master plan for the center of Donau-City and two 200-meter towers in Vienna; the new auditorium for Saint Petersburg's Mariinsky Theater; and the EWHA Women's University campus in Seoul, Korea.

Klaus Rollenhagen

*1943 in Schneidemühl (heute Piła / Polen). Studium der Ingenieurwissenschaften und der Betriebswirtschaft. Projektingenieur bei Siemens in Erlangen und London. Für Lahmeyer International mehrjährige Auslandseinsätze in Saudi-Arabien, im Jemen und in Argentinien. Mehrere Kurzeinsätze in afrikanischen und asiatischen Ländern. Seit 1992 Hauptgeschäftsführer des Verbandes Beratender Ingenieure. Beiratsmitglied u. a. im Nah- und Mittelostverein (NUMOV) und Verwaltungsratsmitglied der Bundesagentur für Außenwirtschaft (bfai).

Born 1943 in Schneidemühl (today Piła, Poland). Studied engineering and business. Project engineer at Siemens in Erlangen and London. Spent several years abroad for Lahmeyer International, in Saudi Arabia, Yemen, and Argentina. Several short-term missions in Africa and Asia. Since 1992 principal managing director of the Association of Consulting Engineers (VBI). Council member of, among others, the German Near and Middle East Association (NUMOV), and member of the administrative board of the German Office for Foreign Trade.

Peter Cachola Schmal

*1960 in Altötting. Lebte in Deutschland, Pakistan und Indonesien. 1981–1989 Studium der Architektur an der TU Darmstadt. Mitarbeit bei Behnisch & Partner, Stuttgart und ABE Architekten, Zeppelinheim. 1992–1997 wissenschaftlicher Mitarbeiter bei Prof. Johann Eisele an der TU Darmstadt. 1997–2000 Lehrauftrag für Entwerfen an der FH Frankfurt. Seit 2000 wissenschaftlicher Mitarbeiter und Kurator am Deutschen Architekturmuseum, Frankfurt am Main. Seit 2006 Direktor des DAM. Generalkommissar und zusammen mit Anna Hesse Kurator des deutschen Beitrags *Ready for Take-Off* auf der 7. BIA São Paulo 2007.

Born 1960 in Altötting. Has lived in Germany, Pakistan, and Indonesia. 1981–1989 studied architecture at the Darmstadt University of Technology. Worked for Behnisch & Partner, Stuttgart and ABE Architekten, Zeppelinheim. 1992–1997 research assistant to Professor Johann Eisele at the Darmstadt University of Technology. 1997–2000 teaching appointment for architectural design at the FH Frankfurt. Since 2000 research assistant and curator at the Deutsches Architekturmuseum, Frankfurt. Since 2006 director of the DAM. General commissioner and curator, with Anna Hesse, of *Ready for Take-Off,* the German contribution to the 7th BIA São Paulo 2007.

Tatjana Steidl
*1966 in Düsseldorf. Studium der Politikwissenschaft in Marburg und Berlin, Ausbildung zur PR-Referentin. Referentin für Fachgruppen und Außenwirtschaft beim Verband Beratender Ingenieure (VBI).

Born 1966 in Düsseldorf. Studied political science in Marburg and Berlin, trained as PR spokeswoman. Spokeswoman for specialist groups and foreign trade for the Association of Consulting Engineers (VBI).

Wolfgang Voigt
*1950 in Hamburg, Architekturhistoriker. Studium der Architektur an der Universität Hannover, Promotion und Habilitation. 1979–1981 Wissenschaftlicher Mitarbeiter an der Hochschule Bremen und 1982–1984 im Stadtarchiv Hannover. Freie Mitarbeit beim Denkmalschutzamt Hamburg. 1986–1995 Wissenschaftlicher Mitarbeiter an der HfbK Hamburg, Arbeit in verschiedenen Forschungsprojekten unter Leitung von Hartmut Frank und Jean-Louis Cohen. Lehraufträge für Baugeschichte an der Hochschule Bremen und der Universität Hamburg. 1993–1994 Vertretungsprofessur für Baugeschichte an der HfbK Hamburg. 1994–1995 freie Mitarbeit am Art Institute of Chicago. Seit 1997 stellvertretender Direktor des Deutschen Architekturmuseums, Frankfurt am Main. Verschiedene Ausstellungen u. a. über Heinz Bienefeld, Helmuth Jacoby, Paul Schmitthenner, Dominikus und Gottfried Böhm, zuletzt *Neu Bau Land . Architektur und Stadtumbau in den neuen Bundesländern 1990–2007.* Zahlreiche Publikationen, u. a. *Atlantropa*.

Born 1950 in Hamburg. Architectural historian. Studied architecture at the University of Hannover, subsequently completed doctoral and post-doctoral (Habilitation) theses. 1979–1981 research associate at the Hochschule Bremen and 1982–1984 at the Hannover City Archive. Worked freelance for the Hamburg Bureau of Protection of Historical Monuments. 1986–1995 research associate at the Hamburg Academy of Fine Arts (HfbK). Involved in various research projects supervised by Hartmut Frank and Jean-Louis Cohen. Teaching positions in building history at the Hochschule Bremen and the University of Hamburg. 1993–1994 proxy Professor of Building History at the HfbK Hamburg. 1994–1995 worked freelance at the Art Institute of Chicago. Since 1997 deputy director of Deutsches Architekturmuseum, Frankfurt am Main. Various exhibitions, including ones on Heinz Bienefeld, Helmuth Jacoby, Paul Schmitthenner, and Dominikus and Gottfried Böhm; most recently *Neu Bau Land: Architecture and Urban Restructuring in Former East Germany 1990–2007.* Numerous publications, including *Atlantropa*.

Thomas Welter
*1969 in Ratingen (Nordrhein-Westfalen). 1990–1995 Studium der Volkswirtschaftslehre und Nordamerikastudien an der Freien Universität Berlin. 1996–2000 freier Mitarbeiter am Deutschen Institut für Wirtschaftsforschung (DIW) sowie als Lehrbeauftragter an der Fachhochschule für Technik und Wirtschaft (FHTW) und am IMK – Privates Institut für Marketing und Kommunikation in Berlin tätig. 2000 Promotion im Fach Wirtschaftswissenschaft. Danach Referent für Wirtschaft und Gesellschaft in der Bundesarchitektenkammer. Seit 2002 Geschäftsführer der verbandseigenen D.A.V.I.D. Deutsche Architekten Verlags- und Informationsdienste GmbH.

Born 1969 in Ratingen (North Rhine–Westphalia). 1990–1995 studied economics and North American studies at the Free University in Berlin. 1996–2000 freelance work for the German Institute for Economic Research (DIW), as well as teaching positions at the University of Applied Sciences (FHTW) and IMK–Private Institute of Marketing and Communication in Berlin. 2000 awarded a doctorate in economics. Subsequently head of department for business and society in the Federal Chamber of Architects. Since 2002 managing director of its Deutsche Architekten Verlags- und Informationsdienste (DAVID) GmbH.

Bildnachweis
Credits

A
Dirk Altenkirch: 187 (5)
Architekturmuseum der TU Berlin: 54
AS&P: 13 (2–3)
B
Bez + Kock Architekten: 83
Valerie Bennett: 176
Bibliothek des DAM: 63
bitterbredt.de: 181 (2)
BMW AG: 84
Andreas Böttcher: 194, 195, 203 (3), 204 (3)
Brandenfels: 69
Zooey Braun: 109
Hans-Christoph Brinkschmidt: 88
Till Budde: 202 (1), 203 (2)
C
Lorenz Cugini: 146
D
Gitty Darugar: 87 (5)
Richard Davies: 27
DBBP 08: 78, 79
Rui Moraes de Sousa: 204 (1)
Deutscher Werkbund: 58 (1)
E
Eberle & Eisfeld: 139
Eller + Eller Architekten: 70
H. G. Esch: 40, 71, 145
F
Georges Fessy: 34, 35
Foster + Partners: 25, 49 (1), 202 (3)
Klaus Frahm: 126, 127, 175
David Franck: 108 (2, 3), 151
Eik Frenzel: 20, 21, 22, 23
G
gmp-Archiv: 15
Reinhard Görner: 26 (2)
GTZ: 18, 19 (1)
H
Roland Halbe: 48 (2), 68, 100, 101
Jörg Hempel: 87 (6)
Moritz Henning: 198, 199, 200 (1–4), 201
Christian Hoffmann: 169 (2–4)
G. Hurkmans: 202 (2)
Werner Huthmacher: 48 (4), 93, 187 (3, 4, 6)
J
Jo Franzke Architekten: 64

K
KCAP: 41, 42, 45
Annette Kisling: 157, 181 (3, 4)
Dietmar Köther: 55
Krost Industrial & Building Company: 89
L
Hans-Jürgen Landes: 115, 131 (5), 133
Veit Landwehr: 121
Lepkowski Studios: 179
Levin Monsigny: 73
M
Norbert Miguletz: 193
Stefan Müller: 156
Stefan Müller-Naumann: 53 (2)
N
Naqsh-e-Jahan Pars: 52
Alexey Naroditskiy: 74
Frank Neumann: 169 (5)
O
OMA: 44
P
Perrault projets: 36, 37
Markus Pillhofer: 28
PULS GmbH: 72
R
Marc Räder: 116, 117, 119
Olaf Rayermann: 140
Christian Richters: 48 (1, 3), 96, 97, 105, 107 (4, 5)
Ricky Ridecos: 12 (3)
Corinne Rose: 104, 107 (3, 6)
Joachim Rostock: 13 (1)
S
Manfred Sack: 32, 38, 39, 49 (2, 3), 50, 51, 52, 53 (1)
Martin Scheuermann: 12 (1, 2), 196, 197, 200 (5, 6)
Hans Schlupp: 161
SANAA: 81
Jan Siefke: 14
Barbara Staubach: 24
T
Ludwig Thalheimer / Lupo: 165, 167
Michael Tsegaye: 19 (2)
V
Jean-Luc Valentin: 163
Rainer Viertlböck: 80
Wolfgang Voigt: 56, 57, 58 (2, 3), 59, 62, 65
Y
Nigel Young / Foster + Partners: 26 (1)

Diese Publikation erscheint anlässlich der Ausstellung
Ready for Take-Off. Aktuelle deutsche Exportarchitektur.
Deutscher Beitrag 7. Internationale Architekturbiennale
São Paulo 2007.

This book is published in conjunction with the exhibition
Ready for Take-Off: Contemporary German Export Architecture.
German Contribution 7th International Architecture Biennial
São Paulo 2007.

São Paulo, Brasilien Brazil
10. November – 16. Dezember 2007
November 10 – December 16, 2007

Frankfurt am Main, Deutschland Germany
7. Juni – 2. November 2008
June 7 – November 2, 2008

Herausgeber Editors
Anna Hesse
Peter Cachola Schmal

Verlagslektorat Copyediting
Clemens von Lucius
Donna Stonecipher

Übersetzungen Translations
Ishbel Flett
Deutsch-Englisch German-English
Jeremy Gaines
Englisch-Deutsch English-German
J. Roderick O'Donovan
Deutsch-Englisch German-English
Annette Wiethüchter
Deutsch-Englisch German-English

Grafische Gestaltung Graphic design
Surface Gesellschaft für Gestaltung
Oliver Kuntsche, Markus Weisbeck

Schrift Typeface
Akkurat

Reproduktionen Reproductions
LVD Gesellschaft für Datenverarbeitung mbH

Papier Paper
Galaxi Supermat, 150 g/m^2

Gesamtherstellung Printing and binding
fgb freiburger graphische betriebe

© 2008 Hatje Cantz Verlag, Ostfildern;
Deutsches Architekturmuseum, Frankfurt am Main;
Autoren und Architekten Authors and architects

Erschienen im Published by
Hatje Cantz Verlag
Zeppelinstrasse 32
73760 Ostfildern
Deutschland / Germany
Tel. +49 (0)711 44 05-200
Fax +49 (0)711 44 05-220
www.hatjecantz.com

Hatje Cantz books are available internationally
at selected bookstores. For more information
about our distribution partners, please visit our
homepage at www.hatjecantz.com

Buchhandelsausgabe Trade edition
ISBN 978-3-7757-2146-2
(Hardcover)

Museumsausgabe Museum edition
ISBN 978-3-939114-02-4
(Softcover, nur im Museum erhältlich
only available in the museum)

Printed in Germany

Umschlagabbildung Cover illustration
Metropol Parasol, Sevilla, J. Mayer H.

Sponsoren Sponsors